MAVERICK GUIDE TO
VIETNAM, LAOS,
and CAMBODIA

mav.er.ick (mav'er-ik), *n* 1. an unbranded steer. Hence colloq. 2. a person not labeled as belonging to any one faction, group, etc., who acts independently. 3. one who moves in a different direction than the rest of the herd—often a nonconformist. 4. a person using individual judgment, even when it runs against majority opinion.

The Maverick Guide Series

The Maverick Guide to Australia
The Maverick Guide to Hawaii
The Maverick Guide to New Zealand
The Maverick Guide to Thailand
The Maverick Guide to Bali and Java
The Maverick Guide to Berlin
The Maverick Guide to Malaysia and Singapore
The Maverick Guide to Vietnam, Laos, and Cambodia
The Maverick Guide to Prague
The Maverick Guide to Hong Kong,
Macau, and South China

MAVERICK GUIDE TO
VIETNAM, LAOS,
and CAMBODIA

Len Rutledge

Researched by
Phensri Athisumongkol

ALL NEW
3RD EDITION

PELICAN PUBLISHING COMPANY
Gretna 1996

First edition, May 1993
Second edition, March 1994
Third edition, March 1996
ISBN: 1-56554-126-X

Information in this guidebook is based on authoritative data available at the time of printing. Prices and hours of operation of businesses listed are subject to change without notice. Readers are asked to take this into account when consulting this guide.

Maps and photos by Len Rutledge

Manufactured in the United States of America
Published by Pelican Publishing Company, Inc.
1101 Monroe Street, Gretna, Louisiana 70053

Contents

Laos

Cambodia

11. The Land, Life, and People of Cambodia

12. Phnom Penh and Other Places

LIST OF MAPS

ACKNOWLEDGMENTS

Some of the strongest memories I have of my travels are of people rather than places. Meeting people is undoubtedly one of the great joys of travel writing. During the preparation of this book, I met hundreds of people who were helpful and friendly. I would particularly like to acknowledge the following:

Ho Xuan Phong, Haig Conolly, Dang Thanh Man, Phensri Asthisumongkol, Ken Morton, Khamseng Soundara, James Kiang, Var Eng Leang, Lisa Mackay, Dr. Chanthaphilith Chiemsisourath, Kham Kheuang Bounteum, Bounteng Vongxay, Tran Vu Phuong Lan, Chang Hu, Eng Nguyen Truong Son, Nguyen Bich Thuy, Hoang Hou Ky, Somruthai Prasart-tong-Osoth.

MAVERICK GUIDE TO
VIETNAM, LAOS, and CAMBODIA

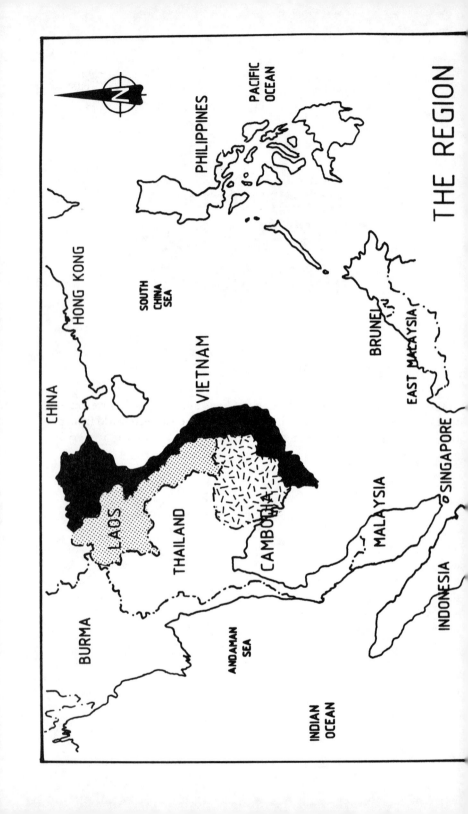

THE REGION

1

Why Go to Vietnam, Laos, and Cambodia?

Four decades of conflict have made Vietnam, Laos, and Cambodia some of the poorest nations on earth. The conflicts and successive governments that shunned the outside world have prevented the Western world from getting a broad picture of life in these countries, so an aura of mystery has developed.

That aura of mystery is about to evaporate. As part of the changing world order, and in order to patch their shattered economies, Vietnam, Laos, and Cambodia are opening their doors to Western tourists and business people. Even the media is being invited to selectively report on conditions and attractions.

The doors are opening to some of the most spectacular features of southeast Asia and to the sublime beauty of the region. Visitors can experience the brilliant achievements of the Khmer, the Cham, and the Vietnamese civilizations. You will be overwhelmed by the brilliant green rice paddies, the white beaches, the blue water of much of the coastal region, the rugged mountains, fertile valleys, and the growing cities which seem to come straight from the pages of an Asian guidebook from the 1950s.

The Vietnamese, Laos, and Cambodians are—almost without exception—friendly to Western visitors. It seems to matter little that, in many cases, they or their parents have either fought against Western colonialism, been

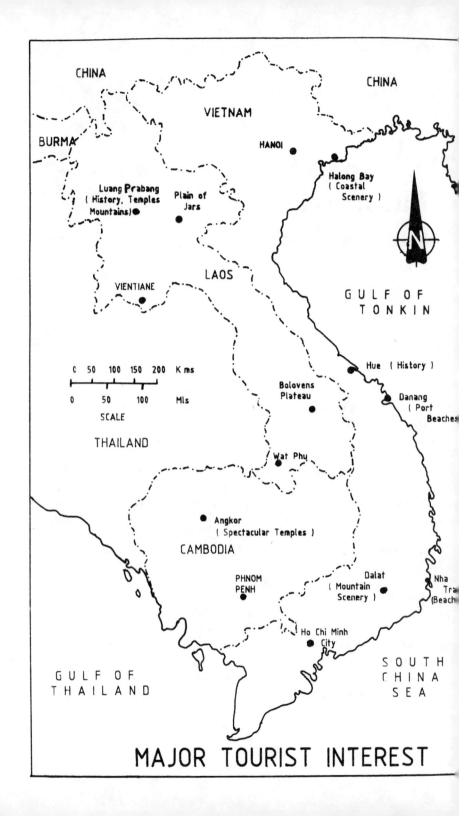

MAJOR TOURIST INTEREST

bombed by Western aircraft, or been betrayed by Western governments that often put their own interests before those of the region and its people.

During these early years, as the area opens to outsiders, each visitor has a special responsibility to ensure that the expectations of the residents are not crushed. It is important that a sense of trust be established, so the potential benefit of full contact with the world community can be seen. For this reason, I encourage you to be a thinking, caring visitor as you pass through a fragile social and political order not yet sure of its place in the world.

Travel to and within Vietnam, Laos, and Cambodia requires quite a bit more perseverance than visiting Thailand, Malaysia, or Singapore for instance. Visa regulations are tough and not always straightforward. Basic infrastructure is poor, so transport reliability is not great. With a few exceptions, the standard of accommodation cannot be compared with neighboring countries. Lack of experience with the West and Western visitors means that bureaucratic attitudes can be difficult to follow at times.

For these reasons, the number of Western visitors in recent years has been small. This has considerable benefits. You can see a countryside unpolluted by mass tourism. On many occasions, you will be the only foreigner at a restaurant, museum, or scenic waterfall. You will find that there is less cynicism, less "rip-off" mentality, and less resistance to visitors than in areas where tourism is a way of life.

Sights that are long gone from most of the world are commonplace in Vietnam, Laos, and Cambodia. Bullock carts share the road in Hanoi with bicycles and the occasional bus. Water buffalo wallow along the roadside throughout the region, while hairdressers, restaurateurs, bicycle repairmen, and T-shirt sellers jostle for a square meter of curbside in the cities. An endless green patchwork of rice fields confronts you in the rich river valleys, while towering rain forests still dominate many of the ranges.

History is all around you. From the mystery of the Plain of Jars in Laos, to the wonder of the structures at Angkor in Cambodia, you can see the rise and fall of successive civilizations and cultures that have all contributed to the people and societies that exist today.

There is considerable natural beauty as well. Halong Bay in the north of Vietnam may one day be a popular international island destination. Farther south, the central highlands have a cool climate, beautiful mountain scenery, and lovely lakes and waterfalls. In Laos, the Khammuan Plateau in the north and the Bolovens Plateau in the south are two areas of natural beauty. In Cambodia, the Cardamon Mountains and the remote southern beaches provide unspoiled areas rarely visited by tourists.

Communism has smothered all three countries with untold restrictions, unimaginable bureaucratic procedures, and mediocrity, which will take a long time to erase; but it hasn't entirely daunted the will of the people to strive for better lives. You see the drive and enterprise emerging in Danang and Ho Chi Minh City in Vietnam. You see hope on the streets of Phnom Penh, and outward criticism of past ways from officials in Laos. It is this energy, this reassessment of direction, and this hope in the future that help make a visit to Vietnam, Laos, or Cambodia an exciting experience.

Tourist Vietnam, Laos, and Cambodia in Summary

•Ho Chi Minh City (Saigon) is by far the largest, most enterprising and thriving city in Indochina. With a population of around four million people, it is a great attraction for those visitors who crave cities.

•Coastal Nha Trang (Vietnam) has an attractive, popular beach, clear water that is excellent for fishing and snorkeling, and good hotel and restaurant facilities.

•The Central Highlands surrounding Dalat (Vietnam) has a cool climate, great mountain scenery, numerous lakes and waterfalls, and many ethnic minority groups.

•Danang (Vietnam) is a major seaport with a sense of dynamism rare to the region. The region has some fine beaches, an interesting history, and the best examples of Cham architecture to be found today.

•Hue (Vietnam) has traditionally been a political, religious, cultural, and educational center. There are museums, pagodas, and palaces within the old city and splendid royal tombs just south of the city.

•Hanoi (Vietnam) is the somewhat drab, but at times charming, capital of Vietnam. The city has some lakes, pagodas, and two museums worth visiting; but the delightful "Old Quarter" will take much of your time.

•Halong Bay (Vietnam) has three thousand islands with beaches and grottos rising sharply from the waters of the Gulf of Tonkin. The region has the potential to become a major tourist attraction.

•Vientiane (Laos) has the charm and atmosphere of a city forgotten by time. There are tree-lined streets and numerous temples along the banks of the mighty Mekong River.

•Luang Prabang (Laos) is a sleepy city in a lovely mountain setting with loads of history, temples, and a great museum. The surrounding area is an excellent place to observe village life little changed by war, ideology, or the twentieth century.

•The Plain of Jars (Laos) has over two hundred huge stone jars of unknown origin scattered about a wide area.

•The Bolovens Plateau (Laos) has traditional Lao villages, an excellent climate, streams and waterfalls, and the beginnings of a tourism infrastructure.

●Wat Phu (Laos) is an Angkor-period Khmer temple near the Mekong River in southern Laos.

●Phnom Penh is still the loveliest of the French-built cities of Indochina, despite three decades of violence and decay. There are palaces, pagodas, museums, markets, and more. South of the city, there are several significant temples.

●The temples of Angkor (Cambodia) must surely rate as one of man's most magnificent architectural achievements. You should try to visit at least three temples: Bayon, Ta Prohm, and Angkor Wat.

The Confessional

Unlike many other guidebooks, this one contains neither overt nor covert advertising. The opinions expressed throughout are mine. You may not always agree with my opinions, but you will know that they are based on my personal experience and are given openly and honestly. As with other books in the Maverick series, no use of friendship or favors is allowed to influence these opinions.

When I was commissioned to write this book, I made five visits to the region over a fifteen-month period. During these visits, I deliberately stayed in a wide range of accommodations, ate at a wide range of street stalls and restaurants, experienced some guided tours, investigated the shopping opportunities, and tried out the nightlife. I traveled by plane, train, car, bus, boat, and bicycle. I visited wats, museums, markets, and national parks. At no time did I ask members of the tourism industry to subsidize this research.

There were travel restrictions in each of these countries. I had the choice of either entering on a tourist visa as part of an organized tour group and breaking away (illegally) to do my independent research, or declaring myself a journalist/writer and asking for government cooperation. After much soul searching, I decided on the latter course. This meant that I had to wait ten months to get a Lao visa; I had to cancel one trip to Vietnam because approval for the visit was so slow in arriving; and I had to chase halfway around the world to get official permission to be totally independent in Cambodia.

These difficulties later proved to be worthwhile. I finally received the cooperation of each government and was given permission to go where I pleased. I thus was able to visit areas and sites where no organized tours yet travel. I was given access to officials and government facilities which would have been impossible to obtain as a tourist. All of this has enabled me to give a much broader picture of life in Vietnam, Laos, and Cambodia and to write about attractions that are only just opening to the outside world. For this new edition I have made three further visits and discovered many changes. Vietnam, in particular, is rapidly opening to the outside world.

It was not possible for me to stay in every hotel that a visitor can use, but the book covers a good range from luxury (what few exist) to basic—likewise with restaurants, night spots, and shops. You will end up eating at or visiting some places not mentioned in this book. Some may not have existed when I did my last inspection. If they are particularly good, friendly, interesting, or a good value, please let me know about them so I can visit before completing the next edition of this guide.

Travel writing has been my life for around twenty-five years, and it has provided me the opportunity to travel throughout the world. I am sure that my travel experiences have made me a more aware, tolerant, and appreciative person, and have helped to keep me young at heart. If you approach traveling in a positive way, you too will receive the same benefits. Don't visit Vietnam, Laos, and Cambodia expecting everything to be a duplication of things at home. If you do, you will be sorely disappointed. Go with the knowledge that these countries have had very limited contact with the Western world for twenty years. Don't complain when facilities and service are less than perfect. Try a smile and a simple request for what you need, and most times you will be rewarded by a positive response. Accept that time may be less important to locals than to "busy" tourists and business people, and plan accordingly. See these things as a broadening of your experience and as insights into new cultures which may just have as many benefits as your own.

Getting the Most out of This Book

This guide is arranged in a pattern similar to that of the other Maverick Guides. It is a format that commenced with the Maverick Guide to Hawaii in 1977, and has been well tried and tested in the years since. It enables you to get a good feel for the country and its people, while at the same time getting the specifics that are so necessary when you are traveling.

After a chapter on how to travel to and within Vietnam, Laos, and Cambodia, there is a chapter on how to minimize the potential hassles involving climate, government, and logistics. I have split the book into three sections—one covering each of the three countries. Within each section, there are chapters on the land, life, and people of the country and specific area chapters covering the main regions of interest to the visitor.

Each of the area chapters is divided into twelve numbered sections. After you become familiar with them in one chapter, you will know where to look for these same subjects in each of the other chapters. The categories are as follows:

1. **The General Picture**	7. **Guided Tours**
2. **Getting There**	8. **Culture**
3. **Local Transportation**	9. **Sports**
4. **The Hotel Scene**	10. **Shopping**
5. **Dining and Restaurants**	11. **Entertainment and Nightlife**
6. **Sightseeing**	12. **The Address List**

The book has been set up to be used two ways. First, you should read it thoroughly before you finalize any plans for your trip. Decide where you would like to visit and what you would like to do when you are there. Consider the choice of hotels; decide if there are some specific restaurants, theaters, or nightspots that you will visit; make a list of the things you would like to buy while you are away; *then* go talk to your travel agent.

Remember that although travel agents are well qualified to advise on airfares and some package tours, it is unrealistic to expect them to be familiar with the details of all destinations around the world. A good agent will appreciate your making informed suggestions, and I know of several who have used the contact names and telephone numbers found in all Maverick Guides to help with the detailed planning and booking for their clients.

The book is also designed to be used when you are in Vietnam, Laos, and Cambodia. Travel restrictions are being progressively eased, so there are many more opportunities to travel as you wish and stay in the hotels of your choice. You will find our recommendations on tours, hotels, restaurants, and shopping will help smooth your travels. The information on sightseeing, culture, and sports will help broaden your horizons and encourage you to explore things that most visitors miss. All of the sections are geared toward helping you save time and money.

In this volume, I have included many maps that will help you orient yourself quickly and show you where hotels, restaurants, sightseeing attractions, and shops are located. There are also some regional maps that give you a wider picture and help you plan a practical itinerary.

Some Quick Comments

This book is a great source of information on Vietnam, Laos, and Cambodia; I also hope you find it to be a good read. The descriptive chapters are designed to give you a good appreciation of the countries, the people, and the cultures. You will find that you will know more about life in these countries than many tourists who have been there on a brief, fully escorted package tour.

There is very little tourist or business information and precious few modern books of any value available about these countries. Your travel agent may be able to give you a little information, and you should try your library, but don't expect too much. There is a whole range of publications that concentrate on history and the Indochina war period in particular. Some of these are excellent, and they provide useful background information on lifestyle and why some attitudes exist today.

Prices in this book are quoted in either U.S. dollars or local currency. In other Maverick Guides I have always used local currency because that is what a visitor will need to be familiar with when traveling around. In Vietnam, Laos, and Cambodia, it is a little different. In many cases, there are both local and tourist prices. If you are non-Asian, it is almost impossible to pay anything but the tourist price, which will almost always be quoted in U.S. dollars. There is a tourist price for most accommodations, some restaurants, most tours, almost all admissions to sightseeing attractions, many shops, and for most transport. It is very frustrating, particularly when you know you are paying up to ten times the local price, but there is little you can do about it. Always ask for the local price and always offer to pay in local currency, but if this is refused, you will just have to grin and bear it.

Collecting information for this guidebook has been a difficult and occasionally frustrating experience. It will never be possible for me to visit every place and experience every aspect of Vietnam, Laos, and Cambodia. Serious travelers and some business visitors to the region will find that they are eating, shopping, or staying in places that I have not mentioned. I would love to hear about these places, so the next edition of the book can be improved for future readers. Please write to me (care of the publisher) and tell me about your experiences.

Use either the enclosed letter/envelope form, or if that is not enough space, copy the address onto your own envelope and include as many pages as you like. Your reactions to both the book and the destinations are earnestly solicited and will be warmly appreciated.

Good Traveling!
LEN RUTLEDGE

2

Happy Landings

How to Get There

The only practical way for Western visitors to enter Vietnam, Laos, and Cambodia is by air. This situation may change shortly if Laos and Cambodia open their land borders with Thailand, and if Vietnam eases restrictions on its Chinese border. Collectively, this area was once known as Indochina and that remains a convenient name even though all three countries are totally independent.

There are regularly scheduled air services linking Saigon (Ho Chi Minh City), Hanoi, Vientiane, and Phnom Penh with the outside world. Each of the three countries has one or more airlines that operate internationally—**Vietnam Airlines, Lao Aviation, Pacific Airlines, Cambodian Airlines,** and **Kampuchean Airlines**—and several Western international airlines also serve the region.

Bangkok originally emerged as the most convenient port of embarkation to the Indochina region, but as services develop, other cities are becoming just as convenient. Hong Kong has become the logical choice for North American travelers because of its excellent **Cathay Pacific** connections to both Hanoi and Saigon and **Dragonair** services to Phnom Penh. Cathay Pacific also has daily Boeing 747 services from both Los Angeles and Vancouver to Hong Kong, so passengers can have

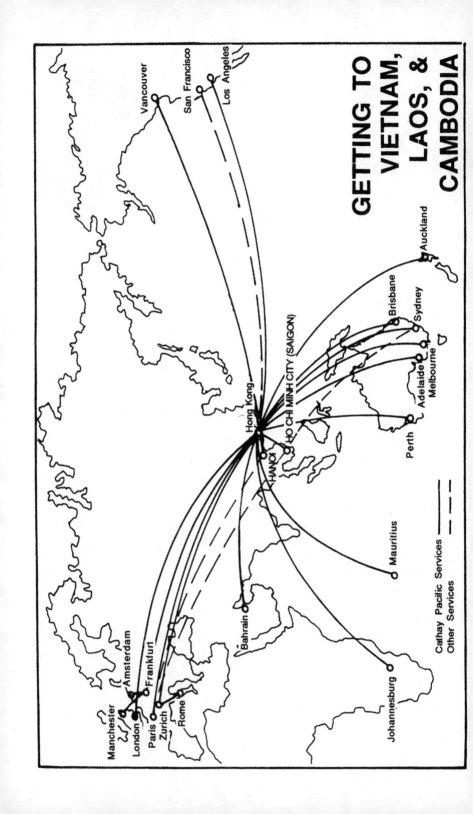

GETTING TO VIETNAM, LAOS, & CAMBODIA

Vancouver
San Francisco
Los Angeles
Auckland
Brisbane
Sydney
Adelaide
Melbourne
Perth
Hong Kong
HO CHI MINH CITY (SAIGON)
HANOI
Mauritius
Bahrain
Johannesburg
Manchester
Amsterdam
London
Frankfurt
Paris
Zurich
Rome

Cathay Pacific Services ——————
Other Services ——————

the convenience of using the same airline for the entire trip. When that airline is consistently rated as one of the best airlines in the world, it becomes a very attractive package. Vientiane and Phnom Penh can then be accessed from Hanoi or Saigon by **Lao Aviation, Kampuchean Airlines,** or **Vietnam Airlines.**

Hong Kong has become an equally convenient gateway for European passengers because of the direct Europe to Hong Kong services that are now available. Cathay Pacific has nonstop connections with London, Paris, Frankfurt, and Zurich, and one-stop connections with Rome, Amsterdam, and Manchester. South African, Australian, and New Zealand passengers are also discovering the benefits of the Hong Kong route. Not the least of these is the opportunity to have a stopover in one of the most exciting cities in Asia.

If you plan to see some other countries in southeast Asia on your trip, you can fly to Kuala Lumpur, Singapore, Taipei, and Manila from some point within Indochina. From these cities, there are direct Cathay Pacific flights back to Hong Kong and then home.

No North American airline currently flies into Indochina, but that is expected to change in 1995. **Air France, KLM,** and **Lufthansa** have some services into Vietnam. **Quantas** operates from Australia.

Transportation within Vietnam, Laos, and Cambodia

Air. Because of government restrictions, poor ground infrastructure, and weather and topographical constraints, most visitors will find that they will travel many internal legs within the region by air. This means using the services of the national airlines. Until very recently, Vietnam Airlines had a poor reputation for maintenance, safety, and service, and the other carriers were not far behind. The situation now is a little different. Air Vietnam and Lao Aviation have new aircraft that operate international routes, and there have even been some improvements internally. Pacific Airlines and Cambodia Airlines both operate modern jet aircraft.

The following is the situation as of December 1994. Vietnam Airlines operates a Russian TU134 flight from Hanoi to Vientiane and return on Mondays, Thursdays, and Sundays, and Lao Aviation has a Tuesday flight using a Boeing 737. Lao Aviation has a Friday B-737 flight from Vientiane to Ho Chi Minh City, which returns to Vientiane via Phnom Penh. Vietnam Airlines has round trip flights from Ho Chi Minh City (Saigon) to Phnom Penh at least daily. Cambodia Airlines operates twice a week with 737 aircraft.

Within Vietnam and Laos, there is a reasonable network of flights. Due to continuing problems in Cambodia, there are far fewer routes there. Vietnam Airlines connects Hanoi with Danang, Ho Chi Minh City, Hue, Nha Trang, and Dien Bien Phu with direct services. From Ho Chi Minh City, there are direct services to Ban Ma Thuot, Dalat, Danang, Haiphong, Hanoi, Hue, Nha Trang, Phu Quoc, Pleiku, Can Tho, and Quy Nhon. Lao Aviation connects Vientiane with Savannakhet, Pakse, Luang Prabang, Oudom Xay, Xieng Khouang, Vien Xay, Xayaboury, Houei Sai, Ahapeu, Thakhek, Namtha, Salavanh, and Xieng Khang. In Cambodia, the only services currently running on a regular basis are from Phnom Penh to Siem Reap (for Angkor), and from Phnom Penh to Stung Treng.

Internal flights are often fully booked several days ahead of time, and on some flights you will see three people squeezed into two seats because of overbooking. Foreigners pay fares that are several times higher than local fares, so there is some encouragement to find a seat for a foreigner even if a flight is full. You are required to pay for airline tickets in U.S. dollars. Traveler's checks are not accepted. Each national airline uses Soviet or Chinese aircraft on most internal services. Some are in very poor condition, and safety instructions and other cabin precautions that are compulsory in the West are unknown here. Nevertheless, most flights arrive at their destination close to their scheduled time. For some reason, Soviet and Chinese aircraft often pour clouds of thick vapor from their ventilation systems—so don't be alarmed when this happens. It is considered normal.

Train. There are no train connections between the three countries. Within Vietnam, the Hanoi to Ho Chi Minh City rail line is slowly being improved, and train services are speeding up; however, they are still painfully slow. Most train services are heavily booked, and except for the more expensive cars of a few express trains, comfort is not great. The trains, however, are about five times better than the buses. Most local trains have wooden seats, but there is usually plenty of leg room. There are no airconditioned cars, and most sleeping berths are a wooden deck with a palm leaf mat.

Laos has no railway, and foreigners are not permitted to travel on Cambodia's rail lines at present because of the security situation. Hopefully that will soon change. I understand that the Thai Rail Authority has undertaken a preliminary survey of the rail line from the Thai border to Phnom Penh with a view to starting Bangkok to Phnom Penh services as soon as possible.

Bus. Buses run every day from Saigon to Phnom Penh, but foreigners are sometimes discouraged from using them. You will need a visa that specifically states that you can enter the destination country at the land border point. If you have this visa but still run into problems with the buses, it is usually possible to hitch a ride with a vehicle belonging to one of the non-government agencies working in this area. They frequently travel this stretch of road.

Currently there are no other border crossings that foreigners can use by

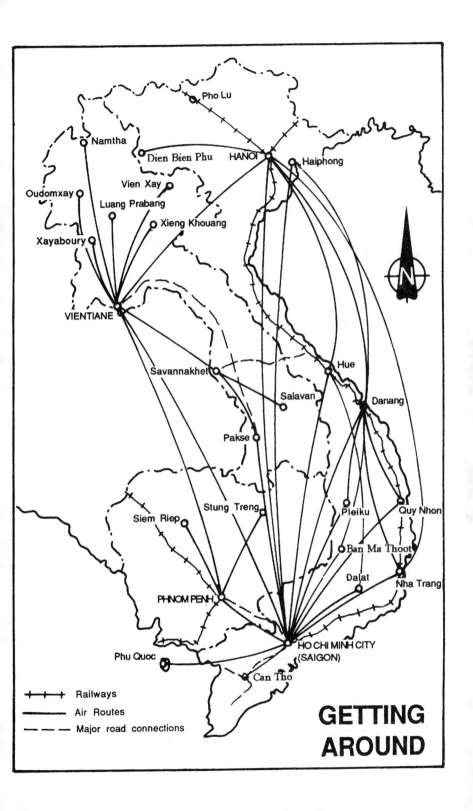

Pho Lu

Namtha

Dien Bien Phu   HANOI   Haiphong

Vien Xay

Oudomxay

Luang Prabang

Xayaboury   Xieng Khouang

VIENTIANE

Savannakhet

Salavan   Hue

Pakse   Danang

Stung Treng

Siem Riep   Pleiku   Quy Nhon

Ban Ma Thoot

Dalat   Nha Trang

PHNOM PENH

HO CHI MINH CITY
(SAIGON)

Phu Quoc

Can Tho

N

+++ Railways

——— Air Routes

– – – Major road connections

GETTING
AROUND

bus. This situation is likely to change in the near future as Laos and Vietnam open up to tourism. An obvious connection is the route from Savannakhet (on the Mekong in Laos) across the border at Lao Bao to national highway 9 in Vietnam. This would have a good connection with Hue.

Within Vietnam, there is an extensive network of buses. Almost all of them suffer from frequent breakdowns, have narrow bench seats, little leg room, and chronic overcrowding. I am not a fan of bus travel under these circumstances. In Laos, there are some long-distance bus services; but many roads are almost impassable during the wet season, and are poor at best during the rest of the year. In Cambodia, there is a limited bus service at present due to the political situation and civil war. Over the past few years, the government has often imposed a ban on bus travel for foreigners.

Boat. There is some boat traffic between Vietnam and Cambodia, but nothing of interest to foreigners. The authorities in both countries are very wary of foreign entry by this means. Along the Vietnamese coastline there are some freighters, but again these are generally off-limits to foreigners. Shorter trips around the Mekong Delta are possible. There are regular boats from Saigon to Mythos for instance, and you can travel on to other destinations from there.

Boat travel is still common in Laos, particularly on the Mekong River. There are regular river ferries from Vientiane to Luang Prabang and from Vientiane to Savannakhet. Some have food stalls on board, while others stop at villages. On-board facilities are very basic. Within Cambodia, boat travel was popular, but like all other forms of travel, it has been curtailed by the civil war. The Mekong is navigable all year to Kratie, and as far north as Stung Treng in flood time. There is a regular service to Kratie (taking 3 days from Phnom Penh), and another to Phnom Kron on Tonle Sap south of Siem Reap.

Rental Cars. There are no facilities to rent a self-drive car; but each country has some cars with drivers. Government rental cars with drivers regularly make the journey from Saigon to Phnom Penh, but this is the only connection between countries at present.

Travel Facts

Climate. Cambodia and southern Vietnam are always hot. Temperatures vary from bearable to sweltering. As you travel north or climb the highlands, the weather moderates and the winter evenings can be positively cool. The mean annual temperature is around 27 degrees Celsius in the south, and 21 degrees Celsius in the far north.

There are substantial local variations; but in general, the hottest period is around April and May, the wettest period is June through October, and the coldest period is December and January. There is no universally accepted "best time" to visit this region, but my personal choice is November through to March.

Packing. My standard advice to all travelers is to travel light, and I repeat that for Vietnam, Laos, and Cambodia. You will never need large quantities of warm clothing, so leave them at home. You will need a supply of light, easy-to-wash, casual clothes, something more formal for business meetings or a special night on the town, and a sweater for evenings in the highlands.

I do acknowledge, however, that you probably need a few "extras" because of the poor supply situation in much of the region. These could include some English language reading material, a flashlight (torch) with batteries, a good supply of film (if you use anything other than ASA100 color print film), sanitary napkins, a first aid kit, a few small gifts, and perhaps a pocket shortwave radio if you wish to keep up with world events.

Like most Asians, the Laos, the Vietnamese, and the Khmers are more conservative than many people in the West. You need to respect that and either keep your micro-bikini in your bag or leave it at home. Remember that shorts, bare midriffs, and bare shoulders are not acceptable in temples or even some museums. Pack some conservative gear to wear on these occasions.

Public Holidays. There are both religious and secular holidays in each country. The religious holidays are generally determined by the lunar calendar, whereas the secular holidays are based on the Christian calendar that we know in the West. Year 1 of the Vietnamese lunar calendar corresponds to 2637 B.C., while in Laos it is 638 B.C.

In Vietnam, the New Year (Tet), which usually falls in late January or early February is the most important festival. It is the time of family reunions, new clothes, flowers, special food, the payment of debt, and new beginnings. The whole country stops for a period of up to seven days. In Laos and Cambodia, the New Year celebrations are held in April. There are festivals, religious gatherings, water throwing, and family get-togethers. Three days in the middle of the month are public holidays.

International Labor Day (May 1) is a holiday in each of the three countries. Cambodian Independence Day is November 9. Vietnam National Day, which celebrates the promulgation of the Declaration of Independence by Ho Chi Minh in 1945, is September 2. Lao National Day is December 2. It celebrates the 1975 victory of the proletariat over the monarchy.

Mail and Telephone Service. Within all three countries, mail and telephone services have improved dramatically over the past few years. Most Western countries are now able to get letters to and from the region in about seven to ten days. The restrictions on letters which caused much mail to go through Moscow are now gone. It is always better to post international letters at the main post offices in Hanoi, Saigon, Vientiane, and Phnom Penh, rather than in local post offices. International mail from Vietnam is relatively expensive. In Laos and Cambodia it is less so. Make sure you see the clerk cancel the stamps while you are there, otherwise you run the risk of someone soaking them off and throwing the letters away.

It is now possible to make direct-dial telephone calls to Vietnam, Laos, and Cambodia from many parts of the world. This is largely due to satellite links provided by Australia's OTC Service. International dialing codes are 84 for Vietnam, 856 for Laos, and 855 for Cambodia. In theory, this also means that you can make direct-dial telephone calls from these countries. Many hotels now have these facilities, and there is a growing network of public telephones connected to the international satellite. The irony is that although you can effectively use satellite technology to telephone across the world, your chances of making a successful call across a city are less than even.

There are rapidly growing fax services, and you will see many fax numbers listed in this book. Although faxes are a good record in case of later disputes, you will find that replies to your faxes will be very tardy or will not be received at all. This is probably because the cost for faxes and telephone calls in local values is very high, and people try to avoid this expense.

Telegraph and telex facilities are still available from each country although these are now declining. A few major centers have extended hours for telegraph, telex, fax, and international telephone service. Vietnam has DHL Worldwide Express document delivery services from Hanoi and Saigon.

Metrics and Electrics

The metric system of weights and measures is used throughout Vietnam, Laos, and Cambodia. If you are not familiar with the system, you can quickly learn a few conversions that will help you make sense of the strange terms. It is strongly recommended that you do this if you wish to be familiar with what tomorrow's temperature will be or how far it is to your planned destination.

Temperature. In the Celsius system, zero degrees is the freezing point of water, and 100 degrees is the boiling point. From a climatic point of view, 10 degrees Celsius is cold, 20 degrees Celsius is temperate, 30 degrees Celsius is quite warm, and 40 degrees Celsius is extremely hot. In Fahrenheit, these are equivalent to 50 degrees, 68 degrees, 86 degrees, and 104 degrees respectively.

Distance. Is it close or far away? Will it take 2 hours or 5 hours to get there? These are the questions that travelers ask, and the answers are relatively easy. All distances shown on signboards are in kilometers. To do a rough conversion to miles, remember that 5 kilometers is approximately 3 miles. Therefore, 10 kilometers equals 6 miles; and 100 kilometers is roughly 60 miles. Travel through the region is slow, so make allowances for poor roads, ferry crossings, and slow trains when calculating times.

For small distances, remember that 5 centimeters equals 2 inches, 30cm equals 1 foot, and a meter and a yard are roughly equal.

Electricity. Voltages, amperages, and cycles are a total mystery to most people, so don't worry too much about that. What you need to know is that Vietnam uses both 110 volts (North American standard) and 220 volts (European/Australian/Asian standard). It is very difficult to tell what outlets are each voltage—even the locals don't know sometimes. This means that whatever electrical appliances you bring with you they will not operate part of the time, and you run the risk of burning them out. In Laos and Cambodia, 220 volts is the common system.

The standard of electrical wiring is frightening. I have not made one trip to the region without running foul of the electrical system. Bare wires are often wound together to make a connection. This is then left exposed—even in bathrooms. In Vietnam and Laos, I have had hotel room hot water systems burn out on me, and it's not a happy situation to be under a shower when sparks and smoke are emanating from the water heater.

In all three countries, electricity outages are common, particularly in the wet season, so you need a flashlight (torch) and some candles. In some rural areas, electricity is only supplied for a few hours each evening. All this can be a real problem. My advice is leave your electrical appliances at home. One advantage of these countries is that labor is very cheap, so it is better to pay someone to press your clothes, wash and dry your hair, and so forth rather than do it yourself.

Money and Prices

Money. The currency in Vietnam is the *dong*. One hundred dong is shown in this book as 100d. You will see bank notes in denominations of 200d, 500d, 1,000d, 2,000d, 5,000d, 10,000d, 20,000d, and 50,000d. There are no coins in use in Vietnam. The inflation rate in Vietnam has varied between high and astronomical, but is now under control. The conversion rate is around 11,500d to US$1. When you change US$100, you are an instant millionaire. You also receive a pile of notes higher than a house brick, so you need a bag to carry your haul.

As a Western visitor, you will find that there are a number of times when you will not be able to pay in dong. Most hotels, some restaurants, Vietnam Airlines, many tour companies, and some other places will only accept payment in U.S. dollars. Traveler's checks are accepted by some banks but few hotels. Credit cards are accepted at a growing number of hotels. This means that the visitor needs to carry U.S. cash—large bills for major payments, and small bills for small expenses and to make up odd amounts in hotel bills and so forth. Make sure that the notes you have are clean and not torn. This was the case in late 1994 even though the government had brought in a law saying that all payments must now be in dong.

The currency in Laos is the *kip.* In the late 1980s, there was rampant inflation and the exchange rate halved in twelve months. Now it has stabilized at around 720 kip to one U.S. dollar. At the same time, you can pay for some things in Thai baht or U.S. dollars. In shops, the currencies are almost interchangeable. You can make a single purchase with a combination of all three currencies.

Traveler's checks and credit cards are still only of limited use in Laos, so you need to bring U.S. dollars cash with you. You can change U.S. dollars at a bank or at a money changer. Most shop owners will be happy to give you kip in exchange for your dollars or baht.

The currency in Cambodia is the *riel.* In 1989, you got about 150 riel for one U.S. dollar, but at the end of 1994, the rate was 2,500. This appeared to be both the official and black market rate at that time. In fact, whereas the black market was quite open in 1989; it was difficult to find in 1994. As in Laos, traveler's checks and credit cards are only of limited use.

Prices. If you can somehow get into the dong, kip, or riel economy, traveling through Vietnam, Laos, and Cambodia can be very inexpensive indeed. This is easier said than done for a non-Asian, English-speaking visitor. Unless you are very firm, you will find yourself being directed to places that think in dollars and are automatically up to ten times the local price. I have managed on a few occasions to pay for hotels, tours, and even a car and driver in local currency, but generally it is difficult to do. I usually only go to restaurants that have local prices, but some hotel restaurants insist on dollar payment. I always bargain for purchases in local currency.

Some of these things may help a little, but I suspect that I still end up paying substantially more than what a local would pay. Foreigners are often overcharged in restaurants on the assumption that they cannot read the bill. I always insist on going through a bill item by item with the waiter or waitress, or if they cannot speak English, with anyone in the place that can talk with me. About 25 percent of the time, things that I did not have were added to the bill or a higher charge was made for an item that I did have. The problem seems to be far worse in Vietnam than in Laos or Cambodia.

Tipping. Many hotels and restaurants add a ten percent service charge to the bill, so tipping is not expected. Even places that do not do this, do not expect you to leave a large tip. I suspect that a healthy figure is already built into the price. Please do not encourage the practice of heavy tipping.

Small gifts for people such as guides and business contacts are always appreciated. If you are working in the region, you will get far greater support if the occasional pack of cigarettes or chocolates is passed around. A duty-free bottle of scotch or brandy is likely to do wonders.

Governmental Fiddle-Faddle

Passports and Visas. You'll need a passport to enter any of the countries in Asia and to get back into your own country. You should ask your travel agent or the relevant government department about how you get a passport.

Additionally, you will need a visa for each country you wish to visit. These are issued by the government of the country to which you are going. In the case of Vietnam, Laos, and Cambodia, they are not as simple to obtain as you might imagine. The difficulty is twofold. First, all three countries have had socialist systems in place for quite a few years. This means you need more perseverance and patience than you would in dealing with other countries. The second problem is the lack of representative embassies in much of the world. Until the late 1980s, all three countries had embassies in the communist block and almost nowhere else. Now there is more representation, but no Western country has embassies of all three countries.

The other problem is knowing exactly what is required to get a visa. This is in a state of flux at present, and is likely to become easier as they become more accustomed to "capitalist" visitors. If you are planning to visit all three countries, or Vietnam and one other, I strongly suggest that you consider going to Vietnam first. You can then arrange your Cambodian and Laos visas in Vietnam.

Vietnam tourist visas were once difficult to obtain, but I obtained my most recent one in four days through the Vietnam embassy in Australia. The peace of mind of having one before leaving home is important to many people. You cannot arrive in Vietnam without a visa.

Most travelers to Laos will enter the country on a tourist visa. When applying from abroad, this will take at least two months (my first application took eight months), but it can be much faster if done through the Lao embassy in Bangkok or Hanoi. If you plan to spend only a short time in Laos, a transit visa—which allows a stay of up to five days—may be the easiest to obtain. The visa is usually granted by an embassy without argument if you present a confirmed air ticket between two external points showing a stopover in Vientiane. Such a visa is obtainable in Vietnam for around US$10.

Visas for travel to Cambodia are issued by embassies or consulates in Hanoi, Saigon, and Vientiane, and by some travel agencies in Bangkok,

Hong Kong, and Singapore. These agencies charge heavily for the privilege, and they will give you a visa on a card separate from your passport or will arrange for someone to meet you at Phnom Penh's Pochentong Airport to deliver the pre-arranged visa.

Business visas are more complicated, but they can be issued for longer periods and they allow for greater freedom within a designated area. For each country, you will require a letter of introduction from some official body within the country. This can take a long time and can be a very frustrating exercise. Saigon is the most likely starting point for business travelers, so a contact with the People's Committee of Ho Chi Minh City at 86 Le Thanh Ton Street, Saigon; the Office for Foreign Economic Relations at 45 Ben Chuong Duong Street, Saigon; or the Chamber of Commerce and Industry at 171 Vo Thi Sau Street, Saigon, could be useful in starting the process.

Travel Restrictions. Independent travel around Cambodia is almost impossible at present; but you will find that when you reach Vietnam and Laos, you can travel independently if you wish.

In Vietnam, all foreigners must register with the immigration police within two days of their arrival. Some of the larger hotels in Saigon and Hanoi have registration offices within their buildings, or they will arrange to register you if you leave your papers with them. If you are staying in a small hotel or privately, you must register yourself. When individual travelers arrive at a place they intend to stay for more than 48 hours, they must register with the local police. This is done automatically if you are staying in a hotel.

Internal travel permits have at last been abolished in Vietnam and Laos, so that is one major administrative hassle out of the way. Unfortunately though, some local bodies in Vietnam are demanding permits (and sometimes official car rental) to visit some specific places within the country. This is probably illegal but there is little a visitor can do about it. One of the problems is in knowing where you currently need a permit. Certainly there are parts of the central highlands and the old DMZ where a local permit is necessary. You will need to check for yourself because the position is changing constantly.

Here is a useful list of some embassies in the West and some within the region where you will be able to get additional information and help:

Vietnam

Australia—6 Timbarra Crescent, O'Malley, ACT 2603 (Tel: 062-866-059)
Cambodia—Son Ngoc Minh Ave, Phnom Penh (Tel: 25481)
Canada—695 Davidson Drive, Ottawa (Tel: 613-744-0698)
Germany—Konstantinstr 37 5300 Bann 2 (Tel: 0228-357-022)
France—62 Rue de Boileau 75016 Paris (Tel: 45-245-063)

Japan—50-11 Moto Yoyogi-Cho Shibuya-ku Tokyo (Tel: 3-466-3311)
Laos—Thanon That Luang, Vientiane (Tel: -5578)
Malaysia—4 Periaran Stonor, Kuala Lumpur (Tel: 03-248-4036)
Thailand—83/1 Wireless Road, Bangkok (Tel: 02-251-7201)
U.K.—12 Victoria Road, London W85RD (Tel: -937-1912)
U.S.A.—U.N Mission, 20 Waterside Plaza, New York, NY 10010 (Tel: 212-685-8001)

Laos

Australia—1 Dalman Crescent, O'Malley, ACT 2603 (Tel: 062-864-595)
Cambodia—111 214th Street Phnom Penh (Tel: -251-821)
Germany—1100 Berlin Esplanade 17, Berlin
Japan—3-3-22, Nishi Azabu, Minato-ku, Tokyo (Tel: 5411-2291)
U.S.A.—2222 S Street N.W., Washington, D.C. 20008 (Tel: 202-332-6416)
Vietnam—40 Quang Trung Street, Hanoi (Tel: -252-588)

Cambodia

Laos—Thanon Saphan Thong Neva, Vientiane (Tel: -2750)
Vietnam—71 Tran Hung Dao Street, Hanoi (Tel: -253-788)
    41 Phung Khai Khoan Street, Saigon (Tel: -292-715)

Travel Agents

Hong Kong—Abercrombie and Kent, 24 Henessy Road, Wanchai (Tel: -865-7818)
Phoenix Services Agency, 96 Nathan Road, Kowloon (Tel: -722-7378)
Traveler Services, 57 Peking Road, Tsim Sha Tsui (Tel: -367-4127)
Bangkok—Exotissismo Travel, 21/17 Sukhumvit, Soi 4, Bangkok (Tel: -253-5240)
Diethelm Travel, 140/1 Wireless Road, Bangkok (Tel: -255-9150)

Customs. Regulations are fairly similar in all three countries. At times, they are rigidly enforced; but at other times, there is a more relaxed atmosphere.

Visitors can bring in almost unlimited quantities of jewelry and foreign currency, but they must be declared on the customs arrival form. Any cameras, watches, radios, tape players, and so forth must be declared as well. When you are leaving the country, you have to fill in another customs form which is compared to the arrival one. You may be asked to prove that you are taking all these items out with you and be asked to show receipts for foreign currency transactions. Fortunately, as more experience is gained with Western tourism and business people, the regulations appear to be easing.

Airport taxes. Each country has a departure tax which is collected at the departure hall. The current rate is US$5-8 to be paid only in U.S. currency.

Traveler's Guide

Safety. I have never encountered any personal safety problems in the region, but there are boundless stories about people who have. Whether these are accurate or not is difficult to determine. Certainly the world economic downturn of the early 1990s—combined with local factors such as the demise of communism, the opening of tourism, and the reduction in size of military forces—has caused an increase in crime. There are gangs of pickpockets in Saigon (I know through personal experience), and there are individuals who attempt to confidence trick unwary travelers. Theft from hotels is more common than it once was, and it is not considered wise to leave anything in a parked car. I believe the situation in Laos is much less dramatic. Cambodia is experiencing a rise in petty (and serious) crime.

The security situation is relatively good in Vietnam and Laos. In some areas, it is considered unwise to travel at night, and there are some stories of tourist vehicles being stopped and robbed. I believe these are fairly isolated incidents. In Cambodia, the security situation is less assured due to the continued fighting. There are several areas that I would be wary of visiting. Fortunately the government agrees and discourages people from traveling there.

It is still unwise to walk in isolated areas due to three decades of bombing, mining, and booby-trapping carried out by various armed forces in the region. Many thousands of local people have been injured or killed by leftover war material, so you should avoid coming in contact with this at all times.

Vietnam, Laos, and Cambodia are all predominantly Buddhist countries and they are generally free of specific hassles for female travelers. Women should be aware, however, that prostitution occurs in many cheap hotels, and this has the potential of being a problem for the visitor.

Business Hours. Most people in the region rise early. This was the established pattern on the farms, and it has carried over into city life. Many offices, shops, museums, and government departments open at somewhere between 7 and 8 A.M. Many then close for 1½ to 2 hours sometime between 11 A.M. and 2 P.M., then operate again until 4 or 5 P.M. Shops often remain open until 7 or 8 P.M.

Almost all offices and government departments are closed on Sunday, and many also close Saturday afternoon.

Tourist Information: It is extremely difficult to get reliable tourist information on any of the three countries. This is partly because the tourism industry is still in its infancy and partly because there is very limited overseas representation.

I have found that embassies have little or no useful tourist literature, and most travel agents know little about the region. Libraries contain many books on the Indochina War but little else.

Airline representative offices do have some material, and this would be my first choice—after reading this book. You could try the following:

Vietnam Airlines

Hong Kong—Peregrine Tower, 89 Queensway (Tel: 2810-4896)
Singapore—Beach Center, 15 Beach Road (Tel: 339-3552)
Thailand—584 Ploenchit Road (Tel: 251-4242)

Lao Aviation

Hong Kong—China Travel, CTS House, 78 Connaught Road (Tel: 853-3888)
Japan—Transindo Ltd., 2-7-16 Mita Minto-ku, Tokyo (Tel: 3454-3391)
Thailand—1/29 Silom Plaza, Silom Road, Bangkok (Tel: 235-5557)
U.S.A.—Lao-American, 338 S. Hancock Avenue, South Elgin, Illinois 60177 (Tel: 312-742-2159)

Cathay Pacific

Australia—28 O'Connell Street, Sydney (Tel: 02-931-5500)
    30 Collins Street, Melbourne (Tel: 03-653-2022)
Canada—18/F, 650 West Georgia Street, Vancouver VGB 4N8 (Tel: 604-682-9747)
France—267 Bld Pereire 75017 Paris (Tel: 406-86160)
Germany—Feuerbachstrasse 26 6000 Frankfurt (Tel: 710-08221)
Hong Kong—Swire House, 9 Cannaught Road (Tel: -747-1888)
Japan—5-2 Yurakucho 1-Chome, Chuyoda-ku, Tokyo 100 (Tel: 03-3504-1531)
New Zealand—Stock Exchange Bldg., 191 Queen Street, Auckland (Tel: -379-0861)
South Africa—Norwich Life Towers, Fredman Drive, Sandown, Sandton 2199 Johannesburg (Tel: 011-883-9226)
Switzerland—Todistrasse 44 8039 Zurich (Tel: 01-202-8156)
Taiwan—129 Min Sheng East Road, 3, Taipei (Tel: 02-712-8228)
United Kingdom—52 Berkeley Street, London WI (Tel: 071-930-4444)
    4/F Arkwright House, Parsonage Gardens, Manchester M2 3LF (Tel: 061-833-0126)
USA—360 N. Michigan Avenue, Chicago, IL (Tel: 800-233-2742)

300 N. Continental Bldg., El Segundo, Los Angeles CA 90245 (Tel: 800-233-2742)

590 Fifth Avenue, New York, NY 10036 (Tel: 800-233-2742)

Vietnam—49 Le Thanh Tong Street, Ho Chi Minh City (Tel: 223-203)

News Media. The news media in Vietnam and Laos is still firmly in the hands of the government and the army. This has little influence on the visitor because almost all the media (press, radio, and television) is in the local language, and it is of almost zero interest to visitors. There are weekly papers in English in Vietnam and Cambodia. Foreign newspapers were banned during the 1970s and 1980s from each of the countries, but now some are available. The Bangkok newspapers in English are available in limited numbers in most of the major centers. Papers from Hong Kong, Singapore, and occasionally Australia are sometimes available in Hanoi, Saigon, and Phnom Penh.

An English language news service is broadcast by Radio Vietnam each morning at 6 A.M. on 1010 KHz (AM band), and the Lao National Radio has English-language news services on its one radio station at 1 P.M. and 8.30 P.M. Shortwave radio broadcasts from Radio Australia, the BBC, and the Voice of America can be received in Hanoi, Saigon, Vientiane, and Phnom Penh.

Vietnamese television has two channels that broadcast to most areas. Vientiane has one TV channel, but Thai TV is readily available. Cambodia has three channels. Satellite TV is available at many of the hotels.

Travel Tips in Indochina

Before you go

● Consider the airline options. Comfort and safety are important. The lowest-priced bargain airfare is not always the cheapest in the long run.

● Stopover options are an important factor in long-haul travel. With the "right" airfare, you can probably stop at a good destination on the way for little extra cost.

● Travel insurance is a "must." I would not travel to this region without a comprehensive policy.

● Arrange unlimited medical insurance, including a policy that provides for your evacuation to a Western country if major medical treatment is required.

● If you are traveling with someone, make sure both of you have some traveler's checks and U.S. cash. Credit cards have limited use at present.

● Travel light. Cool, casual clothes are what you will need.

● Get your timing right. Try to avoid the peak of the hot season, and the worst of the wet season.

- Don't be late at the airport. Airlines often overbook to compensate for "no-shows." If too many people turn up, it is often the last arrivals who suffer.
- Watch out for excess baggage charges. International travel to Asia permits 20 kilos in economy and 30 kilos in business. The excess charge can be very high. Try to carry small, heavy items in your hand baggage if you know you are over the allowed weight.

While you are away

- Always confirm onward flights as early as possible. Most airlines do not have computer links to the Indochina gateways, so manual systems are still in place. It is important to get your name on a flight list early.
- Understand what your money is worth, and try to buy things using the local currency as a bargaining tool.
- Report lost credit cards promptly. Even if this requires an international telephone call, you must do it. Your liability is then small.
- Always carry your travel documents, money, and medical items with you, just in case the airline, busline, railway, or hotel misplaces your main bag.
- In restaurants, do not order items that are not on the menu, and always ask the price of a drink before you order it.
- Always put your valuables in the hotel safety deposit.
- Don't tip unnecessarily. Most people will not expect it.
- Don't wear new shoes while you are away. Comfort is essential when traveling.
- Accept that you will be overcharged for government services at times. There is nothing you can do about it, and getting annoyed will not help the situation.

Visit the Region

Vietnam, Laos, and Cambodia are conveniently placed within southeast Asia, so it is possible to visit some other countries in the region as part of your trip. Because there are very few direct flights into the region from Europe, North America, and Australia, you normally travel via another destination. This can be an important stopover and added bonus.

Hong Kong is certainly the most convenient access point from North America, and it is also convenient from Europe. As a stopover destination it is brilliant. The city is an amazing business center, but it is also a colorful, cosmopolitan city in which traditional Chinese culture survives amid the most modern Western amenities.

You will find some of the most dazzling shopping bazaars in the East,

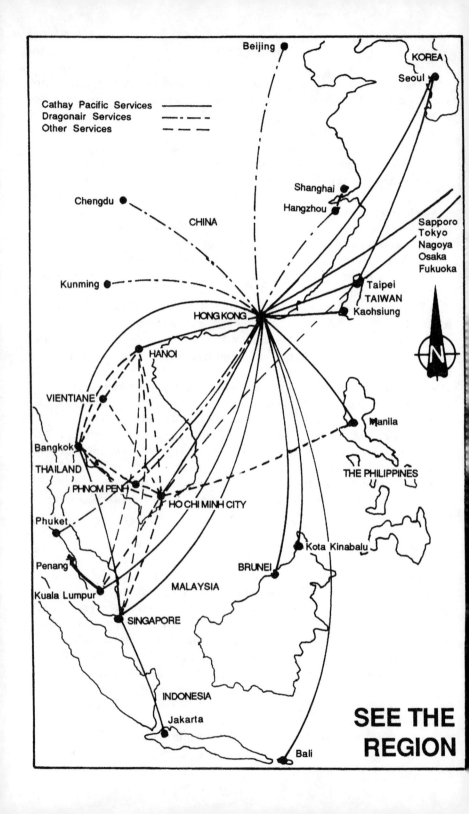

Beijing

KOREA
Seoul

Cathay Pacific Services
Dragonair Services
Other Services

Shanghai
Hangzhou

Chengdu

CHINA

Sapporo
Tokyo
Nagoya
Osaka
Fukuoka

Kunming

Taipei
TAIWAN
Kaohsiung

HONG KONG

HANOI

N

VIENTIANE

Manila

Bangkok
THAILAND

THE PHILIPPINES

PHNOM PENH

HO CHI MINH CITY

Phuket

Kota Kinabalu

Penang

BRUNEI

Kuala Lumpur

MALAYSIA

SINGAPORE

INDONESIA

Jakarta

SEE THE
REGION

Bali

some of the world's best Chinese restaurants, a magnificent harbor surrounded with stunning architecture, great tourist attractions, and the
excitement that is missing from most other destinations in the region. Ride
the Star Ferry across the harbor, or take the super-slick mass transit railway
to a station near your destination. For a wonderful view, ride the Peak Tram
to the top of the mountain on Hong Kong Island. For more details, see
The Maverick Guide to Hong Kong, Macau, and South China.

Taiwan, or Formosa as it was named by the Portuguese, has been occupied
over the centuries by the Chinese, Portuguese, Spanish, Dutch, French, and
Japanese. In 1949, two million mainland Chinese refugees arrived, bringing
with them their culture, artistic skills, commercial abilities, and antique
treasures. The island has some spectacular, rugged scenery; and the capital,
Taipai, has temples, shrines, parks, and the magnificent National Palace
Museum, which contains the world's finest collection of Chinese antiques
and art treasures. Taiwan has become a major investment and trading force
in Asia. It ranks number one as a foreign investor in Vietnam.

Malaysia has palm-fringed beaches, coral reefs teeming with fish, tropical
forests, highland resorts, tea and rubber plantations, and interesting cultures. Kuala Lumpur, the federal capital, is a modern city of tall buildings,
gold-domed mosques, and lush gardens. The islands of Penang, Langkawi,
and Tioman offer excellent facilities for visitors in idyllic surroundings.
For more details, see *The Maverick Guide to Malaysia and Singapore.*

Singapore is a bustling city-state with many contrasts and surprises.
High-density living is the norm in much of Singapore, yet this is probably
one of the cleanest, safest, and most orderly cities in the world. There are
dynamic skyscrapers, quaint old Chinese shop-houses, quiet back lanes,
massive expressways, and bustling bazaars. The population is predominantly
Chinese, with Malay and Indian minorities.

Thailand has sun, sand, sea, mountains, national parks, forests, walled
cities, and ancient ruins. You can find peace and solitude as well as adven-
ture. Bangkok, the capital, has great shopping opportunities, fabulous
restaurants, museums and art galleries, and a nightlife scene that is almost
legendary. All this is supported by one of the most friendly, attractive, and
tolerant people on earth. For more details, see *The Maverick Guide to Thailand.*

The Philippines is an English-speaking nation where visitors can see the
strong influences of Malay, Chinese, Spanish, and American periods of history as well as the considerable achievements of the modern independent
nation. The archipelago of 7,000 islands has a great diversity of ethnic, cultural, and geographic features. The Filipinos are a warm race that love
color, music, dancing, and enjoying themselves.

Vietnam

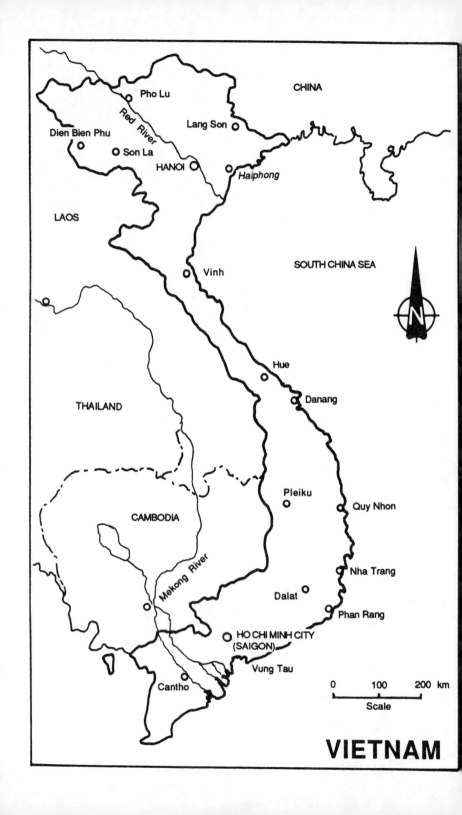

3

The Land and Life of Vietnam

It is said that the Vietnamese have fought for two thousand years to maintain or establish their independence, yet today foreigners are being welcomed like never before. The country has a sublime beauty that it shares with some of its neighbors, that gives it great tourist potential. The country's economy and business establishments have suffered immensely from war, isolation, poor government policies, and too many controls. Now the opportunities are emerging for companies and individuals to be part of the inevitable development that will occur. Vietnam is a challenging and exciting place, yet most visitors know pitifully little about the land, life, and the people.

Many Westerners still think of Vietnam as a war rather than a country. Hollywood perpetuates this idea, as does Vietnam's reticence in revealing its true nature to the outside world. As a result, the country remains one of Asia's great enigmas—a place we seem to know well, yet, in reality, know so little about. One carries with him into Vietnam an exhausting burden of ingested facts, fantasies, and confused images.

Geography

Vietnam's size is deceiving. The country stretches 1,600 kilometers from north to south, from below 9 degrees north to above 23 degrees north.

Although it stretches from 102 degrees east to 109 degrees east, much of it is little more than 200 kilometers wide—and at its narrowest, a mere 60 kilometers. In area, it resembles Italy, and it is a bit smaller than California. The whole country lies within the tropic zone. Hanoi is roughly at the same latitude as Mexico City.

The country has a coastline that is over 3,000 kilometers long, and it has land borders with China (1,150 kilometers), Laos (1,650 kilometers), and Cambodia (950 kilometers). There are two major river systems and agricultural areas—the Red River Delta in the north and the larger Mekong River Delta in the south. Much of the rest of the country consists of mountains or hill country.

The central part of the country is dominated by the Truong Son Mountain Range which forms much of the border with Laos. Swiftly flowing rivers lead from the mountains to the South China Sea and feed to the Mekong River on the western side. Several mountain spurs lead off this range toward the coast, and these produce spectacular coastal scenery backed by striking mountains.

Vietnam controls several islands in the South China Sea and claims others in the Gulf of Thailand and farther offshore in the South China Sea. Some of the islands which are not disputed are the Nam Du archipelago, the Con Dao group, and numerous islands along the coast. Those that are claimed by both Vietnam and other countries include Phu Quoc (Cambodia), the Hoang Sa archipelago east of Danang (China), and the Truong Sa Group (Philippines, Malaysia, Indonesia, China, and Taiwan). Most of these islands have little value, except that ownership brings with it territorial waters that provide fishing grounds and perhaps large undersea oil reserves.

Climate

Although Vietnam is totally within the tropics, it has a diverse climate because of its range of latitudes, altitudes, and weather patterns. Ho Chi Minh City (Saigon) in the south has little temperature variation. Its hottest month is April with an average daily temperature range of 24 to 35 degrees Celsius (76 to 95 degrees F), and the coolest month is December with a range of 22 to 31 degrees Celsius (71 to 87 degrees F). Danang, on the central coast, has a July average of 25 to 34 degrees Celsius (77 to 94 degrees F) and a January average of 19 to 24 degrees Celsius (66 to 75 degrees F). Hanoi, which is in the north, has more temperature variation. Its hottest month is July with a range of 26 to 33 degrees Celsius (78 to 92 degrees F) and a cool January average of 13 to 20 degrees Celsius (56 to 68 degrees F).

Rainfall patterns also vary. In the south, there are two main seasons—the wet and the dry. In Saigon, the wet season lasts from May (220mm) to October (270mm), with January to March being dry. In Danang, it is wet from August (120mm) to December (210mm), with February to May being the dry season. In Hanoi, the wet season is from May (200mm) to September (250mm), with December to March being the dry season. Much of Vietnam receives about 2,000mm of rain each year.

Because of this variation, it is difficult to say which are the good and bad times for visiting the country as a whole. Most visitors would prefer Saigon from December to March, when the humidity is relatively low and rain is infrequent. February through April may be the best time in Danang, while October through January are the favored months in Hanoi. The hot, wet months of May through August are usually poor times to go to either Hanoi or Saigon.

An unusual feature of the Vietnamese climate is the fog and mist along the north-central coast, particularly in February and March. Light drizzling rain is also experienced in Hanoi throughout each of these months, explaining why rain is recorded on fifteen or so days but the average rainfall is only between 30 and 40mm a month (1¼ to 1½ inches).

The hot, wet climate is conducive to the growing of dense tropical rainforests, and at one time almost the whole country was covered with them. Now it is estimated that only twenty percent remain; and at the present rate of change, this will be reduced to ten percent by the end of this decade. The loss of forests may be contributing to climate change and is certainly causing more downstream areas to flood; causing rivers, lakes, and reservoirs to become silted; causing massive soil erosion that is making some areas almost useless; and leading to the destruction of many animal, bird, and fish species in some areas.

The Government

The present Socialist Republic of Vietnam came into being in July of 1976. It replaced the Democratic Republic of Vietnam (North Vietnam) and the Republic of Vietnam (South Vietnam). Until 1980, the country effectively used a 1959 constitution from the north, which had the goal of a communist society with central planning and collective property ownership. In 1980, a new constitution aimed at fully integrating the south into the social and economic fabric of the north was adopted. This constitution was based largely on an earlier Soviet Union model, and contained special reference to the role of the Communist party (the only force leading the state and society) as well as hostile references to the United States and China. In 1988, these references were quietly dropped.

The Socialist Republic of Vietnam initially moved toward becoming a fully socialist state; but in recent times there has been recognition that a more market-based economic system is needed. To date, this has been brought about without official change to the constitution or the government, but it is likely that further softening of socialism may occur, requiring major changes to the constitution, the legislature, and Party directives.

The flag of Vietnam is the previous flag of the Democratic Republic. It consists of a yellow star on a red background.

It is impossible to talk about the government without talking about the Communist party because the two are often bound together as one. The Party influences every aspect of life in Vietnam, but since the death of Ho Chi Minh there has been no chairman or high-profile leader. Major party conferences are held every five years or so—the most recent was in mid 1991. These conferences are where major policy directions are decided and ratified.

The Communist party implements party decisions through the Central Committee, but its decentralized structure allows local party leaders considerable scope for local initiatives. The Central Committee meets only once or twice a year, so it in turn elects the Central Executive Committee and the Political Bureau (Politburo) to oversee day to day activities. The Politburo consists of twelve to fourteen members and is the most powerful organization in the country. It has the power to issue directives to the government which have the force of law.

The National Assembly consists of five hundred or so members who are elected to five-year terms by universal suffrage. They normally meet for about two weeks each year and appear to merely "rubber-stamp" Politburo decisions and party-initiated legislation. The National Assembly in turn elects the Council of State (about fifteen members) who carry out the assembly's duties for much of the year. This council is in effect a "collective presidency."

The National Assembly also elects the Council of Ministers (about forty members) who serve as Vietnam's executive branch of government—its cabinet. The council consists of the prime minister, ministers with portfolio, the heads of state commissions, and others of equivalent status. Communist party members dominate in all these bodies, and even within the bureaucracy, party membership can be more important than competence in the job.

Despite this central organization, Vietnam's forty or so provinces have a significant degree of autonomy. You see this particularly in the south where some areas have adopted a more radical approach to economic development, tourism, and political reform than some of the areas near Hanoi. In addition to these provinces, there are three independent municipalities—Greater Hanoi, Greater Ho Chi Minh City, and Greater Haiphong.

The judicial system is supervised by the Peoples Supreme Court whose members are elected to five-year terms by the National Assembly. There are Peoples Courts located in each province and judges to these are elected by local committees. Local courts handle minor disputes and crimes.

The Economy

Few people in Vietnam would dispute that the country's economy was a total mess as it entered the 1990s. Some blame it on the United States trade embargo, others on war damage, but the realists admit that most of the problem was with policies based on ideology rather than reality. The fact that half of the government's budget has gone to the military hardly helped as well.

The result is that Vietnam was one of the poorest countries in the world. It had massive international debts that it was unable to pay; there is a chronic shortage of spare parts of everything; inflation has been running out of control; and there is considerable under-employment.

The tragedy is that fundamentally Vietnam should be a flourishing, successful country. It has an excellent climate for agriculture, rich soil, a relatively well-educated work force, good basic infrastructure, and a large and potentially hard-working population. In recent years, the Vietnamese have survived largely due to Russian and East European aid. These sources have now dried up along with many of the jobs in those countries that were once available to Vietnamese workers who were desperate for any job and foreign currency.

It appears, however, that at last almost everyone in Vietnam realized that there was a massive problem. Economic realities are a daily obsession with most people. Most workers are on the state payroll, but salaries are so low that few can survive on what they earn. Many have second jobs, others start up small private businesses. Even top government officials talk about a market economy and the relaxing of centralized controls.

Progress has been made in the south, but it is still slow in the north. The entrepreneurial skills and management experience that had been suppressed since the overthrow of the Republic of Vietnam in 1975 have again emerged in the south, and this is propelling the southern economy along at a much greater rate than that of the north. The result is that the gap in the standard of living between the north and south is widening. When I asked in Hanoi about intracountry migration, I was told, "Yes, there is much, but it is all one way. Everyone wants to go to the south." It is not difficult to see why.

However, there appears to be considerable hope on the horizon for the whole country. Vietnam has made dramatic progress since 1990. Until 1990, aid from the Soviet Union worth around US$1 billion a year had been the country's main source of external support. Suddenly the aid stopped. But instead of failing, Vietnam's economy shuddered then lurched ahead. Economic growth since 1991 has been impressive and, more importantly, the rampant inflation that raged up to four-digit figures in the 1980s is now being reined in. The State relaxed its stifling grip on daily life and many people reacted with enthusiasm. It was as if the nation was arising from a deep sleep.

The economy's strength is backed by steadily improving export earnings, particularly from rice. Vietnam is now the world's third largest rice exporter after Thailand and the United States. Rice production soared when the government gave farmers the right to farm on their own, rather than producing for the State.

The government also has high hopes for tourism and has licensed more than five hundred tourist agencies in Saigon alone to meet the anticipated annual growth of around sixteen percent over the next few years. Officials claim that already ten thousand visitors are arriving in Saigon each week, and that a third of these also visit Hanoi and the provinces. Many of these are business people or Vietnamese returning from overseas, of course; but the number of genuine tourists is undoubtedly growing. Tour operators worldwide are weighing the benefits of improved transport links and better government cooperation against the negative aspects of infrastructure and managerial shortcomings.

Agriculture is by far the most important plank in Vietnam's economy. More than seventy percent of Vietnam's population depend on agriculture for a living. Rice dominates as the most important crop, but some corn, sugar cane, and potatoes are grown in some areas. The south has some tropical fruit orchards; and rubber, peanuts, tobacco, coffee, and tea are grown in the uplands.

The Mekong Delta is the country's rice bowl, but the Red River Delta is also important. Over many years, Vietnam has exported its quality rice to acquire foreign currency, then imported cheaper product for its own needs. Due to problems transporting the imported rice from the ports, some rice-growing areas have almost reached starvation levels. This has caused considerable resentment.

Rice cultivation methods have remained almost unchanged for centuries in parts of Vietnam. Water buffalo still pull wooden plows to till the soil. Planting and harvesting is done by hand. Irrigation water is transferred from channel to field by woven baskets manipulated by women. Harvested rice is dried by the sun and threshed by pedal-driven contraptions, or left on the roadways for vehicles to run over. Both dry rice and glutinous rice are grown.

Increasingly, agricultural production is being hindered by floods and droughts. Both are believed to be related to the dramatic deforestation which is occurring throughout the country. There is a need for additional irrigation schemes and better agricultural techniques, but lack of funds and political considerations hamper this development.

Forestry cannot be considered irrelevant to agriculture as Vietnam has discovered to its detriment. Forests are shrinking due to timber harvesting, slash and burn agriculture, fires, and illegal cutting. Replanting is occurring, but it is not keeping up with forest losses. Many of the replanted areas use Australian eucalyptus trees which grow quickly, but are no substitute for the natural rainforest. The government is encouraging the population to take an interest in reforestation, and has included it in the school curriculum, so perhaps all is not lost. It is one of the areas in which foreign investment is being encouraged.

Fishing is a major source of employment for coastal areas, and fish constitutes the most important food after rice. Freshwater fisheries are rapidly declining due to exploitation, pollution from war and agricultural chemicals, and silt from denuded hillsides. Inshore fishing has likewise declined due to areas being over-fished, but reef and deep-sea fishing is probably under-exploited. The government has been cautious with this industry, however, because many of the boats have been used by refugees fleeing the country. As the economy improves, this exodus is likely to stop and fishing would then have scope for expansion. Fish farming occurs on a limited scale, but much less than some other countries in southeast Asia.

Large industries such as cement and steel production, food processing, and textile manufacturing were heavily promoted in the late 1970s and early 1980s, but due to a variety of circumstances, most industries are languishing. These plants are concentrated in the north and are plagued by poor management, the lack of a competitive environment, and insufficient spare parts, fuel, and capital. The government is currently trying to change this.

On the other hand, small industry is flourishing, particularly in the south. Much of it has remained in private ownership, and the government is actively encouraging small industry as a way to get the country growing again. They still have some problems obtaining spare parts and modern equipment, but the Vietnamese are very resourceful and some of their improvisation is quite amazing. Many of the products that have traditionally gone to Eastern Europe are now shipped to Japan, Hong Kong, Taiwan, and Western Europe.

Mineral resources may be the catalyst for Vietnam to rejoin the world trading community. Oil and gas reserves are being identified under the Mekong Delta and in the South China Sea, and many foreign companies have taken up exploration and development rights. Oil has been a major import for the country, thus using much of Vietnam's limited foreign exchange. The development of a significant oil and gas industry, which is underway, will be a major boost to the country.

At present, coal is mined for local consumption, and there are small tin, lead, zinc, bauxite, and copper mines. Mined minerals are supplemented by scrap metal left over from the Vietnam War. Aluminum, copper, and bronze are reworked into household goods; and scrap iron is sold to Japan and Singapore.

The People

The Vietnam population of about 70 million people is composed of ethnic Vietnamese (about 85 percent), ethnic Chinese (perhaps 3 percent), and about 60 minority groups—many of whom are related to Thailand's hill tribes. The country has a population density of about 200 persons per square kilometer, but the heavily settled areas of the Red River and Mekong Delta can rise to 1,000 persons per square kilometer.

The Vietnamese civilization is said to have begun at least two thousand years ago when there was a mixing of Viet immigrants from China with a Malay-Indonesian people from the south. The civilization that emerged was influenced by China, India, and the Khmers in Cambodia; but it had a strong local culture that was distinct from all others.

The ethnic Vietnamese developed as a rice-growing people, and thus tended to congregate in the flat coastal areas. They first occupied the north, then slowly moved south to eventually replace the Chams and the Khmers who had occupied the central and southern parts of the area that is now Vietnam. The economic necessity of rice growing has left its mark on the lifestyle and culture of the Vietnamese. The life of the Vietnamese is closely associated with the village and the structure of the Asian rural commune.

The ethnic Chinese are the largest minority group in Vietnam. The Chinese have been prominent in commerce for many years and this has given them more power than their numbers would suggest. It has also caused considerable friction—at times to the extent of open hostility—between them and the Vietnamese.

The Chinese have attempted to retain their own identity while living within the Vietnamese community. They have built their own schools, kept their own language, and tend to live in their own communities. The ethnic-Vietnamese historic mistrust of China has at times been directed toward the ethnic-Chinese community. In the late 1970s, many Chinese left Vietnam during and after the brief border war between China and Vietnam. The Cholon area of Ho Chi Minh City houses the largest community of ethnic-Chinese in Vietnam.

The Khmers are the next largest group. They are concentrated in the

Mekong Delta near the Cambodian border. These are descendants of the ancient Khmer empire that once stretched from the South China Sea to the Indian Ocean. Its capital was the city of Angkor in Cambodia.

The Chams too are remnants of a lost civilization. The kingdom of Champa once occupied the coastal areas of central and southern Vietnam. This Malay-type race was eventually overrun as the ethnic Vietnamese moved south. The Chams have linguistic and physical similarities to the people of Indonesia and East Malaysia, and have Hindu and Islam-derived customs.

The central hill tribe people live in scattered villages on the high plateau. Many of these people originally lived in bamboo longhouses, but now more conventional structures are favored. Traditionally, many of these people have grown hill rice using the "slash and burn" method of agriculture. This is highly destructive of forests, so the government has initiated a program to encourage them to grow paddy rice or commercial crops such as tea and coffee, and to settle in fixed locations.

The Tai or Zao people live in the far northern portion of Vietnam and consist of several different groups. These people originated in China and speak the Tai-Kadai language. Most work as farmers cultivating rice, but traditionally they have also been traders. The Nung are another group with similar social organizations.

The Muong live to the west and south of Hanoi and have become fairly well integrated into Vietnamese culture. Their dialect is similar to Vietnamese and they are excellent farmers. Traditionally, they live in longhouses built on stilts.

The Meo are fairly recent arrivals in this area as they are in Thailand, Laos, and Burma. They live at high altitudes where they raise cattle and horses and cultivate opium, corn, beans, and fruit.

Many other ethnic minorities exist (there are about sixty), but their numbers and influence is small.

The Amerasians are a legacy of the Vietnam War. The children who are half white or black were raised in a society that largely rejected them, so many were forced to live on the streets. Some have now emigrated to the United States, while others have survived the streets and are now back in mainstream Vietnam society.

Religion

Most Vietnamese are Buddhists, but over the centuries Vietnam has been influenced by several religions and philosophies. Underlying many of the current beliefs is the long-held belief in ancestor and spirit worship. Even among many staunch Buddhists and Christians, there is a tradition of honoring the spirits of ancestors because of a belief that the soul lives on after death and can influence its descendants.

For many years, religious activity was discouraged by the government; but recently there appears to have been a relaxation in government attitude. Certainly pagodas exist throughout the country and much of the population appears to take an active interest in local happenings.

Buddhism, like Christianity, has several strains which have developed in different ways. The major strain in Vietnam is Mahayana Buddhism, which came to Vietnam via China. Within this strain, Zen Buddhism is the largest sect, with Dao Trang important in the south. Theravada Buddhism, which is practiced in India, Burma, and Thailand, has some adherents particularly in the Mekong Delta region.

More than five hundred years before the birth of Jesus Christ, an Indian prince attained Enlightenment and founded Buddhism. Over the next few centuries, the religion spread through much of Asia, molding attitudes and tempering morality. Buddhism arrived in Vietnam during the second century A.D. It was almost simultaneously introduced by Chinese monks and Indian pilgrims. Although there was some initial penetration, the belief grew slowly. It was not until about the tenth century that it became a major force.

Buddhists believe that a person's life does not begin with birth and end with death, but is a link in a chain of lives, each conditioned by acts committed in previous existences. Buddhism is an empirical way of life rather than a strict religion. It is free of dogma and is a flexible moral, ethical, and philosophical framework within which people find room to fashion their own salvation. In Vietnam, there is also a mixing of Taoism and Confucianism, which is all very confusing for the visitor who is trying to understand the influence of religion on the life of the Vietnamese people.

Buddhism's influence reached its peak between the tenth and thirteenth centuries when it received royal patronage. It was proclaimed the official state religion in the twelfth century. This saw financial support for the construction of pagodas and the participation of monks in the governing of the country.

After this period Buddhism declined—except for a period during the sixteenth and seventeenth centuries in the south. A major revival occurred early in this century. During the Vietnam War, some Buddhist monks actively opposed the Ngo Dinh Diem regime in South Vietnam, partly because of its perceived Roman Catholic bias.

Today within many Buddhist pagodas, you can see statues of Buddha, of Quan Am the goddess of mercy, and of various saints who have attained the desired state of "bodhisattva" (perfect in various virtues). Additionally, you may find various Taoist divinities and an altar for worship or remembrance of ancestors.

Confucianism was the second major religious influence. Again, this is not an organized religion, but more of a philosophy. Confucius lived in China about 500 B.C. He drew up a code of ethics to achieve orderly social and governmental interaction. The code has an emphasis on a person's duty to family and society and has appeal to those in power who wish to maintain the status quo.

Confucian philosophy was brought to Vietnam around 100 B.C. by the Chinese. It remained firmly entrenched for the next one thousand years and played a large part in stabilizing family and social systems. In Confucianism, virtue is acquired through learning and education, so this was the catalyst for the establishment of schools and universities throughout the country. For hundreds of years, young people were taught their duties to family and the community according to Confucian philosophy. There was a system of government-run examinations which provided entrance into the ruling class—the mandarins. This whole system encouraged a respect for intellectual and artistic accomplishment which has remained until today.

Confucianism was supplanted by Buddhism thought in the tenth through thirteenth centuries, but was revived again with the Chinese invasion of 1414. In more modern times, the philosophy became conservative and backward-looking; and to a large extent its influence has waned.

Taosim is based on the philosophy of Chinese philosopher Lao Tze. It originated after Confucianism and rejected the demands for strict social order. Taoism emphasizes simplicity of life, but there is also an emphasis on genies, spirits, and demons which represent the forces of nature and great people from the past. Because few people have a full understanding of Taoist philosophy, there is much mysticism and superstition involved in today's beliefs. Taoism has merged many features into Mahayana Buddhism, so today there are very few Taoist pagodas, but considerably wider belief in some of the Taoist concepts for understanding the harmony of humans and nature.

Hinduism was a major force in the Champa civilization of central Vietnam, and many of the famous Cham towers were built as Hindu sanctuaries. When Champa was destroyed in the fifteenth century, Hinduism declined; but even today the remnants of this civilization practice various Hindu rituals and worship some Hindu deities.

Islam has never been a significant influence in the area even though it is believed that the religion was first introduced in the eighth century A.D. Most Muslims are concentrated in the Saigon region and have links with India, Malaysia, or Indonesia. Many Vietnamese Chams call themselves Muslims, but their beliefs and practices vary considerably from conventional Muslim thought. Today it is probably more an Islam-based religion with strong Hindu and animism influences.

Christianity was introduced into Vietnam during the sixteenth century by Roman Catholic missionaries. It grew rapidly for a few years, then it faced three centuries of persecution. It was not until the arrival of the French that the religion started growing again. It was given preferential status by the French, and many churches were constructed. It generally maintained its doctrinal purity, so masses were observed in Latin and other European factors were retained rather than allowing for some Vietnamization.

When the communist government emerged in North Vietnam, nearly a million Catholic refugees fled south and supported the government of Ngo Dinh Diem. Since 1975, Catholics throughout the country have faced restrictions on their activities as well as the stigma of having foreign connections which could be a threat to the state. Despite this persecution, Vietnam has the highest percentage of Catholics in southeast Asia, except for the Philippines. It is estimated that they presently number two million.

Protestantism was only introduced into Vietnam this century and it has never been a major force. Because it has been associated with American and European influence, Protestant religious activities have been restricted by the government in recent years.

Language

The Vietnamese language is derived from a variety of sources, so it is complicated and difficult for most Westerners to understand. Fortunately for visitors, the old Chinese characters and the original Vietnamese system of writing were both replaced early this century by Latin-based script; so it is possible to read street signs and other simple signs if you have a map and a phrase book.

A major complication for most Westerners is the tones that exist to distinguish meanings. In the north there are six tones, and in the south there are five. English speakers accustomed to a nontonal language will have some initial difficulty differentiating between the various tones. Fortunately, visitors are not expected to speak Vietnamese. On the tourist circuit, you will be provided with an English-speaking guide, and elsewhere a combination of signs and a phrase book will often get you the information you need.

There are, however, decided advantages in learning a few Vietnamese words and phrases. You will impress the locals with a few words in their language and you will find that this will encourage some young people to try their limited English on you. In no time, you can be having a conversation with a few words in each language.

In the past, French, then Russian were the preferred Western languages; but now English is encouraged in the schools. In the north, few older people other than those in the tourism industry can speak English, but in the south you can usually find someone who speaks reasonably well—often with a strong southern drawl. Increasingly, the people at hotel reception desks, car rental companies, airline offices, and tourist shops can speak English.

The Latin-based Vietnamese alphabet has twelve vowels, seventeen consonants, and nineteen double consonants. Most of the consonants are pronounced as they are in English, and dictionaries are alphabetized as in English except that various vowel-tone combinations are separated as different letters.

Grammar is less rigid than we know it, but because the language has no articles (a, an, the), no plural endings on nouns, no prefixes or suffixes, and no conjugation of verbs; modifiers and classifiers have to be used to differentiate number and tense. A further complication is that questions are asked in the negative. "Will you go?" is actually asked "You will go will you not." The positive answer would be "No will not," which means that you will go. It is essential that English speakers clearly state a meaning rather than just saying yes or no.

It is also worth knowing a little about names. Vietnamese names are usually made up of three elements—a family name which appears first (there are only a very limited number of these), a middle name which is often used to distinguish sex, and a given name. The Vietnamese use this given name after a title. Thus, Dr. Vu Van Khai is known as Doctor Khai. Vu Thi Khai would be known as Madame Khai (Thi being a common female middle name). Nguyen Hong Khai would also be known as Madame Khai even though she belongs to a totally different family.

Here is a selection of words and phrases that you will find useful in Vietnam.

Numbers

one	—mot
two	—hai
three	—ba
four	—bon
five	—nam
six	—sau
seven	—bay
eight	—tam
nine	—chin
ten	—muoi
eleven	—muoi mot
twelve	—muoi hai
twenty	—hai muoi
twenty-one	—hai muoi mot

thirty	—ba muoi
one hundred	—mot tram
one hundred and ten	—mot tram muoi
one thousand	—mot nghin
one million	—mot trieu
first	—nhat

Days of the Week

Sunday—chu nhat   today—ngay may
Monday—thu hai   tomorrow—hom qua
Tuesday—thu ba   yesterday—ngay mai
Wednesday—thu tu   morning—buoi sang
Thursday—thu nam   afternoon—buoi chieu
Friday—thu sau   evening—buoi toi
Saturday—thu bay

Months of the Year

January—thang nay   October—thang nuoi
February—thang hai   November—thang mot
March—thang ba   December—thang chap
April—thang tu   month—thang
May—thang nam   year—nam
June—thang sau   last year—nam ngoai
July—thang bay   this year—nam nay
August—thang tam   next year—nam sau
September—thang chin

Greetings

Good morning, good afternoon, good evening, goodbye—chao
Good morning, etc. (formal greeting to older men)—chao ong
Good morning, etc. (formal greeting to older women)—chao ba
Good morning, etc. (friendly to men of similar or younger age)—chao anh
Good morning, etc. (friendly to women of similar or younger age)—chao chi
How are you?—Bac co khoe khong?
Fine, thank you.—Cam on, binh throng.
I'm rather tired.—Toi met.
excuse me—xin loi

General

please—xin (pronounced *seen*)
thank you—cam on
yes—da
no—khong
I like—toi thich
I don't like—toi khong thich
I want—toi can
I don't want—toi khong can
beautiful—dep
expensive—dat
cheap—re
interesting—hay
old—cu
new—moi

clean—sach
dirty—ban
fast—nhanh
slow—cham
near—gam
far—xa
hot—nong
cold—lanh
hotel—khach san
room—phong
toilet—car tieu
bathroom—nha tam
doctor—bac si
hospital—nha thuong

Food

chicken—ga
pork—lon
beef—bo
fish—ca
crab—cua
shrimp—tom
spring rolls—nem (*or* cha gio)
noodle soup—pho
rice—com
bread—banh mi
tomato—ca chua
banana—qua chuoi
paw paw (papaya)—qua du du

lychee—qua vai
orange—qua cam
watermelon—qua dura hau
grapefruit—qua buoi
water—nuroe
tea—nuroe che
beer—bia
coffee—ca phe
sugar—durong
restaurant—tiem an
to eat—an
to drink—uong
I'm hungry—toi doi

Traveling

bus—xe buyt
bus station—ben xe
train—xe lua
train station—goi xa lua
airport—san bay
cyclo (trishaw)—xe xich lo
timetable (schedule)—bang gio giac

highway—xa lo
mountain—nui
river—song
island—hon dao
city square—cong truong
market—cho
museum—bax tang vien
pagoda—chua

church—nha tho	south—nam
post office—nha buu diem	west—tay
bank—nha bang	east—dong
north—bac	

Culture and Lifestyle

There are some fundamental differences between Western and Vietnamese attitudes that visitors should consider. Vietnamese culture is built on the agricultural economy of wet rice farming. This demands strong ties to the family and village, and a sensitivity and modesty brought about by close and continuous contact with neighbors. In Vietnam, a person lives, works, and sacrifices not for himself, but for the home, the family, the village and the nation. These strands form the web that defines everyone's place in society. Modern Western culture on the other hand is based on an industrial society and a concern for personal privacy and freedom.

In dealing with the Vietnamese in every situation, you will always achieve a better result if you smile and adopt a pleasant attitude. Becoming angry causes you to "lose face" and will often cause delays in solving a problem. All this can be very hard when you encounter the mentality of officialdom from some government people, and the unbelievable delays that occur for inexplicable reasons at the most inopportune times. Nevertheless, I cannot stress too strongly the need to stay calm. You must visit Vietnam expecting delays and minor problems, and you should build some spare time into your itinerary.

Part of this problem comes from the Confucian attitudes that encourage humility and politeness among the masses; part comes from the centralized Communist/Socialist workings of the State; and part comes from the Buddhist and Hindu concepts of time which say that there will always be another day, another year, or another life in which you can achieve your goals.

Visitors may also notice a reserve in the Vietnamese people that is not evident in the Thais, for instance. This stems partly from their modesty and humility, but it also comes from generations of experience with the foreigners who ruled Vietnam for hundreds of years, and more recently when it was illegal for Vietnamese to speak casually to foreigners. Despite recent changes in government attitudes, some Vietnamese prefer not to run the risk of drawing any attention to themselves by being seen with foreigners. Naturally, this does not extend to people within the tourism industry.

The Vietnamese place great emphasis on maintaining harmonious relationships, so they avoid direct criticism of others and even avoid giving opinions if there is a chance of offending. This leads to much confusion with

Westerners who interpret "yes" as agreement with a statement rather than the Vietnamese interpretation of *da*, meaning "what is being said is understood." You would be wise to ask important questions in several different ways before you accept that you have agreement with a Vietnamese.

There are a number of other do's and don't's that need to be kept in mind. As with most Buddhist countries, it is considered rude to touch anyone on the head or to point your feet toward someone. These taboos are slowly becoming less important, but as a visitor you should assume that everyone could be offended by this. Likewise, public displays of passion are frowned upon. Although some Vietnamese realize that Westerners have different concepts, avoid hugging, kissing, and so forth in public.

You should also be aware that calling someone over (as in a restaurant) with the typical Western hand motion of a finger movement with the palm upright, could offend many Vietnamese. It is much better to adopt their standard of palm downward with four fingers bent. Another thing that the visitor will notice is that Vietnamese rarely look you in the face when talking to you. Some visitors take this to mean that the local is dishonest, but in reality it is just an attempt to refrain from being rude or too bold.

Education has long been a Vietnamese ideal and today it is compulsory and free. Primary education is now universal and an estimated forty percent of students attend secondary school. This has given Vietnam a literacy rate above many other countries.

For thousands of years, primary education was the responsibility of the village schoolmaster, and the curriculum varied from village to village. Now lessons have been standardized across the country. School facilities have often not kept up with the numbers attending school, so class sizes are large, and many schools operate a two and sometimes three shift schedule.

Secondary education has also been standardized, and recent decisions have seen more emphasis placed on practical sciences, technology, and vocational training. Until recently, large numbers of students went to Russia or Eastern Europe for advanced training. Now they want to go to the West.

The traditional national dress of Vietnam, known as *ao dai* is rarely seen in everyday life. It consists of a close-fitting full-length blouse split to the waist for women and a shorter loose-fitting version for men, worn over black or white satin trousers. You will see the *ao dai* worn on formal occasions, and here women wear high-heeled sandals with the outfit.

For normal wear, young people prefer jeans or Western-style trousers, and knitted shirts are popular. Many of these items come from Thailand. Women in the north rarely wear skirts or Western-style dresses; but in the south, where fashion is more important, you can see the latest world trends on some women in Saigon.

It is not common for Vietnamese women to wear shorts (except at the beach), and you rarely see men wearing them in the cities either. In rural areas, men sometimes wear shorts and it is acceptable for children of both sexes to wear shorts anywhere. T-shirts, baseball caps, thongs, and sandals are commonplace all over the country. Cone-shaped hats for women and helmets for men are very common in rural areas particularly in the north.

The Cham civilization of south-central Vietnam has made the most lasting monuments in Vietnamese architecture. These consist of graceful brick towers which were mostly constructed as Hindu temples. The towers were built between the fourth and thirteenth centuries. Apart from the sophisticated masonry techniques that were used, the Chams produced spectacular carved sandstone figures for their sanctuaries. These sculptures were influenced by Indian art; but in later years, they also incorporated Vietnamese and Japanese influences.

The Vietnamese were not great builders, and much that was constructed has been destroyed by either feudal wars, invasions, or the tropical climate. Although many pagodas and temples are still functioning many centuries after they were founded, in most cases they have been rebuilt over the years without much attention to the original plan or style.

Music and theater have had a long history in Vietnam. Much of the theater brings music, dance, and mime together. Traditional Vietnamese music uses the five-note Chinese scale. Choral works have the added restriction that the melody must correspond to the word tones—it must fall when words with a falling tone are sung and rise when the words have a rising tone.

Vietnamese classical music originates from the imperial court and is rather formal. Folk music is more of the people and is usually sung without instrumental accompaniment. Theater music can be based on Chinese opera, adaptations of peasant songs with modern verse, or Western-inspired musical shows.

The ethnic minorities also have their own musical tradition that is often expressed in dances with colorful costumes accompanied by players with reed flutes, bamboo wind instruments, drums and gongs, and various stringed instruments. Some of this music has found its way into popular folk songs.

Conventional puppetry and Vietnamese water puppetry have been popular art forms for hundreds of years; but today there is less support than in the past. Visitors, however, should take the opportunity to see a water puppetry performance in Saigon or Hanoi because of its unique nature.

Rural life is the "norm" for eighty percent of Vietnam's population. These people live in rural villages which often consist of several small hamlets. Each village has a central community center which often serves as temple, meeting room, government administrative office, health clinic, and cooperative headquarters.

In the north, socialization means that many farmers work on communes; but this has been resisted in the south and many privately owned farms still exist there. Recent years have seen a move away from rigid socialism, so it is likely that "free enterprise" will survive.

In both the north and the south, it is customary for three or four generations to share the same bamboo, wood, or mud brick house. Near the house is a vegetable garden, perhaps a small pond, and an outdoor toilet. Water is obtained from a stream, a private well, or perhaps from a government-built communal handpump. Many rural houses are still without electricity.

Rural life is simple and is based on the agricultural cycle. Work constitutes the major part of the day and is undertaken by all the able-bodied people in the village. Young children are cared for by the elderly while the other adults are in the fields. At night after a meal of rice, vegetables, and perhaps fish, the men may sit around with a pipe or cigarette while some of the women will chew betel leaf. Days tend to start and finish early.

Food and Drink

Vietnam, like many southeast Asian countries, has a long tradition of interesting cuisine. While the ordinary rural family may make do with frugal fare, the ruling classes have always eaten well. Today there are a wide variety of Vietnamese dishes (some with strong Chinese and Thai influence), and most are reasonably priced. In general, food in the south tends to be more adventurous and spicy than that in the north. The south also seems to have a much better range of fruits and beverages.

In addition to the small roadside food stalls, private restaurants, and government-run eateries, there are hotel restaurants, some Western-style cafes (mainly in the south), Chinese restaurants, and sandwich bars. Some will be amazingly inexpensive, and none should be expensive by Western standards if you pay the correct charge. Take note that Vietnamese eat an early dinner, so in many parts it will be difficult to get a meal after about 8 P.M.— except perhaps in a hotel.

Western food is better in Vietnam than in many Asian countries, but I still recommend that you eat local food as much as you can. The cost will be less, the quality may be better, and you will have no trouble finding something that suits your needs. Taking a meal at a food stall or local restaurant is also a good way to meet some locals.

At street stalls, the best way to select food is to point to something that looks appealing. Add some rice, fish sauce (nuoc man), and water and you will probably be eating similar food to half of Vietnam. In restaurants, you should order several dishes from the menu and share these with everyone.

You should take some rice from the large shared dish, put it in your own rice bowl, then take some of the other food and add it to your rice. Everyone else will be doing the same. On restaurant menus, dishes are listed together according to their main ingredient.

There are many Vietnamese dishes that you should try. This is a small selection:

Pho is a noodle soup that is very popular in Hanoi, but is available everywhere. The rice noodles are mixed with a boiling broth made from fish sauce, ginger, and prawns; shredded beef or chicken; and shallots and parsley as seasoning. It can be eaten all day but is particularly popular for breakfast.

Bun thang is a rice noodle soup with shredded chicken, fried pork, fried egg, and prawns.

Nuoc man is that special Vietnamese fish sauce that most foreigners initially dislike but later discover as a necessary condiment to many dishes.

Vietnamese spring rolls are made of minced pork, crab, vermicelli, onion, mushrooms, and eggs wrapped in a thin rice pancake and fried. They are usually served with lettuce, carrot, green papaya, and a sauce made from nuoc man, water, vinegar, sugar, pepper, clove, and garlic.

Gio is lean pork that has been seasoned then pounded into a paste before being packed into banana leaves and boiled.

Banh cuon is a steamed rice pancake rolled with minced pork and an edible fungus. It is served with a spring roll-type sauce.

Cha ca is a popular fish dish of fillets broiled over charcoal then served with noodles, green salad, roasted peanuts, and a special sauce.

Bun cha is fried pork cooked over charcoal and served with noodles.

Rau xao hon hop is fried vegetables. It is usually delicious.

Com is sticky rice which is often served in lotus leaves.

Banh com is a sticky rice cake filled with bean paste and pork.

Banh chung is a traditional dish served during Tet, made from sticky rice, bean, onion, and pork packed in leaves.

Mut is candied fruit made from many kinds of fruit and vegetables such as kumquat, tomato, carrot, coconut, ginger, and lotus seeds.

Banh deo is a sticky rice flour cake filled with mut. It is a traditional dish at the mid-autumn festival.

As you travel around Vietnam, you will see thousands of *com pho* signs along the roads. These are advertising the rice and soup stalls which are so popular with Vietnamese travelers.

Visitors will enjoy the fruit which is available throughout Vietnam. In the south, tropical fruits (banana, coconut, pineapple) predominate, while the north has lychees, melons, mandarins, and grapes.

Cold drinks are essential during the hot season, but in many parts they can be a problem. Refrigeration is by no means universal, so the only way to make drinks cold is to use ice. I am very wary of this. It appears that most ice is made from unboiled water, so it is no safer than tap water. As a general rule, don't drink the water and don't put ice into your drinks. To overcome the "cold" problem, pack some ice around the bottle or can before you drink it. It won't produce an icy drink, but it may save you from days of debilitation.

Coca-Cola in cans and bottles has become widely available and has attracted a cult following. If you enjoy soft drinks, this is a good choice because many of the locally made alternatives are pretty terrible. There are several varieties of mineral water available—some sweet, some salty. You will have to assume that these are safe, but I have lingering doubts when I see the condition of some of the bottles. Try several brands before you decide which one you like.

Beer has become a popular drink among the richer Vietnamese. Saigon-produced 333 Export beer is by far the most popular local brand. This sells for slightly less than imported Heineken (from Singapore), and San Miguel (from Hong Kong). Some Australian and American beers are also available, particularly in the south. A can or small bottle will cost around 8,000d. Hanoi beer, Fruda beer, and Thirty-three are other acceptable brands that are somewhat cheaper. Avoid most of the local brews—many are dreadful.

Hot drinks are virtually restricted to Chinese tea (which goes well with most Vietnamese dishes) and instant coffee. If you want milk with your tea or coffee, it will most likely be sweetened condensed milk.

Vietnam produces several types of wine (but none that I rave about) and a locally produced vodka. In some places you can find Australian, French, and Californian wines; and there is a good selection of brandy, vodka, and other alcoholic beverages that originate in Russia or Eastern Europe. Some imported scotch, gin, and bourbon is available.

Festivals

Vietnam has a number of secular holidays and religious festivals, but only a few are universally celebrated. International Workers Day (May 1) and Vietnam National Day (September 2) are the most widely observed holidays, but Tet (Vietnamese New Year) is by far the most important festival of the year.

Tet marks the new lunar year and the advent of spring. It is a week-long holiday which usually falls in late January or early February. Tet is very much a family festival and a time to meditate on the past, to enjoy the present, and to contemplate the future. Transportation and accommodations are often at a premium as the Vietnamese head for home. Great importance is attached to starting the year properly because it is believed that these early days will determine success of the year to come.

The new year is celebrated with firecrackers, gongs, and drums with festivities continuing for seven days. Cultural performances, sporting events, and other celebrations are held. On the seventh day, the New Year tree (cay neu) is taken down to end the festival. If this day is bright and sunny, people believe that good health and good luck will follow for the rest of the year.

Thanh minh is celebrated on the fifth day of the third lunar month. The name means "serene weather," and people use this opportunity to visit and tidy-up the graves of deceased relatives. Offerings are made of food, flowers, and joss sticks.

Buddha's Birth, Enlightenment, and Death is remembered on the full-moon day in May. This day is celebrated throughout the country with people crowding temples and pagodas. Temples and many private houses are festooned with lanterns, and candlelight processions are held in the evening.

Ho Chi Minh's Birthday is celebrated on the 19th of May. The famous leader was born on this date in 1890 near Vinh in north-central Vietnam.

Doan Ngo, the summer solstice day, is celebrated on the fifth day of the fifth lunar month. This is the festival of pest-killing and disease-curing. People take various leaves to make traditional drugs, and offerings are made to spirits and ghosts of ancestors.

Trung Nguyen is the mid-year festival. It falls on the fifteenth day of the seventh lunar month. According to Buddhist tradition, this is the day when faults are pardoned. Offerings are made in homes and pagodas to ancestors.

Trung Thu is the mid-autumn festival that falls on the fifteenth day of the eighth lunar month. The festival coincides with schools opening, so high-ranking Party and State officials send letters of greetings to schools and children and present gifts to some. Moon cakes of sticky rice are eaten and a lantern procession is held in the evening.

National Day is September 2. It celebrates the Declaration of Independence of the Democratic Republic of Vietnam in 1945.

Christmas is celebrated in Christian churches with special masses and services. In the main cities it is a significant event.

Health and Safety

Good health is one of the essentials if you are to enjoy yourself in tropical Third World countries. There are some simple precautions that you should adopt and some facts you should know. If you are careful, you should be perfectly safe in Vietnam; but if major problems arise, you should consider heading for Bangkok, Hong Kong, Kuala Lumpur, or Singapore. A good travel insurance policy is a wise idea, but be sure you understand the restrictions and requirements.

Most travelers carry a small medical kit with them. Tourists and business people rarely do. That is a mistake. I suggest that you pack some adhesive bandages for minor injuries, scissors, tweezers, tablets for pain and fever, antiseptic solution, antihistamine tablets, medicine for stomach upsets, insect repellent, and sunscreen. In Vietnam it may also be useful to have some antibiotics for use in an emergency. These should be prescribed by a doctor and used only if advised by a local medical person. They are only carried because they may not be available locally. Use them only as recommended and use them for the prescribed period.

The golden rule is to be careful with what you eat and drink. Stomach upsets and diarrhea are common and can ruin a visit. Most problems stem from contaminated water, so as a general rule you should avoid water and ice unless you are certain it has been well boiled. In hotels, the hot water in your room flask can be used to make Chinese tea, but I have doubts about the ice—even in hotels. Imported Coca-Cola is fine and some local soft drinks will be safe, but you should be wary of the mineral water. You should check the seal on any bottled water that you buy.

You have to find that fine line between being sensible and being paranoid. Avoiding water is sensible, avoiding local food or local food restaurants is being paranoid. Thoroughly cooked food will generally be safe, but avoid anything that looks as if it has been reheated from a previous meal. Take care with fish and seafood and avoid undercooked meat. Fruit should be peeled and salad washed with boiled water to remove the danger of contaminated water and soil.

Medical attention in Vietnam is reasonable, but equipment and medicines are in chronic short supply. Foreign visitors will often be given priority treatment—especially if they are prepared to pay U.S. dollars for attention—but you should still check the expiration date of any medication and be extremely wary of anything that you cannot read.

Malaria is one illness that you should take precautions against. Ask your home doctor about the advantages of taking anti-malarial tablets while you are in the affected area. Whether you take these or not, you should guard against mosquito bites. This means wearing long-sleeved shirts at dusk, using an insect repellent, and sleeping under a mosquito net at night. Rabies is widespread in Vietnam, so it is a wise precaution to avoid dogs and other animals that may bite.

Sexually transmitted diseases exist in all countries. Syphilis and gonorrhea are fairly common; and due to undermedication with antibiotics, some resistant strains have appeared in Vietnam. Herpes and AIDS are also present. Screening of blood is not widespread, so resist transfusions unless you are in a life-threatening situation.

Be aware that tropical temperatures and insanitation are a potentially dangerous combination. Prickly head, an itchy rash that often occurs on the buttocks; heat stroke, which is a serious condition caused when the body's heat-regulating mechanism breaks down; fungal infections such as athlete's foot; and typhoid fever, cholera, and hepatitis all occur in Vietnam and should be guarded against. Your local physician is best able to recommend precautions.

Crime rates that affect visitors to Vietnam are quite low, but you should be aware that what might be a few unimportant dollars to you may be a month's savings to a local. Don't put this temptation in front of hotel staff or others.

Bag snatching is not common, but you should be aware that snatchers do exist, particularly in Saigon. Take normal precautions. The same goes for pickpockets. It is foolish to flash bank rolls or have a bulging wallet. It is both socially and economically unwise to wear expensive jewelry on the street—you don't need it.

The streets in most Vietnamese cities and towns are much safer at night than many U.S. or European cities. Generally, women can safely walk alone at any time of the day or night. A wise precaution, though, is to ask the hotel receptionist for any precautions you should take in that particular area.

It may well be that the countryside is more dangerous than the cities. At the end of the Vietnam War, there were huge quantities of unexploded ordinance throughout the country. In the past twenty years, much of this has been cleared from the cities and cultivated areas, but it is unwise to wander off into other areas. Thousands of Vietnamese civilians have been maimed or killed; you should take action to avoid adding to the statistics. Don't climb into bomb craters; don't touch any rockets, shells, or mines you come across; don't ever walk across country areas that are not cultivated.

Business Opportunities

Vietnam has come in from the cold since it signed the Paris peace agreement on Cambodia in 1992. It has reopened border trade with China; it has reached its reconciliation with the United States; and it has been invited to join ASEAN. Its hotels are full of Japanese, Taiwanese, Korean, Malaysian, and Singaporean businessmen and women.

The country is at peace at last after fifty years. It has been able to reduce its armed forces by at least half, and its focus is now on economic modernization. Economic reform, financial restructuring, and an expansion of foreign trade have become the new battlegrounds.

Vietnam hopes to become Asia's next newly industrialized economy sometime early next century. It has several things going for it: the cheapest labor force in the Western Pacific, a good central location, rich natural resources, and in the south considerable experience with and enthusiasm for capitalism. It is surrounded by dynamic growth centers in southern China, Taiwan, Hong Kong, and the ASEAN States (Thailand, Malaysia, Singapore, Philippines, Brunei, and Indonesia).

The Vietnamese Communist Party Secretary-General Do Muoi has said that Vietnam will remain a socialist state. However, he has also said that Vietnam's basic aim to the year 2000 is to accumulate material wealth. Vietnam is developing trade, economic, and financial relations with many countries and organizations regardless of their political affiliations.

Increasing exports has become a matter of "paramount importance." The country is reaching out for trade, aid, investment, management skills, and ways to modernize education and develop science and technology resources. Pending the arrival of the Americans, Vietnam is looking to investors from Taiwan, Europe, Australia, South Korea, Hong Kong, Malaysia, Thailand, Singapore, Japan, and the overseas Vietnamese who fled the country in the 1970s and 1980s.

Taiwan has become the biggest investor in Vietnam, ahead of Hong Kong, Australia, France, and Japan. It has committed large amounts in direct foreign investment in various labor intensive projects. The commercial ties between Vietnam and the rest of the world are growing rapidly too. World Bank and Asian Development Bank loans are helping with infrastructure and other activities.

Office space for trade representatives in Ho Chi Minh City (Saigon) is at a premium. Many countries are developing banking and trade offices in Saigon and Hanoi. Vietnam's international telecommunications network with the rest of the world has opened up. The United States has lifted bans and is now participating in many developments. Japanese, Singaporean, Korean, and Taiwanese shipping lines are expanding services to Haiphong and Saigon. Vietnam has opened commercial offices in Beijing, Seoul, Hong Kong, Tokyo, and most of the ASEAN capitals.

Energy resources in Vietnam have attracted widespread interest among Pacific Rim countries. The northern part of Vietnam has perhaps the largest commercially viable coal deposits in Asia. Its cheap labor potentially makes it a competitive source for the Asia-Pacific region. There are also large offshore oil reserves. In the future, Vietnam could rate alongside Australia and Malaysia as an oil and natural gas producer.

A survey by the East-West Center in Hawaii estimates the reserves to be between 1.5 billion and 3 billion barrels. It says that within the next thirteen years, output could be as high as 500,000 barrels a day. Already oil is one of Vietnam's biggest foreign exchange earners. "For the first time, you can say we are an oil-producing country," said Mr. Nguyen Danh, an economic adviser to the government.

Exploration is centered off the coast southeast of Saigon, although some companies are also exploring off the central coast from Danang. The first oil was discovered by Mobil in March of 1975, but in April of 1975 all Americans left South Vietnam and have only recently returned. Today, the fields are being worked by a Russian company. In 1987, one Indian and four Western companies began signing oil exploration contracts. More followed in the early 1990s. Recently, ten blocks in two new areas have been up for grabs. All were snapped up by Western and Asian companies.

Vietnam's economy is still heavily reliant on its agricultural sector with manufacturing goods making up less than 16 percent of exports. However, the Vietnamese government is committed to lifting production in its secondary industries and is seeking to upgrade existing factories. Additionally, some state-owned corporations will be converted into what the Vietnamese call "stockholders companies" in an attempt to increase their efficiency.

Obviously there has been some success. It is estimated that there was a growth rate of 15 percent last year in manufacturing in the Saigon region. This is the heartland of business in Vietnam. Part of this growth is being funded by foreign investment that is being plowed back into factory upgrading. It is most noticeable in the textile and garment manufacturing industry. Some factories have secured contracts with Western countries to supply garments.

Major projects involving foreign funds have to be approved by the State Committee for Co-operation and Investment. Officially, the SCCI has attracted about US$10 billion in foreign investment. Oil and gas, hotels and services, agriculture, forestry, food processing, and general industries were the major growth areas.

Investors are favoring Saigon as a center for investment. It attracts more than of 80 percent of all foreign investment. The government is attempting to address the imbalance by offering special incentives such as lower electricity rates, land costs, and concessional tax treatment to attract foreign investment to the northern part of the country, including Hanoi.

Some of the recent success for joint-venture operators has been in vehicle assembly plants. The first Vietnamese-made vehicle rolled off the assembly line in mid-1992. These are essentially utilitarian vehicles: ambulances, police patrol cars, trucks, and a handful of passenger cars under the name of Mekong Cars. The investors are South Korean and Japanese. A second plant started in 1993 making Japanese cars under license. This is a Japanese-Philippines grouping.

Investors are starting to look to food processing, particularly fruit, vegetables, and seafood. Canned pineapple juice is being produced and exported to Canada. A Taiwanese company employs large numbers of Vietnamese to produce mushrooms for export. Another group grows bananas for export to Africa, the Middle East, and Japan.

The level of interest from foreign investors is growing by the day, and some problems are emerging. Some foreign investors who have obtained licenses to operate joint ventures are offering them to other investors at a fee. Vietnamese authorities are tired of the "cowboys" and are trying to screen them out. They are withdrawing licenses if the foreign investors do not proceed within a given time. So far, about ten percent of licenses issued have been canceled.

Obviously, investment in Vietnam is for the "long-haul." Some foreign companies feel that if they don't get in now, they will miss existing opportunities. The truth is, however, that there are no such things as existing opportunities. Companies have to go into Vietnam and work at creating the opportunities.

A representative of a Western embassy in Hanoi told me that investment in Vietnam will only work if the investor has long-term plans, and the capital to see them through the first two or three years. Anyone aiming to bring proposals to the Vietnamese should already have financial backing, for it is virtually impossible to raise funds in Vietnam now. Corruption is almost endemic throughout the country and smuggling is occurring on a huge scale. Property values have risen to unrealistic levels in Hanoi and Ho Chi Minh City and appalling infrastructure continues to constrain growth.

Stamina and patience are two other ingredients that are needed. Setting up a business deal is often fraught with problems. Increasingly, the Vietnamese are being courted by business people from many countries. Dealing with ministries and State bodies is protracted and often gets bogged down with frustration.

But ventures can be successful. The key on many occasions is the right contact. Increasingly, there are so-called brokers who try to sell their business expertise and contacts to new investors. Some of these are genuine, but others are not. The advice is "get a trusted Vietnamese adviser of one kind or another who knows his way around the government."

This is particularly important when it comes to the law. There are still considerable gaps in Vietnam commercial law. The good news is that the government has accepted that there is a problem and improvements are being undertaken.

Gaps in corporate law are aggravated by the shortage of officials experienced in dealing with private sector companies. Another problem is that the law in Vietnam traditionally involved obligations rather than rights, and the concept of companies hammering out disputes before a judge in court is quite alien to this system. The Asian system involves protracted haggling.

The following is a partial list of areas in need of foreign investment as determined by the Vietnamese government recently. Business people hoping to invest in Vietnam would do well to look at these areas as a first priority.

Agriculture currently employs nearly two-thirds of the labor force. There are a number of specific and general investment opportunities. These include:

• Long Xuyen-Dong Thap Muos rice planting area in the Mekong Delta. Millions of hectares are still fallow. Clearing and irrigation is required.

• Land is available for export-standard rice, rubber, coffee, peanuts, soya beans, green beans, sesame, coconuts, pepper, cashews, tobacco, pineapples, sugar cane, and mulberry plants.

• Fertilizer production, particularly nitrogen fertilizer, is needed for millions of hectares of land in need of supplement.

• Livestock keeping, including high yield pig production and dairy cattle.

• Marine products, including large-scale shrimp farms, refrigerator and processing factories, and fishing fleets.

• Wood pulp production for the paper industry.

Secondary Industry and heavy industry are very weak. General industry is using obsolete equipment and much is operating at only 50 percent of capacity. The following particularly need foreign input:

• Foodstuff industries—rice husking, marine product processing, tea and coffee processing, fruit and nut processing, cigarette manufacturing, meat freezing and canning, beverage manufacturing, feather processing.

• Light industries—assembly of electronic devices, garments, leather, embroidery, stationery, office equipment, paper, furniture.

• Energy—oil refining, coal production.

• Machinery—farm machinery, road vehicles, railway coaches, small ships.

• Chemical industry—fertilizers, pesticides, plant and livestock growth stimulators, paint, soda, alum, phosphorous, phosphoric acid.

• Metallurgy—factories for non-ferrous metallurgy, exploitation and processing of tin, bauxite, chromium, rare earth, lead, and zinc.

• Construction materials—cement, lime, bricks, tiles, sand, and gravel.

• Mining—coal, lignite, phosphate, iron ore, gold, tin, graphite, zinc, lead, antimony, pyrites, manganese, kaolin, limestone, marble, and gemstones.

- Computers—assembly and manufacture.

Infrastructure facilities are poor and underdeveloped due to years of war and socialist dogma. The following require investment and improvement:
- Transportation—enlarging of ports, ship building, railway modernization, road construction, manufacture of buses and lorries (trucks), airport development.
- Communications—inland telephone system, international connections.

Hotels and Tourist Services facilities particularly in Hanoi and the provincial areas are poor. Foreign investment is encouraged and there have been several notable successes.

4

Who Are the Vietnamese?

Early Vietnamese history is shrouded in mystery, but it is known that there were cultures in northern Vietnam ten thousand years ago. Primitive agriculture probably commenced eight thousand years ago and by 2000 B.C. a highly complex and sophisticated society had emerged. This developed into the Dong Son culture which had extensive knowledge of mining, metallurgy, and associated technologies. You can see some of the results of this today in the magnificent bronze drums and other items in the History Museum in Hanoi.

Little is known of this period in the south, but by the first century A.D., the southern part of what is now Vietnam was part of the kingdom of Funam. The Funamese were great engineers and builders, and archaeological excavations have provided evidence of contact between these people and China, Indonesia, India, and even the Roman Empire.

In the third century B.C. , immigrants from southern China settled in the Red River Delta area paving the way for Chinese military excursions. Initially the Chinese established hilltop outposts, but eventually they extended their influence over the entire delta. After a while, the Red River area and portions of southeastern China were reorganized into a single region called Nam Viet. A hundred years later, China completely annexed this into a Chinese province called Giao Chi.

Although the Vietnamese gained much from the Chinese, there were periodic revolts and uprisings. Two well-known events were the rebellion of the Trung sisters in 40 A.D., and the much later insurrection led by Ly Nam De in the sixth century. The Trung sisters formed an army and led a revolt that drove the Chinese governor out of the region. The sisters were proclaimed queens, but their reign was short-lived. Three years later, the Chinese counterattacked and the Trung sisters killed themselves.

The insurrection led by Ly Nam De also caused the Chinese considerable problems, but they reasserted their authority and controlled the area for three hundred more years. During the Chinese period, many innovations were introduced which led to the establishment of the rice-growing civilization much as it is today. It also saw the introduction of Confucianism, Taoism, and Buddhism as well as scientific, medical, and social influences from the powerful Chinese and Indian civilizations. Some Vietnamese took advantage of these new opportunities, and as scholars they started the shaping of a clear Vietnamese identity.

Independence

Chinese rule was shaken by the collapse of the T'ang Dynasty in China in the early tenth century, and the Vietnamese seized this opportunity. Under the command of Ngo Quyen, the Vietnamese secretly placed sharpened timber poles into the bed of the Bach Dang River with the tips hidden below the high tide water level. The Vietnamese then revolted against Chinese rule, luring the Chinese warships up the river when they went to reinforce the ground troops opposing the revolt. The Chinese ships were impaled on the stakes and were quickly defeated. So ended one thousand years of Chinese rule. An independent country called Dai Co Viet was established in 939 A.D. under Ngo Quyen, with its capital at Hoa Lu (75 kilometers south of present-day Hanoi) on the edge of the Red River Delta.

On the death of Ngo Quyen, anarchy broke out and it took three years to restore control. Dinh Bo Linh emerged the leader, and he survived for thirteen years until 980 A.D. To survive, Dinh Bo Linh reached an agreement with China. The Chinese would recognize Dai Co Viet's independence, but the Vietnamese were to recognize Chinese sovereignty and pay taxes to the Chinese rulers. It was a system that had faults, but it provided some stability for the fledgling country.

The Early Dynasties

While the country was nominally independent and controlled by one ruler, there in fact were various clan leaders vying for ultimate control. In 980 A.D. Le Dai Hanh overthrew Dinh Bo Linh to establish what is known as the Early Le Dynasty. This lasted for twenty-nine years and encouraged Buddhism to flourish. This in turn helped to unify the government and provide a basis for improvement in daily life and a new emphasis on education.

Some of this was continued into the Ly Dynasty that commenced in 1010 and lasted for 215 years. This was a vital period in Vietnam's development, because it ensured almost 200 years of stability. The early rulers continued to promote Buddhism at the expense of Confucian scholars who were perceived as being too close to China. Major agricultural works were undertaken to increase the area under irrigation and to provide some protection against flooding. It was during this period that the famous Temple of Literature was established in Hanoi (see Hanoi and the North).

In the south, there were problems with the Champa Empire, then later with the Khmers; but attacks were repelled by the Vietnamese, and the Ly Dynasty slowly extended its influence to the south by annexing good agricultural land then occupying it with armed settlers. In the north, there were attacks from the Chinese Sung Dynasty troops, but these were successfully resisted.

By the early thirteenth century, civil strife had again broken out. Tran Hung Dao eventually overthrew the Ly Dynasty to create the Tran Dynasty, which lasted for 175 years. Within a few years, it was forced to face the threat of a Mongolian invasion. When the Mongolian forces were poised to strike, the Dai Viet and Champa forces agreed to forget their differences and join forces against their common enemy. The Vietnamese withstood three major Mongolian attacks, then defeated the invaders in a brilliant display of bravery and cunning.

The final one hundred years of the Tran Dynasty saw an increase in rice cultivation areas and improvements in the dikes along the Red River. The Mongolian threat had united the various groups living within the area of present-day Vietnam, but eventually this unity broke down. The Chams attacked and overran Hanoi in 1371; then there was a period of disunity which culminated in the overthrow of the Tran Dynasty in 1400 by Ho Qui Ly.

Although Ho Qui Ly was victorious over the Trans, he was unable to assume complete control of the Tran Empire. Many Tran loyalists remained, and the Chams were also proving difficult to deal with. The Ming emperors of China, who had been watching the progress of Vietnam, saw their chance and invaded in 1407. They very quickly took control of Vietnam and imposed a twenty-year hard regime on their new subjects. Although some Vietnamese initially welcomed the Chinese, they were soon disillusioned. The Chinese took the national archives to China, imposed high taxes, discouraged many of Vietnam's intellectuals, and committed crimes against the peasants—some of whom became slaves.

It was inevitable that there would be a revolt against this harsh regime. It was organized by Le Loi and became known as the Lam Son uprising,

after the village in which he was born. It took Le ten years to raise sufficient support, but after several minor defeats, Le and his guerrilla troops
finally overcame the Chinese. In 1428 Le declared himself emperor and
began what is known as the Later Le Dynasty. It was a new era of prosperity
for Vietnam, and even today Le Loi is revered as a great national hero.

The Later Le Dynasty lasted for 360 years, but its major achievements
occurred in the first one hundred years. During this period, the arts and
education flourished, there were significant land reforms, and the most
advanced legal code in southeast Asia was enacted. Women received significant rights in the domestic area, the Vietnamese language gained favor,
and Vietnam's influence spread south and west. The Champa kingdom
was slowly overrun by the advancing Vietnamese, and parts of present-day
Laos came under Vietnamese control. The Le Dynasty made a determined
effort to break free of the cultural domination of China. Fourteen hundred years of Chinese influence was difficult to overcome; but indigenous
beliefs and traditions were encouraged, and there is little doubt that the
Vietnamese nation was shaped by these years.

As the kingdom of Vietnam continued to expand, it became increasingly difficult for the Le government to control the whole country. Powerful
regional families arose. When it became clear that the Le emperor was
unable to assert his authority over them, some of these clans seized lands
and established almost total control over them. At the same time, the first
Europeans arrived in the area. A period of conflict lay ahead.

The Middle Years

While the Later Le Dynasty continued to nominally rule Vietnam during the seventeenth and eighteenth centuries, the real power was held by
various Trunh Lords in the north and Nguyen Lords in the south.

During the sixteenth century, the Portuguese established a trading and
missionary colony and Franciscan missionaries from the Philippines arrived.
By the seventeenth century, the French, Dutch, and British had all seen
the possibilities for trade with Vietnam. The French in particular embarked
on a campaign to convert villagers to Christianity; and by the mid-seventeenth century there was a significant Christian population in Vietnam.

The missionaries were initially welcomed by the emperors for their modern knowledge of medicine, astronomy, and engineering—and in some
cases because they gave the emperor access to modern European weapons.
After a while, however, the situation changed because the new religion
seemed to be against the emperor-as-god system that was inherent in
Confucian education and Buddhist practice. One of the most well-known
missionaries from this period was the French Jesuit Alexandre de Rhodes

who devised the Latin-based phonetic alphabet in which Vietnamese is still written today.

Meanwhile, the Trinh Lords were launching unsuccessful attacks on the Nguyen Lords in the south. To guarantee their survival, the Nguyens negotiated with the French and Portuguese for aid and arms. This in turn spurred the Trinh to deal with the Dutch. In the struggles that followed, it became Portuguese weapons against Dutch.

Both groups nominally recognized the Later Le Dynasty, but the inept and powerless emperor was really only a figurehead. The government lacked strong leadership and by the mid-eighteenth century, the scandalous mismanagement became well known. Unrest was inevitable. The first occurrence was in 1765 in the town of Tay Son, where three brothers lead an uprising. By 1773, the Tay Son rebels had taken over the whole of central Vietnam and the oldest brother, Nguyen Nhae, assumed control. By 1783, the rebels had captured Saigon and the rest of the south. The previously ruling Nguyen Lords were either killed or forced to flee. The second brother, Nguyen Lu, assumed control of the south.

The Tay Son now moved north and overthrew the Trinh Lords from their stronghold. They then reaffirmed their allegiance to the Later Le Dynasty. Almost immediately, the Chinese sent 200,000 troops to northern Vietnam, hoping to exploit the country's political unrest. Nguyen Hue, the youngest brother, raced his troops north in a surprise attack and successfully routed the Chinese. Nguyen Hue became the new emperor in the north and took the name of Quang Trung. He then married the daughter of the old emperor and set about reforming conditions for the peasants and Vietnam's poor.

Meanwhile, one of the defeated Nguyen Lords who had escaped from Vietnam convinced the French missionary bishop of Adran to support his cause. The bishop lobbied in France for military support and eventually managed to convince French merchants to provide two ships, weapons, and supplies. The bishop then set out to recruit army deserters and young adventurers to take part in an attack on southern Vietnam. In 1789, they arrived in the south and had some minor victories over government forces.

In 1792, Quang Trung died and the dynasty began to fall apart. The bishop and his troops took advantage of this and slowly pressed north. They overran most of central Vietnam; then they attacked Hanoi in 1802. Before long, they controlled the whole country. Nguyen Anh was proclaimed emperor, thus beginning the Nguyen Dynasty. It had its capital in Hue. In exchange for their help during the thirteen years of fighting, French merchants received commercial concessions from the emperor.

Although Nguyen Anh had been championed by a Catholic bishop he was somewhat suspicious of the Catholic's motives. When he was succeeded by his son (Emperor Minh Mang) in 1820, the Catholics found that the new emperor was actively opposed to some Catholic teachings which he regarded as a threat to the staunchly Confucian state that he was developing. Minh Mang was succeeded by Emperor Thieu Tri, who set about expelling most foreign missionaries. By now, the missionaries were aggressive and politically active, and the emperors believed that many of the periodic civil uprisings were being fomented by priests. It is likely that they were correct.

The priests and missionaries pressured French public opinion by passing on selective truths and half-truths about conditions in Vietnam. Eventually, outraged protests reached Napoleon III, and he was forced to approve official military action in Vietnam.

One Hundred Years of French Rule

When France decided to take action in Vietnam, it was without an overall plan or long-term strategy. In fact, it took France almost forty years to take control of Vietnam.

The first French action was an attack on Danang Harbor in 1847 in response to Thieu Tri's expulsion of Catholic missionaries. Little else happened until 1858, when the French again stormed Danang, then moved south and overran Saigon in 1859. In 1861, the French won a significant victory at the Battle of Chi Hoa; and in 1862 the emperor gave the French the three eastern provinces of southern Vietnam (Cochinchina). At the same time, missionaries were allowed back into the country, several ports were opened to French (and Spanish) commerce, and the emperor agreed to make a payment to the French.

Despite this concession, there was a general antagonism to the French which caused the rise of a popular guerrilla resistance. The French were ambushed and generally harassed for several years until 1867 when they carried out a comprehensive offensive that broke the back of the resistance. Cochinchina then became a French colony.

The French then swung their attention to the north and seized the citadel in Hanoi in 1872 in what was probably a private action by adventurous troops. These same troops then terrorized towns and villages throughout the Red River Delta, demanding tribute payments and looting and destroying those that refused or were unable to pay.

This activity finally came to an end when the French captain in charge of this operation was killed by a rebel army of Chinese, Vietnamese, and hilltribe people known as the Black Flags. While the French troops no longer terrorized villages, this activity was taken over by the Black Flags and Chinese militias. At the same time, pretenders to the old Le Dynasty throne started emerging and the hilltribes revolted. Central authority had virtually collapsed and the north was in a state of chaos.

By this time, the French had a major stake in Vietnam, and they needed to ensure that law and order returned. With this in mind, the French seized Hanoi in 1882, attacked Hue, and imposed a Treaty of Protectorate on the royal throne. In the next two years, there were four emperors either killed or removed in a major power struggle. The French played a prominent role in this activity; and in 1885 they promoted their own candidate, Dong Khanh, as emperor. In 1887, the French claimed the Indochinese Union consisting of Cochinchina (southern Vietnam), Annam (central Vietnam), Tonkin (northern Vietnam), Laos, Cambodia, and a small area of China.

With the French now firmly in control, ambitious public works were begun. Levees were strengthened, irrigation schemes constructed, the Saigon-Hanoi rail line was built, and ports were developed. At the same time, the French ran alcohol, salt, tobacco, and opium monopolies; levied heavy taxes on the rural community; and began a systematic exploitation of mineral and agricultural resources. The policies devastated the traditional rural economy, made seventy percent of the population landless, and impoverished the country.

Many Vietnamese retained a strong desire to have their independence, and French actions drove many more in this direction. Various uprisings and rebellions occurred, but they were always defeated by the French military forces. A Nationalist Party was founded in 1927, but many of its leaders were guillotined by the French after an abortive uprising in 1930. This opened the way for the Communist Party to develop and prosper by relating to the frustrations and aspirations of the peasants and other groups.

Ho Chi Minh and the Communist Movement

Ho Chi Minh was born in Nghe Tinh Province in 1890. As a young man, he traveled the world working on a French oceanliner, then he worked as a pastry chef in London. He visited the United States in 1915, then went to Paris to work and study. In Paris, he joined the French Socialist Party, then later The French Communist Party. He left Paris in 1923, and after some time in Moscow for training and indoctrination, he went to Canton in China and formed the Revolutionary Youth League with Vietnamese exiles living there.

Ho made a major move when he organized the Communist Party of Indochina in Hong Kong in 1930. This united the Revolutionary Youth League and several smaller Marxist groups. For the first time, there was a strong organization to oppose the French occupation of Indochina. The Communist Party led a movement to set up revolutionary committees

(Soviets) in Nhge Tinh Province of Vietnam—these were quite successful. The party workers listened to the people's grievances, then directed them against the French. They stirred up emotions then channeled them toward mass protest marches, strikes against French plantation owners, and other activities. During 1930 and 1931, this led to the Nghe Tinh Uprising in which Soviets took control of parts of the province.

The French responded strongly. They brutally put down the protests and re-established control. They also exerted pressure on foreign governments. When Ho Chi Minh went on a mission to China, he was arrested as a spy and spent fifteen months as a prisoner.

An uneasy peace existed in Vietnam for a few years until there was another uprising in 1940 supported by the Communist Party of Indochina. The French again reacted strongly, and brutally suppressed the participants. Then they went after the Party's infrastructure and seriously damaged the organization.

At about the same time, Germany overran France. In September, the new French government made an agreement with Japan to accept the presence of Japanese troops in Vietnam. The Japanese decided to leave the French administration in charge of the day-to-day running of the country, so there was Japanese occupation with French cooperation.

Ho Chi Minh returned to Vietnam in 1941 to expand the League for Independence of Vietnam—or as we know it, the Viet Minh. This organization was a coalition of communists and nationalists who shared the ideal of Vietnamese independence. The Viet Minh was the only group that did anything significant to resist the Japanese occupation, and it grew rapidly in membership. The organization cooperated with American intelligence who were attempting to erode Japanese influence in southeast Asia, and from 1944 it received funding and arms from the American O.S.S.

In March of 1945, the Japanese decided to take over Vietnam from the French government. They installed a puppet government under Emperor Bao Dai which declared Vietnam "independent" within Japan's Greater East Asian Co-Prosperity Sphere. The Japanese exported Vietnamese minerals and rice to Japan to supply its war machine which paired with flooding to cause a horrific famine in northern Vietnam that is estimated to have killed two million people.

However, the Japanese occupation was dying, and by August of 1945 the Viet Minh controlled much of the country. In mid-August, Ho Chi Minh formed the National Liberation Committee and called for a general uprising (the August Revolution). Almost immediately, the Viet Minh took complete control of the north and assumed power in a shaky coalition with non-communist groups in the south.

When Japan surrendered to the allies, the Potsdam Conference agreed that British troops would occupy Vietnam below the 16th parallel, while Chinese troops would accept the Japanese surrender in the north. Before this could occur, Ho Chi Minh, with the support of American O.S.S. agents, declared the Democratic Republic of Vietnam independent at a rally in Hanoi's Ba Dinh Square on September 2, 1945. Ho initially made efforts to give his government a broad base by inviting moderates to join in positions of authority, but the response was poor.

British troops arrived in Saigon to find the city in chaos. Various Vietnamese groups were on the verge of armed conflict, French settlers were running out of control, and the economy had collapsed. The British commander quickly realized that his 1,800 troops were not enough, so he released and armed 1,400 imprisoned French paratroopers and encouraged the French civil servants to reinstate the old colonial system. The paratroopers quickly became an independent force, attacking homes and shops and overthrowing the Committee of the South government. In effect, the French were again in control in the south.

In the north, 200,000 Chinese troops were heading south, looting and devastating the country as they went. With the knowledge that the last time the Chinese came to Vietnam they stayed for a thousand years, Ho Chi Minh decided to accept a temporary return of the French in order to get rid of the Chinese. In negotiations, the Chinese agreed to withdraw subject to receiving favorable trade arrangements with the French and access to the Vietnamese rail system.

In November of 1946, full-scale war erupted between the Viet Minh and the French over which government had the right to collect customs at Haiphong Harbor. The French shelled Haiphong, killing hundreds of civilians. Shortly thereafter fighting broke out in Hanoi. Ho Chi Minh and his government and forces retreated to the mountains where they would remain for eight years.

After the communists came to power in China in 1949, they set about helping Ho's military commander Vo Giap with weapons and training. The French countered by asking the United States for help. In 1950, China and the Soviet Union officially recognized Ho Chi Minh's government. The French and the U.S. responded by recognizing the Saigon-based Bao Dai government of Associated States of Vietnam and establishing a Vietnamese national army in the south to fight alongside the French.

The Viet Minh, and later the National Liberation Front, organized the people in the north into paramilitary support units and trained them in guerrilla tactics. This was so successful that by 1953, France had 250,000 armed troops in Vietnam and the Viet Minh controlled much of Vietnam and some of neighboring Laos.

After eight years of fighting, the French were losing faith in their

Indochina territories. The end came suddenly at Dien Bien Phu, a valley near the Laotian border in the northwest of Vietnam. There, the French commander hoped to lure the Viet Minh into a direct confrontation; but instead he found his troops under siege by a well-armed and positioned enemy that was receiving massive help from China. The massacre continued for fifty-five days before 10,000 starving, beaten French troops surrendered and the French Indochina War came to an end.

The next day, the Geneva Conference opened to negotiate an end to further conflict. The agreement provided for an exchange of prisoners, the temporary division of Vietnam at the 17th parallel, the free passage of people across the 17th parallel for a period of three hundred days, and the holding of nationwide elections on July 20, 1956. The agreement was signed by the French and the Viet Minh. Eighty days later, there was an orderly transfer of power from the French to the Viet Minh in Hanoi on October 9, 1954. The Democratic Republic of Vietnam was founded in north Vietnam.

In the south, the situation was different. After the signing of the agreement, the south was ruled by a government led by Ngo Dinh Diem, a fiercely anti-communist Catholic. The Saigon regime had adopted a national flag which was different from that of the Viet Minh and, unlike the Ho Chi Minh government, it refused to recognize the Geneva agreement which had been negotiated by the French.

With the backing of the United States, Diem refused to implement the terms of the Geneva agreement partly because he had no major political party or guaranteed loyal local army to support his policies and election campaign. Instead he held a referendum to confirm his leadership, depose Emperor Bao Dai, and abolish the monarchy. The official result was 98 percent of the vote for Diem. He then declared himself president of the Republic of Vietnam and received recognition from the United States, Britain, France, Australia, Japan, and several other countries.

The Conflict Continues

Diem proved to be remarkably resilient and effective. With American help, he thwarted opposition by disloyal army commanders. He defeated the Binh Xiyen crime syndicate in Saigon and the private armies of the Hoa Hao and Cao Dai sects. For a time, he was known as the "miracle man of Asia;" but he became increasingly nepotistic in making government appointments, and he slowly alienated the Buddhist population by clear favoritism to Catholics.

Meanwhile in the north, Ho and his associates were having their problems. The new government launched a radical land reform program aimed at redistributing land and breaking the traditional authority of the land-lords in the country. Tens of thousands of landlords were arrested, given hasty trials, and executed. Up to 100,000 others were imprisoned. It was clear the whole process was completely out of hand and in response to serious rural unrest, the program was stopped and "grave mistakes" admitted by the government.

This problem and the poor economic conditions throughout the Democratic Republic of Vietnam occupied Ho Chi Minh and his government to the point that happenings in the south were secondary. The party did, however, approve selective acts of violence against officials in the Diem government. In 1957 and 1958, there were several hundred of these, then in May 1959, the Party Central Committee adopted a resolution calling for armed struggle in the south.

To assist the campaign, the Ho Chi Minh Trail, which had been in existence for some years, was further developed and several thousand experienced agents and armed guerrillas were sent south. In 1960, military conscription was introduced in the north, and in December a new organization called the National Liberation Front of South Vietnam (N.L.F.) was formed. In the south and abroad, this became known as the "Viet Cong" or just "V.C."

When the N.L.F. campaign commenced, the military situation of the Diem government rapidly deteriorated. In response to this, the United States Kennedy administration sent sizable numbers of American military "advisors" to the Republic of Vietnam. The Diem government launched a Strategic Hamlet Program where peasants were forcibly moved to fortified villages in order to deny the Viet Cong bases of support. However, the program was carried out so poorly that soon many of the "strategic hamlets" were under V.C. control.

In 1963, it was rumored that President Diem was using French contacts to explore negotiations with Hanoi. The United States made it known to disaffected South Vietnamese generals that it would not block a coup d'etat, and on November first, rebel troops attacked the presidential palace, overthrew the government of President Diem, and killed him. Diem was succeeded by a series of military rulers. The military corruption which was occurring on a massive scale continued.

Hanoi began sending regular North Vietnamese army units into the south in 1964 and the military situation for the Republic of Vietnam rapidly deteriorated. In August 1964, two American war ships in the Gulf of Tonkin reported that they were under attack from North Vietnamese gun boats. The details surrounding these attacks were later proved to be highly suspicious, but President Johnson immediately ordered U.S. jets to bomb North Vietnamese installations on shore. The president then asked the

U.S. Congress for a statement of support, and an almost unanimous vote authorized the president to "take all necessary measures" to prevent further aggression in Vietnam.

The situation in Vietnam stabilized for a while, but in early 1965 the Viet Cong carried out several attacks on U.S. military installations in South Vietnam. American bombers immediately attacked North Vietnam, Gen. William C. Westmoreland became concerned that U.S. bases were vulnerable to attack, so in March 1965 American troops landed at Danang. By the end of the year, there were 184,000 American military personnel in South Vietnam.

Another coup in June 1965 saw a military junta headed by generals Nguyen Van Thieu and Nguyen Cao Ky eventually leading to the election in 1967 of Thieu as president. While this stabilized the political situation, the military problems were continuing. By the end of 1967, there were almost 500,000 U.S. military personnel in South Vietnam joined by small forces of Australians, New Zealanders, Thais, Filipinos, and South Koreans. Together with South Vietnamese troops, they numbered around 1.3 million.

This was not enough, however, to stop a major Viet Cong offensive on January 31, 1968, which became known as the Tet Offensive. In a coordinated attack in over one hundred towns and cities throughout South Vietnam, the V.C. achieved enormous psychological success, but the immediate military benefits were few. The Americans and South Vietnamese counterattacked almost indiscriminately. Within a month, over 2,000 U.S. personnel were killed, an estimated 175,000 civilians were dead, over two million people had become refugees, and countless Viet Cong units were decimated.

Much of the action was captured by teams of television reporters and beamed into the homes of millions of Americans. Suddenly, many Americans were brought face to face with the realities of the Vietnam War and opposition started to grow within the country. Despite this, U.S. military numbers continued to grow for another twelve months, but the emphasis shifted towards a "Vietnamization" of the war effort.

In 1969, the scope of the Vietnam War spread when the United States started bombing Cambodia. Bombers based in Thailand were also saturation bombing parts of Laos. In 1970, U.S. troops were sent into Laos to help some South Vietnamese units. By 1972, the United States was committed to withdrawing from the Vietnam conflict and negotiations were underway with North Vietnam. These were shaken somewhat by a North Vietnamese offensive across the 17th parallel and the American response of heavy bombing of the north and mining of North Vietnamese harbors.

The 1972 "Christmas bombing" of Hanoi and Haiphong finally enabled the United States, North Vietnam, South Vietnam, and the Viet Cong to sign the Paris Agreement which provided for a cease fire, the establishment of a

National Council of Reconciliation, the withdrawal of U.S. combat forces, and the release of American prisoners-of-war.

Despite the agreements, only limited progress occurred. Many American prisoners were released and the Americans withdrew large numbers of troops and equipment; but large numbers of North Vietnamese troops remained in South Vietnam, the Viet Cong continued some activities, and the South Vietnamese government showed little enthusiasm for talking to the north.

In January 1975, a massive North Vietnamese attack took place across the 17th parallel. On April 30, 1975, General Duong Van Minh, South Vietnam's president of only two days, surrendered to the North Vietnamese. Immediately, almost 150,000 South Vietnamese fled the country and this number grew to about 750,000 over the next few years.

Unification

The takeover of the South was unexpectedly easy, and it appeared that the North Vietnamese government had no specific plans in place for an orderly transfer of power. For fifteen months, the south was ruled by a Provisional Revolutionary Government before there was a formal unification of Vietnam in July 1976.

After 1976, there was a rapid transition to socialism in the south. This was accompanied by political repression, persecution of the urban intelligentsia, religious monks, priests, and clergy, and the detention of hundreds of thousands of people who had real or imagined ties to the former South Vietnamese government. It also caused a collapse of the southern economy.

The problem was further compounded in 1978 when the ethnic-Chinese business class was targeted, and 500,000 Chinese fled the country. This caused China to cut off all aid to Vietnam and to briefly invade the northern part of the country in 1979 to "teach the Vietnamese a lesson."

Vietnam's relationships with its neighbors continued to be rocky. In late 1978, it invaded Cambodia before setting up a pro-Hanoi regime there in 1979. This proved to be a costly exercise because Vietnamese forces remained there until 1990.

It soon became obvious that the harsh measures of the late 1970s and early 1980s were not working in southern Vietnam, so there has been a gradual movement toward greater regional autonomy and less emphasis on rigid Marxist theory. During the early 1990s, Vietnam has set about establishing better relationships with China, Thailand, and other countries and has welcomed Western capital and know-how into much of its oil, mineral, and manufacturing areas.

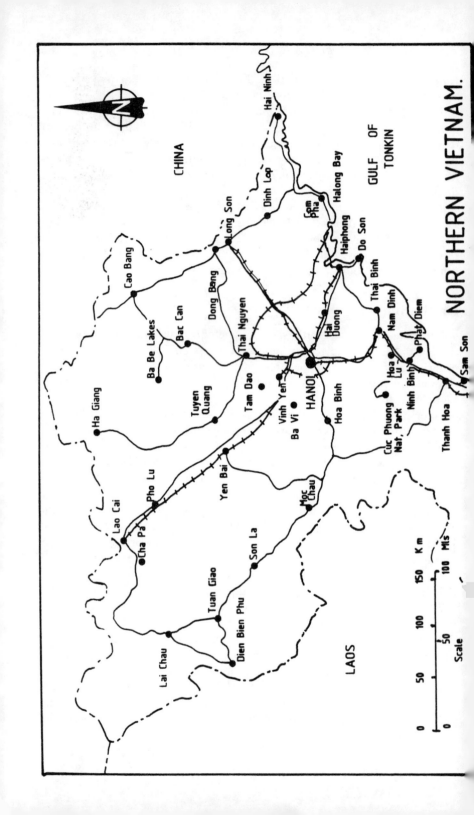

NORTHERN VIETNAM.

5

Hanoi and the North

1. The General Picture

Hanoi is a charming city of lakes, tree-lined boulevards, small squares, and delightful pocket-size parks. Hanoi is drab, dirty, difficult to negotiate, rigid, and bureaucratic. Hanoi is a living museum, a mishmash of 1920s provincial France and 1960s Asian decay. If ever a city had a split personality, it would surely be Hanoi. All of these descriptions are accurate for parts of this relatively small, but very interesting, national capital.

Hanoi city is about 70 kilometers inland from the Gulf of Tonkin. It sits on the right bank of the Red River. The city's urban population is around one million; but greater Hanoi, which includes much of the rich delta flood plain extending quite a distance from the city, has a regional population of over two million. The city reflects its French colonial past in its broad tree-lined streets, squares, and public buildings—including an opera house. Unfortunately, the trees that give the streets their character are gradually ruining the pavement.

The Hanoi area has been the site of major settlement since 1010 A.D. when a local emperor moved his capital here. It has had many names over the years and has only been known as Hanoi since 1831. It was the capital of French Indochina from 1902 to 1953, and it became the capital of North Vietnam after the Geneva Agreement of 1954.

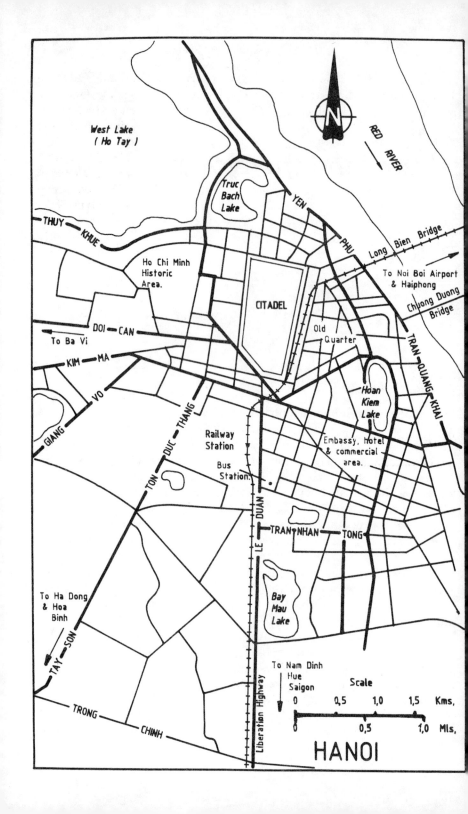

Although Hanoi is the capital of Vietnam, it lags far behind Ho Chi Minh City (Saigon) when it comes to development, enterprise, and facilities. Ambitious young people, foreign businessmen, and even many bureaucrats head for Saigon rather than Hanoi. This has left the city with an inferiority complex that is only slowly being overcome.

This inferiority is evident in tourism infrastructure and facilities, and comes as a shock to many first-time visitors. It is still difficult to get a clean, modern, well-furnished hotel room in some parts of Hanoi. Transport facilities are still frustrating at times, and in many areas of the city it is impossible to get a bottle of chilled soda or beer in the heat of 38 degrees Celsius. Wooden carts packed with squealing pigs still rumble on the streets, waking visitors early before the sun appears. If you peer out the window in this predawn hour, you will see peasants on bikes, men pedaling cycles, and women carrying baskets in yokes across their shoulders, bringing the products of the countryside for sale in the city. In many ways, life in this city is still village life. It's a life both readily visible and veiled in mystery.

Despite these difficulties, Hanoi and the north is an appropriate place to start your Vietnam experience. You can experience the best and worst of the Socialist Republic in this region knowing that if things ever become too difficult or overpowering, you can head south and they will probably improve.

2. Getting There

Hanoi is linked with a number of world capitals and other cities by several international and regional airlines; and services are slowly growing. The busiest routes are Bangkok-Hanoi and Hong Kong-Hanoi. These are convenient entry routes for visitors from North America, Europe, and Australia. Services from Bangkok are offered by Thai Airways International and Vietnam Airlines. Services from Hong Kong are provided by Cathay Pacific Airways and Vietnam Airlines.

All flights arrive and depart from **Noi Bai Airport** which is about 35 kilometers north of the city. A new toll road has cut traveling time to the city to about 40 minutes. There are separate terminal buildings for international arrivals, international departures, and flights within Vietnam. Facilities are being upgraded progressively, but standards are generally poor. If you are coming from the gleaming Hong Kong, Singapore, Kuala Lumpur, or Bangkok terminals, arrival in Hanoi is like going back thirty years.

International aircraft park some distance from the terminal, and passengers are ferried in ancient buses which are often jammed to bursting point. On entering the building, you form several lines which slowly pass through **immigration.** As you enter the baggage collection area, you will be

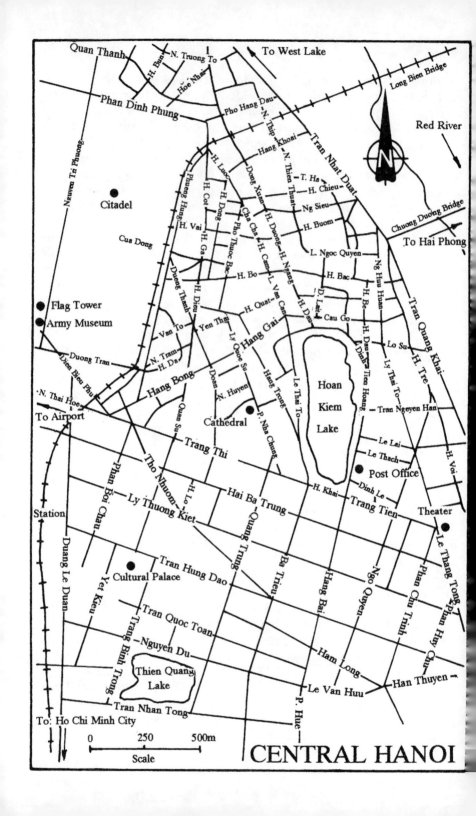

CENTRAL HANOI

met by an armada of people carrying signs identifying individual passengers or incoming groups. Look carefully for your name if you expect to be met at the airport because this is your only chance to establish contact.

The baggage collection area is chaotic and crowded, and bags take an amazingly long time to travel from the aircraft to the collection area. This will be your first test of patience in Vietnam, but resist any tendencies to show annoyance. Customs and police at the airport have a reputation for unpleasantness; and although I personally have had no problems, others certainly have. Showing anger or impatience may just be the trigger that will cause you trouble.

After collecting your baggage, you pass to the **customs hall** where the forms you completed on the aircraft are examined. There appears to be no orderly lines or system to this operation. The object is simply to have your form stamped, so charge in and battle with the other passengers who are doing the same thing.

Finally you are through. If you have not been met, you should head for the **taxi counter** which is directly behind the line of customs officers. If you are lucky, you will have the choice of a non-airconditioned car, an airconditioned car, or a twelve-seat microbus. Costs for the vehicle are around US$20, 25, and 30 respectively. You may be able to negotiate cheaper prices.

The arrivals terminal has a few other facilities. There is a small **exchange bureau** where you can purchase some dong. Only change a small note because you can get a better rate in the city. There are telephones, a post office, and a restaurant.

There are no international rail services to Hanoi, but there is a reasonable **domestic rail network** which can now be used by foreigners. Most long-distance trains arrive at **Hanoi Station** on Le Duan Street near the central city. The main exceptions are some southern trains which arrive and depart from **Thuong Tin Station**, which is about 10 kilometers south of Hanoi. The main station is reasonably efficient, there is a waiting room and bar, but English speakers are few and far between. Cyclos wait outside for customers.

There are no international bus services to Hanoi. Visitors are most likely to arrive from southern and central Vietnam. These buses arrive at the very basic **Kim Lien Bus Station** on Le Duan Street about three-fourths of a kilometer south of the railway station. Most services are operated by very cramped Russian-built mid-size vehicles which are often grossly overcrowded and very uncomfortable. Fares are cheap.

3. Local Transportation

Hanoi, fortunately, is a city where walking is often the best and most enjoyable way of moving around. Many of the streets are well shaded, and the sidewalks are a constant source of surprises. Public transportation is poor.

Hanoi has a **bus system** and you can even buy a map showing the bus routes. Visitors, however, have three problems. The information on the map is inaccurate, so you are never quite sure if a bus will arrive at all. The service on some routes, particularly outside rush hour, is infrequent and unreliable. Then most buses have no legible destination board and few drivers or conductors will speak any English. All in all, I don't recommend bus travel unless you know exactly where you are going.

Taxis are slowly appearing in Hanoi, but in late 1994 they were still fairly rare. There are several companies which you can telephone to order a car. It is still not possible to get a self-drive rental car. The best you can do is rent a car with a driver. The normal rental is one day which means from about 8 A.M. to 5 P.M. Even if you rent from 2 P.M, you are likely to be charged for one day and you will be expected to pay extra if you want to use the vehicle after 5 P.M Day rental rates vary between US$20-35—depending on the company and the vehicle—and this only includes travel around the city. You need to make other arrangements if you plan to use the car for out-of-town travel.

If you can't reach somewhere in Hanoi by walking, you can get there by **cyclo.** These three-wheeled vehicles are called "samlors" in Thailand and "trishaws" in some countries. Fares are cheap, but they require intense bargaining before boarding. A kilometer or so in Hanoi should cost no more than 5,000d (about US$0.50). Cyclos congregate around the hotels and are eager to transport foreigners because they often agree to pay far more than locals. You can hail a cyclo driver in the street, but it is more likely that he will approach you offering his services. Most cyclo drivers in Hanoi speak little or no English. Cyclos can also be rented for around 15,000d per hour.

If you are independent and plan to stay in Hanoi for some time, you should join the locals and travel by **bicycle.** Hanoi has hundreds of thousands of bicycles on its streets, and you will quickly learn the local system. The most important principle is "might is right." Bicycles give way to everything except pedestrians. Bicycles can be rented by the hour or by the day from a few locations in the city (typical rates are 3,000d per hour and 15,000d per day) or you can buy your own from a department store or bicycle shop (there are hundreds) for around US$25-30.

4. The Hotel Scene

Hotel accommodations in Hanoi have improved dramatically over the past three years. There is now a good range of medium-price accommodations in

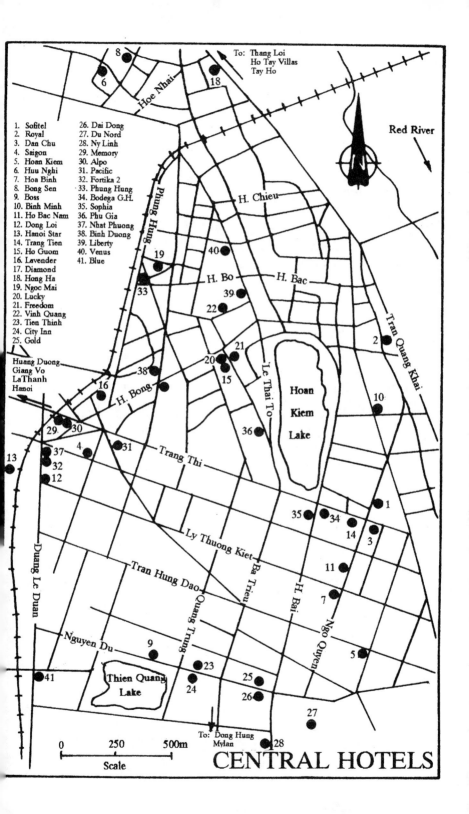

CENTRAL HOTELS

several different areas of the city. Cheaper accommodations are still somewhat difficult for visitors because there is a great reluctance to let foreigners
stay in many of these hotels and an even greater reluctance to let them pay
in local currency. At present, the city has only two hotels that I consider to
fall into the top-notch category, but more are on the way.

Note that in Hanoi, single refers to a room with one bed, which may be
a double bed. Most hotels let two people stay in a "single" room. Double
rooms have two beds and are usually larger in size.

EXPENSIVE HOTELS

The **Hotel Sofitel Metropole** (Tel: 266-919) is the old Metropole Hotel,
completely gutted and rebuilt to four-star standards. It is located in an excellent position at 15 Ngo Quyen Street. There are 109 rooms including sixteen
suites with a new wing scheduled to open in mid 1995. All rooms are airconditioned and have attached bathrooms, refrigerators, mini bars, IDD telephones, TV with satellite facilities, private safe deposit boxes, desks, slippers,
and robes. Many of the standard rooms are fairly small, but they come with
lovely high ceilings and polished wooden floors. The corridors have carpet.

The hotel has a lounge with music from 5 P.M., a bar called Le Club, and
the Le Beaulieu restaurant featuring both French and Asian cuisine from
6:30 A.M. until midnight. The regular menu has prices similar to good Western restaurants, but at lunch there are dishes from US$6-9. There is an
excellent Sunday buffet for US$15.95.

There is a small shopping arcade, a swimming pool which will improve
with time, laundry and dry cleaning facilities, and a business center. The
hotel operates an airport shuttle for US$25. All this comes at a price, but it's
a breath of fresh air for Hanoi's hospitality industry which has not been
known to date for its friendliness or efficiency. Standard rooms are US$179,
premium rooms US$204, deluxe rooms US$234, and suites go up to
US$394. (Book with the hotel by Fax: 844-266-920, or by phone or Tel: 237-
1305 in Thailand.)

The **Hanoi Hotel** (Tel: 252-240) is housed in the old Thang Long Hotel
building, but there is no reminder of the old place. The 76 guest rooms and
suites are all spacious and stylish with full facilities. The 10-story building
overlooks Giang Vo, a small lake about three kilometers west of the city, and
this provides nice views from the Tea Terrace, the Lakeside Bar, and some of
the rooms.

The hotel has the Lily Coffee Shop with buffet selections and a-la-carte
dining, a Chinese restaurant with Cantonese and Sichuan cuisine, the Volvo
Night Club, tennis, billiards, sauna, massage, and a shopping arcade. Rooms
are from US$130 and suites from US$200. (Book with the hotel at 08 Giang
Vo Street, Hanoi; Fax: 844-259-209.)

MEDIUM-PRICE HOTELS

There is now a wide choice in this category, from the 175-room Thang Loi Hotel to a one-bedroom private mini-hotel. Some of the hotels are reasonably modern, while others are in old French-style buildings that may be up to one hundred years old. Most of these hotels are in central Hanoi, but there are a few places near West Lake, Giang Vo, and elsewhere. All mid-market hotels have self-contained rooms with hot and cold water.

The **Royal Hotel** (Tel: 244-233), 65 rooms, is the city's first three-star privately run hotel. It has been established inside a French Renaissance-style building on the edge of the old quarter of town. Rooms are nicely furnished and have all the necessary facilities. There is a restaurant serving Western, Asian, and Vietnamese food, and a conference hall and bar. Room prices start at around US$120, so it is at the top end of the medium-priced hotels. Suites are from US$250. (Book with the hotel at 20 Hang Tre Street, Hanoi; Fax: 844-244-234).

The **Thang Loi Hotel** (Tel: 268-211), 175 rooms, is the largest hotel in the city and, for ten years or more, it was top of the heap. I am very much in two minds about this place. It has a nice location beside West Lake, an attractive open lobby, and more facilities than most other hotels.

The low-rise concrete structure was built on piers over the edge of West Lake, and the extensive grounds have been landscaped. You enter the open-air lobby through a wide entrance and the reception desk is on your extreme right. Staff speak English and are helpful and friendly. The lobby sports clumps of bamboo, a small stream, waterfall, and timber bridges. It is most unusual for Hanoi. There is a hairdresser, a barber, a sauna and massage, a gift shop, tennis courts, and a swimming pool.

Rooms are a reasonable size, but the standard of furniture is just adequate. There are individual airconditioners, and rooms are equipped with TV, telephone, refrigerator, mosquito nets, desk, and two lounge chairs. Rugs cover parts of the stone floor. The bathrooms are reasonable but a little dark. Each room has a balcony. The hotel has two restaurants, three bars, and a disco every Saturday evening. Room rates start at around US$70 or US$90 for single or double respectively, and this includes breakfast in the restaurant. Room service is available at a fifteen percent surcharge. (Book with the hotel at Yen Phu Road, Hanoi; Fax: 844-252-800.)

The **Dan Chu Hotel** (Tel: 253-323), 41 rooms, is in an excellent central location close to the Municipal Theater and Hoan Kiem Lake. The building was constructed about one hundred years ago as the Hanoi Hotel, and it was one of the favorites during the French era. The lobby is fairly basic, but the large lounge bar and dining room is clean and has some style. The hotel has sauna and massage facilities and a souvenir counter.

There are four classes of room, starting from US$60/80 for single/double. Rooms at the back of the building are less noisy and are my choice. The friendly staff on the reception desk will try and meet your requests. (Book with the hotel at 29 Trang Tien Street, Hanoi; Fax: 844-266-786.)

The **Saigon Hotel** (Tel: 266-631), 44 rooms, opened in 1994 and is run by Saigon Tourist. There are four smallish rooms at US$85/100, while other rooms start at US$100/120. This is a pleasant place with good facilities and efficient and friendly staff. (Book with the hotel at 80 Ly Thuong Kiet Street, Hanoi; Fax: 844-266-631).

The **Hoan Kiem Hotel** (Tel: 264-204), 20 rooms, is similar in style to the Dan Chu Hotel, but the location is not quite as good. The old French-style building with its timber shutters has received little modernization and is fairly basic, but it is reasonably clean.

There are four classes of room with little apparent difference between them. Rooms are airconditioned and have a telephone, TV, fan, desk, mosquito nets, and refrigerator. All the rooms I saw had modern sinks and toilets, but there is no separate shower recess so the entire room (including the toilet seat) gets wet whenever you take a shower. Facilities include two bars and sauna and massage. The hotel has a reasonably priced restaurant with an English menu on the ground floor. (Book with the hotel at 25 Tran Hung Dao Street, Hanoi; Fax: 844-268-690.)

The **Huu Nghi Hotel** (Friendship Hotel) (Tel: 253-182), 38 rooms, is a newly constructed hotel that opened in 1990. It is situated in the old quarter of town about a kilometer from Dong Xuan market. There is a small but attractive lobby, and the rooms are clean and quite large. The hotel has four suites at US$60/72 single/double, and 34 first-class rooms at US$45/50 single/double. All prices include breakfast and service. By Hanoi standards, this is good value. Rooms come with airconditioner, refrigerator, TV, telephone, and carpet. Many have small balconies.

On the ground floor next to the lobby, there is a restaurant, a bar, and a small shop that sells handicraft items. Unfortunately, these areas are not airconditioned, so they are very hot at the height of summer. There is a sauna on the ground floor. (Book with the hotel at 23 Quan Thanh Street, Hanoi; Fax: 844-259-272.)

The **Hoa Binh Hotel** (Tel: 253-315) is an old favorite that has been given a new lease on life. Rooms are a nice combination of classic French 19th-century style with reasonably modern facilities.

The hotel is well placed for sightseeing, shopping, and restaurants. It has numerous classes of room starting at third-class single for US$22. Most travelers looking for mid-range accommodations would be satisfied with any of the first-class rooms (A, B, or C). Prices range from US$40-60 for singles to US$47-66 for doubles. There are some special class rooms US$78/88 single/double. First-class rooms are airconditioned and have refrigerators, telephones, and reasonable bathrooms.

One of the attractions of the hotel is the lobby and large internal court with its winding staircase. There is a shop, bar, massage, and a large dining room. On the top floor, there is a delightful open-air bar/lounge that provides a good view of the surrounding area. (Book with the hotel at 27 Ly Thuong Kiet Street, Hanoi; Fax: 844-269-818.)

The **Bong Sen Hotel** (Tel: 254-017) is a modern hotel opened in 1991 by the Hanoi Tourism Company. It is located close to the Huu Nghi Hotel and, in my opinion, the Huu Nghi is more attractive. The 26 large bedrooms are all airconditioned and have TV, refrigerator, desk, and two lounge chairs. There is no carpet. The attached bathrooms have hot and cold water and modern fixtures.

The hotel has a small, clean, non-airconditioned lobby with a reception desk, handicraft counter, and adjacent restaurant. The hotel brochure describes it as "very much, clean-limbed, elegand (sic.) decorated and very circumspectly for service," which I interpret as very clean, elegantly decorated, and designed for service. I believe it. Rooms cost US$45/54 single/double including breakfast and service. (Book with the hotel at 34 Hang Bun Street, Hanoi; Fax: 844-233-232.)

The **Boss Hotel** (Tel: 252-690), 15 rooms, is operated by the OSCAN group who are heavily involved in operations in Vung Tao in southern Vietnam. The hotel is modern and clean, and all rooms are airconditioned and have TV, telephone, and refrigerators. Bathrooms have full baths and separate showers with hot and cold water. The Blue Diamond Restaurant has a good selection of food, and the VIP Lounge is one of Hanoi's most popular after-dark locations. There is a business center with international telephone and fax facilities, and tours and rental cars can be organized here. Rooms are US$70-86 per night. (Book with the hotel at 60 Nguyen Du Street, Hanoi; Fax: 844-257-634.)

The **Ho Tay Villas** (Tel: 258-261) is one of those strange places only found in socialist countries. There are nine villas, 62 hotel rooms, a restaurant and bar, and a shop set in huge gardens by Lake Tay. When I visited, there were dozens of staff sitting around, watching TV, and generally filling in time. There were few guests. Until very recently, this was reserved for the use of high government officials; but in these "enlightened times" it is being opened to foreign visitors. Rooms vary in size and facilities, but if you need a place away-from-it-all, this could be the answer. Room rates are from US$35 including breakfast. (Write to Xa Quang An, Tu Liem, Hanoi; Fax: 844-232-126.)

The **Binh Minh Hotel** (Tel: 266-441), 76 rooms, opened late in 1992. It is a nice-looking building with pleasant English-speaking receptionists. I have not stayed here. All rooms are airconditioned, have telephones, satellite TV, refrigerators, and bathrooms with hot and cold water. The location is good—close to the old quarter and the lake and within walking distance of many other parts of central Hanoi. Room prices are a bargain at US$30-40 but are likely to rise as renovations are completed. (Book with the hotel at 27 Ly Thai To Street, Hanoi; Fax: 844-257-725.)

The **Ho Bac Nam Hotel** (Tel: 257-067), 21 rooms, is just north of the Hoa Binh Hotel. I have not stayed here, so I cannot make any authoritative comment. All rooms are airconditioned and have a telephone and hot and cold water. The better rooms have all the other usual facilities. There is quite a reasonable restaurant. Room rates are from US$25 to US$65. (Book at 20 Ngo Quyen Street, Hanoi; Fax: 844-268-998.)

The **Tay Ho International Hotel** (Tel: 232-380), 118 rooms, is an impressive place out in the middle of nowhere. If you are a business person or an official being looked after by the government and you have access to a 24-hour car, the location is no problem; but otherwise you will be isolated here once your transport leaves.

The hotel has above average facilities to compensate for the location. There is a huge lobby, a good restaurant, a bar, a large pool, huge gardens by the edge of the lake, a post office, sauna and massage, and car rental facilities. There is music in the lobby and a dancing room at night. The rooms are airconditioned and have TV, refrigerator, and telephone. Many have balconies. The suites occupy two full rooms and are a particularly good value. Room prices are US$55/64 and US$66/78 for single/double. (Book with the hotel at Quang An, Tu Liem, Hanoi; Fax: 844-232-390.)

The **Dong Loi Hotel** (Tel: 255-721), 30 rooms, was once a scruffy budget hotel but it has been upgraded into something quite reasonable. The location is excellent for rail passengers, and the restaurant is good. There is a bar and massage facilities. Rooms are US$50 double or single. (Book with the hotel at 94 Ly Thuong Kiet Street, Hanoi; Fax: 844-267-999).

The **Hanoi Star Hotel** (Tel: 250-935), 21 rooms, is a similar standard but the area is not quite so convenient. There are two restaurants, a bar, and friendly staff. Rooms have all the usual facilities. Room prices are US$35/40 single/double. (Book with the hotel at 14-225 Street, Hanoi; Fax: 844-250-934.)

The **Quoc Tu Giam Hotel** (Tel: 257-106), 20 rooms, is in a similar area. It has a cafe on the ground floor and restaurant above with Western and Asian food. Rooms are adequate and prices are US$30/37 single/double. (Book with the hotel at 27 Quoc Tu Giam Street, Hanoi; Fax: 844-264-338.)

The **Mylan Hotel**, 40 rooms, is south of central Hanoi in a residential area. The rooms are above average, and there is a restaurant, a nightclub, and Karaoke facilities. It seems to be quite popular at US$60/70, single/double. (Book with the hotel at 334 Ba Trieu Street, Hanoi.)

Back nearer the city center, the **Trang Tien Hotel** (Tel: 256-115), 40 rooms, has some appeal. There is an upstairs restaurant and adequate rooms; those near the front are a bit noisy. Room prices are US$32 and US$40. (Book with the hotel at 35 Trang Tien Street, Hanoi; Fax: 844-251-416.)

Still farther in, the **Ho Guom Hotel** (Tel: 252-225), 25 rooms, has a nice courtyard entrance and reasonable, quiet rooms. There is a restaurant and bar and plenty of action at night. Room prices are US$40, 45, and 60. (Book with the hotel at 76 Hang Trong Street, Hanoi; Fax: 844-243-564.)

The **Lavender Hotel** (Tel: 236-723), 12 rooms, is worth a particular mention because of its exceptional friendly, helpful staff. Rooms have all the necessary facilities including satellite TV, and there is a small restaurant. Room rates in late 1994 were a real bargain at US$30. (Book with the hotel at 3 Tong Duy Tan, Hanoi; Fax: 844-231-474.)

The **La Thanh Hotel** (Tel: 254-123) is a classic old French-style three-story building about four kilometers from the center of town. This is not the place to be if you plan to spend your evenings wandering the old quarter because transport to and from the hotel can be a problem.

The advantages of the hotel are the space you have, the cost, and the cheapest car rental prices in Hanoi. The building has no elevator, but there is a shop, a lounge with a pool table, a restaurant, sauna, and massage. There are grounds to wander through or for jogging if you are so inclined. Room prices start at around US$25 but the better rooms are from about US$30. (Book with the hotel at 218 Doi Can, Hanoi.)

The **Diamond Hotel** (Tel: 232-708), 23 rooms, opened in late 1994. It has standard rooms from US$38 to suites at US$98. The rooms are good, the location is convenient, and the staff is friendly. Price includes breakfast. (Book with the hotel at 95 Hang Bong Street, Hanoi; Fax: 844-246-331.)

The **Hong Ha Hotel** (Tel: 253-688), 30 rooms, is not a bad place at 78 Yen Phu Street. This is the main riverside road, and the hotel is just north of the railway bridge. It is not a great location, but it is within walking distance of the old quarter of town. The hotel is reasonably clean, there is very friendly staff, the restaurant is good, and the rooms are quiet but not particularly stylish. I stayed in a second-class room which had airconditioning, refrigerator, telephone, TV, and bathroom with hot and cold water. It costs US$30 a night. Special rooms are US$40, and third class is US$25.

The **Giang Vo Hotel** (Tel: 253-407) overlooks the same lake as the Thang Long Hotel, about three kilometers from the city center. It is often said that this is the largest hotel in Hanoi, but most of the rooms are rented on a semi-permanent basis, so the number of rooms available to short-stay visitors is limited.

The best rooms are on the second floor of a long apartment block.

Foreigners pay US$20 for these rooms and Vietnamese pay 60,000d. Each consists of a bedroom, a separate lounge, and a bathroom with hot and cold water to the shower and a modern toilet. Rooms are airconditioned and have a refrigerator and telephone. There is a restaurant and there is dancing on Thursday and Saturday evenings. (Book with the hotel at Giang Vo Dong Da, Hanoi.)

In the past couple of years, a large number of privately owned mini-hotels have appeared. Almost universally they are narrow, single-fronted buildings, five-stories high, with two or three rooms per floor and with no elevator. All seem to have reasonable-size rooms, all the usual facilities (TV, telephone, refrigerator, airconditioning, hot and cold water) and small bathrooms. There are far too many of these in the city to list them all, but the following have been inspected and are considered satisfactory.

The **Ngoc Mai Hotel** (Tel: 267-104; Fax: 844-267-104), 10 rooms, is at 7 Cua Dong Street in the old quarter of the city. Rooms are from US$40. The **Lucky Hotel**(Tel: 251-029; Fax: 844-251-731), 9 rooms, at 12 Hang Trong Street, and the **Freedom Hotel** (Tel: 267-119; Fax: 844-243-918), 11 rooms, at 57 Hang Trong Street, are in the area just west of Hoan Kiem Lake. Rooms are from US$35. The **Vinh Quang Hotel** (Tel: 243-423; Fax: 844-251-519), 15 rooms, at 24 Hang Quat Street, has a small restaurant and bar and rooms from US$30.

In the area south of the central city, there is plenty of choice. There are four good places on Nguyen Du Street. The **Tien Thinh Hotel** (Tel: 226-406; Fax: 844-227-713), 7 rooms from US$40 at Number 52, the **City Inn** (Tel: 226-263; Fax: 844-227-282), 5 rooms from US$33 at Number 55A, the **Gold Hotel** (Tel: 265-186; Fax: 844-226-017), 6 rooms from US$40 at Number 12, and the slightly larger **Dai Dong Hotel** (Tel: 227-867; Fax: 844-227-296) with its restaurant and 12 rooms from US$40 at Number 5. The more up-market **Hotel Du Nord** (Tel: 243-410; Fax: 844-228-405), 11 rooms from US$55 at 58 Tran Xuan Soan Street and the **My Linh Hotel** (Tel: 268-800; Fax: 844-226-994), 9 rooms from US$70 at 328 Pho Hue Street, are in the same area.

In the area near the railway station you will find the **Memory Hotel** (Tel: 232-668; Fax: 844-232-668), 8 rooms from US$30 at 25 Nguyen Thai Hoc, and the **Alpo Hotel** (Tel: 236-138), 8 rooms from US$30, is at Number 9. Close by, the **Blue II Hotel** (Tel: 233-541; Fax: 844-236-393), 8 rooms from US$60, is at 6 Dinh Ngang Street, while the **Pacific Hotel** (Tel: 250-773; Fax: 844-250-785) 6 rooms from US$40, is at 35 Tho Nhuom Street. The **Fortika Hotel 2** (Tel: 265-537; Fax: 844-281-133), 10 rooms from US$30, is at 49 Le Ovan Street.

To the west of the railway line you could try the **Star Hotel II** (Tel: 269-251; Fax: 844-269-251), 5 rooms from US$30 at 51B Quoc Tu Giam Street, the very friendly **Hotel Bich An** (Tel: 232-701; Fax: 844-234-981), 8 rooms from US\$30 at 189 Son Tay Street, or the **Huong Duong Hotel** (Tel: 232-153; Fax: 844-231-453), 6 rooms from US\$45 at 71E Kim Ma Street.

BUDGET ACCOMMODATIONS

I have somewhat of a problem with down-market hotels because I have encountered considerable reluctance to allow foreigners to stay at many of them. I initially thought this was because management thought that foreigners needed better facilities than those being offered, but on several occasions when I insisted I wanted a room and produced money to pay for it, I was still told that foreigners couldn't stay there. In some instances I know that foreigners have previously stayed there, so I am not sure exactly why this has changed. Perhaps it is an attempt to get more foreign currency; but if this is so, it is not in the best long-term interests of Vietnam tourism. I have personally checked out the following hotels, so you should have no difficulty in these cases.

The **Phung Hung Hotel** (Tel: 252-614; Fax: 844-269-279) was a well-known "cheapie," but the hotel has been slowly renovated and most of the very cheap rooms are gone forever. Airconditioned singles and doubles are small rooms with reasonable facilities. The attached bathrooms are also very small, but they have hot and cold water. Costs are US\$20/25, single/double. The people at reception do not speak much English, but "sign language" will get you by. There is a restaurant and cafe. The hotel is about one kilometer from the railway station at 2 Duong Thanh Street.

The **Victory Hotel** (Tel: 258-725; Fax: 844-260-539), 20 rooms from US\$25 just sneaks into this category. The facilities are good (TV, refrigerator, airconditioning, etc.) but the location at 9-225 Street west of the railway line is only fair. The **Blue Hotel** (Tel: 263-572; Fax: 844-269-976), 15 rooms from US\$20 at 209 Le Duan Street, is also a bit out of the way but the facilities are OK. If you want to be in the center of things, the **Bodega Cafe Guesthouse** at 57 Trang Tien Street is the place to go. There are only a few rooms and it is clean and very popular so you have to be lucky to get one of the US\$15/20 rooms.

The **Sophia Hotel** (Tel: 255-069) also seems very popular. There are eight rooms which cost US\$15/20 for single/double. Rooms are small, but they are reasonably clean and each has hot and cold water. The hotel is on the third floor above a cafe at ground level and a restaurant on the second level. This place is very popular. The last time I was there, it was completely booked by foreign visitors. The location of this hotel is excellent. The address is 6 Hang Bai Street, near the lake and the post office.

Not far away, the **Phu Gia Hotel** (Tel: 255-493) is also popular. The location at 136 Hang Trong Street is opposite Hoan Kiem Lake and close to many attractions of the city. Rooms are self-contained and are reasonably clean. The ones I have seen have been a decent size with adequate furniture. At US$12 per night, they represent good value. Close to the railway station, the **Nhat Phuong Hotel** (Tel: 250-376; Fax: 844-243-131) at 39 Le Duan Street has a range of rooms starting at US$15.

The **Giang Vo Hotel** (Tel: 253-407), which was mentioned in the medium-price section, also has some cheaper rooms which foreigners can rent. The rooms are quite large, fairly basic, and have no hot water, but the hotel said that foreigners can rent these rooms at the Vietnamese rate of 50,000d per day. That is very good value.

The **Nha Khach Guest House** at 41 Hang Ba Street has ten aircondi-tioned rooms with refrigerators and hot and cold water. At US$18 they are good value even though the building is nothing to rave about.

The alternative to all these is to stay at one of the now privately owned mini-hotels which are appearing throughout the city. Generally they provide airconditioned rooms with telephone and TV and sometimes a refrigerator, with a small bathroom. The smallest rooms in some of these rent for US$20. Here are some that I have inspected.

The **Pacific Hotel II** (Tel: 259-282; Fax: 844-250-785), 5 rooms from US$20 at 52P Ly Thuong Kiet Street, is one of the most central. The **Thanh An Hotel** (Tel: 267-191; Fax: 844-269-720), 8 rooms from US$25 at 46 Hang Ga Street and the **Binh Duong Hotel** (Tel: 253-187; Fax: 844-243-127), 11 rooms from US$25 at 40 Hang Da Street, are both on the western edge of the old city. Closer to Hoan Kiem Lake, you will find the **Liberty Hotel** (Tel: 267-566; Fax: 844-245-362), 12 rooms from US$20 at 14 Luong Van Can Street and the friendly **Venus Hotel** (Tel: 261-212), 11 rooms from US$20 at 10 Hang Can Street.

South of the center, the **Dong Hung Hotel** (Tel: 269-758; Fax: 844-269-759), 10 rooms from US$25 and its attractive lobby with circular staircase, is at 156 Ba Trieu Street, while the **Hotel Van Lan I** (Tel: 226-225; Fax: 844-226-226), 14 rooms from US$15 and its roof-top swimming pool, is at 55 Tran Nhan Tong Street.

The **Golden Dragon Hotel** (Tel: 233-585; Fax: 844-234-665), 10 rooms from US$25, is at 40 Cat Linh Street. The **Ngoe Bae Hotel** (Tel: 237-540; Fax: 844-237-465), 8 rooms from US$25, is at 195 Son Tay Street. Both are west of the city center.

5. Dining and Restaurants

Hanoi is a city with a poor reputation for dining opportunities for visi-tors. The situation has, however, dramatically improved in the last two years, and now there are a number of places outside the hotels that are worth seeking out. Most visitors will nevertheless take their first meals in the hotels, so here is a brief run-down on the opportunities.

HOTEL RESTAURANTS

The **Le Beaulieu Restaurant** at the Hotel Sofitel Metropole is by far the most stylish and the most expensive hotel restaurant in the city. It is run by a very competent European food and beverage manager, and it shows. Expect the food to be excellent, expect the service to be good, and expect to pay Western prices for the privilege. The Sunday buffet lunch is a highlight.

The **West Lake Restaurant** at the Thang Loi Hotel is large, matter-of-fact, clean, and friendly. The menu is in English and the food has a definite Western influence. Popular dishes are roast chicken, smoked beef, and meat pie. Costs range from US$2 to US$5 for main dishes. A beer is US$1 and an orange juice US$0.40. This restaurant has a disco after dinner every Saturday night. The Thang Loi Hotel also has a small restaurant off the main lobby which serves Vietnamese specialties. This is a good introduction to local tastes if Vietnamese food is new to you.

The **Chinese Restaurant** at the Hanoi Hotel serves good Cantonese and Sichuan cuisine in nice surroundings. The **Lily Coffee Shop** in the same hotel serves both European and Asian food either buffet style or a-la-carte.

The **Dan Chu Hotel Restaurant** has more style than most. The old French colonial-style dining room has high ceilings and fans attached to the large columns. It is clean and there is a lounge area and a bar. Menus are available in English, French, and Vietnamese. I recommend the crab soup (5,000d for two) and the spring rolls. The fried vegetables were not very good. Mineral water, both sweetened and natural, is available at 1,500d per bottle. Coca-Cola and 333 beer is around 9,000d.

The **Hoan Kiem Hotel Restaurant** is relatively small, but the service is good and there is a friendly feel about the place. The English menu is not very extensive, but you will find that the soup, fried rice, pork, and steamed snails with ginger leaves are all excellent.

The **Hoa Binh Hotel Restaurant** is bright and airy and the staff is attentive and friendly. Not all of the staff can speak English, but the manager will assist and even suggest dishes that may or may not be on the menu. A meal for two can cost less than 50,000d.

The **La Thanh Hotel Restaurant** is situated in a separate building at the rear of the hotel. Prices here are very reasonable with an omelette costing 2,500d, spring rolls 3,500d, meat and potatoes 3,500d, and rice and mixed pork also 3,500d. I can't say that I thought the food was fantastic, but it is cheap for hotel fare.

The **Sophia Hotel Restaurant** is popular because it is in the area where

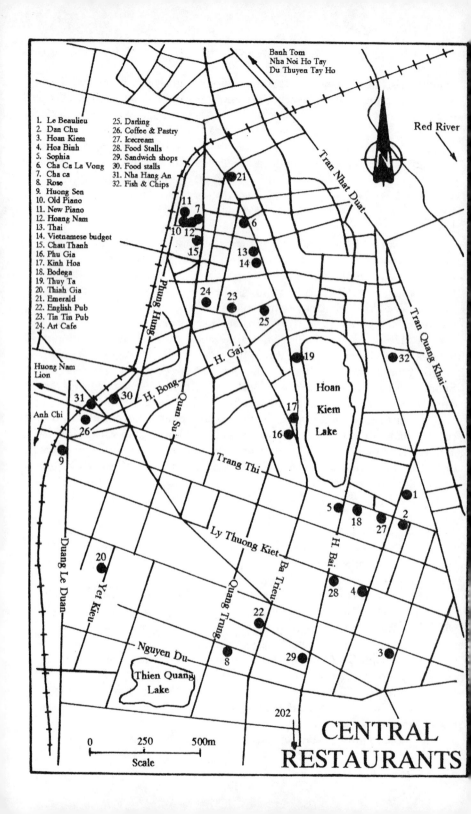

1. Le Beaulieu
2. Dan Chu
3. Hoan Kiem
4. Hoa Binh
5. Sophia
6. Cha Ca La Vong
7. Cha ca
8. Rose
9. Huong Sen
10. Old Piano
11. New Piano
12. Hoang Nam
13. Thai
14. Vietnamese budget
15. Chau Thanh
16. Phu Gia
17. Kinh Hoa
18. Bodega
19. Thuy Ta
20. Thiah Gia
21. Emerald
22. English Pub
23. Tin Tin Pub
24. Art Cafe

25. Darling
26. Coffee & Pastry
27. Icecream
28. Food Stalls
29. Sandwich shops
30. Food stalls
31. Nha Hang An
32. Fish & Chips

Banh Tom
Nha Noi Ho Tay
Du Thuyen Tay Ho

Red River

Tran Nhat Duat

Tran Quang Khai

Phung Hung

H. Gai

Huong Nam
Lion

Anh Chi

H. Bong

Quan Su

Trang Thi

Hoan
Kiem
Lake

Duang Le Duan

Yet Kieu

Ly Thuong Kiet

Ba Trieu

H. Bai

Quang Trung

Nguyen Du

Thien Quang
Lake

202

0   250   500m

Scale

CENTRAL RESTAURANTS

many tourists find themselves at mid-day. The English menu has no prices, but dishes average out at about 9,000d. Seafood can be much higher. This is one place that you can find some Thai influence in some of the cooking. Note that the restaurant will not take dinner orders after 8 P.M.

The **Royal Hotel**, the **Saigon Hotel**, **Huu Nghi Hotel**, the **Boss Hotel**, the **Tay Ho International Hotel**, the **Bong Sen Hotel**, and many of the small mini-hotels all have restaurants, but I have not eaten in any of them. They all look clean and have English menus.

OTHER RESTAURANTS

One of my favorite restaurants is **Restaurant 202** at 202 Hue Street, east of Bay Mau Lake. The restaurant is upstairs and is not particularly large, so it has a nice intimate atmosphere. Some nights, the front is opened and tables are put on a small balcony. This can be very pleasant. The menu has both Vietnamese and Western dishes. Crab is one of the specialties and the spring rolls are delicious. Another dish that I particularly like is the skewered chicken which is flame-cooked. It is served with boiled rice. The menu has no prices, so don't be afraid to ask before you order. There will be someone who can speak good English, and all the staff are friendly. A selection of local and imported beers is available together with a good range of other drinks. Two people can eat for around 50,000d, including drinks.

Another favorite is **Cha Ca La Vong Restaurant** at the other end of the city in Cha Ca Street, about 500 meters north of Lake Hoan Kiem. *Cha Ca* means "fried fish," and this restaurant specializes in fish and vegetables that you cook yourself at your table. The place is usually crowded, so just wait for a table, sit down, and the meal will be brought to you. You can eat either upstairs or downstairs. Neither area is airconditioned, but that helps to give it a nice local flavor. Coca-Cola, juice, and beer are available. A meal for two will cost around 50,000d. Just to confuse things, there is a **Cha Ca Restaurant** (Tel: 267-881) at 66 Hang Ga Street. The food is quite good if you happen to end up here.

At the other end of town, the **Rose Restaurant** (Tel: 254-400) at 15 Tran Quoc Toan Street has a large clientele. It is open from 8 A.M. to 10 P.M. every day, and it serves both Asian and Western cuisine. There is one large room with about twelve tables, and four small rooms for more intimate surroundings. All rooms are airconditioned. The restaurant has a staff of young waiters and waitresses, some of whom speak English. You will be welcomed and looked after by someone who could well be Rose herself. It's well worth trying.

The **Nha Hang An** at 3 Dien Bien Phu, beside the railway line, is one of those places most people would not enter unless they had a recommendation. It appears to be old, dirty, and run-down, but in fact it manages to produce some excellent food and is justifiably popular. The owner sits out on the sidewalk and talks in Vietnamese or French to passing walkers. The restaurant menu is in the same languages, but English speakers will be able to find some dishes that they understand. A meal here should not cost more than 25,000d for two, and you are likely to be dining with locals rather than visitors.

The **Huong Sen Restaurant** is upstairs at 52 Le Duan Street, just north of the railway station. This is an upscale restaurant that is aimed at tourists, but you will find that there are many Vietnamese here as well. Prices tend to be higher than in many other places. A meal for two will cost 75,000-100,000d. There is an extensive English menu with many strange but interesting dishes. You can sample such things as eel, goat, frog, snails, and pigeon. If something conventional is more to your liking, there is pork, beef, fish, or chicken. The restaurant is airconditioned, but I have been there when the only chilled drink available has been Vietnamese beer. Western pop music is often played to help digestion.

Music of a different kind is played at the **Piano Restaurant**. Actually there are two of these. The original is at 50 Hang Vai Street, and the new restaurant run by the daughter of the original family is just around the corner on Phung Hung Street. The original restaurant opens at 8 A.M. for breakfast and remains open until midnight. Music starts at 7 P.M. and goes until late. Typical costs for two are 60,000-75,000d. The new restaurant, which is slightly more upscale, opens from 11 A.M. to 2 P.M. for lunch and from 6 P.M. for dinner. I recommend the grilled shrimp, and there are a variety of beef, pork, and other dishes. Cream caramel is a popular dessert. Australian Lindemans wine is available, as is San Miguel Beer. A pianist and a violinist play from 7 P.M. This is a popular place for embassy and United Nations personnel to dine.

One of the best Vietnamese restaurants in the city is close by. **Hoang Nam Restaurant** (Tel: 232-436) at 46 Hang Vai Street looks like many others, but the food is outstanding. Don't be surprised to see several expatriate faces among the customers. The same can be said for the **Thai Restaurant** (Tel: 260-214) at 30 Hang Can Street. There is a bar downstairs and a nice dining area upstairs. Vietnamese and Chinese dishes are also available. On the same street, the **Vietnamese Restaurant** (Tel: 267-160) at Number 22 is a find for budget travelers looking for good food. The restaurant is down an alley then upstairs, but it is worth finding.

The **Chau Thanh Restaurant** at 48 Hang Ga Street is a small place with a good reputation. This restaurant was originally at another address about a kilometer from here, but obviously some of the clientele have followed to the new location. The very friendly owner speaks some English and runs a nice, brightly lit airconditioned restaurant. When I visited in mid-summer, this restaurant scored top marks for having the coldest drinks in Hanoi—cold drinks are a rare commodity in many places. I can also recommend the food.

The **Phu Gia Restaurant** at 136 Hang Trong Street was once one of the top restaurants in town. It has become rather run down, but the food is still quite good. There are several dining areas but you are probably best off using the upstairs airconditioned area. There is an English menu and prices are reasonable. Nearby, you will find the **Kinh Hoa Restaurant** (Tel: 258-057) which has good Vietnamese food at 6 Le Thai To Street.

Restaurant Thong Bao is above the **Bodega Cafe** at 57 Trang Tien Street, near the southern end of Hoan Kiem Lake. It is not airconditioned, but at night it is pleasant in the opening nearest the street—there is often a breeze. I have only eaten here once and on that occasion I had a very friendly English-speaking waitress who was extremely helpful. Unfortunately, it didn't help with my food selection because although the sweet and sour pork was excellent (5,000d), the beef with soya sauce and ginger was awful. The meal for two cost 35,000d. Downstairs at the Bodega, things really hum along at night. The cafe specializes in cake, ice cream, and coffee and is packed most of the time with locals enjoying the video clips of Western hit songs. Without a doubt, they serve the best ice cream in Hanoi.

The **Restaurant Banh Tom** is very popular with Vietnamese out for a good time. It overlooks West Lake (Ho Tay) just near Truc Bach Lake. If the weather is good, the place to go is upstairs where there is a large eating area under a huge spreading tree. There is no English menu, but you will be able to guess at some of the dishes because of the small drawings indicating beef, fish, pork, eel, and so on. Avoid the chicken because it is as hard as leather; some other dishes are fair. The orange juice is good. Shrimp cakes are the specialty.

In this same area, the **Nha Noi Ho Tay Restaurant** and the **Du Thuyen Tay Ho Restaurant** both float on West Lake. These seem to be popular places for Vietnamese to take visitors, but I think they are overrated and I have never had particularly good food there. I have similar feelings about **Thuy Ta Restaurant** which overlooks Hoan Kiem Lake. The two-story building has been painted, but the service is poor. Both food and drinks are overpriced and very limited.

For those staying on the western edge of the central city, the **Huong Nam Restaurant** on Giang Vo Street is a good find. This is actually situated in a large building called Block II. The restaurant faces the street and is not hard to find. There is a nice atmosphere and the food is well above average. Across the road, you will find the new **Lion Restaurant** (Tel: 230-409) which has Western and Asian dishes and Vietnamese food in a modern airconditioned atmosphere. Back toward the railway at 3A Quoc Tu Giam Street, the **Anh**

Chi Restaurant (Tel: 259-520) has a good reputation for Vietnamese food. It sometimes has live music. Back near the Workers Culture Palace, the **Thiah Gia Restaurant** at 24 Yet Kieu has good food, an extensive English menu, and an upstairs airconditioned section. Just down the road, the **Hoan Thien Restaurant** is worth trying for good Vietnamese food.

A recent development has been the appearance of Western-style pubs and bistros serving a variety of Western food. Three of these are **The Emerald** (Tel: 259-285) at 53 Hang Luoe Street where you will find a genuine pub atmosphere, English beer on tap, and English, Italian, and Vietnamese food; the **English Pub** (Tel: 228-398) at 66 Ba Trieu Street where a set dinner costs 100,000 dong and coffee is 5,000 dong, in a smart atmosphere; and the **Tin Tin Pub** (Tel: 260-326) at 14 Hang Non Street where there is Vietnamese food together with pizza, hamburgers, and crepes.

The **Art Cafe** (Tel: 258-000) at 57 Hang Non Street has cocktails, pizza and spaghetti, and great coffee. **Apocalypse Now** at 46 Hang Vai Street is called a dive bar, and it lives up to that name. **Darling Cafe** at 33 Hang Quat Street (there is another cafe with the same name in the same street) is a popular hangout for budget travelers. The **Coffee and Pastry Shop** at 252 Hang Bong Street serves breakfast, yogurt, French pastries, and good coffee until late.

OTHER PLACES TO EAT

Apart from the formal restaurants, there are a growing number of small eating stalls appearing on the sidewalks. These provide very limited choice of food, but in my experience what is available is usually good. Additionally, it is inevitably cheap because it is aimed at the locals. No prices appear at these places but even if you are charged more than the locals, it will still be an amazingly cheap meal (rarely more than 4,000d).

You will find these stalls in many areas, but there are concentrations of them at **Dong Xuan Market** on Hang Bong Street near Phung Hung Street, in Tong Duy Tan Street near the railway line, and on Ly Thuong Kiet Street down from the Hoa Binh Hotel. You will find that you can sample the famous *Hanoi Pho* (a noodle soup) at one of these places for around 1,500d.

There are also small sandwich shops scattered around the city selling French bread filled with various mixtures. There are several good outlets along Hang Ba Street, south of Tran Hung Dao Street.

6. Sightseeing

Lakes, temples, and museums are just some of the highlights of sightseeing in Hanoi. The city has a good selection of natural attractions, ancient monuments, and modern structures to provide something for almost everyone.

EAST OF THE RAILWAY

Hoan Kiem Lake is the natural starting point for Hanoi sightseeing. The lake provides a quiet and peaceful area in the busiest part of the city. Like almost everything in Vietnam, the lake has a legend attached to it. This concerns a magic sword and tortoise and it still influences names in the area today. The lake's name means "Restored Sword," and in its center is the historic relic called "Tortoise Tower." The lake and surrounding lawns and gardens serve as a major outdoor recreational outlet for locals. In the early morning, residents can be seen exercising and walking; during the day, young children play under the shade trees while parents sit on the benches; and at night, Hanoi's young come to eat, walk, cuddle, and find a private space for themselves.

This part of Hanoi can best be explored on foot, so let us start at the southern end of the lake and walk east along Trang Tien Street. Immediately in front of you is the grand French Opera House, now called the **Municipal Theater**. This lovely building was constructed in 1911 and was a high point in the cultural life of the city. Even today the building is well used, and it is quite an experience to see a performance in its main hall. During one of my visits in 1991, Shakespeare was being performed. Ticket prices are very reasonable. If you are a guest of a hotel in this area, the front desk may help you purchase a ticket.

Immediately behind the Municipal Theater is the excellent **Museum of History**. This was founded in 1910 as the Louis Finot Museum, and the present impressive building dates from 1932. Exhibits cover almost five thousand years of Vietnamese history, and there are some individual pieces that are quite magnificent. Highlights include the Ngoc Lu bronze drums (from at least four thousand years ago), one thousand-year-old gold ornaments from central Vietnam, and some ancient ceramics. Many of the displays are well presented, but unfortunately there is no explanation in English. The museum is open from 8 A.M. to 3:45 P.M.

The **Museum of the Revolution** is literally across the road from here. Visitors are encouraged by Vietnamese officials to visit; but frankly I found it rather boring because there is no English explanation and there are strong political overtones to many of the exhibits which are of little interest to foreign visitors. I suspect that many other people feel the same way because when I visited, there was not another person in the whole museum. While there are some displays from Vietnam's long-running struggle with China, much of the emphasis is on the struggle against Japan, the French,

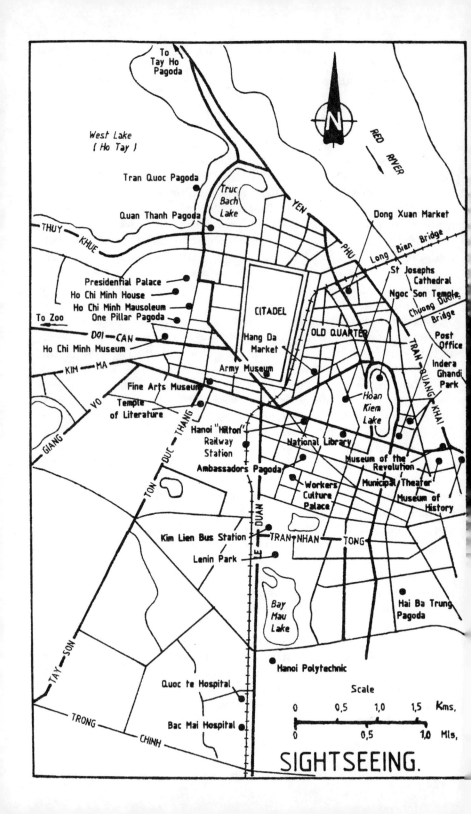

SIGHTSEEING.

and the United States. This museum was established some years ago, and in some ways it has been overtaken by the new Ho Chi Minh Museum (described later). There is a 1,000d entrance fee.

It's now a matter of making your way across the small park and down some side streets back to the lake. On the way, you may pass the **Government Guest House** where important visitors are often housed, and you may walk through **Indira Gandhi Park**. To your left is the **General Post Office** and **International Telephone Office**. The post office is open from early morning until 8 P.M. You can purchase stamps, send letters and packages, and buy philatelic items. The telephone and telex office is in the building to the right. Charges for all these services are extremely high by international standards, so ask before you use the facilities.

Now that you are back at the lake, take the path north around the shore. Near the north end of the lake you will see the **Ngoc Son Temple** on a small island. It is linked to the shore by a red wooden bridge called the Hue which dates from the nineteenth century. The temple is well worth a visit, mainly because of its lovely location. It is open daily from 8 A.M. to 5 P.M. As with almost everything in Hanoi, there is an entrance fee. As you exit the bridge note the paintbrush obelisk and the inkwell slab which were erected 130 years ago to honor a famous Vietnamese scholar.

To your left is the heart of the **Old Quarter**, a fascinating area of narrow streets, old French architecture, bustling commerce, and interesting restaurants. Many of the streets bear the names of the businesses that were once conducted here. There is Silver Street (Hang Bac), Basket Street (Hang Bo), Fish Street (Hang Ca), Brass Street (Hang Dong), Paper Street (Hang Giay), and so on. It is fun to wander around this area, looking into shops, venturing up alleys, and generally taking in the atmosphere. Most of the streets are lined with mature trees and are quite attractive. Many old homes still exist. Wrought-iron balconies, windows with louvered wooden shutters painted in tones of green and blue, and decorative details at sky level, embellish them. Curbside vendors offer oven-fresh baguettes, live ducks, dead chickens, Madonna T-shirts, pith helmets, and fresh flowers.

Your aim now is to reach **Dong Xuan Market** on Hang Khoa Street, the largest general market in Hanoi. Most of the old French buildings have disappeared, replaced by a modern characterless concrete building, but the stalls and atmosphere are still interesting. There are food stalls and vendors selling fresh fruit and vegetables, clothing, footwear, household goods, plants, live animals and birds, and herbal medicines. While there may be nothing you need to buy, you will enjoy wandering around the large building and taking in the sights. Unfortunately, a major fire in late 1994 had closed the market on my last visit. A reopening time was not forthcoming from officials.

If one market is not enough for you, head for Ngo Tram Street and the

Hang Da Market. This is a smaller version of Dong Xuan with more emphasis
on imported goods, clothes, and shoes. From here, it is worthwhile to make a
detour down Ly Quoc Su Street to **St. Joseph Cathedral**. The building is something straight out of Europe. The main door of the cathedral is often closed
and the side gate to the compound has a chain on it. But don't despair, to your
left is the Diocese of Hanoi and you will find a way through to the cathedral if
you persevere. It is worth the effort. The interior is attractive with an elaborate altar and some delightful stained-glass windows. A mass is held early in the
morning and late in the afternoon most days.

When you leave the cathedral, turn right and walk to Trang Thi Street.
This will take you by the **National Library** and two hospitals. Turn left and
you will find yourself walking along the side of **Hoa Lo Prison**, a grim structure made infamous by the U.S. prisoners of war who were kept here in
the "Hanoi Hilton." The building was constructed by the French early in
this century, and it still functions as a prison today.

One block west, on Quan Su Street, you will find the **Quan Su Pagoda**
which is often called the Ambassador's Pagoda. Originally there was a guesthouse here for ambassadors of Buddhist countries. When it became the
headquarters of Vietnamese Buddhism in 1934, it was decided to build a
new pagoda which was completed in 1942. The building is open to the public, but is often closed at lunch time.

From here, you can see the large **Workers Cultural Palace** on Tran Hung
Dao Street. The building was financed by the Soviet Union and contains
theaters, classrooms, libraries, and meeting rooms. It is one of the few
impressive modern buildings in Hanoi, and it is enhanced by its landscaped
surroundings. There is a good view of the area from the roof. The **Railway
Station** is one block away to the west.

WEST OF THE RAILWAY

Directly north of the railway station is a walled area known as the **Citadel**.
What you see today is of fairly modern construction, but this area was once
the location of the Imperial Palace of Thang Long. The original citadel
was built progressively from 1010 when Ly Thai To moved his capital to the
site of Hanoi. At its peak, the palace, court yards, gardens, apartment
blocks, and other structures were considered to be one of the most beautiful complexes in Asia. Unfortunately, nothing survives today.

When Gia Long came to power two hundred years ago, he established his
capital in Hue rather than Thang Long (Hanoi), but he was well aware of
the military significance of Hanoi. He ordered the remains of the ancient
citadel of Thang Long to be torn down and a smaller, more defensible for-
tification to be built. All that remains of that structure is the hexagonal

Watch Tower on Dien Bien Phu Street, which has been a symbol of Hanoi for many years.

Next to the Watch Tower is the **Army Museum**. This is open daily except Mondays. There is a 2,000d admission charge. Military museums are not normally my favorite places, but this one left a strong impression on me. It made me realize that this region has experienced war for thousands of years. Early conflicts with China are depicted together with the Trung sisters uprising (see Hai Ba Trung Temple), the battles with the French and South Vietnam, Pol Pot's Kampuchians, and China's invasion of the northern border area in 1979.

Outside the museum, there are Soviet and Chinese weapons alongside captured French and American-made tanks and guns. Inside, there are scale models of various major battles and other objects including U.S. military dog tags, I.D. cards, and other personal items. Many people will find this in very poor taste. The most well-known feature of the museum is a full-size MIG-21 jet fighter sitting atop a pile of wreckage made up of F-111, B52, and other U.S. aircraft metal.

It's a short walk from here along Tran Phu Street to Chu Van An Street and the **Fine Arts Museum**. The collection of paintings, sculpture, clothing, and lacquerware is spread over three levels of a fine old French building. Unfortunately the building is not airconditioned so at times it is extremely hot, and I'm sure the art is suffering badly from heat and humidity. Much of the work will have only passing interest to most visitors, but there are a few items of traditional crafts and embroidery and some modern paintings that are well worth seeing. The museum is open Tuesday through Sunday from 8 A.M. to noon and 1 P.M. to 4 P.M. There is a 1,000d entrance charge.

The Fine Arts Museum is close to the back wall of the **Temple of Literature National Institute** (Van Mieu). This is the most important historic site in Hanoi and certainly one of the most interesting. The temple was founded in 1070 and was dedicated to teaching the proper Confucian way of thinking and behaving. Vietnam's first university (Quoc Tu Giam) was established here in 1076 to educate the sons of the emperor and some high-ranking officials. In the thirteenth century, the school was enlarged and renamed Quoc Hoc Vien, or National Institute. The National University was transferred to Hue in 1802 by Gia Long.

A visit to the Temple of Literature today is a relaxed and restful experience. There are rarely crowds inside the complex and it is easy to find a corner where you can sit and appreciate the atmosphere. The two-story entrance gate is near Quoc Tu Giam Street. Note the stone dragons as you enter. The Temple consists of four courtyards divided by brick walls. The first two areas are now mostly devoid of buildings, but there are some lovely old trees, tiled walkways, and the Khue Van Pavilion is the second area. This building is only a few hundred years old, but it is considered to be a fine example of traditional architecture.

The third area contains the most precious items in the temple. From 1442 until 1779, it was the practice to engrave on stone slabs called stelac the names, places of birth, and achievements of those scholars who succeeded in obtaining the Doctor of Literature degree. The eighty-two stelac that remain today can be seen sitting on stone tortoises.

The fourth area consists of a large yard and several halls and other buildings. The highlight here is the temple dedicated to the memory of Confucius and his disciples. It is well worth seeing. The Temple is open every day except Monday. There is a 2,000d entrance charge.

It is about a kilometer from here to the **Ho Chi Minh Museum.** This is the newest major attraction in Hanoi and it must be on everyone's sightseeing list. The museum traces the life of Ho Chi Minh and the establishment of communism in Vietnam. There is a huge amount of symbolism and a surprisingly hard-line approach to capitalism, the West, and all things that don't fit into "glorious socialism." It must even be strange to faithful Vietnamese that Coca-Cola is highlighted inside the museum as one of the evils of "decadent capitalism" but is being offered for sale at a drink stand on the forecourt. The guide who took me around had no problem with the standard commentary on the "imperialist Americans" and how they "raped and killed the poor Vietnamese people." It was even more strange for me because I had just come from a meeting with officials who told me that it was important for Vietnam to establish a close relationship with the United States in order to learn and obtain the many benefits of a market economy. The museum is closed Mondays and Fridays.

Close by is one of the most famous Hanoi landmarks. The **One Pillar Pagoda** (Chua Mot Cot) was built by Emperor Ly when he founded his city at this location in the eleventh century. The wooden pagoda that is built on a single stone pillar resembles a lotus blossom rising from a pond. Over the centuries, the structure was repaired several times until the French deliberately destroyed it as they were leaving Hanoi in 1954. The structure you see today has been rebuilt since then. Because of its location, it now tends to be overshadowed by the Ho Chi Minh Museum on one side and the Ho Chi Minh Mausoleum on the other.

Despite a specific request to be cremated, Ho Chi Minh has a glass-enclosed platform within a monumental building as his final resting place. The **Ho Chi Minh Mausoleum** is situated in Ba Dinh Square and it has become a place of pilgrimage for many Vietnamese and visitors. It is not just a simple matter of walking in though. All visitors must register and check any carried items into a reception area near the Ho Chi Minh Museum. A passport can be helpful here. After you have received approval, an armed guard will escort you for the last two hundred meters or so to the entrance of the mausoleum.

You are then turned over to the guards who man the inside of the building. It is all done in an efficient manner, but the air of authority is very heavy over the whole procedure. Within the mausoleum, you must maintain a respectful demeanor at all times. When I tried to stop for a better view, I was immediately moved along even though there was no one else behind me. Please note that visitors wearing shorts, t-shirts, or other casual clothes are not admitted, and you are not permitted to carry anything (including purses or cameras) into the building.

You exit the mausoleum into the park which surrounds the Presidential Palace and Ho Chi Minh's house. The **Presidential Palace** is a beautifully kept French colonial building which was built early this century for the governor-general of Indochina. Vietnam's recent rulers have not lived in this house, but it is used for official receptions and some other functions. **Ho Chi Minh's House** is where the leader lived for several years beginning in about 1958. The house is simple but attractive and it is maintained in excellent condition. A guide will explain various features and customs of Ho Chi Minh's lifestyle, then you can wander down to the fish pond where he kept some carp. The area surrounding here was and is a botanic garden.

Directly north of here is the **West Lake** (Ho Tay) area. West Lake is the largest lake in Hanoi and was once the site of some elaborate houses and pavilions. Adjacent to the southeast corner of the lake is another small lake called **Truc Bach** (White Silk). The first point of interest is **Quan Thanh Temple** on the southwest shore of Truc Bach Lake. This was originally established during the Ly Dynasty (eleventh and twelfth centuries A.D.) and although nothing remains from those days, the temple is well worth visiting. The tree-shaded courtyard is a lovely place to wander through, and the temple, which is dedicated to Saint Tran Vo, has some statues and other items from the seventeenth century. There is no admission charge. Adjacent to the temple is the site of one of the city's old gates.

After exiting the Quan Thanh Temple, you can walk north along Thanh Nien Road on a causeway between the two lakes. About half a kilometer along, you can visit the **Tran Quoc Pagoda** which is built on a small islet that you reach via a small causeway. It is believed that this pagoda was built about 1,400 years ago on the banks of the Red River. When the banks eroded in the seventeenth century, the pagoda was moved to its present site. It was renovated in 1991.

Farther north, there are two floating restaurants, and another kilometer brings you to the Thang Loi Hotel. If you go farther, you can visit the **Tay Ho Pagoda** near the Communist party guest house. The pagoda is in a very rural setting amid duck farms, rice paddies, and orchards. It looks ancient, is a bit run down, and the people at the temple all seem old;, but it is quite attractive and not at all "touristy."

If you continue out this road another ten kilometers or so, you will eventually come to the large two-level **Thang Long Bridge** across the Red River, built with Russian aid funds. The bridge is now linked to Hanoi Airport by a toll road.

Within the city, there are a few other sightseeing attractions. The **Thu Le Zoo** is situated about six kilometers west of the city center. It covers a large area and there is an attractive lake, but the animals are poorly displayed and the species are not extensive. It is a place to wander around if you have an afternoon to kill.

The area south of the city center is of some interest. This area includes the **Kim Lien Bus Depot** from which most long-distance buses depart. Facilities are poor. Close by is **Lenin Park** with its Lake Bay Mau. Walking paths, lawns, and gardens have been established here and the area continues to develop. Within the park is the headquarters of the **Vietnam Circus,** and performances can be seen at certain times of the year. The circus closely follows the pattern of those in East Europe with jugglers, trained animals, and gymnasts. A kilometer east of the park is the **Hai Ba Trung Pagoda** (Trung sisters), which was founded in 1142 to honor two sisters who led an unsuccessful uprising against the Chinese in the first century.

The so-called Liberation Highway leads south from Lenin Park. On the left is the campus of the **Hanoi Polytechnic**—one of the top technical institutes in the country. Also along here are two of Hanoi's better hospitals—**Quoc Te Hospital**, and **Bach Mai Hospital.**

AROUND HANOI

Extensive touring around northern Vietnam is still difficult, but there are a number of worthwhile places that can be visited on day trips from Hanoi. Few organized tours exist, so in many instances the only way to reach these places is to rent a car and driver. A good first trip is to head north across the Chuong Duong bridge (you have to pay a toll) following Route 2 toward the airport.

Co Loa Citadel is the remnants of a once glorious capital city which was founded in 200 B.C. Only a small part of the ancient earthen fortifications still exist, but there is enough to indicate the strength of the moats and ramparts that once protected the city. You enter the area through a gate which has statues of a king and his daughter. You can then visit the communal house and a small pagoda, and farther on there is the upper temple which is believed to have been built on the grounds of an ancient palace. The citadel is about fifteen kilometers north of Hanoi, close to the road to the airport.

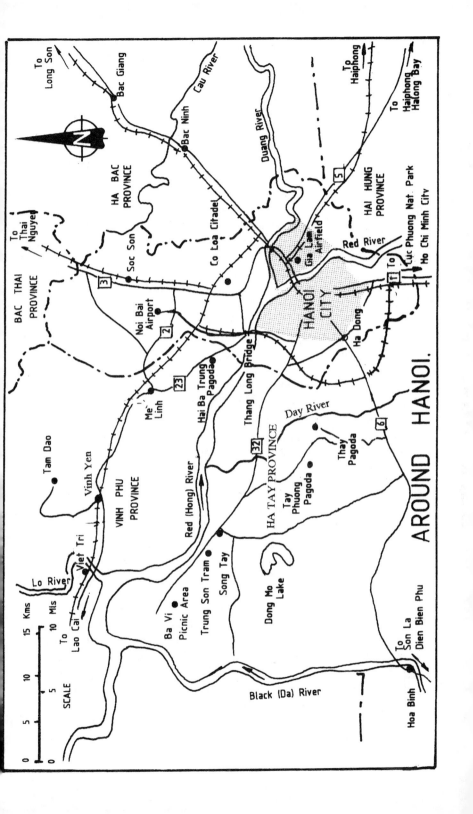

AROUND HANOI.

Hai Ba Trung Pagoda and **Me Linh** are two reminders of the Trung sisters who lead an uprising against the Chinese in 40 A.D. The sisters lived in Me Linh (about forty kilometers northwest of Hanoi) and remains of citadels that they constructed are still standing in this area. The best example is probably the Den Citadel built on a hill near the Nguyet Due River. The remnants of the walls are ten meters thick. The pagoda, about twelve kilometers to the south on Route 23, honors the sisters.

Tam Dao is a small settlement at an elevation of 930 meters about eighty-five kilometers northwest of Hanoi. The area was established by the French early this century as a place to escape from the heat and humidity of the river plain. Most of the old colonial buildings are now in a state of disrepair, but there are some more modern structures which have been built by the government and are used as guest houses by various ministries.

There is also a hotel which is open to the public. The Tam Dao Hotel was built in 1968 and renovated in 1990. The thirty-eight rooms are classified into A (2 rooms), B (29 rooms), and C (7 rooms). "A" rooms are suites with bedroom, sitting room, and bathroom. They have no airconditioning nor fans, but they have mosquito nets and a balcony. The bathrooms are adequate and reasonably clean. "B" rooms are the same as the suites without the sitting room. "C" rooms are similar, but they have no hot water. Room rates are US$25/20/18. There is a restaurant and a bar. When I visited, the hotel had no guests. Reception is not in the main building but in a little hut across the road.

All visitors pay an entrance fee to Tam Dao. For a car and four people, it was 11,000d. Once you enter the area, you notice the cooler weather, the good views, the temperate plants, and the birds and butterflies. The area is good for walking, there is an attractive waterfall and a small temple which is reached by a steep climb into the forest. You often see hill-tribe people in the area, but unfortunately many of these people appear to be damaging the native and planted forest in their quest for income selling timber.

Tam Dao, Hai Ba Trung, and Co Loa can all be combined in a long day trip into the heart of the Red River Delta that will give you many glimpses of Vietnamese rural life. It may also be possible to visit **Thai Nguyen** (80 kilometers north of Hanoi). The attraction here is the Museum of Vietnamese Ethnic Minority Culture where there are displays of the relics and lifestyles of the 54 ethnic groups living in Vietnam. Another interesting day trip takes you west of Hanoi to waterfalls, a lake, and several pagodas.

Ba Vi is both a mountain and a popular day trip, swimming, and picnic location. Some confusion exists because these two locations are not identical. For visitors the swimming-picnic location probably has more appeal. It is about eighty kilometers west of Hanoi along Route 32. You pay an entrance fee to the area (currently 8,000d for foreigners), and find that there is a small restaurant, a nice pool at the base of the lowest waterfall, walking trails, a number of little "day huts" for rent, and a still-to-be-completed hotel. The Ao Vua Hotel has very basic bare rooms, with a bed and a standing fan as the only furniture. Most rooms have a balcony, but there is not even a sink. The communal bathroom was locked and the downstairs toilet was dirty and smelly. Rooms rent for 35,000d (for one or two people). The hotel has a small restaurant.

A few hours at Ba Vi is enough for most visitors, so you may decide to head to Dong Mo Lake for lunch. On the way, you pass several villages with old Christian churches—it is not too difficult to imagine that you are in rural France or Germany. One such church worth visiting is in the village of **Trung Son Tram**. Leave the car on the main road and walk through the village to the church. You will be joined quickly by some village children, and while you walk you get a good insight into the standard of houses and facilities in a typical village. The church itself is large, well maintained, and holds a mass every Sunday. It is a very unexpected side of Vietnamese life.

Dong Mo Lake is used primarily for irrigation purposes, but there is one area which has been set aside for tourism. You pay an entry fee into this area, then find a restaurant, picnic tables, a small boat to rent, and a seven-room hotel. The food at the restaurant is quite good, and the rooms at the hotel are quite reasonable. For 40,000d you get an airconditioned room with attached bathroom. The furniture is adequate, but you will share the bathroom with thousands of mosquitos. Fortunately the beds have nets. This is a far better value than the hotel at Ba Vi.

Tay Phuong Pagoda is about ten kilometers closer to Hanoi near the village of Thach That. This hilltop pagoda which you reach by 240 steps, is considered to be one of the most significant in the Hanoi region. It is believed to have been founded in the fourth century A.D., but has been rebuilt and enlarged several times. Some substantial restoration was carried out in 1991. Apart from its attractive location, the pagoda is famous for its striking curved roofs that are covered with tiles and ceramic animals, and its outstanding works of traditional Vietnamese wood sculpture. This is a place in which most people will find something of interest.

You need to travel about six kilometers east to reach **Thay Pagoda**. This is a personal favorite of mine, partly because of the unusual and attractive setting of the village near the pagoda. The pagoda was established in the eleventh century. Little exists from that time, but the present buildings are quite old and there is statuary dating several centuries. There is a very friendly guide who speaks good English. I have the feeling that this place receives relatively few visitors outside festival time, which is usually in March. The small village spreads out from the pagoda around a delightful small lake cradled by hills. In the lake, there is a stage on stilts where water puppet shows are staged during festivals. To the right is a steep path to a hill-side viewing point from which there is a lovely view over the lake, the village, and the surrounding countryside. It is now about forty kilometers back to Hanoi.

If you still have some time, a visit to **Huong Pagoda** (Perfume Pagoda) should be considered. For various reasons, I have never quite made it there, but friends tell me that it is in a lovely area with much to do and see. I am told there is a series of pagodas and Buddhist shrines built into the cliffs of a mountain close to the Yen River. The river once provided the only access, but I believe road access is now possible to part of the area. The pagoda has a month-long festival (usually March) during which it receives many pilgrims and other visitors. Huong Pagoda is about sixty kilometers southwest from Hanoi.

EAST FROM HANOI

One of the almost mandatory trips from Hanoi is to the port city of **Haiphong** and nearby regions. You leave Hanoi via Chuong Duong bridge, then turn right onto Route 5 which passes Gia Lam airfield. The road is divided, barren, and treeless for several kilometers while you pass through the outer urban confusion, then the countryside quickly reverts to the rich riceland of the delta. Midway between Hanoi and Haiphong, you pass though Hai Duong, a vaguely attractive town with little of interest to visitors.

The busy road negotiates two long one-way bridges which can cause considerable delays, so the hundred-kilometer trip often takes three or four hours. Haiphong is Vietnam's third largest city and the most important seaport in the north of the country. The Haiphong urban area has around 500,000 inhabitants, and the greater Haiphong area has a population of about 1.5 million. The port and most of the industries were established by the French early in this century. The city was bombed by the French in 1946, and was attacked by American air and naval forces in the late 1960s and early 1970s.

Most of today's city is generally unattractive, hot, dusty, and barren. Like many industrial port cities, parts of it are an ecological disaster. You see this as you approach Haiphong from Hanoi. In fact, this is probably the worst side of the city. The older central area has much more appeal. Tourists are unlikely to spend more than one night in Haiphong, but business people may have longer needs. The best hotel in town is the **Hang Hai Hotel** (Tel: 48576) at 282 Da Nang Street. The thirty-eight rooms are quite nice with airconditioning, refrigerator, telephone, and clean attached bathrooms. There are two restaurants and a top-floor disco that operates on Tuesday and Saturday nights (5,000d entry). Room rates are US$30/27/25 for different classes of room. The only problem with the hotel is its location in a depressed area about three kilometers from the city center.

If a central position is important, there are two reasonable options. The **Hotel of Commerce** (Tel: 47206) at 62 Dien Bien Street has forty airconditioned rooms with attached bathrooms. This French-era hotel has been renovated and improved, but it retains its nice feel. Rooms are from US$25. There is an attractive restaurant on the ground floor. The alternative is the **Duyen Hai Hotel** (Tel: 42134) at 5 Nguyen Tri Phuong. This is another French-era hotel that has renovated most of its rooms. Standards and prices are similar to the Hotel of Commerce. Cheaper alternatives are the **Bach Dang Hotel** (Tel: 47244) at 42 Dien Bien Street or the **Ben Binh Guest House** across the road on the corner of Ben Binh Street.

I don't think that I am being unfair in saying that Haiphong has few sights of interest to visitors. An exception perhaps is the three-hundred-year-old **Du Hang Pagoda** which is a good example of traditional Vietnamese architecture. The **Hang Kenh Communal House** is known for its wood carvings. Nearby is a factory that produces tapestries for export.

Outside the city, there are three major points of interest. **Do Son Beach** is about twenty kilometers south of the city and is the most popular seaside resort in the north. The road from Haiphong passes through barren, dreary country, but as you approach Do Son, the atmosphere improves. You pay an entry fee to the Do Son area (4,000d for four people and a vehicle) and you can then drive for about four kilometers along a hilly promontory. There are palm trees, tables for picnics under the trees, many open-air restaurants, numerous hotels, a sparkling new casino, very little sand, and very dirty water.

The casino is operated by Macau's Mr. Stanley Ho, and it is situated in what was once the rather run-down Van Hoa Hotel. At present it is the only casino in the country.

There are many hotels for visitors at Do Son, and it is difficult to select the best. I thought the **Hai Au Hotel**, 45 rooms, which is run by Haiphong Tourism, was quite good. The rooms are airconditioned and have attached bathrooms. Most have balconies, mosquito nets, portable fans, hot and cold water, and reasonable furniture. The hotel has a shop, a large restaurant, and dancing on Friday, Saturday, and Sunday evenings. Room prices are US$30/25 for rooms with airconditioning, or US$20 without. Another hotel also operated by Haiphong Tourism is the **Hoa Phuong**. This is also reasonable. In this same area, you can stay at villas which were once used by the politburo. The newest accommodations are at the **Ministry of Energy Guest House**, 98 rooms. The better rooms have a balcony, airconditioning, tele-

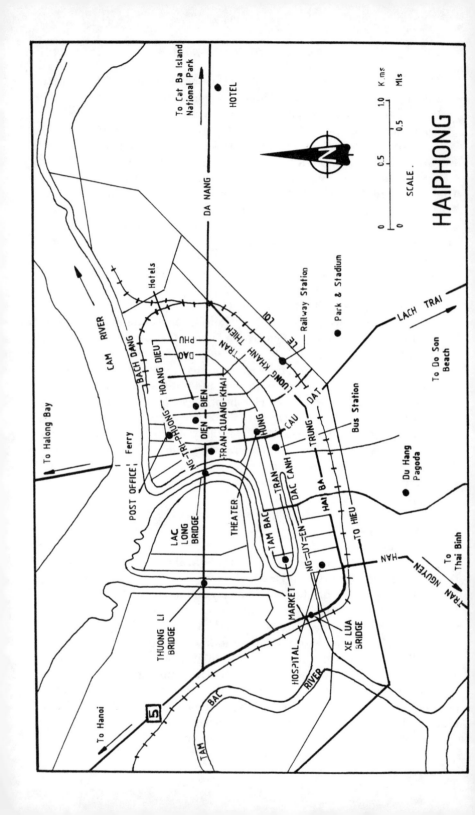

phone, above average furnishings, and nice clean bathrooms. Unfortunately it is not fronting or overlooking the beach. Prices are US$35/30/20 for foreign visitors.

The second place of interest is **Cat Ba Island**. This is the largest island in the Halong Bay area, and much of it has been declared a protected region. The island has a permanent population of around 12,000 who are engaged in fishing, forestry, and agriculture. The appeal to visitors is the diverse topography, flora, and fauna. There are spectacular limestone and dolomite hills rising to over three hundred meters (1,000 feet), tropical evergreen forests, freshwater swamp forests, mangrove forests, numerous lakes, waterfalls, caves, and sandy beaches. Offshore, there are some coral reefs.

The island has been inhabited for a long time. Stone tools and bones left by humans who lived here seven thousand years ago have been found at many sites. The island is also home to a range of mammals (including the Francois monkey) and many birds. At certain times of the year, you will see tens of thousands of waterfowl using the island as a resting place on their migratory trek. You reach Cat Ba Island from Haiphong by taking Da Nang Street to the boat terminal, then riding the ferry the twenty-five kilometers to the island. This trip takes around three hours.

While Cat Ba Island has appeal, for many people it is **Halong Bay** that is the big draw. Some Vietnamese see this as the site for major tourism development, and they talk about it as a potentially world-renowned destination such as the French Riviera. It is light years away from that at the moment, but certainly there is much natural beauty in the three thousand or so islands in this small area of the Gulf of Tonkin.

The center of Halong Bay tourism is the small beach resort of **Bai Chay**. The road from Haiphong reaches here after two ferry crossings and many twists and turns. While it is only about sixty kilometers from Haiphong, the trip will take about 2½ hours by car and four hours by bus. There are three sections of town: the commercial center, the major accommodation center by the beach, and the area near the jetty. Most visitors, both foreign and local, stay in one of the hotels or guest houses near the beach. By some standards the beach is poor, but there is some sand, people do actually go swimming, it is nice to stroll along under the trees, and there is always something to see. This is also the area where you find the most restaurants.

I stayed at the **Trade Union Guest House**, probably the largest building in town. It is in a good position overlooking the beach. While it is intended mainly for Vietnamese having a vacation by the sea, it encourages foreigners if there is room as part of the government push for tourism. The building is relatively new, but it appears that little maintenance is carried out, so many facilities in my room such as the airconditioner, the bathroom window, and the radio did not operate. Because of this, the US$20 charge was only a fair value. The guest house restaurant had poor food and service. In contrast, I thought the **Bach Long Hotel**, 40 rooms, which is right next door, was good value. Bright clean rooms with airconditioner, mosquito nets, and hot and cold water in a clean bathroom were provided for US$25 double and US$22 single. The staff here were very friendly and were able to provide information on this and some other areas of Vietnam. In my experience, that was very rare. The hotel has a nice dining room which can provide drinks and a meal for two people for around 25,000d. The **Manh Cuong Hotel** (Tel: 46342) has rooms with private facilities from 70,000d. There are also several mini-hotels with good rooms at around US$20.

At this point, it is worth commenting on the **Thuan Loi Restaurant** which is in this same general area. This was the only restaurant in the north of Vietnam that blatantly cheated me, and you should avoid this place. The **Hong Minh Restaurant** next door may be better, but ask the price before you order.

Boat tours of Halong Bay leave from a jetty about a kilometer from here. There are organized tours, but their frequency is doubtful. None operated while I was at Bai Chay. It is possible to rent a motorized launch to tour the bay and visit some of the islands, beaches, and caves. The going rate seems to be about US$20 an hour, but I am sure this changes depending on demand. I was able to join a party of locals from the guest house who were taking a three-hour cruise on the guest house launch. This ended up costing me about US$1.50. For those on a tight budget, you should consider staying at the **Van Hai Hotel** which overlooks the jetty. Room prices are US$8/6/5 depending on room size and location. The best rooms are those in the front which look out through shuttered windows on the bay and islands. There is a central male and female bathroom, with separate shower and toilet stalls. It's not great, but it is reasonably clean. On the ground floor, there is a busy restaurant and bar.

Better accommodation is available at the **Suoi Mo Hotel** (Tel: 46381; Fax: 8433-46284), 45 rooms, and another **Van Hai Hotel** (Tel: 46403; Fax 8433-46287), 76 rooms, both on Bai Chay Road, Hongai. Prices at both are around US$30 a room.

SOUTH FROM HANOI

The main highway and the main railway linking the central and southern provinces to Hanoi head due south from the central city. These are the main land communication routes, but you would hardly know it when you travel about twenty kilometers out from the city. The railway is single track on a fair alignment, but train speeds are low. It takes between forty-two and sixty hours to travel the 1,700 kilometers to Ho Chi Minh City (Saigon). Much of the highway is narrow; it accommodates heavy trucks, army vehicles, oxen-drawn carts, bicycles, and motorcycles; and it acts as a rice-drying pavement twice a year.

There are, however, several noteworthy points of interest south of Hanoi. Most are accessible via the highway. It is worthwhile to travel via **Ha Dong**, which is on Route 6 at the edge of the Hanoi urban area. The city is famous for its silks and brocades, but the area also produces rattan, bamboo, and wooden articles which are available in roadside stalls or at small manufacturing plants adjacent to the road. There is a connecting road from here to Highway 1 for those going farther out.

Nam Dinh City is the first major center south of Hanoi. It is linked to Hanoi and Haiphong, so it has developed as a significant transport and industrial center. There is very little visitor interest in the city, but around this area there are several places to visit. The excavation site at **Phu Luong** has produced many valuable items from a Bronze Age civilization called Van Lang. You can see some of these items in the Museum of History in Hanoi. Some thirty kilometers northeast of Nam Dinh, you can visit **Keo Pagoda** which was founded in the twelfth century. The timber bell tower is regarded as a masterpiece.

Hoa Lu is south of the city near the village of Truong Yen. This was the capital of Vietnam for a period in the tenth century after Co Loa was abandoned. The ancient city was surrounded by several massive ramparts, but little remains today. There are two pagodas that can be visited. Both have been extensively rebuilt over the years, but each contains stone and bronze work from the early days. One of the temples has some ancient drums and gongs. The area around here is very attractive with sharply rising limestone hills somewhat reminiscent of Halong Bay without the water. From the highway, you see some lovely village churches in this region.

Cuc Phuong National Park is the first such park to be established in Vietnam. Much of the park is tropical forest and it is home to a vast variety of wildlife. Several species of plants and animals have first been discovered here. Wild animals still found in large numbers include boas, bears, leopards, antelopes, and monkeys. Don't expect to see them as you drive or walk the areas which are readily accessible. What you will see is a good variety of birds—parrots, pheasants, grouse, orioles—and if you visit in April or May you will be thrilled by millions of butterflies.

The park covers 22,200 hectares in three provinces. The area is hilly and the limestone country has many caves, pot holes, and strange rock formations. Vestiges of human life from twelve thousand years ago have been found in Con Moong cave. You can visit here by walking through the jungle and climbing the stairs that have been built against the rocky hills. The highest peak in the park is 650 meters above sea level.

Foreign visitors are expected to pay US$3 for entry into the park, and there is an extra US$1 charge if you have a camera. There is a small restaurant at park headquarters and you can sometimes get a guide from here to accompany you as you travel around the park. There are various options if you wish to stay in the park. At the top of the list are several bamboo houses which have airconditioning and attached bathroom and toilet. These rent for US$35 a night. Close by is the Foreign Guest House which has nine rooms at US$15 a night, or you can stay in the Vietnamese Guest House for US$10 a night. Meals are available at the two guest houses. In this same area, there is a botanic garden with concrete foot paths that allow you to see many of the plant species that grow in the area.

Getting to Cuc Phuong without a car is not easy. You can get to within about ten kilometers of the park entrance by public bus (there are three changes of bus between Hanoi and the park exit) but you will have to walk from where the bus leaves you. This bus trip will take at least five hours. Even by car, the 150-kilometer trip takes about three hours and some of the road is in very poor condition. If you have no interest in nature, don't go.

Back on Highway 1, **Ninh Binh** is a typical regional town. A town like this is well worth a look, particularly if you have previously spent time only in Hanoi. Life in the Ninh Binh's of Vietnam is quite different in many ways from life in the major cities. The **Ninh Binh Hotel** provides reasonable accommodations, but you may be better off traveling the forty kilometers south to Thanh Hoa City or going an extra sixteen kilometers to the beach at Sam Son.

It may also be worthwhile to leave the highway at Ninh Binh and travel about twenty-five kilometers southeast to the market town of **Phat Diem**. The market here is one of the most interesting in this region, and foreign visitors are well received. The town is also outstanding because of its huge cathedral which was once an important center for the Catholic church in Vietnam. Go inside to see the wood and stone sculptures and the huge soaring columns. There is also an unusual hundred-year-old covered bridge in the town.

Thanh Hoa City also has a large attractive church, ancient Ly Cung Palace, a frequently bombed road and railway bridge, and several hotels and restaurants along Highway 1. The city is a convenient stopping point between Hanoi, 155 kilometers to the north, and Vinh, 140 kilometers to the south (see Hue and North-central Vietnam). Thanh Hoa province was where Vietnamese hero Le Loi launched a successful uprising against the Chinese in the fifteenth century which lead to the re-establishment of an independent Vietnam. Ruins of Le Loi's capital city at Lam Kinh still remain. Elsewhere in the province, there are archeological sites of the Bronze Age Dong Son culture, and modern day Muong and other hill-tribe villages in the west.

Sixteen kilometers southeast of Thanh Hoa City, the **Sam Son Beaches** are some of the best in northern Vietnam. As with Do Son and Halong Bay farther north, there are government guest houses, hotels, and more basic cabin accommodations. At most times, you can drive along the beach road and take your pick of which accommodations appeal to you.

FURTHER AFIELD

The far northern and northwestern provinces of Vietnam are seldom visited by international travelers. The reasons are many: Vietnam doesn't encourage visitors to the Chinese border region, air services are poor, roads deteriorate rapidly as you travel north and west of Hanoi, and there have been few recognized visitor attractions or facilities in these areas.

But now intrepid travelers are venturing into these areas by train and by jeep, and air services have commenced to Dien Bien Phu. You will have no problem visiting **Hoa Binh City**. Route 6 passes through Ha Dong, then through typical agricultural land until you reach Hoa Binh beside the Black (Da) River. On the way, you will pass by the area where the ancient Hoa Binh society developed thousands of years ago. This civilization produced some beautifully decorated bronze articles which still survive today. An excellent example is a huge drum which is now in Hanoi's Museum of History. As you pass through this area today, you will notice many hill-tribe people. It is possible to visit some of these villages and see how life has changed little for hundreds of years. You can reach this area in a day trip from Hanoi.

West of here the area changes. There are fewer people and less traffic, and the inhabitants are more likely to be hill-tribe people than ethnic Vietnamese. You will see tea plantations and orchards as well as rice fields. It is a long, hard three-hundred-kilometer drive to **Son La**, the capital of a province with the same name. There are some fairly basic accommodations in town, and a choice of fair restaurants. The next 120 kilometers to **Dien Bien Phu** takes almost all day. In parts, the road winds through attractive mountains and high plains. The area is largely populated by hill-tribe people, and facilities for visitors, including accommodation and food, are poor. So too are the roads. This region was the site of the major battle between the French and Viet Minh forces which resulted in the French abandoning their attempts to keep control of Indochina. The French forces in the Dien Bien Phu garrison were eventually captured after a two-month siege. In the process, twenty-five thousand Viet Minh were killed or injured and three thousand French troops lost their lives. There is a small museum and some old French tanks and guns on the site. The Laos border is a short distance from here.

There is a road north from Dien Bien Phu which eventually leads to **Lao Cai**. This passes through the most remote region of Vietnam and is not recommended to any but the pioneer-type. The last half of the journey is through the Hoang Lien Mountains which include Vietnam's highest peaks. You can see Phan Si Pan Mountain (3,140 meters), the highest peak, but there is no road there. You can visit the old hill resort of **Sa Pa** (1,400 meters) which was developed by the French. This is a beautiful area noted for its temperate gardens and orchards. There are some waterfalls and dramatic scenery. Some Hanoi tour operators are promoting visits to the area, but appreciate that it is frontier country, high in interest but still difficult to reach. Once there, accommodation in one of the refurbished villas can be reasonably comfortable. Lao Cai is the major town in this region, but because it is very close to the Chinese border, access is often restricted and its commercial activities have shrunk. If relations with China improve, Lao Cai will assume its previous importance as a railway town and border crossing. At present, passenger trains from Hanoi only travel as far as **Pho Lu**, which is about fifty kilometers from Lao Cai. There is a road back to Hanoi via **Yen Bai** and **Vinh Yen** which can be negotiated in about twelve hours.

I have never had the time or the patience to attempt to see the far northern regions of Vietnam. Most of this area has been closed to individual travelers, but now it is opening up. It's even possible for foreigners to exit Vietnam into China at a border crossing at Huu Nghi Quan. The main centers are **Cao Bang** (270 kilometers north of Hanoi) and **Lang Son** (155 kilometers north). Cao Bang is connected to Hanoi by road, while Lang Son can be reached by road or rail (in six hours). Both towns are on traditional trade routes with China, and, despite some problems, trade is booming. The populations of these regions is made up largely of ethnic minorities. Part of Lang Son, and the frontier village of Dong Dang (fifteen kilometers north) were destroyed by invading Chinese forces in 1979. This whole northern region has mountains, caves, waterfalls, and lakes. The most well-known area is **Ba Be Lakes** which is 240 kilometers north of Hanoi and ninety kilometers southwest of Cao Bang.

7. Guided Tours

Vietnam Tourism or **Vinatour** (Tel: 252-986) is the organization most active in promoting guided tours. It has a number of standard tours that cover the whole country, or you can choose to do just one or two regions. They are well run, but are not necessarily what a tourist wants and they are expensive. There is no day tour industry as we know it in the West. No tour buses show up outside the hotels in the morning hoping for passengers. Tours need to be organized well in advance. Vietnam Tourism likes to deal with groups and to arrange special itineraries for them. I get the impression that individual tours are too difficult. The best they can offer here is a rental car and driver. That is not a bad idea, but you need to have some input into where you go and what you see. A car for the day around the city will cost around US$35. It goes up when you go further afield.

Many small "travel agents" can book hotels, tickets, cars, bicycles, etc.

8. Culture

It is immediately apparent to visitors that Hanoi is an excellent place to see much of what is best in Vietnamese culture. The cultural experience can include visits to major buildings such as the National Library and the Workers Cultural Palace, as well as activities staged in theaters, schools, and other locations and festivals such as Tet, National Day, and more local festive days. There are also several folk traditions that either originated in the north or are unique to the north.

Water puppetry is probably the most interesting cultural form in this region. The art probably originated in the Red River Delta about a thousand years ago. It is designed to depict scenes from rural life or history and has been embraced by both village people and the aristocracy. The puppetry is performed in a lake with the audience sitting on the lake's edge and the puppeteers controlling the wooden puppets with rods and wires that are concealed under the water. The puppets can appear to be walking on the water, then they can quickly disappear. It is a unique art that will appeal to most visitors. Unfortunately, it is not always easy to see a water puppet display. Performances have been held from time to time in Hanoi at Bay Mau Lake, Hoan Kiem Lake, and less frequently at other locations including the Thay Pagoda. Now a special theater has been built in central Hanoi, and performances are held every evening at 8 P.M. Contact the Kim Dong Theater at 57B Dinh Tien Hoang Street (Tel: 260-553) for details.

The **Quan Ho Ritual** is popular in the north particularly in Ha Bac province. These folk songs are often sung by two competing teams made up of young men and women. One member of one team starts singing, then a member of the opposite sex on the other team responds by making up lyrical verses in reply. The third person continues the theme with the fourth person responding. It is an opportunity for young people from different villages to meet, mix, and eventually marry. The Lim festival, which is held in mid-February, is one of the best-known occasions for this ritual.

Classical theater, known as **Hat Tuong**, is based on Chinese opera. It is very formal, stylized, and loud. To most Westerners, it looks similar to opera seen in Hong Kong, Taiwan, and Singapore, where make-up and dress are extreme to make sure that the audience has no doubt about who is who and whether they are good or evil. You can often see performances of Hat Tuong at the Workers Cultural Palace and elsewhere.

The **Children's Theater** on Ly Thai To Street often has some interesting performances for young people. Language has less importance in some of these shows, so they may be suitable for visitors. The **Hanoi School of Music and Art** also has some performances which can be identified by your hotel receptionist.

The **Hanoi Ballet** was established a long time ago and has traditionally performed classical ballet in the European style. Recently, it has had input from an Australian modern dance company, and this has considerably broadened its repertoire. If you are in Hanoi during a ballet season, it is worth checking out one of the performances. So too with the **Cheo Ensemble**. I am not sure where these performances are held, but your hotel receptionist should be able to help. The **Vietnam National Symphony and Choral Orchestra** has adopted a more professional approach after 35 years of lethargy, and performances are now worth seeing.

The **Youth Theater** (Tuoi Tre) on Ngo Thi Nham Street near Le Van Huu is an attempt to combat the influence of foreign videos and pop music which are hugely popular in Vietnam. The theater has performances every evening and they vary from modern Vietnamese music or singers and dancers aping the latest Western hit song to fashion parades, modern dance, and so forth. The audience is by no means only young, but in general the performers are. It is bright, loud, and somewhat amateurish; but it is received well by an enthusiastic audience. While all the dialogue is in Vietnamese, it is not difficult for English-speaking visitors to follow what is happening. This is an unusual insight into another aspect of Vietnamese life.

Tet, the Vietnamese lunar New Year festival, which falls in either late January or early February, is the most important festival of the year. In Hanoi, many entertainments take place during the period of Tet. Most notable are the Flower Market held along Hang Luoe Street (near Dong Xuan Market) during the seven days before new year, the Spring Flower Competition held in Lenin Park for the first two weeks of the new year, and the Dong Ky Firecracker Festival in which huge, beautifully decorated firecrackers are lit in a noisy contest on the fourth of the month.

The **Dong Da Festival** is based around the Dong Da Mound (five kilometers from central Hanoi) where Emperor Quang Trung led a peasant uprising in 1788 which defeated 200,000 troops that a Chinese leader had sent to occupy Hanoi. The festival, which takes place on the fifteenth of the first lunar month, includes well-attended wrestling bouts. The activities at the **Huong Pagoda Festival** (Perfume Pagoda) are quite different. This is held from the middle of the second lunar month to the end of the third month. Thousands of people make a pilgrimage to this lovely area for religious purposes and for boating, mountaineering, and sightseeing.

The **Thay Pagoda Festival** starts on the fifth day of the third month and lasts for three days. As well as visiting the pagoda, pilgrims enjoy mountaineering, exploring the caves, and watching water puppet shows. It is a long time until the **Mid-Autumn Festival**, which is held on the fifteenth day of the eighth lunar month. In Hanoi, people pour into Hang Ma Street to buy toys and lanterns for children. There are lion dances, processions, and much drum beating.

Vietnam's **National Day** is September 2. This celebrates September 2, 1945, when President Ho Chi Minh read the Declaration of Independence, founding the Democratic Republic of Vietnam. During National Day, a rally is held at Ba Dinh Square (in front of Ho Chi Minh's Mausoleum), boat races are held on Hoan Kiem Lake, and there is a fireworks display at night.

Painting enthusiasts may wish to visit the exhibition held at the **Hanoi Charity Fine Art School** on Phan Chu Trinh Street. This is some of the best modern Vietnamese art you will see anywhere in the country.

9. Sports

The opportunity to participate in sporting activities is small. There are no golf courses, few tennis courts, and most hotels do not have swimming pools. There is no hotel with a sports club. Some hotels have table tennis and billiards facilities. Public tennis courts are available in front of the Thang Loi Hotel. Rackets and balls can be rented. There are swimming pools at the Thang Loi Hotel, Tay Ho Hotel, and Hotel Sofitel; and public pools are located on Tang Bat Ho Street and Le Hong Phong Street. You will see public billiards tables in many places around the city; and table tennis and badminton are also popular. Soccer games are held on a regular basis. The Kings Island Golf Resort and Country Club, 45 kilometers north of Hanoi, has opened its 18-hole lakeside course and expects its mountain view course to open in late 1995. Tennis facilities are also available. There is a golf driving range in Hanoi near West Lake. Fishing platforms are available on Hoan Kiem Lake and on Giang Vo Lake. Foreigners pay around US$2 per hour.

10. Shopping

Hanoi is not a great shopping center, but there are opportunities to buy some reminders of your visit. The best buys are probably handmade handicrafts, paintings, and antiques.

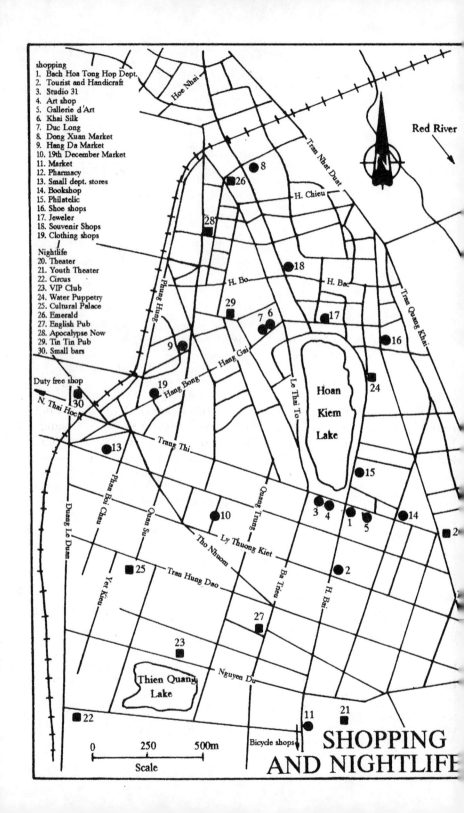

shopping
1. Bach Hoa Tong Hop Dept.
2. Tourist and Handicraft
3. Studio 31
4. Art shop
5. Gallerie d'Art
6. Khai Silk
7. Duc Long
8. Dong Xuan Market
9. Hang Da Market
10. 19th December Market
11. Market
12. Pharmacy
13. Small dept. stores
14. Bookshop
15. Philatelic
16. Shoe shops
17. Jeweler
18. Souvenir Shops
19. Clothing shops

Nightlife
20. Theater
21. Youth Theater
22. Circus
23. VIP Club
24. Water Puppetry
25. Cultural Palace
26. Emerald
27. English Pub
28. Apocalypse Now
29. Tin Tin Pub
30. Small bars

Red River

Hoc Nhai

Tran Nhat Duat

H. Chieu

H. Bo

H. Bac

Phung Hung

Hang Gai

Le Thai To

Tran Quang Khai

Hoan Kiem Lake

Duty free shop

N. Thai Hoc

Hang Bong

Trang Thi

Quang Le Duan

Phan Boi Chau

Quan Su

Yet Kieu

Tho Nhuom

Ly Thuong Kiet

Quang Trung

Ba Trieu

H. Bai

Tran Hung Dao

Nguyen Du

Thien Quang Lake

Bicycle shops

0   250   500m

Scale

SHOPPING
AND NIGHTLIFE

Your shopping choices include a few department stores, state-run tourist stores, markets, privately owned souvenir and antique stores, and street markets.

The largest store in Hanoi is the **Bach Hoa Tong Hop** department store on Hang Bai Street just south of Hoan Kiem Lake. The ambience is from the 1940s, and much of the stock looks as if it has been there almost as long; but it is interesting to walk through and see what is for sale. If you have a need for cheap household goods, this is a good place to look. They also have a large range of bicycles at around 250,000d.

Souvenir shops are appearing all over Hanoi. Most hotel lobby shops now have a selection of items, but these tend to be overpriced. The best place that I found was the **Tourist and Handicraft Shop** (Tel: 255-516) run by Hanoi Tourism on the corner of Ly Thuong Kiet Street and Hang Bai Street. On first appearance it could be considered a tourist trap, but items are priced in both U.S. dollars and dong. Pay the dong price and you will get reasonable value. There are ceramics, lacquerware, paintings, wood carvings, jewelry, and various other objects.

Similar goods are available at a number of small stores in the vicinity of Hoan Kiem Lake. This is also the best area to buy antiques and art objects. There are many stores along Le Thai To Street, Hang Khay Street, and Trang Tien Street. Some of the better ones in my experience are **Studio 31** at 31 Hang Khay Street, where well-known artist Pham Dinh Khanh can be found among his best paintings and drawings; the **Art Shop** at 25 Hang Khay Street, where there is a good selection of art works; and the **Souvenir Shop** at 17 Hang Khay Street, where there is a range of cheaper items as well as art objects. The **Gallerie d'Art** at 61 Trang Tien Street is more up-market with a good selection of watercolors, oil paintings, and carvings. Most of these shops close for an hour or more at lunch time. Art prices are spiraling as foreign tourists and business people swoop down on the works of local artists now free of government shackles and censorship. The government no longer requires artists to provide paintings of workers, peasants, and soldiers, so standards have improved dramatically.

At the northern end of Hoan Kiem Lake, you will find the **Intimex Shop** (Tel: 256-148) on Le Thai To Street; while just around the corner on Hang Gai Street, there are several antique shops and a number of places that have embroidered work and silk. Two of the better-known silk shops are **Khai Silk** (Tel: 254-237) at 96 Hang Gai Street, and **Duc Long** (Tel: 269-151) at Number 100. Farther along this street, when it changes to Hang Bong Street, there are several small tailors and material shops. I don't recommend trying to get the latest Western fashions made for you, but casual clothes and hand-sewn or embroidered articles are reasonably priced and quite serviceable. You can get some good quality T-shirts from several shops along here.

Going north from Hoan Kiem Lake, your best shopping opportunities are along the street which is first named Hang Dao, then Hang Ngang, then Hang Duong before it reaches Dong Xuan Market. This is considered to be the main shopping and commercial area by many Hanoi residents, and it is always bustling with activity. In this area, it is worth checking out the **Souvenir and Art Shop** (Tel: 252-622) at 48 Hang Ngang and the **Art Souvenir Shop** (Tel: 242-576) at 21 Hang Giay. A bit closer to the lake, **Ngoc Tuyet** (Tel: 259-498) at 6 Cau Go is a good jeweler. Around this area, there are many shoe shops just bursting with stock. Unfortunately, if you have large feet you are out of luck. The **Dong Xuan Market** itself offers numerous shopping opportunities ranging from fresh food, cooked food, and household goods to clothing, cassette tapes of Vietnamese music, books, and greeting cards. A similar range of goods (with less of a selection) is available at the **Hang Da Market** on Ngo Tram Street.

Greeting cards, note paper, and postcards are good purchases. These items are available at many curbside stalls and some shops around Hanoi. My experience is that you don't need to bargain for these items, but you can always try to get the price down a bit. The handpainted cards are quite attractive and quite inexpensive by Western standards. There is a good bookshop on the corner of Trang Tien Street and Ngo Quyen Street where you can buy these items. It also has a small selection of books in English, some posters, and philatelic items. I didn't have the opportunity to check philatelic items elsewhere, but prices here seemed high. A better choice if you wish to buy stamps as souvenirs would be to go to the philatelic counter at the main post office in Dinh Tien Hoang Street. There is a **Foreign Language Bookshop** at 61 Trang Tien Street. This is not to be confused with the **Foreign Languages Publishing House** (and Vietnam-Language Publishing House) at 40 Tran Hung Dao Street.

One of the newer developments in Hanoi is the growth of modern photo stores offering fast printing services. There are several of these on Hang Khay Street, Hang Bai Street, and Ba Trieu Street. There is quite an efficient operation in the **CTST Building** on Hang Khay. The same building has photocopying and international telecommunication facilities.

Ready-made clothes are available at several street markets that operate around town. A good night market appears in the Le Van Huu Street region of Hang Bai Street. Some of the items are locally made, but you can also find Chinese and Thai goods. Similar goods are found in the street market which operates between Hai Ba Trung Street and Ly Thuong Kiet Street near the "Hanoi Hilton" prison. In the area near the railway station, you can browse through items displayed on the sidewalks and there are two small department stores in Trang Thi Street which are of "looking interest" rather than for buying anything special.

For those planning a long stay in Hanoi, the area of Hue Street south of Nguyen Cong Tru Street will be of interest because there is a collection of bicycle and motorcycle shops in this area. Likewise, the length of Cat Linh Street west of the stadium has numerous shops offering timber, plumbing fixtures, and other household goods.

Duty free items are available in the departure terminal of Noi Bai Airport and at a store in Giang Vo Street.

11. Entertainment and Nightlife

Hanoi has a reasonable collection of theaters, some cinemas, a few dancing spots, numerous bars, a growing number of discos, and one or two other interesting entertainment places. Many of the more cultural spots were mentioned previously, but it is worth repeating that visitors should check out the offerings at the **Municipal Theater**(Nha Hat Lon), the **Youth Theater** (Nha Hat Tuoi Tre), and the **Workers Cultural Palace** (Cung van hoa Viet xo). There are performances most evenings at these locations.

The **Hanoi Circus** (Rap Xiec Circus) has its headquarters in Lenin Park. It follows closely the format of Eastern European circuses, and many of the performers were trained in Russia, East Germany, and Poland. There are gymnasts, jugglers, animal acts, and clowns. Although it may not be top world standard, it is entertaining. Tickets are inexpensive.

The **Billabong Club** is one of the most popular meeting places for the English-speaking community in Hanoi. If you can arrange an invitation, you will meet interesting people and gain an insight into aspects of Hanoi life that otherwise may remain unknown. Contrary to some published information, this is a club and entry is restricted to members and invited guests. The club meets every Friday evening at the Australian Embassy on Ly Thuong Kiet Street.

Hanoi seems to lack any intimate nightclubs where there is a show or a pocket-size dance floor in a smokey atmosphere. There are, however, venues for **dancing**—both ballroom and disco—which are generally large, open, and fairly bright. Many hotels, restaurants, and bars have developed Karaoke facilities. The **Sunset Pub** at the Dong Do Hotel is currently popular for live jazz or pop music Thursday and Saturday evenings. If you just want a pub atmosphere, try **The Emerald** at 53 Hang Luoc Street, or the **English Pub** at 66 Ba Trieu Street. Others have recommended the **Pear Tree** at the Eden Hotel, 78 Tho Nhuom Street, and the **Fun Pub** at 168 Quan Thanh Street. This latter place and **Ngoc Hoa** at 236 San Tay Street both have hostesses.

Some hotels have **music** in their lounges. The best is the **Hotel Sofitel Metropole** with live music every evening from 5 P.M. There is a nice atmosphere and the music is appropriate for the time and the setting. The **Tay Ho Hotel** often has a rock group in the lobby who play a mixture of Western "oldies" and Vietnamese tunes.

The **VIP Club** (Tel: 252-690) at the Boss Hotel is unusual for Hanoi. For a US$4 entrance fee, you have a club that offers Karaoke, dancing, slot machines, and a games room. The crowd is a mixture of locals, overseas visitors, expatriates working in Hanoi, singles, and groups.

One of the surprising features of Hanoi is the number of small sidewalk **bars and cafes** that appear after dark. Many of these places are just "holes-in-the-wall" with seating for half a dozen people, but most try to increase customer numbers by setting up small tables and chairs on the pavement outside. People drink Saigon 333 Export beer, cheaper Fruda beer, Coca-Cola, Nuoc Suoi (mineral water which is inexpensive at around 1,500d a bottle), or coffee. You will find these small bars all over Hanoi with strong concentrations in Dien Bien Phu Street near the railway line, on Pho Hang Bong, and on Pho Hang Bai. Stop off for a drink one evening. You could find yourself talking with the locals very quickly.

12. The Hanoi Address List

Airlines—Cathay Pacific Airlines, 27 Ly Thai To Street (Tel: 269-232); Thai Airways International, 1B Quang Trung Street (Tel: 267-921); Vietnam Airlines, 1 Quang Trung St. (Tel: 255-229).

Bank—Bank for Foreign Trade, 47 Le Thai To Street (Tel: 252-831).

Bus Station—Kim Lien Station, 100 Le Duan Street (Tel: 255-230); Kim Ma Station, Nguyen Thai Hoc Street (Tel: 253-846).

Business—Ministry of Commerce and Tourism, 31 Trang Tien Street (Tel: 254-915); Vietnam Trade Information Center, 49 Ngo Quyen Street (Tel: 262-318).

Car Rental—Vicarrent, Ngo Quyen Street (Tel: 264-007).

Churches—St. Joseph Cathedral, Nha Chung Street.

Doctors—Ask your hotel or contact your embassy.

Embassies—Australian, 66 Ly Thuong Kiet Street (Tel: 252-763); Cambodian, 71 Tran Hung Dao Street (Tel: 253-789); French, 49 Ba Trieu Street (Tel: 252-719); Lao, 24 Tran Binh Trong Street (Tel: 254-576); Malaysian, A3 Van Phuc Street (Tel: 253-371); United Kingdom, 16 Ly Thuong Kiet Street (Tel: 252-510); Russian, 58 Tran Phu Street (Tel: 254-633).

Express Delivery—DHL, 49 Nguyen Thai Hoc (Tel: 267-020).

Government—Ministry of Foreign Affairs, 1 Ton That Dam Street (Tel: 257-279); Ministry of Information, International Relations Department (Tel: 253-152); Chamber of Commerce, 33 Ba Trieu Street (Tel: 252-961).

Hospitals—Quoc te (International), Kim Lien Street (Tel: 256-063); Back Mai, Duong Giai Phong Street (Tel: 254-385); Viet Duc (German-Vietnam), 40 Trang Thi (Tel: 253-531).

Information—Vietnam Tourism, 54 Nguyen Du Street (Tel: 255-963), and 30A Ly Thuong Kiet Street (Tel: 264-319); Hanoi Tourism, 18 Ly Thuong Kiet Street (Tel: 254-209); TOSERCO, 8 To Hien Thanh Street (Tel: 263-541).

International Organizations—FAO, 3 Nguyen Gia Thieu Street (Tel: 257-208); UNDP, 27 Phan Boi Chau Street (Tel: 257-495); UNESCO, 15 Le Phung Hieu Street (Tel: 253-261); UNFPA, 3B3 Giang Vo Street (Tel: 254-763); UNICEF, 72 Ly Thuong Kiet Street (Tel: 252-109).

Library—National Library, 31 Trang Tien Street (Tel: 252-643).

Police—(Tel: 01).

Postal—GPO, 75 Dinh Tien Hoang Street (Tel: 257-036).

Press—Foreign Press Center, 10 Le Phung Hieu Street (Tel: 254-697).

Railway—Hanoi Station, Le Duan Street (Tel: 252-628).

Taxi—Hanoi Taxi (Tel: 535-252).

Telecommunications—International Telephone (GPO) (Tel: 252-030); International Operator (Tel: 01); CTSC, 1 Ba Trieu Street (Tel: 265-244).

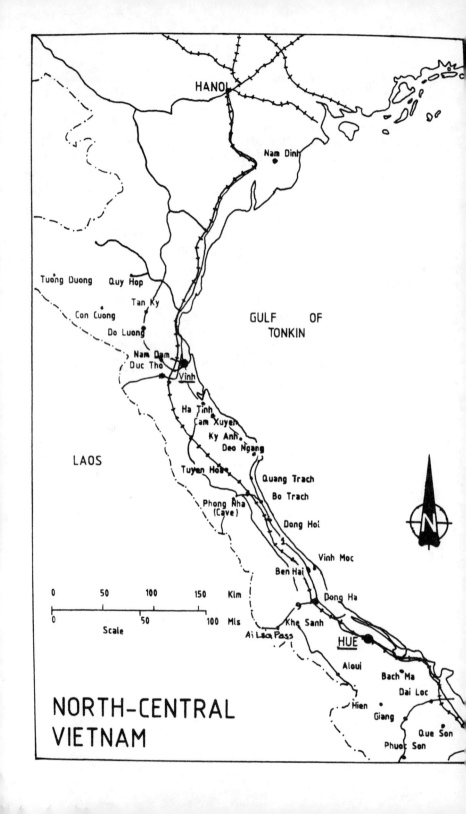

HANOI

Nam Dinh

GULF OF
TONKIN

Tuong Duong   Quy Hop

Tan Ky

Con Cuong

Do Luong

Nam Dam
Duc Tho
Vinh

Ha Tinh
Cam Xuyen
Ky Anh
Deo Ngang

LAOS

Tuyen Hoa

Quang Trach
Bo Trach

Phong Nha
(Cave)

Dong Hoi

Vinh Moc

Ben Hai

0   50   100   150   Klm   Dong Ha

0   50   100 Mls
Scale   Khe Sanh

Ai Lao Pass

HUE

Aloui

Bach Ma

Dai Loc

Hien
Giang

NORTH-CENTRAL
VIETNAM   Que Son

Phuoc Son

N

6

Hue and North-Central Vietnam

1. The General Picture

It is believed that there has been a town on the site of present-day Hue for at least two thousand years. At first it was a command center for the Chinese army, then it was the capital of a small principality. It became an important center within the Champa kingdom, then was captured by the Vietnamese, named Phu Xuan, and made the capital of an autonomous region. In the mid-eighteenth century, Phu Xuan became the capital of the southern part of Vietnam. By the late eighteenth century, the town had been taken over by the Tay Son Rebels, but these were defeated in 1802 and the new Nguyen Dynasty that was formed selected Hue as its seat of power. For 150 years, Hue was the capital of Vietnam.

Hence, it is no surprise to learn that the city has been one of Vietnam's prime cultural, religious, and educational centers. It has also been a center for political action and influence—leaders Ho Chi Minh, Pham Van Dong, Nge Dinh Diem were all educated here.

Hue is sixteen kilometers inland from the South China Sea on the Perfume River. The old imperial city is on the left (west) bank of the river, while the new city is on the right bank. Most of the major items of interest within the city are on the left bank. All the major hotels and restaurants are on the right bank. The city has some notable pagodas and the splendid tombs

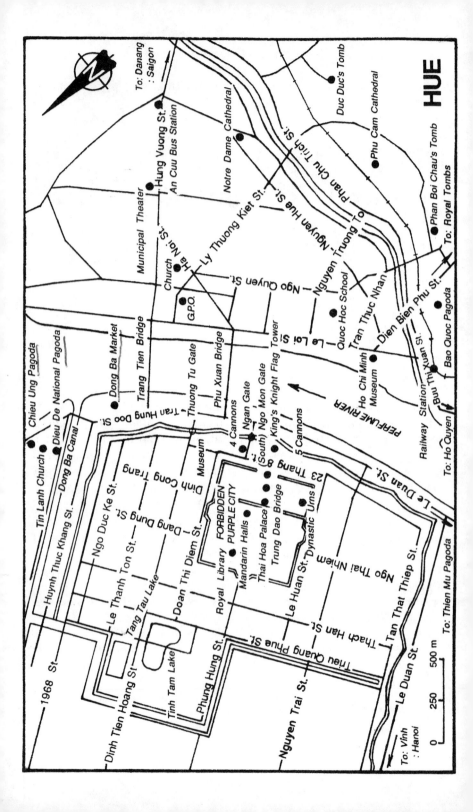

of the Nguyen emperors, which are all southeast of the city, are a major attraction. Despite suffering many wounds of war, the people have preserved their unique soft drawling speech, and the city has preserved much of its alluring beauty and architectural poetry.

About seventy-five kilometers north of Hue is the old Demilitarized Zone (DMZ)—a five-kilometer strip on either side of the Ben Hai River. For twenty years, this served as the border between the Democratic Republic of Vietnam (North Vietnam) and the Republic of Vietnam (South Vietnam).

Farther north, the mountains start to crowd the coastal plain. They provided a natural boundary between the Vietnamese and Champa civilizations, and later between the French regions of Tonkin and Annam. Over the mountains lies Vinh and the most populated province in Vietnam.

2. Getting There

At the end of 1994, Vietnam Airlines had two flights a week from Dalat and five each from Hanoi and Ho Chi Minh City, all using smallish ATR-72 aircraft. The airport (Phu Bai) is about fourteen kilometers south of the city. The flight from Hanoi takes one hour and twenty minutes, and from Saigon it takes one hour and forty-five minutes.

The city is served by a number of local and long-distance trains. There are about three trains a day from both Saigon and Hanoi, although seats to Hue are severely limited on some of these. All of these trains have both sleeping and sitting berths. Additionally, there is one train a day from Nha Trang and two trains from Danang. Train travel from Danang to Hue is quite spectacular, particularly around the Lang Co area.

Buses operate from Hanoi, Vinh, and other points north as well as from Danang, Nha Trang, and Saigon; but I don't recommend bus travel to anyone at the moment.

3. Local Transportation

On a **bicycle** is the ideal way to explore Hue. The city is small and flat, and it is fun to join the rest of the population in the apparent chaos that chokes the streets. Somehow it all works. Bicycles can be rented from several hotels and guest houses, and I have found that staff at these places are more than willing to rent their private bicycles for a small fee.

A chauffeur-driven **motorbike** is the best way to get out to the royal tombs. You will find someone willing to take you there by just asking at your hotel or guest house. Allow half a day for this excursion.

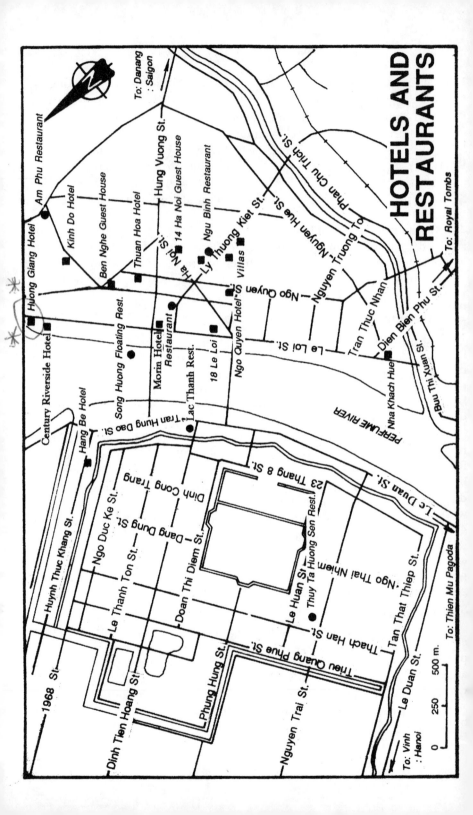

HOTELS AND RESTAURANTS

To: Danang : Saigon

To: Royal Tombs

Am Phu Restaurant

Kinh Do Hotel

Ben Nghe Guest House

Thuan Hoa Hotel

Hung Vuong St.

14 Ha Noi Guest House

Ngu Binh Restaurant

Ha Noi St.

Ly Thuong Kiet St.

Ly Thuong Villas

Huong Giang Hotel

Nguyen Hue St.

Phan Chu Trinh St.

Nguyen Truong To

Song Huong Floating Rest.

Ngo Quyen St.

Ngo Quyen Hotel

Tran Thuc Nhan

Century Riverside Hotel

Morin Hotel Restaurant

18 Le Loi

Le Loi St.

Dien Bien Phu St.

Nha Khach Hue

Buu Thi Xuan St.

Lac Thanh Rest.

Hang Be Hotel

Tran Hung Dao St.

PERFUME RIVER

Huynh Thuc Khang St.

Ngo Duc Ke St.

Dinh Cong Trang

Dang Dung St.

23 Thang 8 St.

Le Duan St.

To: Thien Mu Pagoda

1968 St.

Le Thanh Ton St.

Doan Thi Diem St.

Huong Sen Rest.

Ngo Thai Nhiem

Dinh Tien Hoang St.

Phung Hung St.

Tieu Quang Phuc St.

Thuy Ta

Le Huan St.

Thach Han St.

Tan That Thiep St.

Nguyen Trai St.

Le Duan St.

To: Vinh : Hanoi

0   250   500 m.

Rental cars with driver are available from the Hue Hotel, the Huong Giang Hotel, and from Hue City Tourism. Several other places around town can arrange for official or private vehicles for you.

Many tourist sites can be reached by **boat**. There are organized sightseeing tours on the Perfume River, and private boats can be rented from near the Huong Giang Hotel.

4. The Hotel Scene

Hue has no expensive hotels. There is a reasonable selection of medium-price hotels and budget accommodations.

MEDIUM-PRICE HOTELS

The **Century Riverside Inn** (Tel: 23390), 150 rooms, is the biggest and newest hotel in the city. The building occupies a large site right on the river and is built in a grand "East European" manner. The hotel opened in 1991, but it looks as if it has been there for twenty years. There are extensive facilities including two restaurants, a discotheque, Karaoke, steam bath, massage, barbers, hairdressers, post office, tennis court, swimming pool, table tennis, and shop. You can organize local tours, the hotel has its own boat for river cruises, and you can rent a car and driver for business or sightseeing.

The rooms are adequate but not brilliant. The first-class bedrooms are a reasonable size, but the furniture and furnishings are about two-star quality. Rooms are airconditioned and most have a refrigerator, television with satellite programs, and telephone. The larger rooms have a table, chairs, and a desk. Bathrooms are fairly basic, and they have baths and hot and cold water. Rooms are clean. Room rates are US$45-80. (Book with the hotel at 49 Le Loi Street, Hue; Fax: 84-54-23399.)

The **Huong Giang Hotel** (Tel: 23958), 75 rooms, is right next door. This was the top hotel in Hue for several years. It has all the facilities and a friendly staff, but it is all a little worn. Facilities include two restaurants, a cafe, steambath and massage, shop, dancing hall, and car and bicycle rental. Sightseeing and boat trips can be arranged at reception.

First-, second-, and third-class rooms are airconditioned and have refrigerators and fans. The attached bathrooms have hot water. There are a couple of suites which have lounge facilities and television. Current room rates are: suite US$90-160, first-class US$48-60. (Book with the hotel at 51 Le Loi Street, Hue; Fax: 84-54-23424.)

The **Kinh Do Hotel** (Tel: 23566) is at 1 Nguyen Thai Hoc Street—two blocks away from the river. The hotel opened in 1990 and it has modern facilities and friendly staff. There is a restaurant with reasonable food, a video bar, dancing, massage, and sauna. The hotel has its own minibus that can be used for sightseeing. Room rates start at US$28. (Book on Fax: 84-54-23036.)

The **Thuan Hoa Hotel** (Tel: 22553) is an overpriced place with average facilities at 7B Nguyen Tri Phuong Street. This is popular with Vietnamese because they pay a fraction of the US$35 asked of foreigners. There is a restaurant, sauna, massage, and dancing. (Book on Fax: 84-54-22470.)

There are a series of **villas** in Ly Thuong Kiet Street that are run by Hue City Tourism. The standards vary considerably between them, and I have very mixed feelings about the value. All have hot and cold water and fans, but no telephones or refrigerators in the rooms. Each villa has a dining room. On a recent visit to Hue, I arrived here at 6 P.M. and could not find anyone who could speak a word of English. Room rates start at US$20. The villas are at No. 11 (Tel: 23753), No. 16 (Tel: 23679), and No. 18 (Tel: 23964).

BUDGET ACCOMMODATIONS

The hotel at **18 Le Loi Street** (Tel: 23720), 8 rooms, has my strong recommendation in this category. There is one nice room with airconditioning and hot water for US$15, but other accommodations are available from US$5. The delight of this place is the wonderful staff who go out of their way to please. Meals are not normally available, but someone went to the market and prepared a delightful dinner for me when I was not feeling well one evening. They also produce the best fresh lemon drinks in the whole of Vietnam (using ice made from boiled water). Bicycles are available for rent at about 8,000d a day.

The **Le Loi Hue Hotel** (Tel: 22153), 140 rooms at 2 Le Loi Street, is only about too hundred meters from the railway station. There are gardens and plenty of space, a good restaurant, and cars and bicycles to be rented. Fan rooms with communal baths are from US$6, and airconditioned rooms with private baths are from US$12. All rooms are fairly basic. At times, this guest house also opens the palatial villa at 5 Le Loi Street. Accommodations here are good.

The **Morin Hotel** (Tel: 23526) is an old place with interesting atmosphere. Some of the hotel has been renovated, and rooms in this part are US$30. Other rooms are from US$12. The location at Le Loi and Hung Vuong Streets is good.

The **Ben Nghe Guest House** (Tel: 23687) is a small place at 4 Ben Nghe Street, not far from the Kinh Do Hotel. Rooms are basic but clean, and the people are friendly. Room rates start at US$6.

The **Hang Be Hotel** (Tel: 23752) at 73 Huynh Thuc Khang is one of the few hotels on the left bank. It is nothing special, but some rooms overlook

Dong Ba Canal and there is a fair restaurant on the ground floor. Rooms cost from US$15 for foreigners.

I am told that the **Ngo Quyen Hotel** (Tel: 23278) at 9 Ngo Quyen Street is a reasonable place, but I have not seen it myself. A similar comment applies to the guest house at **14 Ha Noi Street.** You could try these if the other recommendations are full.

5. Dining and Restaurants

The restaurant on the top floor of the Huong Giang Hotel serves acceptable Vietnamese and Western food at reasonable prices. The terrace of the Century Riverside Inn can be very pleasant and the food is adequate. The restaurant at the Hang Be Hotel serves Vietnamese food. There is little atmosphere, but the food is good at the restaurant in the Kinh Do Hotel.

The best restaurant in town is probably the **Song Huong Floating Restaurant** (Tel: 23738) on the river between the Hue Hotel and the Trang Tien Bridge. This is run by Hue Tourism. It can be delightful on the river on a balmy night, and this place produces quite reasonable food. Prices are in U.S. dollars (usually a bad sign), but I actually thought the prices were acceptable. Soup is 40 cents, fried rice 80 cents, and main meals from $1.50 to $3.00. 333 beer is 8,500d, Heineken is 10,000d, and China beer 5,000d. You need to check the bill carefully because there seems to be systematic overcharging here.

There is a restaurant at **7 Hoang Hoa Tham Street** opposite the post office. English is in short supply here, but they serve good soup and other Vietnamese favorites. As with most other Hue restaurants, it is closed by 9 P.M.

One of the few places that is open late is the **Ngu Binh Restaurant** (Tel: 22167) at 7 Ly Thuong Kiet Street. This place is not great on food, but it has music, dancing, and a supply of local singles who like to meet visitors.

The **Am Phu Restaurant** is on Nguyen Thai Hoc Street near Ba Trieu Street. It has good Vietnamese food.

Across the river on the left bank, there is limited choice. The place with the most atmosphere is the **Thuy Ta Huong Sen Restaurant** (Tel: 23201) at 40 Nguyen Trai Street. This open-sided pavilion is built out over a small lake. The food is mainly simple Vietnamese and they have a good selection of drinks. It is open all day until midnight.

There are a few small eating places on Tran Hung Dao Street between Phu Xuan Bridge and the Dong Ba Market, but none are worthy of particular mention. Most will sell you *com hen* (rice with mussels), *banh khoai* (a pancake filled with bean sprouts and meat dipped in a thick sauce), *banh la cha tom* (shrimp fritters), and *huong giang* (rice seasoned with sesame seeds, herbs, onions, and chilies). The best local restaurant in this area is **Lac Thanh** at 6A Dinh Tien Hoang Street. Try one of the soups. Locally brewed Huda beer is worth trying.

6. Sightseeing

Although Vietnam Tourism and the local tour agencies will encourage you to spend your time in Hue cruising the Perfume River, the real attractions of the city are the Citadel, the Royal Tombs, and the pagodas.

THE CITADEL

The place to start sightseeing is the Citadel. This huge moated and walled area was begun in 1804 by Emperor Gia Long. Originally the ten-kilometer-long walls that are twenty meters wide and seven meters high were built of earth. Around 1820, it was decided to cover them with bricks, so thousands of laborers spent several years on the task. The Citadel enclosed the whole city at that time. However, within this area there were two other sections—the Imperial City and within it, the Forbidden Purple City.

The Citadel had ten gates, each of which was reached by a bridge across the moat. There were also a number of bastions and observation posts. The most imposing was the one in the northwest corner—the **Mang Ca**. This is still used today as a military fortress. The **King's Knight** was built in 1809 as an observation and defense post at the main entrance to the Imperial Palace. It is about seventeen meters high and commands a good view of the Perfume River and the surrounding country. Vietnam's largest flag pole (thirty-seven meters tall) was erected here in 1949. During the 1968 Tet Offensive, the National Liberation Front flag flew from this pole for twenty-five days while the Communists occupied the city.

Close by are the **nine holy cannons**, symbols of the Nguyen nobles and protectors of the kingdom. They were cast from brass articles which were captured from the Tay Son Rebels and were never intended to be fired. Each is five meters long and weighs about ten tons. The cannons also represent the four seasons and the five elements of fire, water, earth, metal, and wood.

The **Museum of Hue**, formerly the Khai Dinh Museum, is at 3 Le True Street. The building was built in 1845 and was restored when the museum was founded in 1923. Unfortunately, the most precious artifacts were lost during the war, but what remains is still worth seeing. Outside the building, you can see bronze sculptures, cannons, and vases; while inside there are objects from the palace. You will see a royal sedan chair, different ceremonial robes, furniture with lacquer and mother-of-pearl decorations, traditional musical instruments, a game that was popular with the emperors, and some Hue porcelain. The museum is open from 7:30 A.M. until 5:00 P.M.

The Citadel is divided by the Ngu Ha canal. This was started in 1805 and not completed until 1825. There are two small lakes near here, Tang Tau Lake and Tinh Tam Lake, which were used by the emperors for relaxation and study.

The **Imperial City** (Hoang Thanh) is a complex of palaces, pavilions, and areas for civil and religious ceremonies. The area is enclosed by a 2,400-meter-long and five-meter-high wall, which has four gates—the Gate of Peace, the Gate of Humanity, the Gate of Virtue, and the South Gate. The South Gate is the main entrance. This has five doorways whereas each of the others has three.

The **South Gate**, called **Ngo Mon Gate**, faces the King's Knight and is the main entrance for visitors to the Imperial City. It is open from 6:30 A.M. until 5:30 P.M. each day. There is an admission charge of 10,000d. The central entrance with its yellow doors was once reserved for the emperor. Now it is used as a bicycle check-in area. On top of the gate is Ngu Phung (the Belvedere of the Five Phoenix) where the emperor appeared on important religious and ceremonial occasions. It was here that Emperor Bao Dai ended the Nguyen Dynasty in 1945 when he abdicated under extreme pressure from Ho Chi Minh's provisional revolutionary government.

Beyond the Ngo Mon Gate, you cross a lotus-filled pond via the **Trung Dao Bridge**. This leads to the paved **Esplanade of Great Welcome** and the **Palace of Supreme Harmony** (Thai Hoa Palace). The courtyard was where the nine ranks of court mandarins gathered during official ceremonies. The upper level was reserved for the highest-ranking mandarins and the lower was used by those of lesser rank. Civil mandarins stood on one side and military mandarins on the other.

The palace is built of wood and is painted bright red and gold. It was built in 1803 and moved to its present site in 1833. The huge hall has massive beams supported by eighty carved columns. The attractive roof is decorated with dragons. The emperor received dignitaries and held festivals and court ceremonies here.

To the left of here was the former site of the **Temple of the Generations** (the Mieu), which was constructed in 1821 and consecrated to the emperors and empresses of the Nguyen Dynasty. In the courtyard in front of here are nine **bronze urns** which were cast in the nineteenth century to symbolize the nine Nguyen nobles that had reigned to that time. Each weighs about two tons and is two meters tall. The central urn, which is the most ornate, is dedicated to Gia Long, founder of the dynasty. The urns have traditional ornamentation chiselled into them—sun, moon, stars, clouds, animals, trees, rivers, and mountains—symbolizing the harmony between the emperor and the universe.

Beyond Thai Hoa Palace, you enter a courtyard containing two bronze cauldrons dating from the seventeenth century. Facing the courtyard are the **Halls of the Mandarins,** where the mandarins prepared for court ceremonies. The buildings have recently been restored and the one on your right contains a small museum and shop.

The **Forbidden Purple City** (Tu Cam Thanh) was the royal palace area used only by the imperial family and the concubines and eunuchs who served them. The palace consisted of sixty buildings arranged around twenty courtyards. It was organized into two sections—"feminine" affairs to the west and "masculine" affairs to the east. Unfortunately, this whole area was almost totally destroyed during the Tet Offensive and is now a collection of vegetable gardens, trees, and ruins.

Prior to the 1968 offensive by the Viet Cong and North Vietnamese army, Hue had remained fairly isolated from the major fighting since 1945. On January 31, however, North Vietnamese forces attacked and occupied the eastern sections of the Citadel. Assaults were also aimed at police headquarters, radio stations, the American military command, and government buildings. Within the next few days, Communist troops and political cadres conducted house-to-house searches for "uncooperative elements." Over the next three weeks, almost three thousand civilians including Buddhist monks, Catholic priests, intellectuals, and South Vietnamese government officials were shot or beaten to death. They were then buried in shallow graves which were discovered in the next few years.

The South Vietnamese army units proved unable to shift the invaders, so American troops were called in to conduct house-to-house fighting. After ten days, most of the Citadel was still in Viet Cong control, so restrictions against bombing the area were lifted. In the days that followed, whole neighborhoods were leveled by V.C. rockets and American bombs and artillery. Eventually, the Viet Cong were driven out, but an estimated ten thousand people had been killed, and the ancient city had been ruined forever.

Today there is little to see here. The two-story **library** (Thai Binh Lau) has been partly restored and some other work is underway, but the magnificent buildings are mostly gone. Vietnam had lost one of its best potential tourist attractions.

SOUTH OF THE CITADEL

So far, all our sightseeing has been done within the Citadel, but there are other places of interest outside. Three kilometers southwest is the **Thien Mu Pagoda**—one of the most famous structures in the country. The pagoda was founded early in the seventeenth century on the ruins of a Cham temple, but none of the original buildings remain. The present complex includes an elaborate octagonal tower (twenty-one meters and seven stories high) which was built by Emperor Thiev Tri in the 1840s. Each level of the tower is dedicated to a manushi-buddha who has lived on earth in human form.

To the right of the tower is the Pavilion of the Great Hero, which contains a stelac dating from 1715 set into a huge marble turtle. Here also is the main sanctuary. To the left of the tower is a pavilion housing an enormous two-ton bell cast in 1710. Behind the sanctuary is the car that transported the bonze who immolated himself in Saigon in 1963 to protest the actions of the Diem government.

The Thien Mu Pagoda complex is set on a small hill overlooking the Perfume River. To reach here from the Citadel, you head southwest on Le Duan Street, cross the railway line, and keep going along Kim Long Street. You can also reach here by sampan—a delightful trip. Boats are available from near the market.

NORTH OF THE CITADEL

Dong Ba Market is interesting. This is still a major shopping center for Hue residents, and it is fascinating to walk around and see what is on sale. If you go north and cross Dong Ba Canal, you enter Phu Cat Sub-District and a fascinating collection of pagodas, temples, churches, and Chinese congregational halls.

You first reach **Dieu De National Pagoda** which was built in 1845 at 102 Bach Dany Street. The pagoda has four towers—one on either side of the gate and two flanking the sanctuary. Two of the towers have bells and one contains a drum. During the early 1960s, the pagoda was a stronghold of Buddhist and student opposition to the South Vietnamese government and the war. This lead to a famous police raid in 1966 in which many people were arrested and equipment was confiscated.

Just north of here in Nguyen Du Street is the **Tin Lanh Church**—the only church on the left bank in Hue. Just around the corner on Chi Lang Street is the **Chieu Ung Pagoda**. Founded by the Hai Nam Chinese community about 150 years ago, it was rebuilt early this century and repaired in the 1940s, but the original ornamentation remains and is well worth visiting. Just opposite here is the old Indian Muslim community mosque which was used until 1975 when the whole community fled from Hue.

The **Chua Ba Pagoda** is farther north along Chi Lang Street. It was founded about a century ago, but was reconstructed after it was fairly seriously damaged during the Tet Offensive. If you go west along Ho Xuan Huong Street, you will reach the **Tang Quang Pagoda** which is the largest Hinayana pagoda in Hue. This is a relatively modern structure (1957), but it has distinctive architecture showing its links with India and Sri Lanka.

Two bridges cross the Perfume River. The downstream Trang Tien Bridge had been there for many years, but it was blown up in 1968. It has since been repaired on several occasions, but seems to close periodically. The newer Phu Xuan Bridge is now the main crossing point.

ACROSS THE RIVER

The right bank of the river contains some points of interest. The G.P.O., Municipal Theater, and several interesting pagodas, churches, schools, and museums are here.

The most interesting pagoda on this side of the river is the **Bao Quoc Pagoda** off Dien Bien Phu Street near the railway line. This was founded in 1670, but nothing remains from that time. The present sanctuary is located in a parklike setting with several stupas and tombs, including a three-story affair dedicated to the founder of the pagoda, Giac Phong. Both Buddhists and Taoists worship here.

A short walk south along Dien Bien Phu Street brings us to the **Tu Dam Pagoda** which was founded at the end of the seventeenth century. In the 1950s, this pagoda was instrumental in establishing the Unified Vietnamese Buddhist Association which aimed to modernize Buddhism and spread its message through conferences and workshops. In the 1960s, the pagoda was a major center of anti-Diem and antiwar sentiment. This was effectively stopped by the 1968 Tet Offensive.

If you go east along Tu Darn Street, you will come to the tomb of the anti-colonialist revolutionary Phan Boi Chau. There is a small museum here. Continue along Duong Tran Phu Street to Nguyen Truong To Street, and turn left. On the right is the **Phu Cam Cathedral** which is the headquarters for the Hue diocese. Masses are held here every day, and the congregations are growing. The building was started in 1963 and has not yet been completed.

The other major church is the **Notre Dame Cathedral** (Dong Chua Cuv The) on Nguyen Hue Street, north of the railway line. This is a modern building that was constructed about thirty years ago with both Eastern and Western elements in its design. There are daily masses here.

The **Ho Chi Minh Museum** will have little to interest most visitors. The small building, which was once the residence of the French government delegate, is at 9 Le Loi Street, not far from the railway station. It contains some photographs and some of Ho's personal belongings and documents. If you have seen the museums in either Hanoi or Saigon, forget this one. Just across the road is **Quoc Hoc Secondary School**—one of the most famous schools in Vietnam. It was founded in 1896 and produced such famous alumni as the president of North Vietnam, Ho Chi Minh (who was expelled for being "rebellious"), and the president of South Vietnam, Ngo Dinh Diem.

About three kilometers west of Phu Xuan Bridge on the right bank of the river is **Ho Quyen**, the Imperial Amphitheater. This was constructed in 1870, but is now in ruins. Fights were held here between tigers and elephants—one domesticated and one savage—representing the forces of nature. The last fight was held in the late nineteenth century.

Two kilometers directly south of Hue is where you will find **Nam Giao**. At one time there was a straight road from here to the main entrance to the Imperial City because it was the most important religious site in Vietnam. The emperor came here to honor the earth and heavens and to conduct a sacrifice to the gods. The monument consists of several levels—the underworld, the earth, and Heaven—linked by four sets of stairs. It is surrounded by pine trees. Despite huge opposition, which is still expressed by locals, the provincial government has erected an obelisk to North Vietnamese soldiers killed during the war with the South on the exact spot where the sacrificial altar once stood. It makes it meaningless for visitors to go there.

THE ROYAL TOMBS

The tombs of the rulers of the Nguyen Dynasty are along the banks of the Perfume River south of Hue City. They are open from early morning until 5 P.M. each day. There is an entrance fee of 30,000d at each tomb. Almost all the tombs were planned and built by the Nguyen emperors during their lifetimes. The tombs consist of a collection of pavilions and traditional buildings amid courtyards. The designs included artificial hills, streams, ponds, cascades, and gardens. Most of the tombs contained precious ornaments.

Today the tombs are in various states of decay. Some have been damaged by war and the elements, all have had the precious objects stolen from them. Some have suffered serious erosion, and others have been altered by random modernization. Despite this, they are worth seeing and together they constitute Hue's biggest attraction.

The tombs are scattered over an area which is about ten kilometers long and several kilometers wide. They are on both sides of the river (and there is no bridge), so it requires a major effort to see all of them. Most people will be happy to see two or three; and in my mind the choice is clear. I would visit the tomb of Khai Dinh, the tomb of Minh Mang, and the tomb of Tu Due, in that order. You can do this on bicycle, in a rented car, or you can take an organized tour from Hue.

The **Tomb of Khai Dinh**, who ruled Vietnam from 1916 to 1925, is gaudy and garish, but to many visitors it is the most spectacular of the royal tombs. It was built from 1920 to 1931, and is the least "Vietnamese" of all the tombs. The reinforced concrete complex makes little attempt to blend with the natural surroundings, and it is a strange blend of French and Vietnamese architecture.

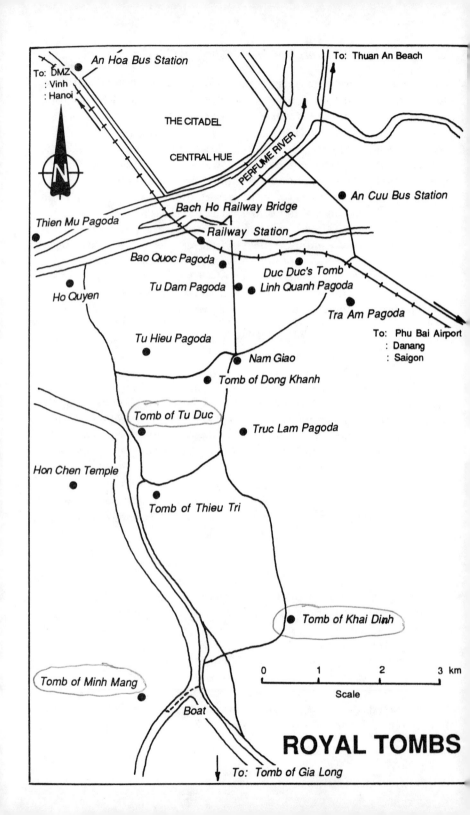

ROYAL TOMBS

The entrance to the complex is up a broad dragon-flanked staircase, which leads to a courtyard formed by two pavilions. Another staircase leads to the next spectacular courtyard with its rows of elephant, horse, and mandarin statues. In the center of the courtyard is an octagonal stele pavilion with ornate columns. Additional dragon-protected stairways lead to other levels and eventually to the top, where the main building is located. The walls and ceilings of this hall are decorated with broken porcelain and colored glass embedded in concrete. In the place of honor is a gilt statue of Khai Dinh beneath a large concrete canopy.

The tomb is located ten kilometers from Hue, right on the road that comes directly south from Nam Giao. Because is it so accessible, there are more visitors here than at any of the other tombs. Local vendors set up outside the complex offering cold drinks, food, and bicycle storage. A visit will take about an hour.

If you continue south then west for about three kilometers, you reach the river. Turn left, and near the center of the village you will find a path leading down to a boat landing. You will need to charter a boat, so hone up your bargaining skills. The boat will take you across the river and a little upstream and will wait for you while you walk or cycle to the **Tomb of Minh Mang.**

Minh Mang ruled Vietnam from 1820 to 1840. The tomb was started during his lifetime and finished in 1843. It is perhaps the grandest of all the tombs, but parts of it are not well cared for, so it has lost some of the majesty that it once had. The visitor entrance is on the right side of the inner courtyard. This leads to the funeral courtyard and to the square stele pavilion. From here, terraces rise to Hien Due Gate and the Sung An Temple which contains the funerary tablets of the emperor and empress.

The Lake of Pure Clarity (Trung Minh Ho) surrounds this area and is crossed by several bridges. On the other side, the Minh Lau Pavilion is on top of a three-tiered terrace representing the heavens, the earth, and the water. Beyond is the crescent-shaped Lake of the New Moon (Tan Nguyet Tri) and, after crossing a bridge, you will find a dragon-graced monumental staircase which leads to the circular Sacred Wall surrounding the imperial burial mound. The burial place is accessed through a bronze gate and is covered with pine trees and shrubbery.

After visiting the tomb, you must return to the boat and again cross the river to the right bank. It is about seven kilometers from here downriver to the **Tomb of Tu Duc**. This is probably the most harmonious of the tombs, possibly because it was used by the king before his death as a second royal residence. Tu Duc came here to fish, to compose poetry, and to lead the "good life" with his many wives and concubines.

You enter the tomb via Vu Khiem Gate. A paved path leads from here to the shore of Luu Khiem Lake. Across the water to the left is the Pavilion of the Emperor's Boat (Xung Khiem), which was built in 1865 and restored one hundred years later. If you cross the courtyard and go through a gate, you reach Hoa Kiem Temple which was used by the emperor as a palace. Today there are two funerary tablets, two thrones, and a collection of other items.

If you follow the path around the lake, you will come to the Honor Courtyard with its two rows of human and animal figures and the Pavilion of the Stele, which contains an enormous stone tablet said to weigh twenty tons. The stele was transported five hundred kilometers to this site. It has inscriptions which were drafted by Tu Duc himself. It is unknown where Tu Duc was actually buried. In an attempt to protect the tomb from raids by thieves, all two hundred workers who buried the king were beheaded after the work was finished.

The **Tomb of Gia Long** is the farthest from Hue, is difficult to reach, and is in a poor state of repair. It is believed that the emperor himself chose the site on White Mountain. Gia Long was the founder of the Nguyen Dynasty and reigned from 1802 to 1820. The tomb is on the left side of the river about fifteen kilometers from Hue.

NORTH FROM HUE

Highway 1 goes northwest from Hue through very poor sandy country to **Quang Tri**. This was once an important city but it was almost obliterated in four months of intense fighting in 1972 when North Vietnamese troops occupied the area. Today little remains except parts of the moat and ramparts and a number of destroyed buildings. An estimated ten thousand troops died in these battles. The area has been renamed Trieu Hai in recent years.

It is another twelve kilometers to **Dong Ha**, capital of Quang Tri Province. In the late 1960s, this was a U.S. Marines command and logistics center. Later it was the site of a South Vietnamese army base, and today it is a fishing port on the right bank of the Cam Lo River. The town was the closest major population center to the Demilitarized Zone (DMZ), and many American bases existed in the region.

Dong Ha is at the junction of Highway 1 (linking Hanoi with Saigon) and Highway 9, which follows the Cam Lo River to the Han River toward the Ai Lao Pass and Laos. This route eventually continues to Savannakhet on the Mekong River in Laos. It is the southernmost route from the sea to the Mekong via the Truong Son Mountains. There are the remains of several American fire bases along this road, but little of interest is left. It is difficult to visualize the intense fighting and dreadful conditions that occurred here during the late 1960s and early 1970s. You can see some evidence of **Camp**

Carroll about twelve kilometers west of Cam Lo. The area around here now belongs to the State Pepper Enterprise. A few kilometers farther west, you can see the **Rockpile**, a 230-meter-high pile of boulders that served as a U.S. Marines lookout and long-range artillery station.

It is twenty-five kilometers farther to the site of **Khe Sanh Combat Base**. It was located in a very beautiful region, but it became the site of one of the most controversial battles of the Vietnam War. In 1966, the base was turned into a Marine stronghold, and the number of troops and aircraft were significantly increased in 1967. After a series of hill fights and hit-and-run attacks, the North Vietnamese army moved tens of thousands of regulars into the hills around Khe Sanh and started a siege in January of 1968 which lasted for seventy-five days. The world's media focused on the battle, and it became front-page news around the world. During the next two months, the base was subjected to continuous ground attacks and artillery fire. The Americans responded by dropping over 100,000 tons of explosives on the area surrounding the base.

In April of 1968, U.S. troops reopened Highway 9 and ended the siege. An unknown number of Americans were killed during the battle, but it is estimated that the North Vietnamese forces lost 10,000 men. Three months later, American forces were pulled out. Holding Khe Sanh was no longer considered necessary. Today, the area is littered with rusting shells and local people scavenging for scrap metal. There are still deaths caused by unexploded mortar rounds and mines, so it is very unwise to walk anywhere but on well-worn paths.

It is much more pleasant in the town of **Khe Sanh**, which is at an elevation of about five hundred meters in an area of attractive hills and valleys. There were once French-owned coffee plantations here, but today the local inhabitants—many of whom are Bru tribespeople—make a living as best they can. It is eighteen kilometers from here to Ai Lao Pass and the town of Lao Bao on the Vietnam-Laos border. At present, foreigners are unable to use this border crossing in either direction.

Back in Dong Ha, there are accommodations in the difficult-to-get-to Dong Truong Son Hotel (Tel: 52415), 48 rooms, which is three kilometers from the main town. I am told that cars can be arranged here for local sightseeing and there is a nice restaurant. Foreigners can also stay in the Nha Khach Dong Ha Guest House (Tel: 52361). There are many places to eat along Highway 1 northwest of the bus station.

Highway 1 continues north where there is more evidence of the war years. **Doc Mieu Base** is next to the highway, eight kilometers south of the Ben Hai River. This and the **Con Thien Firebase** to the west were once part of the so-called McNamara's Wall, an elaborate defense line with mines, infrared detectors, and acoustic monitors designed to prevent infiltration of North Vietnamese into the South. There are still areas around here that are considered too dangerous to walk around.

A few kilometers north of Con Thien Firebase, you can visit the **Truong Son National Cemetery**. This is a memorial to the tens of thousands of North Vietnamese troops who were killed in the mountains along the Ho Chi Minh Trail. Row after row of markers stretch in all directions. The remains that are buried here were brought from other locations after the war ended. Many of the graves are empty and bear the names of some of Vietnam's missing.

The **Ben Hai River** is twenty-two kilometers north of Dong Ha. For twenty-one years, this was the line of demarcation between North and South Vietnam. The area five kilometers on either side of the river was declared a **Demilitarized Zone** (DMZ) as part of the Geneva agreement of 1954 between the French and Ho Chi Minh's government. During the Vietnam War, the area just south of the DMZ was the site of some of the most bloody conflicts imaginable. The area north of the DMZ was, in turn, pounded by long-range artillery and bombing. Neither area has been able to recover satisfactorily in the twenty years since the end of the conflict. Today it is an area of history but little else.

Cua Tong Beach is on the coast, a little north of the mouth of the Ben Hai River. This was a popular place with Bao Dai, Vietnam's last emperor, and it is the start of a long stretch of beach that extends north to Vinh Moc and beyond. At Vinh Moc, it is possible to visit the remarkable tunnels that were constructed during the 1960s. The tunnels were built by villagers who were tired of regular U.S. aerial and artillery attacks. Over a period of eighteen months, the entire village of almost twelve hundred people relocated underground.

The tunnels look pretty much as they did twenty years ago, although some work has been done on some of the entrances to preserve them. You can go through almost two kilometers of tunnel, but only with a guide. It is hard going for anyone who is more than about 1.6 meters, or 5 feet 4 inches tall. Each family had a small chamber connected to a passage. There were community wells, a medical clinic, a central meeting hall, and electricity was installed in 1972. The tunnels were repeatedly bombed or shelled by ships, but they were never destroyed.

The next point north is the fishing port of **Dong Hoi**, capital of Quang Binh Province. The highway here is poor, which may account for the light traffic from Dong Ha to here. Another reason, of course, could be that there is still relatively little contact or internal trade between the north and the south despite reunification. The city, which is built on an estuary, suffered considerable damage during the war years, and it is not particularly interesting. A citadel was built here in the early nineteenth century, and there are some remnants of the fortress left today. The Hoa Binh Hotel is expensive but has acceptable rooms if you have to stay here. Off to the right, there are several kilometers of sand dunes and beaches; but this is a poor region, so development is sparse.

At Bo Trach, a road to the west leads to **Phong Nha Cave**. This is about forty-five kilometers northwest of Dong Hoi. The caves have been used as sanctuaries for thirteen hundred years, first by a Malay people, then by their relatives the Chams, and in more recent years by the Vietnamese. You can travel through the caves for several kilometers by boat and on foot. There are small passages, large caverns, stalactites and stalagmites, and the remains of altars, statues, and medallions.

North of Bo Trach, the highway parallels the coast while the railway heads inland. Both are attempting to find an easy way over the Hoang Son Mountains, which form the boundary between Quang Binh Province and Nghe Tinh Province. In earlier times, this formed a natural boundary between the Vietnamese in the north and the Kingdom of Champa. Later, it was the frontier between the Trinh and the Nguyen nobles; then it became the border between the French regions of Tonkin and Annam. The eastern section of the mountains forms the **Annam Gate** (elevation about 1050 meters).

The country north of here is poor and the weather is even worse. The area is prone to typhoons, floods, and hot, dry summers. Poor soil contributes to the problems. The result is that this is probably the poorest province in Vietnam. Its capital is **Vinh**.

This city of 200,000 inhabitants is one of the least impressive in the whole of Vietnam. The original citadel of earlier days was severely damaged by French aerial bombing in the 1950s; it suffered a huge fire shortly thereafter; then was almost obliterated by hundreds of bombardments in the late 1960s. The present city was partially rebuilt by the East Germans in the 1970s, using their own grim, uniform architecture. Many buildings have since become dilapidated. There are several hotels in town—the Kim Lien Hotel and the Huu Nghi Hotel are the two biggest and best in town. Rooms cost from US$25.

Nghe Tinh Province has long been noted for its revolutionary spirit. It was in the center of the Tay Son Rebellion from 1771 to 1802; and the ancient capital of Trung Do, founded by Nguyen Hue in 1790, is just twenty-five kilometers northwest of Vinh. The Nghe Tinh Uprising against the French (1893-95) and the Nghe Tinh Soviets Movement (1930-31), in which peasant groups seized control of some areas, occurred here. The most famous revolutionary of all, Ho Chi Minh, was born in Kim Lien, fifteen kilometers northwest of Vinh. Much later, the well-known Ho Chi

Minh trail started here—with much of the war material shipped through the port of Vinh.

It is a long 290 kilometers from here to Hanoi. You can visit a Ho Chi Minh museum in Kim Lien, or you can spend some time at the attractive beach resort of Duo Lo, twenty kilometers north of Vinh. After you travel about seventy-five kilometers, you enter Thanh Hoa Province and areas covered by the previous chapter.

SOUTH FROM HUE

The trip by road or rail from Hue south to Danang is one of the best in Vietnam. You pass through pleasant, but ordinary country immediately south of Hue; but as you proceed south, it becomes more interesting and certainly more spectacular. **Lang Co** is one of my favorite places in Vietnam. It is totally removed from the rush and grime of many areas. The town is built on a peninsula with an idyllic blue lagoon on one side, and a long stretch of clean sandy beach facing the South China Sea on the other side. If you take the local train from Hue to Danang, you are likely to spend some time with the enthusiastic food vendors at Lang Co Railway Station while an extra engine is attached to the train to help with the steep climb to the south.

If you travel by road, you will cross the mountain range just south of Lang Co, at Hai Van Pass (500 meters). Originally this area was heavily forested, but twenty years of fighting, organized clearing, and use of defoliants have made it bare. At the top of the pass, you will see an old fort that was built by the French and later used by the South Vietnamese and the American armies. The railway avoids much of the climb by following the coast and plunging through a number of tunnels. Both the road and railway track provide spectacular views.

7. Guided Tours

Regular guided tours are common in Hue, but one or two of the larger hotels can offer a half-day city tour and a half- or full-day tour to the royal tombs.

The city is much better at organizing "one-off" tours. All you have to do is tell the hotel—or just about anyone else—that you are interested in going somewhere or seeing something specific, and you will be offered a tailor-made tour. These tours will be planned for just one person, although it will obviously be less per head if there are more people. Some of these will be "official" tours, run by regular operators; but others will be "private" by people looking for extra money.

Apart from your hotel, you could try several other organizations to see what is being offered while you are in town. The **Office of Hue Tourism**(Tel: 23577) is at 9 Ly Thuong Kiet Street, not far from the telecommunications tower and there is another office at 18 Le Loi Street. They have some information and can arrange for a rental car and driver. The Hue office of **Thua Thien-Hue Tourism** (Tel: 23288) is at 9 Ngo Quyen Street. This office can make hotel reservations, provide interpreters and guides, and organize tours around Hue, the former DMZ, and the Ho Chi Minh Trail. They can also arrange car and boat rental and book domestic air and train tickets.

Thua Thien-Hue Tourism operates another outlet called the **Center for Planning of Tours** (Tel: 22369). It is at 30 Le Loi Street in the old Morin Hotel building. I have had little contact with this office, but I am told that it can "arrange sightseeing and tourist itineraries throughout Vietnam for both individual and group travel." The **Tourism Car Enterprise** (Tel: 23513), at 60 Tran Phu, is an organization that has rental cars and a mini-coach.

Boat rides on the Perfume River can be very pleasant.

8. Culture

Obviously most of the sightseeing attractions in Hue have cultural connections, but there is little else of great interest to the visitor. Frankly, I have been disappointed by this aspect of the city. Hue is supposed to have its own special music that is "passionate yet dreamlike," but I have yet to hear it. It is supposedly possible to see performances of ancient royal dances, yet I have so far been unsuccessful in my attempts to do so. Some of the hotels advertise *ngu thien*, a royal meal, but I have been told that you need to order ahead of time or that it is just "not available at the moment." This is an area that needs to be improved.

9. Sports

The Century Riverside Inn, with its swimming pool and tennis court, is just about the only place with sporting facilities aimed at the visitor. Swimming is available at Thuan An Beach, thirteen kilometers northeast of the city, near the mouth of the Perfume River. There are also tennis courts at the old Circle Sportif on Le Loi Street near the Phu Xuan Bridge.

10. Shopping

Don't believe any of the tourist blurb; Hue is not a great shopping mecca. **Dong Ba Market** is an interesting place to browse, but there is little there that is not available in any large market in the country. The shops along Tran Hung Dao have a few souvenirs and handicrafts, but they are not very special. You might try **Bach Hoa Tong Lop**, the **Intershop**, or **Kim Loan Phu Hoa** along here. There are limited shopping opportunities on the right bank of the river. One exception is the excellent **Galarie Morin** at 30 Le Loi Street, which has a large selection of paintings and other art objects.

11. Entertainment and Nightlife

As with most cities in Vietnam, nightlife is starting to reappear after quite a long absence. Within the hotels, the main choices are the Karaoke room and the discotheque at the Century Riverside Inn, and the dancing hall at the Huong Giang Hotel.

Across the road from the Century Riverside Inn, one or two **bar/discos** have started up. They seem to be popular with the young local crowd, and there are some single ladies who seem to be permanent residents. There is a **video bar** on H. Hoa Street opposite the post office; and there is often some entertainment at the **sports club** by the river close to the Phu Xuan bridge. The restaurant at 7 Ly Thuong Kiet Street has **music and dancing** each night.

12. The Hue Address List

Airline Office—12 Na Noi Street (Tel: 22249).
Bank—Bank of Industry and Trade, 21 Le Quy Don Street (Tel: 22558).
Bus Station—41 Hung Vuong Street (Tel: 23817).
Car Rental—60 Tran Phu Street (Tel: 23513).
Customs Office—17 Nguyen Hue Street (Tel: 22276).
Entry and Exit Formalities—4 Ben Nghe Street.
Hospital—16 Le Loi Street (Tel: 22325).
Hue City People's Committee—13 Le Loi Street.
Hue Provincial People's Committee—14 Le Loi Street.
Hue Tourism—9 Ly Thuong Kiet Street (Tel: 23577).
Police—42 Hung Vuong Street (Tel: 23749).
Post Office—8 Hoang Hoa Tham Street.
Railway Station—2 Bui Thi Xuan Street (Tel: 22175).
Thua Thien-Hue Tourism—9 Ngo Quyen Street (Tel: 23288).
University Library—18 Le Loi Street.

7

Danang, Nha Trang, Dalat, and South-Central Vietnam

1. The General Picture

The area known as South-Central Vietnam is quite different from its northern neighbor. The soils are better, the weather is kinder, and the people are friendlier. The Truong Son Mountain Range moves away from the coast, but this does not give more coastal plain in many areas. Instead, there are highlands with a cool climate and lovely scenery that is home to several minority groups. This central region was home to the Champa Kingdom, which developed about 1,900 years ago. By the fourth century, a Cham religion had emerged, mixing elements of Indian culture with indigenous religions. Not long afterward, a language evolved using the Indian alphabet. It was the first written language in southeast Asia. The Chams established a capital at Simhapura and a major religious center at My Son, near Danang. By the year 1000, the Chams had established a new capital at Vijaya, near Quy Nhon, which was not conquered until 1471. Today the remains of the Champa kingdom are one of the top attractions of this region.

Danang is the major center for the region. This port city of 600,000 people is the fourth largest city in Vietnam. In addition to being of major importance to Vietnam, it acts as an outlet for the southern part of land-locked Laos. Nha Trang is the important coastal city for the southern part of the region. Dalat is a major tourist city in the highlands.

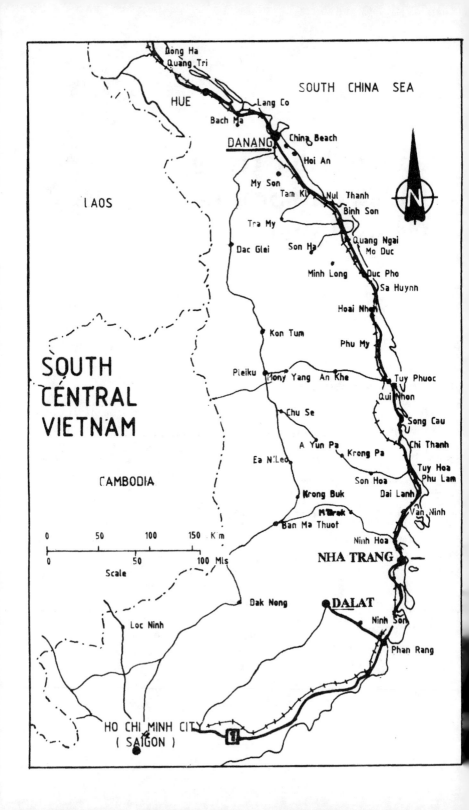

As Vietnam develops wider industrial, commercial, and tourism industries, this region is set to assume greater importance to the country. Danang is already attracting attention from international airlines looking for access into the region. The independent-minded city officials have undertaken economic reforms and social progress which will soon see further development in the area. Nha Trang is progressing as well. Its fishing industry is one of the country's largest, and agriculture is expanding. Tourism is already important and set to grow.

2. Getting There

DANANG

Danang Airport is the third most important in the country. There are several daily flights to both Hanoi and Saigon, and there are connections to Nha Trang, Pleiku, Haiphong, Ban Ma Thuot, and Quy Nhon. The airport is capable of handling international flights, and discussions are currently proceeding with airlines who wish to fly here. Some such as Thai International already have traffic rights. During the Vietnam War, this was one of the busiest airports in the world. Danang Airport is about four kilometers from many of the major hotels. There is no convenient public transport, so if the hotel has no vehicle, the only option is to get there by cyclo. The office of **Vietnam Airlines** (Tel: 21130) is at 35 Tran Phu Street.

Danang Railway Station is served by all the trains that operate between Hanoi and Saigon. In addition, there are local trains to centers such as Hue and Nha Trang. It takes around twenty-four hours to get from Danang to both Hanoi and Saigon, and about four hours to Hue. The fare for foreigners to Hue is about US$3, and the fare to Hanoi or Saigon is around US$30. The station is about one kilometer from the central city area and two kilometers from many of the major hotels. Cyclos meet all trains and will take you to a hotel for around 5,000d. The railway station (Tel: 23810) is on Haiphong Street.

The **Danang Bus Station** (Tel: 21265) is on Dien Bien Phu Street about 2.5 kilometers from the central city. There are "express" buses from here to Hanoi, Saigon, and several other centers.

NHA TRANG

Nha Trang Airport is receiving more flights as Vietnam Airlines develops its internal route network. There are flights to Saigon five days a week, to Hanoi four days a week, and connections to Danang twice a week. The airport is three kilometers from the central city and many of the hotels. The office of Vietnam Airlines (Tel: 21147) is at 82 Tran Phu Street.

The **railway station** (Tel: 22113) is right in the center of town. It is served by Hanoi-Saigon trains, and there are dedicated services to Saigon and north to Quy Nhon and Danang. Cyclos operate to and from the station.

There appears to be a proliferation of **bus stations** in Nha Trang. The main express bus station (Tel: 22397) is on Le Thanh Ton Street. Buses go north, south, and inland to the highlands. A more limited service operates from the Youth Tourism Express Bus Office (Tel: 22010) at 6 Hoang Hoa Tham Steet. There are also services from the Lien Tinh Bus Station (Tel: 22192) on Ngo Gia Tu Street.

DALAT

Dalat Airport (Lien Khang) is about thirty kilometers south of the city. There are three services a week between Dalat and Saigon. The city has recently upgraded the old military airfield called Cam Ly, and this is also available for flights to this area. The Vietnam Airlines office (Tel: 0330) is at 5 Truong Cong Dinh Street. Dalat was once linked to the coast by a cog railway line that climbed the hills in a spectacular fashion. This was closed in 1964 due to attacks by Communist guerrillas. The station at Dalat is well preserved, but much of the line has now gone. It is unlikely that it will ever be operated again. Most visitors arrive by road. There are many daily bus services from Saigon and less frequent daily services from Nha Trang. The **bus station** (Tel: 2077) is at the circle at the western end of Lake Xuan Huong.

Danang is 970 kilometers from Saigon, 770 kilometers from Hanoi, and 540 kilometers from Nha Trang. Dalat is 310 kilometers from Saigon and 205 kilometers from Nha Trang. Nha Trang is 450 kilometers from Saigon and 540 kilometers from Danang.

3. Local Transportation

Danang is built on a coastal plain, so it is flat and ideal for walking, cycling, or traveling by cyclo. The cyclo drivers can be fairly aggressive, but after you negotiate a fare, they are reliable. The airport, railway station, and bus station are all too far from the major hotels to walk. It is possible to rent a bicycle from some of the hotels, but I have not found a place that rents motorcycles. Rental cars with drivers are available from Tourist Transport (Tel: 22104) at 25 Trung Nu Vuong Street. Ferries across the Han River depart from a dock just north of the Han Market.

Nha Trang is also built on the coast. The city is surprisingly spread out, so it is too far to walk if you plan comprehensive sightseeing. The best bet is to rent a bicycle from your hotel (about US$1 a day) or negotiate a half-day deal with a cyclo (about US$4). Motorized Lambrettas, tiny three-wheeled trucks, are available if you wish to travel a bit further afield. There is a Lambretta station near the Dam Market. Cars with drivers can be rented from the Tourism Car Service (Tel: 22377) at 1 Nguyen Thi Minh Khai Street.

Dalat is too hilly for cyclos, and you may find bicycling rather difficult. You can get a motorcycle (Honda ong) driver to take you to the more distant points, and there are lambrettas operating relatively fixed routes. The city has a few taxis that you will find near the bus station, and cars with drivers can be rented from Lam Dong Province Tourism (Tel: 2125), at 12 Tran Phu Street.

4. The Hotel Scene

There are no hotels in this region that are considered to meet international standards. The three cities do have some mid-range hotels that are of reasonable quality—a few of which are particularly interesting. There are numerous cheap hotels that cater to the local market. Some of these refuse to take foreigners, while others will let you stay at a price somewhat higher than what the locals pay. Some represent good value, but others are overpriced by Vietnamese standards for the poor facilities provided.

MEDIUM-PRICE HOTELS

Danang

In my opinion the following are the five best hotels in the city.

The **Hoa Biah Hotel** (Tel: 23984) is the newest in the city. All rooms are airconditioned and have the usual three-star hotel features. There is a Vietnamese restaurant and a souvenir shop. (Book with the hotel at 3 Tran Quy Cap Street, Danang; Fax: 84-51-23161.)

The **Phuong Dong Hotel** (Tel: 21266) is also known as the Orient Hotel. The building has six floors, an elevator, and, rather surprisingly, only thirty-six rooms. The lobby area is large and impressive, but a bit dingy. The best rooms currently rent for US$53/43 double/single and come equipped with airconditioning, TV, refrigerator, cassette player, and bathroom with hot water. There are some smaller rooms without TV at a slightly lower price. The hotel has a good restaurant on the top floor. (Book with the hotel at 93 Phan Chau Trinh Street, Danang; Fax: 84-51-22854.)

The **Pacific Hotel** (Tel: 22137), 48 rooms, is directly across the road. This has eight floors served by elevator. The building is not quite as good, but the facilities are similar to the Phuong Dong Hotel, and the best rooms currently rent for US$35. There are some cheaper rooms without TV or refrigerator for US$22. The hotel has a restaurant on the top floor with mediocre food and service. (Book with the hotel at 92 Phan Chu Trinh Street, Danang; Fax: 84-51-22921.)

The **Bach Dang Hotel** (Tel: 23649), 91 rooms, is the largest in the city. It is situated overlooking the river and is popular with business people. The rooms are well equipped, the restaurant serves Asian and Western food, and there is dancing and a shop. Room prices are US$40-50. (Book with the hotel at 50 Bach Dang Street, Danang; Fax: 84-51-21659.)

The **Hai Au Hotel** (Tel: 22722), 39 rooms, is a relatively new place, but there is nothing very special about the rooms. My room had airconditioning, a telephone, and a bathroom with hot water, but the furniture was fairly basic, and the light was not good enough to read at night. It cost US$30 after some negotiation. Other rooms rent for US$45, and these probably had better facilities. The hotel has a large restaurant and dancing hall on the first floor, a bar and lounge at the rear of the lobby, and a very popular sauna and massage facility out back. I found the hotel reception staff helpful and friendly. (Book with the hotel at 177 Tran Phu Street, Danang; Fax: 84-51-24165.)

There are three other properties with some rooms that squeeze into this category. The **Song Han Hotel** (Tel: 22540), 50 rooms, overlooks the Han River at 26 Bach Dang Street. Airconditioned rooms with the usual facilities rent for US$30. The old-style **Thu Bon Hotel** (Tel: 21101) at 10 Ly Thuong Kiet Street has nineteen rooms with airconditioning, telephone, and bathroom with hot water. There is also a restaurant and massage facilities. First-class rooms are available for US$26 single and US$30 double. The newly named **Marble Mountain Hotel** (Tel: 23258), 60 rooms, has a few first-class rooms with airconditioning, refrigerator, and shared sitting rooms. The hotel has no restaurant, but they will provide room service. The best rooms rent for US$25. The hotel is at 5 Dong Da Street in the same area as the Thu Bon Hotel.

Nha Trang

The place to stay in Nha Trang is along the excellent beach that runs from near the central city to Cau Da, about six kilometers south. There are a number of hotels and guest houses along here.

The **Thang Loi Hotel** (Tel: 22241), 57 rooms, is a low-rise property one block back from the beachfront. It is well located within walking distance of the market and several restaurants. Rooms are pleasant, but a bit old-fashioned. However, each has airconditioning, TV, telephone, refrigerator, and bathroom with hot water. There are two restaurants, a barber, a small shop, and a nice outdoor eating and relaxing area. Room prices range from US$25 to US$40 for two people. (Book with the hotel at 4 Pasteur Street, Nha Trang; Fax: 84-58-21905.)

The **Hai Yen Hotel** (Tel: 22828), 106 rooms, is the largest hotel in the city. The room that I had was not very special; but it was clean, the staff were helpful, and this hotel must have the most efficient laundry system in the country. The room was large and the bathroom had hot water, but there was no refrigerator, no TV, and no telephone. I could not complain about the cost of US$20. Other rooms are from US$26 to US$80 with better facilities. There is an excellent restaurant with live music every evening, a dancing hall for evening relaxing, and a tennis court. (Book with the hotel at 40 Tran Phu Boulevard, Nha Trang; Fax: 84-58-21902.)

The **Vien Dong Hotel** (Tel: 21606), 80 rooms, is directly behind the Hai Yen Hotel, and guests can share facilities. The first-class rooms have airconditioning and telephone but no refrigerator, while second-class rooms lose the telephone, and third-class rooms have no airconditioning. Costs vary from US$10 to US$30 for a double. There are six deluxe rooms, which are large suites with a balcony. These come fully equipped and have a price tag of US$60. There is a nice restaurant, a swimming pool (which was bright green when I was there), and twenty-four-hour room service. (Book with the hotel at 1 Tran Hung Dao Street, Nha Trang; Fax: 84-58-21912.)

The **44 Hotel** (Tel: 22445), 20 rooms, is an old mansion recently turned into a hotel. Before 1975, this was the headquarters of the army in Nha Trang. During the 1980s, it was used as a resort by Communist Party chiefs. Now it is open to the public. Rooms have airconditioners, refrigerators, fans, televisions, and telephones. Some rooms have nice views of the beach. There is a large restaurant and a small lounge. English speakers can be a bit hard to find. Room sizes vary considerably, and so do prices: US$20-40. (Book with the hotel at 44 Tran Phu Boulevard, Nha Trang.)

The **Maritime Hotel** (Trung Tam Thuong Mai Hang Hai II) (Tel: 21969) is a new hotel about five kilometers from the city center. This probably has the best rooms and facilities of any place in the city, but it is in an unfortunate location in the middle of nowhere—even access to the nice beach is tortuous. Rooms have airconditioners, refrigerators, televisions, and bathrooms with hot water. There is a nice restaurant, several meeting rooms, a disco, massage, and a swimming pool. Suites are US$60, normal rooms US$35, and rooms without refrigerators US$25. (Book with the hotel at 34 Tran Phu Boulevard, Nha Trang.)

The **Cau Da Villas Hotel** (Tel: 22449), 24 rooms, is potentially a delightful place, but the rooms are poorly maintained. This was the property of Emperor Bao Dai and was built in the 1920s. It was used by high-ranking South Vietnamese government people in the sixties and early seventies, and by Communist officials in the eighties. The five villas are built on three rocky hills, and they have great views over the South China Sea. Rooms have high ceilings, huge bathrooms, and have now been airconditioned.

Unfortunately, they badly need a coat of paint and some refurbishing. Rooms cost from US$25 to US$35. There is a seafood restaurant. Because the buildings are of historic importance, a 3,000d entry fee is charged at the gate. This is refunded for house guests. (Book with the hotel at Tu Do Street, Cau Da, Nha Trang; Fax: 84-58-21906.)

Dalat

The two most stylish hotels in Dalat were both closed in the second half of 1994. Both were under renovation and when they reopen, it is expected that they will be the best places to stay in the city. The **Palace Hotel** (Tel: 2203), about 40 rooms, is a grand old place. It has nice grounds, extensive views, and large public areas. It has the potential of becoming a grand hotel in the European manner. I will look forward to seeing it when it reopens. The **Dalat Hotel** (Tel: 2363), about 65 rooms, is almost as old. When I saw it in 1992, it was in a poor state of repair and could not be recommended. I hope the renovation recreates its former glory. There are large public areas that could be very attractive. Rooms are large and have high ceilings and lovely timber shutters. The Palace is at 2 Tran Phu Street, and the Dalat Hotel is close by at 7 Tran Phu Street. Both properties should be open in 1995.

The most expensive rooms currently available in Dalat are at the **Hotel Dinh II** (Tel: 2092), which has been established within the former governor general's residence. When I say that rooms are not airconditioned and have no refrigerator nor telephone, you will get the wrong idea. Actually they are quite impressive—very large, nice bathrooms, polished floors, big windows, and good quality furnishings. Suites with a dining room and balcony rent for US$50 and ordinary rooms for US$40. Ideally, you need your own transportation if you are staying here. (Book with the hotel at 2 Tran Hung Dao Street, Dalat.)

In this same area, there are a group of villas that are marketed together under the name **Khu Biet Thu Tran Hung Dao** (Tel: 2203). There are twenty rooms among the seven villas at prices ranging from US$18 to US$35—including breakfast. Some are airconditioned, most have private bathrooms, and some have dining rooms and lounge areas. There is an attractive restaurant on the ground floor of the central villa. (Book by writing to 25 Tran Hung Dao Street, Dalat.)

On my recent visit, I spent a night at the **Hotel Trixaco** (Tel: 2789), close to the center of the city, overlooking Lake Xuan Huong. This small, friendly establishment only has seven rooms, and you share the lounge room with the owner and his family. It is a lovely atmosphere. Rooms vary considerably, so you should look at the rooms before you agree to stay. I had a large upstairs corner room with a delightful view of the lake. It cost US$22. The hotel runs a restaurant on the lakeshore, just across the road. (Book by writing to 7 Nguyen Thai Hoc Street, Dalat.)

The **Minh Tam Hotel** (Tel: 2447), 20 rooms, is a nice hotel set in quite outstanding gardens out on the edge of town. This is not the place to be if you want to party or spend every waking hour sightseeing—it is too far to walk to the city and transportation facilities are not great. There is a nice restaurant and excellent views across the valley. Big rooms with TV, telephone, and bathroom with hot water are available for US$45. Smaller rooms without TV are US$30. There are a few rooms with three beds for US$25. (Book with the hotel at 20 Khe Sanh Street.)

The **Hai Son Hotel** (Tel: 2379), 62 rooms, is centrally placed close to the market. Externally, the hotel looks impressive, and inside the public areas are large and often full of people. However, to me the rooms are a disappointment. The three special-class rooms have plenty of space and good facilities; but in my opinion, the other rooms are not a great value for money. There is a restaurant, dancing hall, coffee shop, handicraft shop, hairdresser, and tour services. These are all fine. If you have come to Dalat for shopping and nightlife, this could be the place to stay. (Book with the hotel at 01 Nguyen Thi Minh Khai Street, Dalat; Fax: 84-92889.)

Then there is the **Duy Tan Hotel** (Tel: 2216), 26 rooms, in a low-rise building of little interest. I have never stayed here, so I know little about the facilities and service. First-class rooms start at around US$20. Second-class are US$15.

BUDGET ACCOMMODATIONS

Danang

The **Danang Hotel** (Tel: 21986), 80 rooms, is the best budget hotel in the city that will accept foreigners. Airconditioned rooms with refrigerator and hot and cold water rent for US$12 for double and US$10 single. The rooms are fair, and the hotel has a restaurant, dancing hall, massage, tourist shop, hairdresser, bar, and tours desk. It is located a long way from most places of interest in the city, but cyclos are available outside the hotel all day. Rooms with no airconditioning and no hot water are only US$7. The hotel is at 3 Dong Da Street.

The **Marble Mountain Hotel** (Tel: 23258), 68 rooms, is next to the Danang Hotel. All rooms are airconditioned and have hot and cold water. The hotel has no elevator and has trouble filling its fifth-floor rooms, so it offers these at US$8 a night.

Immediately next door is the **Huu Nghi or Dong Da Hotel** (Tel: 22563). This has some airconditioned rooms at US$12 and fanned rooms which get cheaper the higher you go. The fifth floor rents for US$5. There is a reasonable restaurant.

I have been told about the **Hai Van Hotel** (Tel: 21300), 45 rooms, but have never seen it myself. Rooms with airconditioning go for around US$9. The hotel is in an area north of the central city at 2 Nguyen Thi Minh Khai Street.

The city has several low-cost places close to both the railway station and the intercity bus station. All are reluctant to take foreigners; but if you insist, you may be allowed to stay. Most have mats on the floor rather than beds.

Nha Trang

The central city hotels are your best bet. The most upscale of these is the **Nha Trang Hotel** (Tel: 22347), 75 rooms. It has a restaurant, and most rooms have hot and cold water. The concrete medium-rise building is at 133 Thong Nhat Street. Budget rooms with fan cost from US$8.

The **Thong Nhat Hotel** (Tel: 22966) is on the beachfront at 18 Tran Phu Boulevard and seems to be an acceptable place. Fanned rooms are US$10. The **Hai Duong Bungalows** (Tel: 21150), on Tran Phu Boulevard are rather dilapidated but this is a lovely location with direct beach access. There is a restaurant and massage facility here. Bungalows cost around US$10 a night.

The **Khach San 58 Tran Phu** (Tel: 22997), 35 rooms, is another place worth trying. It is set back from Tran Phu Boulevard, so it is fairly quiet, and the beach here is wide and clean. I had a problem finding someone who spoke English, but it appears that airconditioned rooms cost US$10 and non-airconditioned rooms are US$5.

There are dormitory accommodations at the railway station and at the Lien Tinh Bus Station, but be warned that they are very basic and you may not be allowed to stay.

Dalat

There are many well-priced hotels, guest houses, youth hostels, and dormitories in Dalat that cater to the local market. Some have hot water and clean rooms and would be quite suitable for budgeting international visitors. There is some reluctance, however, by some of these places to accept foreigners. I believe you will have no problem with those listed below, so this would be the place to start.

The **Anh Dao Hotel** (Tel: 2384), 12 rooms, is up the steps from the market and the Hai Son Hotel, on Hoa Binh Square. The hotel has gone up-market and room prices now start at around US$20. The **Ngoc Lan Hotel** (Tel: 2136) is in a convenient location overlooking the bus station and the lake. Doubles are around US$10 but the rooms are in fairly poor condition. Its address is 42 Nguyen Chi Thanh Street. The **Thuy Tien Hotel** (Tel:

2444) has spacious rooms for around US$15. It is on 3-2 Street near Hoa Binh Square. The **Phu Hoa Hotel** (Tel: 2194) is probably better value. The building is old and hot water may be doubtful but singles are US$5 and doubles US$10. The address is 16 Tang Bat Ho Street, close to downtown. Away from the central area a bit, the **Mimosa Hotel** (Tel: 2656) at 170 Phan Dinh Street, has become a popular backpacker place. Rooms start at US$6.

The **Doi Cu Hotel** (Tel: 2517), 32 rooms, is a nice place a little out of town. It is run by the Youth Tourist Center and specializes in comfortable accommodations for young people. Foreigners are charged US$12 for a nice room. There is a restaurant that serves Vietnamese food. The address is 11A Dinh Tien Hoang Street. It is alongside the old golf course.

Pensee 3 Minihotel on 3-4 Street (the road to Saigon) is a homey place with acceptable rooms for around US$8. Its sister at No. 7, just down the street, is not as good.

5. Dining and Restaurants

Both Danang and Nha Trang are noted for their excellent seafood. Both cities have restaurants that specialize in fish, prawns, and lobster. Dalat, on the other hand, has by far the best fresh fruit and vegetables in Vietnam. Because of its elevation, it can grow temperate plants, so strawberries, black currants, peaches, plums, apples, and cherries are all available here in season. The surrounding hills grow peas, beans, carrots, tomatoes, lettuce, potatoes, and squash. You may be interested to try *thanh long* when you are in Nha Trang. This fruit, which is as large as a small pineapple, tastes a bit like a kiwi fruit.

Danang

A number of restaurants that are worth trying are along Tran Phu Street. **Restaurant 72,** at 72 Tran Phu Street, has Chinese, Vietnamese, and Western dishes. It is a friendly place with reasonable prices. Try the Rocket Shrimps—large spring rolls made from shrimp. At 8,000d, they are a good value. All the food that I have had here has been good. Dinner and drinks for two will cost around 40,000d. You can eat in an airconditioned or non-airconditioned room.

A good alternative is the **Tu Do Restaurant** (Tel: 22039) at 180 Tran Phu. The food here is good but prices have climbed as it has developed somewhat of a reputation. The service is friendly, and you will be invited to make a comment in the visitors book. If the weather is nice, I suggest you dine in the open-air courtyard out back.

There are several popular Vietnamese eateries along Tran Phu Street as well. Those at No. 174, No. 190, and No. 194 are three of the best. The **Thanh**

Huong Restaurant at the corner of Hung Vuong Street is also adequate.

The **Thanh Lieh Restaurant**, at 42 Bach Dang Street across from the river, has an extensive menu in Vietnamese and English. It attracts a wide clientele, including many government officials and visiting business people. In the same area, the **Restaurant Mien Trung** is somewhat down-market but the staff is friendly.

Nha Trang Restaurants

There are several good restaurants between the market and the beach. **Thanh Lich Restaurant**, at 8 Phan Boi Chau Street, is one of the nicest. The food is good, the restaurant is clean, and the service is friendly. The **Lac Canh Restaurant** is just around the corner at 11 Hang Ca Street. Both of these places have good fresh seafood as well as other dishes. One block away is the restaurant at **33 Le Loi Street**. It is slightly down-market; but it is clean, the food is good, and it is popular with the locals. The same can be said for **Phuong Cau Restaurant** (Tel: 22752) at 10 Phuong Cau Street. The **Thay Trang Restaurant** at 9A Le Loi Street has good seafood.

Farther west in the downtown area, the **Binh Minh Restaurant** has been serving up its Vietnamese specialties for around forty years at 64 Hoang Van Thu Street. Obviously it is doing something right. In contrast, the **Ngoe Sang Restaurant** (Tel: 21370), at 54 Yersin Street, is relatively new. It has airconditioning, music, and good food and is one of the more upscale restaurants in the city. I would like to mention the small Vietnamese restaurant on Yersin Street near Hai Ba Trung Street. There is nothing particularly distinguishing about the food, but the restaurant is bright and clean, and the owners have gone to some trouble to provide a nice decor. You can get a meal for two for under US$2.

Along the beachfront, the restaurants in the **Thang Loi Hotel**, the **Hai Yen Hotel**, and the **Vien Dong Hotel** are recommended. I particularly commend the Hai Yen because it has some excellent musicians from around 6:30 P.M. to 8 P.M. The restaurant at **26 Tran Phu Boulevard** is fair. Farther out, the restaurant at the **Seamen's Club** (Tel: 21195) is fine. The bar seems to be given a fair bit of prominence, and the place loves country and western music. There is no English menu. It is also worth trying dinner at **62 Tran Phu Restaurant**. There are several large **open-air cafes** on the beach side of Tran Phu Boulevard. These sell drinks and a few light snacks. They are very popular in the evenings. One of the best is the **Thuy Duong Restaurant**.

Dalat Restaurants

Dalat has many interesting restaurants. Some have huge wood fires at night that provide an unusual atmosphere in this tropical country. Three restaurants around Lake Xuan Huong are particularly appealing. **Thuy Ta Restaurant** (Tel: 2268) is surrounded on three sides by water, and there are lovely views of the lake shoreline. It opens at 6 A.M., so it is a great place for breakfast. Lunch is also popular, and the food is quite reasonable.

The **Thanh Thuy Restaurant** (Tel: 2262) is across the lake at 4 Nguyen Thai Hoc Street, immediately below the Trixaco Hotel. This is a large place where you can eat either inside or on a patio along the shore. On some evenings, they have dancing here. It is a popular and well-known spot. The **Xuan Huong Restaurant** (Tel: 2317) is within the Xuan Huong Mini Hotel. This is a lovely spot at 4 Tran Quoc Toan Street with a great view over the lake.

The other area with several restaurants is the town center. **La Tulipe Rouge Restaurant** (Tel: 2394) is at 1 Nguyen Thi Minh, between the market and the Hai Son Hotel. It is open all day and offers Vietnamese, Chinese, and Western dishes. Up the stairs and two blocks north, at 8 Khu Hoa Binh, the **Shanghai Restaurant** obviously has Chinese food; but there are also some Vietnamese and Western dishes on the menu. This is one of the few places that stays open after about 8:30 P.M.

The **Long Hua Restaurant** on Duy Tan Street across from the Thuy Tien Hotel is a popular foreign travelers' hangout. For the ultimate 1960's experience, try the **Stop and Go Cafe**, a coffee house lost in time.

6. Sightseeing

Danang city has one attraction that nobody should miss. The city's **Cham Museum**, which was established in 1915 and expanded in 1935, has the finest collection of Cham civilization remains in the world. There are over three hundred artifacts dating from the seventh to fifteenth centuries. The material comes from throughout the kingdom of Champa and is displayed by area. There are rooms called My Son, Thap Nam (now Binh Dinh), Dong Duong (Indrapura), and so on. Many of the sandstone carvings are marvelous, but you get more from them if you buy the guidebook called "Museum of Cham Sculpture" which is available at the entrance. There are two clear periods: before the tenth century, when the art and carvings showed Malay and Indonesian influences, and afterwards, as the region came under Khmer influence. The museum is located where Tran Phu Street and Bach Dang Street merge, about a kilometer south of the central city. The entrance fee in late 1994 was 10,000d.

The **Tam Dao Pagoda** is not far away at 253 Phan Chu Trinh Street. The pagoda was built in the 1950s and is interesting for its five-tiered tower that is a landmark in the area. The older **Pho Da Pagoda** is a little farther south. Possibly the most interesting temple is the **Caodai Temple** on Hai Phong

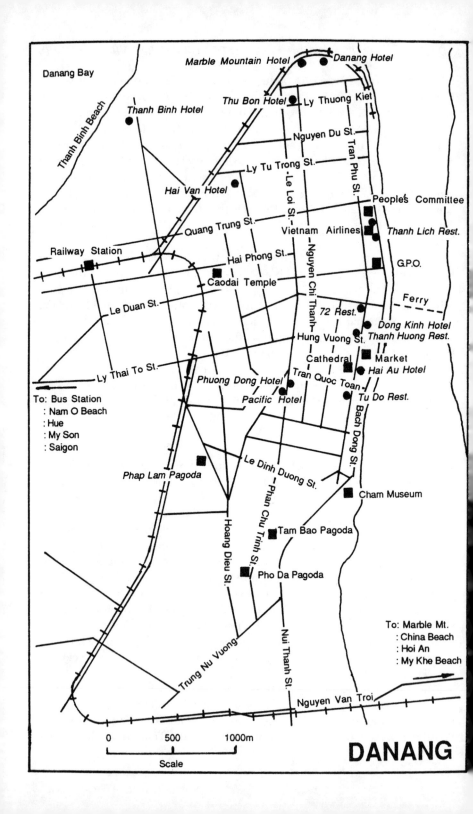

Street, a few blocks from the railway station. (I give some details on this religion in the Saigon sightseeing section.) If you are not planning to visit Tay Niah, you should visit here. **Danang Cathedral** is a nice French-style building on Tran Phu Street. It was built in 1923 and is still very active.

Two of Danang's markets are worth a visit. The **Con Market** is the largest. It is on Ly Thai To Street, near the railway line. If you travel east, you will reach the **Han Market** on the river at the other end of the central city.

There are some excellent beaches in the Danang area. **Thanh Binh Beach**, two kilometers to the northwest of the city, is not one of them. This is the nearest beach to the city and it is often crowded with people, but it is dirty and the water is often polluted. There is a hotel here—the **Nha Nghi Mat Thanh Binh**—if you simply must stay near a beach. **My Khe Beach** is much better. This is about six kilometers from the central city. There is a ferry from a wharf one block north of the Han Market, and you can get a bus from the other side to My Khe. The beach is reasonable, but is not ideal for swimming because there is often a dangerous current.

Nam O Beach is about fifteen kilometers northwest of the city. You see this from the train and bus when you travel south from Hue. There is some nice sand, but because this is on the bay rather than directly facing the South China Sea, there is less water movement and there is sometimes some pollution. Nevertheless, it is a nice spot for a walk and a good place to see some village life. There are some huge fishing nets and some interesting boats.

The best beach in the area is undoubtedly **China Beach**. This has become well known in the West due to the TV series of the same name which told about life during the Vietnam War when this was a rest-and-relaxation center for U.S. troops. The beach is about fourteen kilometers south of Danang. It has a large hotel and restaurants, shelters, and beach chairs and umbrellas on the sand. Foreigners must pay an entrance fee of a few thousand dong to enter. The **China Beach Hotel** (Tel: 36216), 96 rooms, provides reasonable lodging. A regular room has airconditioning, telephone, and a bathroom with hot and cold water. It costs US$34. Special rooms are huge with a lounge suites and refrigerators in addition to the other facilities. These cost US$48. There are three restaurants, a conference hall, tennis courts, and a large massage facility. Local buses operate from Danang to China Beach.

About two kilometers inland from the beach are the **Marble Mountains**. These are actually five small hills made of marble that were actually islands at one time. Each has been given the name of one of the five basic elements of Chinese philosophy: Moc Son (wood), Tho Son (earth), Hoa Son (fire), Thuy Son (water), and Kim Son (gold). The mountains were sacred to the Chams who ruled this area for over one thousand years, and later to the Vietnamese. Many of the caves within the mountains have Hindu, and now Buddhist shrines in them. The caves were used by the Viet Cong during the Vietnam War and were subsequently subject to bombing raids. Many of the temples were damaged, and some of the caves had holes blown in them.

There is a reasonably easy-to-follow circuit around Thuy Son which takes you to a number of the caves and provides good views over the other hills and across to China Beach. The main entrance is up a staircase from Non Nuoc village. If necessary, you can get a guide from here for less than US$1. Don't miss **Van Thong Cave** with its soaring roof, or **Gio Cave** with its steep, narrow passages. The Marble Mountains are twelve kilometers south of Danang. At a point about a third of the way to the mountains, you pass the remains of a huge American military base where concrete aircraft barricades and roadways are still visible.

One of the most interesting places in this region is **Hoi An**. This riverside town, thirty kilometers south of Danang, was a contemporary of Malacca in Malaysia and Macau in China. In its heyday, it was a major international port. Excavations in the area indicate that Hoi An was populated at least 2,200 years ago, but it was the Chams who developed the port. From the third century, when this region was the center of the Champa kingdom, Hoi An had contact with Persian, Arab, Indian, and Chinese traders. By the fifteenth century, it had become a major provisioning stop; and traders from China, Japan, Portugal, Spain, Holland, England, the Philippines and elsewhere came to Hoi An during the next four hundred years.

This was the first place in Vietnam to know Christianity, and it was the first Chinese settlement in southern Vietnam. The town was almost totally destroyed during the 1770s at the time of the Tay Son Rebellion, but it was rebuilt and continued to serve as an important port until about one hundred years ago, when the Thu Bon River began silting up. The town that you see today comes mainly from the nineteenth century, but there are some features from much earlier. It is probably the best place in Vietnam to experience living-history. Some parts of Hoi An look almost exactly as they must have looked 150 years ago. The best way to see Hoi An is to walk. If you have the time, just wander around looking in all directions. It is amazing what you will see. If you are limited to a few hours, check out the following suggestions.

The **Japanese Covered Bridge** is a highlight. This is several centuries old and is quite unique in these parts. The structure is very solid, but the decoration reflects the Japanese preference for restrained finishes. There is a small temple incorporated into the structure. The bridge is eighteen meters long. At the east end, there are a pair of monkey statues; and at the west end, there are statues of two dogs. It is said that the bridge was started in the year of the monkey and finished in the year of the dog. The bridge is at the western end of Tran Phu Street.

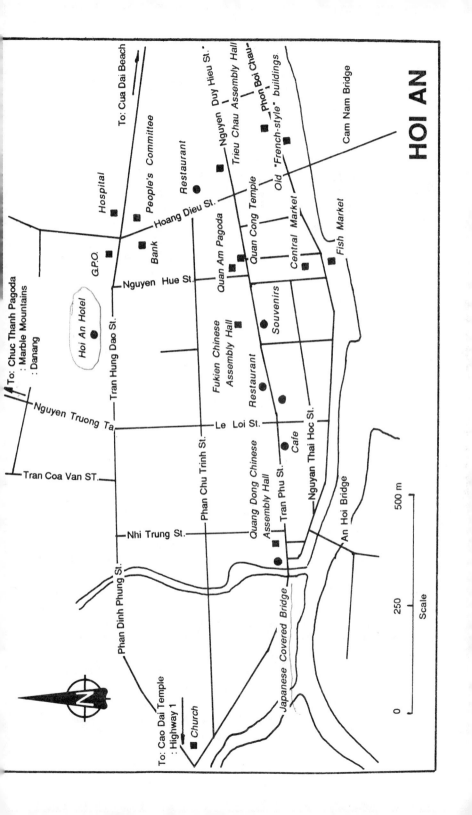

HOI AN

To: Cua Dai Beach

Hospital

People's Committee

Restaurant

Nguyen Duy Hieu St.

Trieu Chau Assembly Hall

Phon Boi Chau

Old "French-style" buildings

Cam Nam Bridge

Hoang Dieu St.

Quan Am Pagoda

Quan Cong Temple

Central Market

Fish Market

Bank

G.P.O.

Nguyen Hue St.

To: Chuc Thanh Pagoda
: Marble Mountains
: Danang

Hoi An Hotel

Tran Hung Dao St.

Souvenirs

Fukien Chinese Assembly Hall

Restaurant

Nguyen Truong Ta

Le Loi St.

Nguyen Thai Hoc St.

Cafe

Tran Coa Van ST.

Phan Chu Trinh St.

Quang Dong Chinese Assembly Hall

Tran Phu St.

An Hoi Bridge

Nhi Trung St.

Phan Dinh Phung St.

Japanese Covered Bridge

To: Cao Dai Temple
: Highway 1

Church

500 m

250

Scale

0

N

There are a series of temples and Chinese assembly halls along Tran Phu Street that shouldn't be missed. From east to west they are the **Trieu Chau Assembly Hall**, which was built more than two hundred years ago and contains some wonderful carving on the temple beams and walls; the **Hai Nam Assembly Hall**, which is only 110 years old, but has a particularly fine elaborate dais; the **Quan Cong Temple**, which was originally formed in 1653 and is particularly interesting because of its statuary; the large **Fukien Chinese Assembly Hall**, which has been transformed into a temple for the worship of the goddess of the sea, Thien Hau; and the spectacular **Quang Dong Assembly Hall**, which is also for the worship of Kuan Kung. The restaurant at Number 2 is a good place to try the local cao lau, a mixture of flat noodles, croutons, bean sprouts, and sliced pork. Reader Barbara Luksch writes to say that the **Cafe des Amis** at 52 Bach Dang has excellent vegetarian food.

The other two streets that should not be missed are Nguyen Thai Hoc Street and Phon Boi Chau Street. Nguyen Thai Hoc Street has some wonderful examples of Chinese-style residences. Some have been well preserved, and a couple have been restored. You can see Chinese, Japanese, and Vietnamese influences in the architecture. Some of these places are open for a small fee. In contrast, the houses on Phon Boi Chau Street are predominantly buildings that could have come from nineteenth-century provincial France. Many are columned, and they present some wonderful photographic opportunities.

The **Hoi An Market** is a good place to explore. I particularly recommend that you go out on the wharf and look at the fish market and the women in their fishing boats as they come and go. This is a place of great activity, and if you go quietly you can watch the action without causing any problems. You can catch a boat from here to **Cam Kim Island** to see some of the boat builders who are still at work here. Many of the wood carvings in Hoi An came from this island.

The **Hoi An Hotel** (Tel: 373), 16 rooms, at 6 Tran Hung Dao Street, is the place to stay if you plan a longer visit to Hoi An. Rooms with fans are available for US$10 and airconditioned rooms cost US$15-18. There is quite a reasonable restaurant and nice shady grounds. Staying here allows you time to visit **Chuc Thanh Pagoda**, which is Hoi An's oldest. It was founded in 1454. The building doesn't date from that time, but some of the ritual items do. The pagoda is almost one kilometer directly north of the hotel. You have to walk the last half kilometer. While you are here, you should also go a four hundred meters farther to see the **Phuoc Lam Pagoda**, which was founded in the mid-seventeenth century. A final suggestion is to go to **Cua Dai Beach**, about five kilometers east of Hoi An. There are kiosks that sell snacks and drinks. Cham Island is offshore.

One legacy of the French that Vietnam will value in the future is the hill resorts that were established to escape the coastal heat. In the Danang area, **Ba Na** was where the French used to go. The center is along the crest of Mount Ba Da (1460 meters), about forty-five kilometers west of the city. The road to Ba Na needs plenty of attention and there is currently nowhere to stay, but the views are quite spectacular and the air is fresh and cool. There are mountain paths that lead to various view points, waterfalls, and so on. I predict that this will again be a popular place to stay in the future.

Back in Danang, take Highway 1 and head south. It is a long 970 kilometers to Saigon, but there is much to see on the way. Approximately sixty kilometers from Danang, you can see the most important Champa civilization sites in Vietnam. They have not yet become great tourist attractions, so you may have trouble finding them. If you have your own transportation, you turn right off the highway at a point thirty-three kilometers south of Danang. This is two kilometers past the Thu Bon River bridge. The first capital of Champa (fourth to eighth centuries) was seven kilometers along this road. Unfortunately, nothing remains of **Simhapura** other than some vestiges of its earthen ramparts. You can best see these from the church on the top of Buu Chau Hill in Tra Kieu town. This was once the site of a Cham tower. Some artifacts from Simhapura can be seen in the Cham Museum in Danang, and there are some others in the Catholic church in the center of Tra Kieu.

You need to travel twenty more kilometers to reach the vicinity of **My Son**. This was the most important Cham religious center in Vietnam, and it is often spoken of in the same terms as the more well-known royal cities of Angkor (Cambodia), Ayuthaya (Thailand), Borobudur (Indonesia), and Pagan (Myanmar). The site was developed over a period of nine hundred years—far longer than any other southeast Asian center. Anyone expecting a grand city like Angkor, however, will be disappointed. At its prime, there were about a dozen sanctuaries totaling more than seventy buildings placed haphazardly along a small river. Today, about twenty of these buildings remain in various states of repair. Some restoration has taken place, but there are few buildings that are anywhere near complete.

The main area of interest at My Son has been labeled "Group B" and "Group C" by archaeologists. This consists of two square temple enclosures standing side by side. The main sanctuary within each temple was destroyed, but some of the smaller buildings are reasonably intact. Within Temple B, building "B5" in the southeast corner is an imposing pavilion with a flaring roof and superb decorations on the inside walls; and "B3" in the southwest corner and "B6" in the northeast corner are both well preserved and worthy of a visit.

My Son was abandoned for four hundred years, until archaeologists started cleaning the site about one hundred years ago. At that time, dozens of buildings were in good condition. Some restoration work was done, but after World War II things again went into decline. The year 1969 was catastrophic for the site as the Americans carpet-bombed and shelled everything in an attempt to dislodge Viet Cong guerrillas. Now, once again, restoration is underway and it is hoped that this can be continued so this can become a major tourist attraction for the south-central region. There is a charge (5,000d in late 1994) to enter the site, and this is supposed to be used for restoration and maintenance. At present there is no road connection to the site, so a visit here involves a walk of about four kilometers. There is a small snack bar for drinks and noodles.

Farther south on Highway 1, about sixty-two kilometers from Danang, you can see three Cham towers enclosed by a wall at Chien Dang. Eight kilometers farther on, there are a group of three towers about five hundred meters from the road on the right side. At Chu Lai, the highway parallels the remains of a huge American base. Buildings and concrete revetments can still be seen.

A few kilometers north of Quang Ngai, there is a road to the east which goes to the district of **Son My**. This was the location of the tragic My Lai Massacre in which hundreds of civilians were killed by American soldiers in a search-and-destroy operation that occurred in 1968. The area was known as a Viet Cong stronghold, but at no time did the troops come under fire or encounter any resistance. Groups of civilians were rounded up and shot, fleeing people were machine-gunned, and wounded people were summarily shot. It was an inglorious exercise that was initially covered up by the military command, but later led to several investigations. There is a memorial in a park where a village once stood. A few kilometers east of here, **Bien Khe Ky Beach** is a long, white sand beach lined with casuarina trees.

Quang Ngai is the major center in these parts. It is the capital of Quang Ngai Province and is built on the south bank of the Tra Khue River. You can almost go through the city without stopping because there is little of interest. A few kilometers south are the remains of the large Cham temple of **Chanh Lo**.

Sixty kilometers south of Quang Ngai, the little seaside town of **Sa Huynh** provides a nice stopping point. The semicircular beach bordered by coconut palms is one of the nicest around. Ninety kilometers farther on is the former Cham capital of **Vijaya** (called Cha Ban by the Vietnamese). This was the Chams' power base for nearly five hundred years, until 1471 when the city was captured by the Vietnamese and the Cham civilization was destroyed. The city was built within a rectangular wall five thousand meters long. The brass tower stands on a small hill in the center of the complex. The city was attacked and plundered repeatedly by the Vietnamese and the Khmers. In return, the Chams occupied Angkor for several years in the twelfth century.

The site today is somewhat disappointing. You have to make a concerted effort to find areas of interest, and even then only ruins remain in many cases. You will find some examples of paved roads and small bridges. In the surrounding countryside, there are several towers and ruins. Probably the most interesting are the **Duong Long** towers, about five kilometers southeast of Vijaya. These show marked Khmer influence and were probably built in the thirteenth century.

The square citadel of **Binh Dinh** was built much later by the Nguyen Lords. This was attacked and occupied in the eighteenth century by the Tay Son, and they also occupied the site of Vijaya in 1776. The Tay Son renamed the city Hoang De and rebuilt and enlarged the citadel. In 1799, it was captured by Nguyen Anh, then it was abandoned in 1813 and the site has been pillaged for building material since then.

Quy Nhon, a city of around 200,000 people, is the capital of Binh Dinh Province and a significant seaport. There is little of great interest here, but it does provide a convenient stopping point between Danang and Nha Trang. The city is ten kilometers off Highway 1, right on the coast. There is a fair beach that is shaded by coconut palms. There are two Cham towers on the road from the highway toward town, about two kilometers before you reach the central area. The **Dong Phuong Hotel** (Tel: 2915), 20 rooms at 39 Mai Xuan Thuong Street, not far from the stadium, is a reasonable and cheap place to stay. The **Olympic Hotel** (Tel: 2375) nearby is also fine. The **Quy Nhon Tourist Hotel** (Tel: 2401), 47 rooms, at the Municipal Beach is supposed to be the best place in town, but it is poorly maintained and highly priced.

Quy Nhon is 240 kilometers from Nha Trang. The road more or less parallels the coast for most of the way, but there are few great attractions. There are some good beaches and the **Cu Mong Pass** area is interesting and provides some good views. **Song Cau** and **Dai Lanh** are suitable places to stop. Dai Lanh beach is attractive, and there are a few hotels here for those with plenty of time to explore the area. **Ba Ho Falls** are twenty kilometers north of Nha Trang and a good place for a picnic. There are three falls and pools in an area of forest.

Nha Trang has become a popular tourist city due to its nice beaches and clear waters that are suitable for snorkeling and diving. Approaching from the north, **Hon Chong Beach** is a series of coconut-palm-fringed stretches of sand off to the left. They run south to the Hon Chong Promontory, which provides superb views of the mountains, the coast, and the islands. There are food and drink stalls, and the **Nha Nghi Hon Chong Hotel** (Tel: 22188) is here.

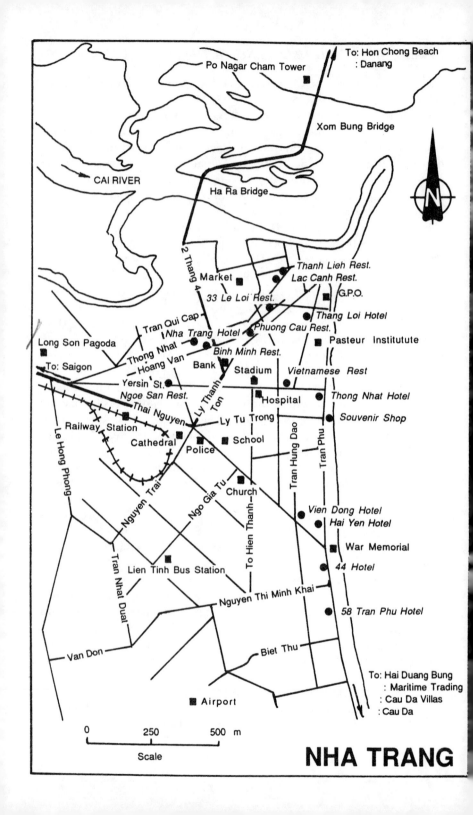

NHA TRANG

One of Nha Trang's major attractions is on the highway, about two kilometers north of the city. The **Po Najar Cham Towers** were built between the seventh and twelfth centuries on a terrace at the top of a small hill on the north bank of the Cai River. The temples have been kept by the Vietnamese as a place of worship, and the towers that remain have suffered relatively little damage over time.

There were once seven or eight towers in this complex, but today only four remain. All the towers face east (toward the highway), and in front of them is the remains of a pillared meditation gallery which once led to a staircase to a platform in front of the north tower. The largest tower is the north tower, built in 817 A.D. and a superb example of Cham architecture. It has a terraced pyramidal roof, a vaulted interior, and some wonderful carvings and inscriptions. There is a gong and drum in the antechamber, and a black stone statue of the goddess Ulma is in the main chamber.

The central tower is less ornate and not so well constructed. It is believed that this was built in the twelfth century. Inside is a linga of Kauthara. There is also a linga in the small south tower. The northwest tower is richly ornamented and quite exquisite. There is a small museum near the north tower and a small souvenir stall near the south tower. Don't miss this place. It is most interesting.

In the city itself, the **Long Son Pagoda** is worth visiting. It is located at 23 Thang 10 Street, about half a kilometer west of the railway station. The modern building is decorated with dragons covered with glass and ceramic tile. If you visit around 10:30 A.M., you can see the monks participating in their luncheon ceremony. On the top of the hill behind the pagoda is a huge, white Buddha that was built in 1963. You can reach it by climbing 150 stone steps up the hill. There are excellent views over Nha Trang from the top.

Nha Trang Cathedral is the main Christian church in the city. It was built in French Gothic style in 1930. Masses are held twice daily. The cathedral is on Thai Nguyen Street, near the railway station. The **Pasteur Institute** was founded by Dr. Alexandre Yersin, a Frenchman much admired by the Vietnamese. He came to Vietnam in 1889, after working under Louis Pasteur in Paris, and spent the next four years traveling and researching through the central highlands. He was the man who recommended the establishment of Dalat. He established the institute in 1895 to carry out research and practical hygiene programs. The institute continues that work today. Dr. Yersin's library and office are now a museum which is well worth seeing. It is on Tran Phu Boulevard, north of Yersin Street.

The **Oceanographic Institute** (Tel: 22536) is another organization that has a museum open to the public. You can see thousands of dead specimens of sea life, and there is an aquarium which is home to various live marine plants and animals. The institute is six kilometers south of Nha Trang at Cau Da.

Mier Island can be reached from Cau Da by ferry or charter boat. The island has a fish farm where various species of fish and crustaceans are bred in large ponds. A cafe provides your food and drink needs.

Nha Trang's six kilometers of public beach are very attractive. Within the city, Tran Phu Boulevard is a divided road that is bordered by gardens on the beach side. There are palm trees, flowering shrubs, a paved walking path, three clusters of cafes which serve drinks and snacks, and a large souvenir shop. The sand is clean and the water is usually reasonably clear. As you proceed south, there are fewer people and the beach remains good.

The highway south from Nha Trang is interesting at first, but it varies greatly in condition. Some sections are good while others are appalling. When I last traveled along here, hundreds of laborers were hand digging a trench beside the road for tens of kilometers. There was no mechanical equipment to be seen. About fifty kilometers south of Nha Trang, **Cam Ranh Bay** has been developed into a major military facility. The Russians used this area early this century, the Japanese docked here during World War II, and the Americans built a huge port and repair facility here in the 1960s. The Russians returned in the 1980s, but at present it is not well utilized. There are some nice deserted beaches along here.

Traveling south, the country rapidly changes and becomes desert-like. This area is bypassed by the monsoons, leaving an inhospitable climate that is one of the most arid regions in the country. As you approach the twin centers of **Phan Rang** and **Thap Cham**, you will see that many of the houses have grape trellises reminiscent of the Mediterranean coast. Table grapes are produced here and sent to Saigon. This is where Highway 20 heads inland to Dalat and eventually on to Bao Loe and Saigon. There are a couple of hotels in Phan Rang, and the **Huu Nghi Hotel** (Tel: 74) is probably the best bet. The railway line goes through Thap Cham, which is about six kilometers northeast of Phan Rang.

By far, the most interesting sight here is the **Po Krong Garai Cham Towers**, which are on a hill about a kilometer north of Thap Cham. The four towers were built around 1300 and sit on a large brick terrace at the top of a cactus-covered granite hill. Inside the main sanctuary is a statue of a bull—a symbol of the agricultural value of the country. Farmers would come here to pray for a good crop. There is also a linga with a human face on it.

A short way inland from here is the former site of **Krong Laa**, a fortified town built by the Cham kings after the fall of Vijaya. It was the capital of the reduced Champa Kingdom throughout the sixteenth and seventeenth centuries. Today only a few brick ruins remain. You can see **Po Ro Me Tower**, however, on a hill about eight kilometers southwest of Phan Rang. This was one of the ritual sanctuaries that always encircled a Cham capital. With some effort you can get there by renting a vehicle from town.

There was an eighty-six-kilometer rail line from Thap Cham to Dalat. It operated from 1930 until about 1963, when it was closed after repeated Viet Cong attacks on the line. It would have been a spectacular trip. Some of the grades were extremely steep and required chains to pull the trains up the mountainside. Since 1964, the line has been stripped of some of its track, and other sections have become overgrown or washed away. Even though it would be a great tourist attraction, it is unlikely that the line will ever operate again. You see sections of the formation from Highway 20 as you travel to Dalat. Fortunately, a seven-kilometer section between Dalat and Trai Mat has been retained, and a daily trip is offered to tourists.

After crossing the coastal plain, you reach the town of **Ninh Son**. The central highlands tower ahead of you, and the water pipeline down the mountain to the power station dominates the scene. The road now starts a steep climb toward **Ngoan Muc Pass** (about 980 meters elevation). You pass under the water pipeline on two occasions, and you can see the concrete fortifications which housed armed guards in earlier times. From the top of the range, you can see the coast in the distance.

A bit farther on, you see **Danhim Lake** on the right of the highway. This was built in the 1960s by the Japanese as war reparation. Presently it is closed to the public. The road now climbs and winds through lovely country and pine plantations toward Dalat.

Dalat is a delight. It could be my favorite place in Vietnam. It is at an elevation of nearly fifteen hundred meters, so the climate is temperate. There are lakes, waterfalls, forests, and walking trails. This site for a hill resort was suggested by Dr. Alexandre Yersin, and the city was established in 1912. It quickly became popular with the French as a cool retreat, and many lovely villas were constructed. During the Vietnam War, Dalat was largely bypassed, and the city was taken over by the North Vietnamese in 1975 without a fight. The result of all this is that Dalat remains a European-looking hill town with a 1950s air about it.

The center of Dalat is the area surrounding the central market. **Xuan Huong Lake** is its southeastern extreme. The small area northwest of the market is a nice area in which to walk. So too is the western end of the lake. Paddle boats can be rented from a few locations, and there are places to sit and just relax.

Emperor Bao Dai's Summer Palace is something not to be missed. The

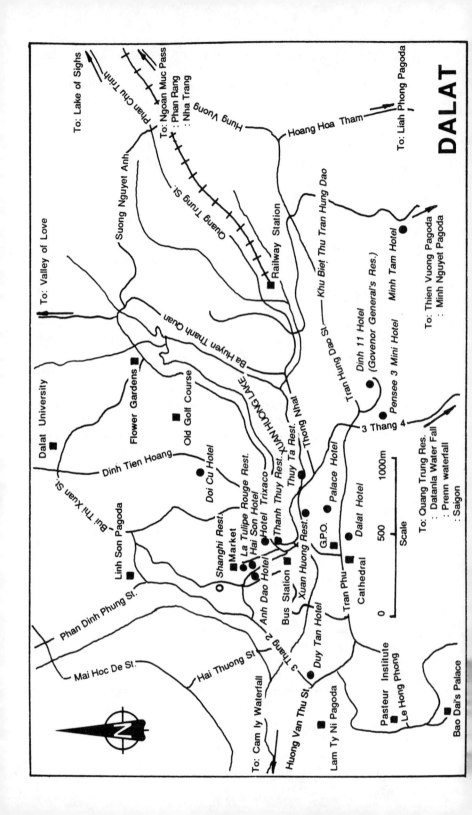

thirty-five-room villa has remained much as it was when Bao Dai last used it in the 1940s. This is very much a hands-on museum. You can sit in the emperor's chair behind his enormous desk. You can be photographed in the sunny garden room among hunting trophies and family memorabilia. Upstairs, you can visit the royal living quarters. The palace is open daily for a 6,000d entrance fee. It is off Trieu Viet Vuong Street, near the Pasteur Institute.

The **Cam Ly Falls** are along Huong Van Thu Street, about two kilometers from the central city. This area was developed as a tourist site when Dalat was established, and it has been popular ever since. The falls are about fifteen meters high, and the areas surrounding them have stuffed animals placed so tourists can be photographed with them and the falls as a backdrop. There are plenty of people to offer to take your photograph and several refreshment stalls.

The **Dalat Flower Gardens** (Tel: 2151) have been in existence for about thirty years. You reach here by driving along the north shore of Lake Xuan Huong. The gardens have a good display of temperate plants, and there are also several buildings used for orchid growing. There is an entrance fee and refreshments are available. You get the recorded music for free.

If you take the side road by the gardens, you will arrive at **Dalat University** (Tel: 2246). This was originally established as a Catholic university in 1957 by the older brother of President Ngo Dinh Diem. It was closed in 1975, but reopened as a state university two years later. Permission is needed to visit.

Dalat Cathedral was built during the 1930s in French style. There are stained glass windows and a forty-seven-meter spire. Masses are held twice daily. The building is on Tran Phu Street next to the Dalat Hotel.

Linh Son Pagoda is about a kilometer north of the town center on Phan Dinh Phung Street. It was founded in 1938 and is notable for its huge bell. Other pagodas that you could visit are the **Lam Ty Ni Pagoda** with its many gardens and interesting decorations, the **Thien Vuong Pagoda** on a hilltop in a pine plantation about five kilometers southeast of town, and the nearby **Minh Nguyet Pagoda**.

The **Valley of Love** is a popular spot about five kilometers north of central Dalat. There is a lake with paddle boats and canoes, and riding horses can be rented. Refreshments are available for sale. You reach here via Phu Dong Thien Vuong Street. The **Lake of Sighs** has similar facilities. This is northeast of the city, out Phan Chu Trinh Street.

When it is time to leave Dalat you can continue along Highway 20 to Saigon. This is a 310-kilometer trip of great interest. Immediately south of Dalat, you wind down Prenn Pass through lovely pine forests. About five kilometers from town, there is a turn off to **Quang Trung Reservoir**, which is being developed as a tourist spot. There are some restaurants, some walking tracks, and boats for rent. It is only a few hundred meters farther along the highway to **Datania Falls**. The falls are deep in a rainforest, about five hundred meters from the highway. The **Prenn Falls** are another seven kilometers along the highway. This is an attractive fifteen-meter-high free fall. You can follow a path behind the falls to see the surrounding forest through the falling water. There is a small restaurant here.

Farther on, you can visit **Lien Khang Falls** at a point about thirty-five kilometers from Dalat, and the **Gougah Falls** about five kilometers thereafter. The area around here contains many tea plantations. **Di Linh** is the major settlement. It is eighty kilometers from Dalat. If you travel another fifty kilometers, you come to **Bao Loc**. There are tea factories and waterfalls to see, and a couple of hotels if you wish to stay. You are still 850 meters above sea level, so the weather is cooler than the coast, but it is not nearly as interesting or picturesque as Dalat.

7. Guided Tours

There are government agencies in Danang, Nha Trang, and Dalat that can arrange tours, guides, and vehicles within each area. They also claim to be able to organize nationwide tours, but I believe you would be better off dealing with Vietnam Tourism or Saigon Tourist if you want a comprehensive tour through the country.

In Danang, the **Quang Nam-Da Nang Tourist Company** (Tel: 21423) at 68 Bach Dang Street are the people to see (Fax: 84-51-22854). This organization has several hotels, restaurants, and entertainment centers in Danang and it operates day tours and rents cars and guides. They are happy to organize a two- or three-day tour to Hue, and this can be worthwhile if your time is limited.

In Nha Trang, **Khanh Hoa Tourism** (Tel: 22753) does exactly the same thing. It is located at 1 Tram Hung Dao Street (Fax: 84-58-21912). This organization has several hotels, a restaurant, a tourist car service, and it runs a guide and information center. One-day and extended tours are readily available, but they are usually organized for each individual or group.

The **Voiles Vietnam Scuba Diving Center** at Cau Da Village (Tel: 23966) has regular two-day cruises on board the sailing junk *Song Saigon*.

In Dalat, **Dalat Tourist**, also known as the **Lam Dong Tourist Company**, (Tel: 2125) at 12 Tran Phu Street can help with transportation and guides. It is a very active organization that is eager to help foreign visitors to come and enjoy the city. It has a Saigon office at 470 Ngo Gia Tu Street (Tel: 250-973) and a regular bus connection between Dalat and Saigon.

8. Culture

South-central Vietnam is a wonderful place to learn about Cham culture, but there are also opportunities to get a glimpse of some living cultures trying desperately to survive. Many minority groups live in the highland regions of south-central Vietnam. The French called these people *montagnards* (highlanders), while the Vietnamese often refer to them as *moi* (savages).

These people had no written languages and were divided into many clans. They lived mostly in tribal villages and had no organized political life. They practiced animist religions, sometimes accompanied by ritual sacrifices. Most engaged in slash-and-burn agriculture. For centuries, the highland areas were allowed a large degree of autonomy, as long as the tribes paid some sort of taxes and recognized Vietnamese sovereignty. This drastically changed during the Vietnam War. Many montagnards were recruited by both sides as fighters, and others were forced to move to "strategic hamlets" where they could be protected or watched. Many saw their traditional lands devastated by war and taken over by refugees or settlers from other areas.

This brutal wrecking of the entire social structure and ecological equilibrium of the various tribes is now leading to the disappearance of whole cultures. The present government is trying to integrate these people into mainstream Vietnamese culture by Vietnamizing their culture, language, and social pattern. There is little doubt that it will succeed such that most of these people will have disappeared by the twenty-first century. You will have to be quick to see what is left.

These days, you have to go to the more remote areas to see the life and culture of the highlands. In some villages, you will see the high-roofed men's houses and their accompanying longhouses. Buffalo sacrifices are still made in some places. There is a hill-tribe museum in Ban Ma Thuot, the capital of Dac Lac Province.

9. Sports

Water sports are by far the most popular sporting activities in this region. Both Danang and Nha Trang have excellent beaches within short distances of the cities. There is the opportunity to fish at many places along the coast, and a small scuba diving industry has started in both cities. In Nha Trang, the **Ship Chandler Company** (Tel: 21195), at 74 Tran Phu Boulevard, can organize a boat and diving equipment.

If you don't like swimming in the ocean, there are a few hotels with swimming pools. Unfortunately, they don't often look very inviting because the water is green or brown rather than clear. That's a fact of life in Vietnam.

A few hotels have tennis courts, but you may have to bring your own racket and balls. Danang, Nha Trang, and Dalat all have public facilities where visitors can play. The Dalat Golf Course has re-opened as an 18-hole layout after the expenditure of US$40 million.

10. Shopping

There seems to be little available here that is not available in the markets or shops of Saigon. It is difficult to compare prices, but I suspect there is little difference. Two possible exceptions are the sea shells and shell souvenirs that are available in Danang and Nha Trang. There are some in the markets, but you will also find them in shops, souvenir stalls along the beachfront, and in hotels. Also worth looking for are the handicrafts made by the highland hill-tribes. There are reed mats, bamboo items, and some woven cloth. You see a little of this in Dalat, but you will be better to try in some of the surrounding villages.

If weight is no problem, there are some excellent carvings in the shops at the Marble Mountains and at China Beach. I think that the better items are very highly priced and probably a mediocre value.

Film is readily available throughout the area and hour-processing is common. There are tailors in Danang and Nha Trang that are just as good as those in Saigon.

11. Entertainment and Nightlife

Cinemas, hotel discos, a few dancing restaurants, and massage parlors are about the extent of the nightlife throughout the region.

My experience is limited, but in **Danang** you could try the **dancing restaurant** between the Marble Mountain Hotel and the Danang Hotel or the one at the **Pacific Hotel**. The **Municipal Theater** on Hung Vuong Street occasionally has a visiting troupe in town. The **massage parlors** at the Hai Au Hotel and the Thu Bon Hotel (both run by Danang Tourist) seem to be very popular.

In **Nha Trang**, the **Hai Yen Hotel** has a popular dancing hall that operates a few nights each week. The **Ngoc Sang restaurant** is a good place to enjoy the music and atmosphere, and the **open-air cafe** on the beach near the end of Le Thanh Ton Street sometimes has a live band and a big crowd.

In **Dalat**, the **Hai Son Hotel** has a popular dancing hall with a live band. The **Youth Hostel** has a discotheque some nights, and the **Palace Hotel** and the **Dalat Hotel** (when they reopen) are likely to have dancing and music. Anyone walking beside the northern shore of the lake after about 8

P.M. will be offered company for the night. In the dim light, it is very hard to see exactly what you would get if you took up the offer.

12. The Address List

Danang

Airport—(Tel: 22094).
Bank—Foreign Trading, 104 Le Loi Street (Tel: 22110).
Bus Station—33 Dien Bien Phu Street (Tel: 21265).
Consulate of Laos—12 Tran Quy Cap Street (Tel: 22628).
Culture Information Service—74 Le Loi Street (Tel: 21203).
Customs Service—210 Bach Dang Street (Tel: 22869).
Dept for Entry/Exit—7 Tran Quy Cap (Tel: 22075).
Directory Assistance (telephone)—(Tel: 16).
Emergency Telephone Call—(Tel: 15).
Fire—(Tel: 21270).
Hospital—76 Hai Phong Street (Tel: 21118).
Long-distance/International Telephone—(Tel: 11).
People's Committee—31 Tran Phu Street (Tel: 21088).
Post Office—52 Bach Dant Street (Tel: 23881).
Railway Station—126 Hai Phong Street (Tel: 23810).
Tourist Information—68 Bach Dang Street (Tel: 21423).
Vietnam Airlines—35 Tran Phu Street (Tel: 21130).

Nha Trang

Airport—(Tel: 21147)
Bank—Foreign Trade, 17 Quang Trung Street (Tel: 21054).
Bus Station—Lien Trang, Ngo Gia Tu Street (Tel: 22192); Express, 46 Le Thanh Ton Street (Tel: 22397).
Hospital—Yersin Street (Tel: 22175).
Oceanographic Institute—Cau Da (Tel: 22536).
Post Office—2 Tran Phu Boulevard (Tel: 22442).
Railway Station—Thai Nguyen Street (Tel: 22113).
Tourist Information—1 Tran Hung Dao Street (Tel: 22753).
Vietnam Airlines—82 Tran Phu Street (Tel: 21147).

Dalat

Bus Station—(Tel: 2077).
Hill Tribe Museum—1 Me Mai Street, Buon Ma Thuot.
Post Office—14 Tran Phu Street (Tel: 2351).

Tourist Information—12 Tran Phu Street (Tel: 2246).
University—1 Phu Dong Thien Vuong Street (Tel: 2246).
Vietnam Airlines—5 Truong Cong Dinh Street (Tel: 0330).

Decoration on Royal Palace in Hue, Vietnam.

A small market town in Vietnam.

Vietnamese fishing ladies.

Halong Bay.

A small Vietnamese village with a water puppetry stage.

The main entrance to the Imperial Enclosure in Hue.

Cham Towers in south-central Vietnam.

Lao children.

A market outside Saigon.

Decoration is a feature of Lao architecture.

Bai Dua Beach in Vung Tau.

Luang Prabang peeks out from jungle greenery.

The amazing Wat Xieng Khwan (Buddha Park), south of Vientiane.

Khmer architecture at Angkor Thom.

Angkor Wat.

Museum Phnom Penh.

8

Ho Chi Minh City (Saigon) and the South

1. The General Picture

Ho Chi Minh City covers an area of about 2,000 square kilometers and has a population of over four million. It is a predominantly rural area of high population density. Its bustling, downtown heart is what the world knows as Saigon.

This is the commercial heart of Vietnam. Fifteen years of Communist rule dampened, but failed to extinguish the enthusiasm, dynamic spirit, and entrepreneurial ideas that have given this one city nearly a third of the country's manufacturing output and retail activity. This is a different world from Hanoi, and its people are determined to keep it that way.

Saigon streets are bustling and filled with motorcycles and pedestrians. Shops rub shoulders with restaurants, bookstalls, hotels, and markets. French and American architecture contrasts with Vietnamese, while international styles are finally making their appearance in this, the most outward-looking of all Indochina cities.

Central Saigon consists of an area between the Saigon River and Le Duan Boulevard, bounded roughly by Hai Ba Trung Street to the north, Ham Nghi Boulevard to the south, and Nam Ky Khoi Nghia Street to the west. Its central point is probably the Le Loi Boulevard-Nguyen Hue Boulevard intersection. This area contains almost all the major hotels, the best selection of restaurants, and the greatest shopping opportunities.

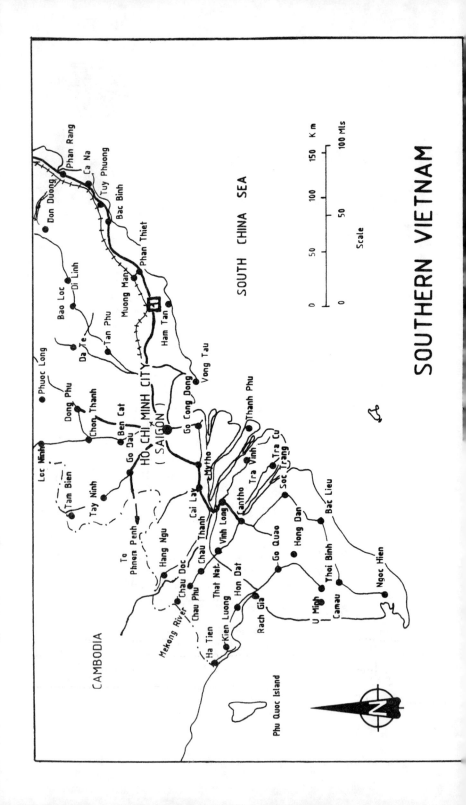

SOUTHERN VIETNAM

The other main area of interest is Cholon, several kilometers southwest of downtown Saigon. This was originally a Chinese town, built toward the end of the eighteenth century. Today it is a crazy mixture of shops, offices, warehouses, and houses crowded together in too little space. This is still the largest ethnic-Chinese community in Vietnam, but hundreds of thousands of Chinese have left here in the last twenty years due to government persecution, causing the area to lose much of its traditional Chinese character. It is still a good source of budget hotels and restaurants, but it is too far from downtown Saigon for my liking.

Sixty years ago, Saigon was the "Pearl of the Orient," with beautiful villas, wide tree-lined boulevards, and neat parks. It was a vibrant city with open-air cafes, a prominent social set, and string quartets playing under wide tamarind trees. In the 1960s, it took on aspects of an American city with bars, restaurants, and strip joints to entertain the visiting troops. In the late seventies and throughout the eighties, the city had a forlorn nature tinged with fear as the weight of an uncaring bureaucracy caused despondency. Now Saigon is changing again. It is trying to be a nineties city, but it is still largely within the confines of a sixties Communist straightjacket. It will be very interesting to see what the next five years bring.

2. Getting There

Ho Chi Minh City Airport (known as Tan Son Nhut Airport) is by far the largest and most important in the country. It is a major domestic terminal with connections to Hanoi, Ban Ma Thuot, Danang, Dalat, Haiphong, Hue, Nha Trang, Phu Quoc, Pleiku, Can Tho, and Quy Nhon. The airport is around seven kilometers from central Saigon. Most services are operated by **Vietnam Airlines**, but there are some services with **Pacific Airlines**.

International services are growing dramatically. Saigon is now linked to Hong Kong, Bangkok, Manila, Singapore, Kuala Lumpur, Guangzhou, Taipei, Kao Shung, Dubai, Paris, Seoul, Amsterdam, Frankfurt, Phnom Penh, Vientiane, Sydney, and Melbourne. Arrival at Tan Son Nhut airport will not present too many problems. If you arrive on a domestic flight, you will be bused or walked to the domestic terminal, where you will wait in the arrival hall for your baggage to be brought from the aircraft. You collect your bags, present the baggage tabs to the security checkers, then walk out into the public terminal. It is usually possible to find a taxi driver here and in 1994 meters were installed, so that avoids the problem of bargaining. If there are no taxis here, you will have to walk the one hundred meters to the international terminal to find one. There are no buses or cyclos at the

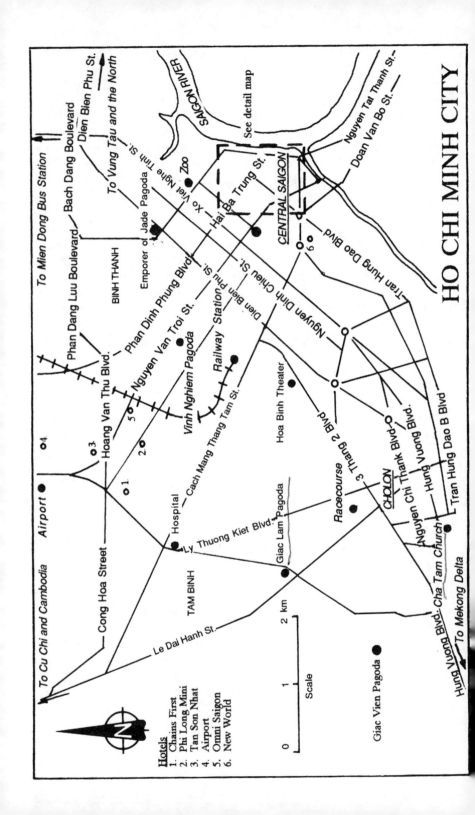

HO CHI MINH CITY

Hotels
1. Chains First
2. Phi Long Mini
3. Tan Son Nhat
4. Airport
5. Omni Saigon
6. New World

airport. You will have to walk the 0.8 kilometers to the airport gate if you wish to travel like this.

Arriving at the international terminal provides a few more difficulties with customs and entry/exit forms, but otherwise the procedure is similar. Leaving, however, is another matter. The departure side of the airport has almost a total lack of directions or English language signs, and the present procedure is complicated and unnecessarily difficult. Before you can enter the airport terminal, you must fill in your departing customs forms. These forms are obtained from an unmarked booth next to a small area marked post office. In theory, you can fill in these forms by yourself; but in practice, the people with the forms are extremely reluctant to give you one. Instead, they ask for your passport, entry/exit form, and a copy of your incoming customs form; then they fill the form in for you. You are then expected to pay US$1 per person. Don't argue—pay up. By now, you should be accustomed to this semi-official fleecing of visitors.

With forms in hand, you now proceed to the entry gate, and the official allows you to pass. Once inside, your first stop is customs. Here you present the two copies of the forms which were filled in for you outside the terminal and the copy of your incoming customs form, which you have carefully kept throughout your Vietnam visit. The forms are compared, your baggage may be examined, then you are allowed to pass to the baggage security checkpoint where all baggage is x-rayed or manually checked. You now proceed to the airline check-in counter where you deposit baggage, receive seat allocation, and pay your US$8 departure tax. From here you can go upstairs to the departure lounge.

Final departure formalities occur as you enter the lounge. Your visa will be checked to see if you are departing within the time limit and from the correct exit point, your duplicate entry/exit form will be taken, and your passport photograph will be compared to the real thing. If all goes well, you will receive a departure stamp in your passport and you can spend your last few minutes in Vietnam buying duty-free and other items from the reasonable assortment offered. You will, however, find that the excess dong that you were unable to change because the exchange counter was not manned, are useless here. You need U.S. dollars—even to buy a cold drink.

If you are arriving from an area north of Saigon by train, you will find yourself at **Ga Sai Gon (Saigon Railway Station)** which is about two kilometers from central Saigon. The station is fairly unimpressive and it is located between encroaching buildings. Cyclos meet all trains, and you should be able to negotiate a ride to the central city for 5,000d. It is too far to walk and there are no buses.

Buses from northern areas usually arrive at the **Mien Dong Bus Station** on Xo Viet Nghe Tinh Street, about five kilometers northwest of central Saigon. A cyclo from here to town will cost at least 10,000d, or if you are really adventurous, a local bus goes from here to the bus station near the Ben Thanh Market.

3. Local Transportation

Central Saigon is a wonderful city for **walking**. The area is flat; the sidewalks are good; there is plenty to see; and in many parts, the buildings or large trees provide shade. All the area that I previously described can be covered on foot.

If you are tired, lazy, or want to go further afield, the standard form of public transportation is the three-wheeled **cyclo**. The standard cyclo fare (arrived at after some negotiation) seems to be 5,000d. For this, you can travel several kilometers. If you only want to go a few blocks, you may be successful with 2,000d. It is imperative to settle on a price before you board. Some cyclo drivers speak a little English, some can read a map if it is in Vietnamese, and some have a fair idea of the geography of the city. If you find one with all these qualities, you should keep him all day. That will cost around US$8. Prices rise in the evening and during rain.

If speed is important or you wish to go farther, the back of a **motorbike** is the answer. There are professionals waiting for customers on many corners, or you can try hailing any passing bike that is going in the general direction. Most riders will be pleased with the extra cash, particularly if you pay in dollars. The regular riders expect about twice the standard cyclo fare. A round trip from central Saigon to Cholon will cost 15,000d to 20,000d.

Traveling by **bus** is possible, but difficult. There are no route maps available and no formal schedules. The major terminal is on Ham Nghi Boulevard opposite the Ben Thanh Market.

Seeing the city by **bicycle** is a good option, although extreme caution is necessary because all other vehicles believe their larger size allows them the right of way. There are numerous places in the central city that rent bicycles for around US$2 a day. If you plan a long visit, you could consider buying a second-hand model for around US$15. Try on Le Loi Boulevard between the Rex Hotel and the bus terminal.

Rental cars are readily available from every hotel and tourist office. An airconditioned Japanese vehicle with driver for use within the city costs around US$25. Longer trips are calculated on a per kilometer basis. This ranges from around U.S. fifteen cents per kilometer up to a high of around thirty-five cents per kilometer.

Taxis are available for short trips around the city, but their numbers are

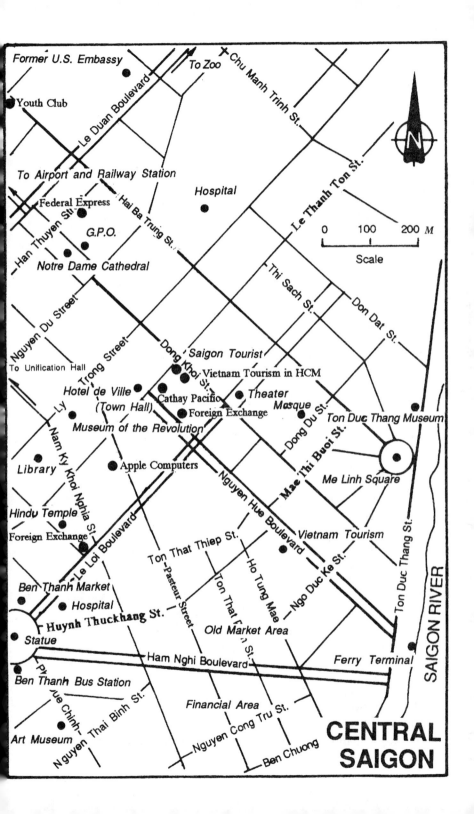

small. They can be hailed on the street or called by telephone. There is a taxi stand on Le Loi Boulevard near the Rex Hotel.

Boats are available for sightseeing, for crossing the Saigon River, and for traveling to several areas of the Mekong Delta. They operate on the river between the Floating Hotel and Ham Nghi Boulevard.

4. The Hotel Scene

Saigon has a better selection of hotels than the rest of the entire country put together. It has Vietnam's only five-star property, a good range of business hotels, an adequate selection of tourist hotels, and numerous budget properties—some of which are suitable for overseas visitors. Room rates vary from about US$5 up to over US$300 for some suites. Most represent good value when compared to other worldwide destinations.

Many hotels in the city are run by government agencies such as Vietnam Tourism, Saigon Tourist, and Ben Thanh Tourist; but there are a growing number of private companies—some of which are international—involved in the hotel industry. Here is a personal selection. Note that a ten percent service charge will usually be added to the quoted rates.

EXPENSIVE HOTELS

The **Saigon Floating Hotel** (Tel: 290-783), 200 rooms, is the best and most expensive hotel in Vietnam. The structure was built to float on the Great Barrier Reef in Australia; but since it was moved to Saigon in 1990, it has developed into the yardstick by which all other hotels are measured. The hotel now floats on the Saigon River at Hero Square on one edge of the central city. There is a swimming pool, a tennis court, two restaurants, 24-hour room service, ice machines with purified water, a seven-day-a-week business center, saunas, fitness center, boardroom, discotheque, cafe, two bars, a large shop, meeting rooms for up to two hundred people, and the efficiency and professionalism of a highly respected multinational operator.

The rooms themselves are on the small side, but they are delightfully furnished and have individually controlled airconditioning systems, remote control color TVs, radios with three-channel CD music, two in-house 24-hour video channels, refrigerators and mini bars, bathrobes, complimentary personal grooming items, valet service, laundry service, complimentary shoe cleaning, and international direct dial telephones. Furnishings are of a high quality and, in contrast to most other Vietnam properties, everything seems to work all the time.

The hotel will accept and change all major currencies, and payment can be made with selected credit cards and traveler's checks. Most staff speak some English, and all reception personnel are fluent in both Vietnamese and English. Interpreter service is available for several other languages. It really is a breath of fresh air in a country where "second best" is often accepted as perfect.

This is the place for business people or tourists who want to enjoy Western hospitality and efficiency, and are prepared to pay for it. After plunging into exotic Asia during the day, you can retire to luxury at night. Standard rooms start at US$195, with suites rising to US$425. (Book with the hotel at P.O. Box 752, Ho Chi Minh City, Vietnam; Fax: 848-290-784; U.S./Canada Tel: 800-835-SPHC.)

The **Omni Saigon Hotel** (Tel: 449-222), 248 rooms, is a fine hotel but its location is less than ideal. The rooms are large and well appointed. The public areas are classy, the restaurants and business centers are well run, and the health club, with its gym, sauna, and swimming pool, is excellent.

The Thai restaurant is casual and friendly, the R & R Pub has fine music and a relaxing atmosphere. and there are Karaoke facilities so you can sing the night away. Sounds almost perfect, doesn't it? My problem with the hotel is that you are several kilometers from most places of interest in the city so you have to catch a car or cyclo every time you want to move. If that's not a problem to you, this hotel would be perfect. Room rates start at US$140. Omni Club rooms start at US$260. (Book with the hotel at 251 Nguyen Van Troi Street, Phu Nhuam District, Ho Chi Minh City, Vietnam; Fax: 848-449-200.)

The **New World Hotel** (Tel: 295-310), 574 rooms, opened in late 1994. This is by far the largest hotel in the city and it is causing some readjustment to the established properties. There are many restaurant choices and good business and sporting facilities. Rooms are large and fully equipped. It is equivalent to a four-star property anywhere in Asia. While it is not right in the center of the city, it is possible to walk to some areas. (Book with the hotel at 76 Le Lai Street, Ho Chi Minh City, Vietnam; Fax: 848-230-710).

MEDIUM-PRICE HOTELS

This category provides a good choice of modern well-run business hotels, remodeled old favorites, and a few others that just seem overpriced. There is no clear favorite suitable for everyone; but the Norfolk, the Rex, and the Continental would be my top choices.

The **Norfolk Hotel** (Tel: 295-368), 120 rooms, is a boutique business hotel in central Saigon. It opened in early 1992 and has been very heavily booked since then. It is not hard to see why. The standards of comfort and service are very high, and it has a lovely feel about it from the moment you enter the quiet, elegant lobby. The hotel occupies a building that has been there for quite a few years, but the Australian owners/managers have completely refurbished the structure from the frame out. The result is quite

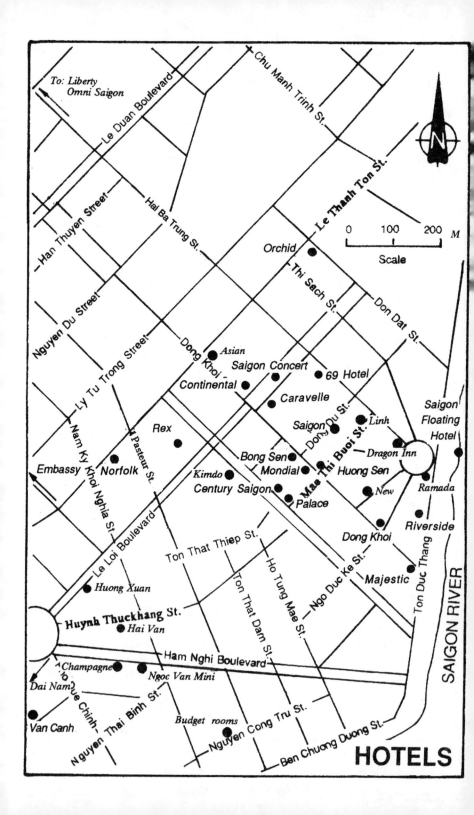

HOTELS

appealing. The rooms are fairly small, but they are very well furnished, clean, and fresh. Each has an attached bathroom with hot water, a color TV with satellite programs, IDD telephone, airconditioning, radio, and refrigerator/mini bar.

The hotel has a business center that provides secretarial, typing, and facsimile services as well as conference and meeting facilities. There is a delightful downstairs restaurant, an atrium bar with a good selection of Australian wines, a lobby lounge with newspapers and easy chairs, an upstairs "club bar," and a rooftop barbecue. Most guests are international businessmen. A new section opened early in 1995, and this has added to the facilities. Room rates are from US$75 to US$95 single and US$90 to US$110 double, with suites from US$150 to US$165. (Book with the hotel at 117 Le Thanh Ton Street, Saigon; Fax: 848-293-415.) Major credit cards are accepted.

The **Rex Hotel** (Tel: 296-042), 207 rooms, is something quite different. It is situated on what is probably the most prominent corner in downtown Saigon. The hotel has been around for quite some time in various forms. In 1992, it took over an adjacent hotel, and since then the hotel has been completely refurbished. All rooms how have individual airconditioners (which are very quiet), IDD telephones, color TV, music, refrigerators with mini bars, electronic safes, hair dryers, and clean bathrooms with hot water. Some rooms have cassette players.

One of the delights of the hotel is the art deco kitsch that appears unexpectedly. You see it in the art gallery on the first floor, in the recreation area on the second floor, and on the rooftop terraces where bonsai plants compete for space with caged birds and giant statuary and topiary. There are three restaurants, a business center, a dance hall, a huge gift shop, a tailor, and a cinema. Somehow, it all fits together. Rooms rates are US$70-90 single and US$85-105 double; and suites are US$100-200 single and US$120-800 double. (Book with the hotel at 141 Nguyen Hue Boulevard, Saigon; Fax: 848-291-469.) The hotel has a rooftop swimming pool and a tennis court behind the Museum of the Revolution.

The **Continental Hotel** (Tel: 299-201), 87 rooms, is in many ways the queen of Saigon hotels. The building is over one hundred years old, but a complete renovation earlier this decade has converted this into quite a modern establishment. The large rooms are airconditioned and fitted with all the necessary furnishings and fixtures. Service is good and small extras—like a flower on your pillow at night—help raise this above the general mass.

The building has considerable nostalgia with war correspondents and fans of the novel *The Quiet American*. Unfortunately, recent changes have eliminated much of this appeal. The Bamboo Bar, which operates from 6

P.M. to midnight, and the terrace adjacent to the restaurant are two of my favorite places. The Palace Restaurant itself, with its high ceiling, scalloped columns, and large chandeliers, is open all day and provides good food at acceptable prices. The Chez Guido Italian restaurant, which occupies the old veranda, has excellent food at high prices. Rooms rates are US$80-130 single and US$105-150 double. Suites are US$155 single, US$177 double. (Book with the hotel at 132 Dong Khoi Street, Ho Chi Minh City; Fax: 848-290- 936.)

The **Mondial Hotel** (Tel: 296-291), 40 rooms, opened in 1991 in a well-renovated building on Dong Khoi Street. Rooms are a reasonable size, and some of those at the front have miniature balconies. The ancient elevator has been made a feature of the building and appears to work well. The lobby area, which runs into a bar and lounge, is somewhat crowded, but the fifth-floor restaurant is attractive and the French-trained chef produces some excellent local and European cuisine. Rooms rates are from US$55. (Book with the hotel at 109 Dong Khoi Street, Ho Chi Minh City; Fax: 848-293-324.)

The same management has recently opened the **Asian Hotel** (Tel: 296-979), 47 rooms, close by. Room rates here start from US$70. Both properties have some style. (Book at 148 Dong Khoi Street, Ho Chi Minh City; Fax: 848-297-433.)

The **Kimdo International Hotel** (Tel: 225-914), 135 rooms, opened in the heart of the city in 1994. The entrance is elegant and the rooms have all the usual facilities including satellite television and electronic safes. The hotel sports a restaurant, coffee lounge, bar, fitness center, business center, massage and sauna, and so forth. Service standards are high. Room prices start at US$120 single and US$135 double. Suites are from US$320. (Book with the hotel at 133 Nguyen Hue Avenue, Ho Chi Minh City; Fax: 848-225-913.)

The **Caravelle Hotel** (Tel: 293-704), 115 rooms, has been around for a while—at one time, it was owned by the Catholic Church. It has seen some recent renovations that have kept it up to a reasonable standard. I have been here several times, but have never stayed because the hotel never seemed to have quite the right feel for my needs. The rooms are adequate, the hotel facilities are good, and the location is excellent. Most people could be well satisfied with all this. The ninth-floor restaurant and terrace have a good reputation and are worth visiting for the decor, the food, and the view. The hotel has a shop, a gymnasium, steam room and massage, a tailor, and a dancing hall. Room rates, which include breakfast, are US$52-85 single and US$63-102 double. Suites are US$144-177 single and double. (Book with the hotel at 17 Lam Son Square, Ho Chi Minh City; Fax: 848-299-746.)

The **Majestic Hotel** (Tel: 295-515), 100 rooms, was once the most elegant hotel in the city; then time caught up with it, and a top-floor fire almost finished the hotel. However, Saigon Tourist refused to give in, and recent renovations have added new life to the building. Many of the rooms are rather dated, but the furnishings are fine. The riverview rooms at the front have appeal. On my last visit to Saigon in late 1994, further renovations were underway and the hotel was closed. The results of these won't be known for some time. The hotel might emerge as one of the most desirable places to stay. Its location and ambiance are certainly attractive. (Book with the hotel at 1 Dong Khoi Street, Ho Chi Minh City; Fax: 848-291-470.)

The **Palace Hotel** (Tel: 292-860), 150 rooms, occupies one of the taller buildings in downtown Saigon. Rooms are fair to good, and all have attached bathrooms with hot water. Furnishings are adequate. The hotel has a rooftop swimming pool, a popular restaurant and bar on the floor below, and a lobby that always has activity. There is also a health club, dancing hall, business center, and gift shop. The hotel is used by some Asian groups, and the occupancy rate is high. Room rates are US$40-120 single and US$55-140 double. (Book with the hotel at 56-64 Nguyen Hue Avenue, Ho Chi Minh City; Fax: 848-299-872.)

Just down the road from here is the **Century Saigon Hotel**, (Tel: 293-168), 109 rooms. The old building has been totally renovated, but unfortunately the owners decided to retain the very small elevators which are a problem. The hotel has good decor and a nice ambience down to the pianist playing in the lobby. The Garden Court Restaurant has 24-hour casual dining, while the Starlight Disco is a popular nightspot. Rooms are nicely decorated and are well equipped, and the business center has all you need. The location is excellent. Room rates are from US$115 single and US$175 double. (Book with the hotel at 68A Nguyen Hue Avenue, Ho Chi Minh City; Fax: 848-292-732.)

The **Orchid Hotel** (Tel: 231-809), 30 rooms, is a privately operated property on the northern edge of central Saigon. The seven-floor building has a lobby lounge, coffee shop, restaurant, business center, and thirty airconditioned rooms with bathrooms, refrigerators, and telephones. The surrounding area is primarily residential, but it is just a short walk to downtown. The hotel was being renovated in late 1994. (Book with the hotel at 29A Don Dat Street, Ho Chi Minh City; Fax: 848-292-245.)

The **Riverside Hotel** (Tel: 224-038), 78 rooms, opened in 1991 in a renovated old French colonial building that looks across Ton Duc Thong Street to the Saigon River. It opened another wing in late 1994. Most of the rooms have high ceilings and plenty of space. They come equipped with TV, refrigerator, telephone, and self-contained bathrooms; and they rent from US$45 single and US$60 double. Suites are US$100-230. All prices include breakfast. The hotel has a small business center, a popular restaurant with Western and Asian cuisines, and a bar. (Book with the hotel at 18 Ton Duc Thang Street, Ho Chi Minh City; Fax: 848-298-070.)

Chains First Hotel (Tel: 441-199), 92 rooms, is a nice property in an out-of-the-way location near the airport. The rooms and facilities are fine, and management includes a buffet breakfast, a downtown shuttle, airport transfer, fruit basket, and nightclub admission in the price. There is tennis, massage, sauna, 24-hour restaurant, business center, and shopping facilities. Room rates are from US$65, suites from US$100. (Book with the hotel at 18 Hoang Viet Street, Tan Binh District, Ho Chi Minh City; Fax: 848-444-282.)

Not far away is the **Phi Long Mini Hotel** (Tel: 448-793). This is one of a growing number of privately operated small hotels which have all the regular facilities, are clean and friendly. I stayed here for two nights on a recent visit, and thoroughly enjoyed it. There is a small restaurant and car rental facilities. At around US$30 a night it is good value, and it's nice to have a personal touch. (Book with the hotel at 295 Le Van Sy Street, Ho Chi Minh City; Fax: 848-448-794.)

Also in this area is the **Tan Son Nhat Hotel** (Tel: 441-039), 41 rooms, which is run by the Vietnamese army. This was once a guest house for important officials, and it shows. There is plenty of space and above-average fittings. Prices are excellent with rooms from US$25 and suites from US$44, and there is a restaurant and a small pool. The location, near the airport, is less than ideal for most people, however. (Book with the hotel at 200 Hoang Van Thu Phu Nhuan Street, Ho Chi Minh City; Fax: 848-441-324.)

A final option in this area is the **Airport Hotel** (Tel: 445-761), 112 rooms. The hotel is too far from the terminals to walk with baggage so it is not particularly convenient. The facilities are acceptable but the whole place needs to smarten up. There is a restaurant, swimming pool, tennis court, massage, and sauna, and room rates at US$25. Suite are US$50. (Book with the hotel at 108 Hong Ha Street, Tan Binh District, Ho Chi Minh City; Fax: 848-440-166.)

The **Hotel Saigonconcert** (Tel: 291-299), 25 rooms, is a great illustration of how everyone in Saigon wants to get into the hotel industry. The hotel is housed in part of the old opera house that is now the Municipal Theater. Ten years ago, these were empty rooms. Five years ago, a small mini-hotel opened and has now been expanded into twenty-five rooms. The rooms are only average, but they have the usual facilities. The lobby is small and pokey, but the staff are friendly and the location is good. There is a restaurant with fair food, but the surrounding area has a wide choice of eating and drinking establishments. Room costs are US$35-47, including breakfast. (Book with the hotel at 7 Lam Son Square, Saigon; Fax: 848-295-831.)

The **Huong Sen Hotel** (Tel: 290-259), 50 rooms, is in a remodeled building that once housed the Astor Hotel. The new rooms are comfortable, but not outstanding. They have all the necessary amenities—airconditioning, TV, telephone, refrigerator, and clean bathroom with hot and cold water. The sixth-floor restaurant and rooftop patio are worth a visit if you stay here. Room rates vary, depending on their size and location, from US$34-64 single and US$49-84 double, including breakfast. The best are the front rooms on the upper floors. (Book with the hotel at 66-70 Dong Khoi Street, Ho Chi Minh City; Fax: 848-290-916.)

The Huong Sen and the nearby **Bong Sen Hotel** (Tel: 291-516), 136 rooms, are both managed by Saigon Tourist, so there is cooperation between them. The rooms at Bong Sen are quite nice with airconditioning, refrigerator, satellite TV, personal safe, and telephone; and there is a small but nice restaurant. Room rates are from US$50 for a standard room, US$200 for an executive suite. (Book with the hotel at 117 Dong Khoi Street, Ho Chi Minh City; Fax: 848-298-076.)

The **Hai Van Hotel** (Tel: 291-274), 21 rooms, is a little tucked away, but it is still within easy walking distance of the main downtown area. The rooms are reasonable and have the usual amenities, and the large Chinese restaurant with dancing and music shows is very popular. Room rates are a reasonable US$22 single, and US$27 or US$30 double. (Book with the hotel at 69 Huynh Thuc Khang Street, Ho Chi Minh City; Fax: 848-291-275.)

There are three hotels in the lower Hai Ba Trung Street area that are worth considering. The **Saigon Hotel** (Tel: 230-231), 105 rooms, has been renovated and had the prostitutes thrown out. It is now quite an acceptable place with rooms from US$36. (Book at 41 Dong Du Street; Fax: 848-291-466.) The **Dragon Inn** (Tel: 292-190), 10 rooms, is a bit pokey, but it's friendly and has a nice bar and restaurant on the roof. Room prices start at US$40. You find it as 3 Hai Ba Trung Street, overlooking Me Linh Square. Then there is the **New Hotel** (Tel: 230-656), 12 rooms, at 14 Ho Huan Nghiep Street. Rooms are from US$27. (Book by Fax: 848-241-812.)

The **Embassy Hotel** (Tel: 231-981), 98 rooms, has emerged from the Ben Nghe Guesthouse. Whereas the guest house was a good value, the hotel seems to be highly overpriced, despite the upgrading that has taken place. All the rooms are airconditioned and have reasonable bathrooms and the usual fixtures; but at US$70-120, they are not a great value. The hotel has an Oriental seafood restaurant, an Asian/Western restaurant, a disco nightclub, and a business center. There are pinball machines in the lobby. The hotel seems to like Chinese, Japanese, and Korean groups and business people. (Book at 35

Nguyen Trung Truc Street, Ho Chi Minh City; Fax: 848-295-019.)

BUDGET ACCOMMODATIONS

There are plenty of low-price, minimum-facility accommodations in Saigon, but not too many within the downtown area will allow foreigners to stay at reasonable rates. The best area to try is south of Ham Nghi Boulevard. If it is imperative that you find a room for less than US$25, try one of the following.

The **Vien Dong Hotel** (Tel: 393-001), 140 rooms, is a smart-looking place with most of the usual facilities. Standard airconditioned rooms rent from US$32 but budget travelers will be delighted to find that there are a few economy rooms with fan and telephone for US$12. There is a restaurant, shop, dancing hall, and Karaoke. (Book with the hotel at 275A Pham Ngu Lao Street, Ho Chi Minh City: Fax: 848-332-812.) In the same street you will find the **Hoang Tu Hotel** (Tel: 322-657), a popular but run-down place at Number 193. The cheapest rooms here are around US$10 but this is away down-market from the Vien Dong. On the parallel Le Lai Street, you will find the **A Chau Hotel** (Tel: 331-571) at Number 12. Rooms with fans start at US$8.

Moving slightly closer to downtown, the **Van Canh Hotel** (Tel: 294-963), 27 rooms, has similarly priced rooms plus some airconditioned ones for around US$12. There is a restaurant with dancing every night so noise can be a problem but it is worth checking it out at 184 Calmette Street. The **Ngoc Van Mini Hotel** (Tel: 231-935), 9 rooms, has some third-floor rooms with airconditioning and hot water for US$15. Add a refrigerator and the price rises to US$20. You find it at 113 Ham Nghi Boulevard. Around the corner at 82 Nguyen Cong Tru, there are four large, clean rooms with airconditioning, refrigerator, fan, and attached bathroom (no hot water) for US$15. They are quiet and safe.

The **Dong Khoi Hotel** (Tel: 294-046) is in a good central location but is in urgent need of attention. The old French-style building has heaps of potential and will be renovated in time. At present, a few airconditioned rooms rent for around US$12, while fan rooms with bath, but no amenities are around US$9. The staff is friendly and helpful and security seems fine. (Book with the hotel at 8 Dong Khoi Street, Saigon.)

The only other downtown bargain is the **69 Hotel** (Tel: 291-513), 20 rooms, at 69 Hai Ba Trung Street. Some upgrading has occurred recently and prices have risen but you can still get a room for less than US$20.

5. Dining and Restaurants

It is easier to get a good meal in Ho Chi Minh City than in any other part of the country. In general, you have to pay more for the privilege. The cheapest food is sold on the streets. Next comes the market, then the government-run restaurants, then traditional Vietnamese and Chinese restaurants, hotel restaurants, and finally a few specialized restaurants. Meal prices can range from less than US$1 to about US$15 per person. I will assume that those who live on a tight budget will be able to find the "pho" stalls which are numerous throughout the city. Here is a run-down on some of the restaurants available if you want something more substantial in somewhat better surroundings.

HOTEL RESTAURANTS

The best Western food in a hotel is available at the **Marina Cafe** at the Saigon Floating Hotel. There is an international buffet each lunchtime, and an a-la-carte menu which includes U.S. sirloin steak, weiner schnitzel, grilled fish, and a jumbo beef burger. The food is prepared and served as you would expect it in Europe, North America, or Australia. There is a full range of beverages, including decaffeinated coffee, cappuccino, fresh fruit juices, milk shakes, and a large range of beers and imported wines. A meal from the a-la-carte menu could cost around US$20, but it is great to know that you can get some home-grown food when you really need it.

Actually, the hotel's premier restaurant is the **Oriental Court** which specializes in Asian cuisines. This is a fine restaurant with great atmosphere and service, but the competition is more intense in this area. The food here is slanted a little toward Western tastes, so it cannot rate as the best Asian restaurant in town. That's not to say that you will not enjoy it here—in fact, some people will enjoy the food and atmosphere more because it is slightly sanitized. If you are staying at the Floating Hotel, make sure you have at least one meal here.

Another restaurant that I enjoy is on the fifth floor of the **Rex Hotel**. With its high ceilings, its correctly dressed waiters, its live classical music, and its good food at decent prices; it has almost everything to make anyone happy. My belief is that the Asian food is slightly better than the Western cuisine. When I last visited here, there were around eighteen serving staff and only about twelve diners, so the service should have been wonderful. However, I would rate it as adequate. Apart from the food, the restaurant is worth a visit just to see the decor and experience the ambiance. You should also visit the outdoor rooftop restaurant, even if it is only for a drink. The atmosphere is casual and fun. An alternative is the ground floor restaurant across the road at the back of the hotel. This serves an excellent lunch at a reasonable price, and it is a delightful place for dinner because of the garden setting. I strongly recommend it.

On the ground floor of the Rex Hotel, you will find the **Nhon Bashi Japanese Restaurant**. It offers all the standard Japanese dishes served in

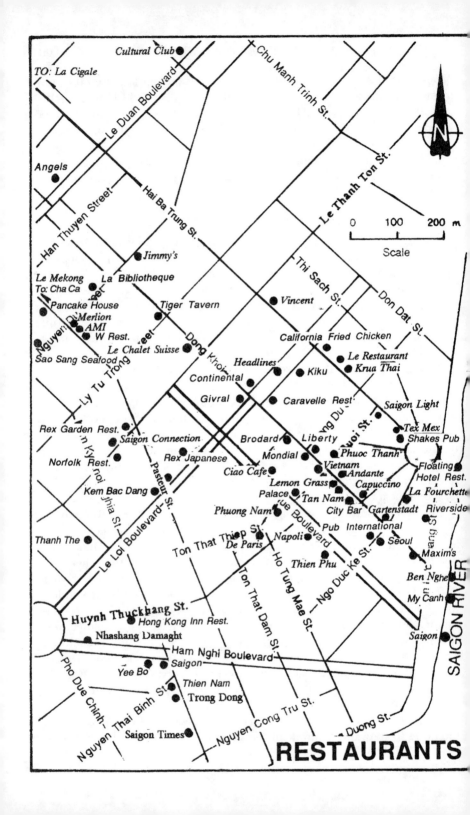

RESTAURANTS

traditional Japanese surroundings. It is all very nice. The food is good, but the portions are small and the prices are too high. You can end up paying US$25 a head without trying too hard.

Over at the **Continental**, there are two choices. The main dining room has a tradition of good food and good service, and the atmosphere is smart and charming. This is what many European hotel dining rooms were like twenty years ago. I liked them then as I like the Continental today. An alternative is the **Chez Guido**, which specializes in Italian food for lunch and dinner. The food is good, presentation is excellent, portions are large, and so is the price. This is another place where US$20 per person should come as no surprise once drinks, extras, and service are added to the bill. Obviously, many people are prepared to pay these prices.

The Marco Polo Restaurant at the **Dai Nam Hotel** is providing Chez Guido with some strong competition. It has make-it-yourself pizza and imported grain-fed steak.

I have never eaten at the restaurant on the fifteenth floor of the **Palace Hotel**, but I have friends who say the food is fine. Certainly the view is great because this is one of the tallest buildings in all of Saigon. Prices seem reasonable.

The ground-floor restaurant at the **Norfolk** is stylish and delightfully simple. I understand why business people enjoy this "no-fuss" place so much. A similar comment can be made about the fifth-floor restaurant at the **Mondial**. I have never heard anyone rave about the food at either place, but I've never heard any complaints either, so they must be doing something right.

The **Riverside Hotel** has a large ground-floor restaurant that is a good place for lunch. At dinner, there is music that gets louder as the night progresses. The Western food is just adequate, but some of the Asian dishes are excellent. Prices for such a place are quite reasonable, and the service is friendly, if a bit sloppy.

Many people consider the Hong Kong Restaurant at the **Hai Van Hotel** to have the best hotel Chinese food in the city. As you would expect, it is Hong Kong-style cuisine and it seems to equal many of that city's fine eateries. Saigon people have discovered this, and there are often parties here that fill the entire restaurant. Check that it is open before you go.

The Thai Restaurant at the **Saigon Omni Hotel** has excellent food at prices that are not outlandish. There is a free shuttle bus leaving from a booth on Nguyen Hue Avenue.

OTHER RESTAURANTS

Several outside restaurants rival the Floating Hotel for Western food. The first is **Le Mekong Restaurant**, which is situated just outside central Saigon at 32 Vo Van Tan Street, near Pasteur. French food is prepared and served here just as it is in Paris. The restaurant specializes in sauces, so select a dish in which the chef can show off his expertise. Main dishes cost up to US$15, but the elegant atmosphere and the attentive service make that worthwhile.

La Cigale (Tel: 443-930) at 158 Nguyen Dinh Chinh, near the Omni Saigon Hotel, is making a bid for top spot. The food is good, service excellent, prices high, and flambes a specialty. **Ami** (Tel: 242-198) at 170 Pasteur Street is a good alternative. A daily set lunch is available for 75,000d, and a house speciality menu with wine costs 150,000d. It is a friendly place with top food. Similar comments can be made about **Le Restaurant** (Tel: 906-105) at 54 Hai Ba Trung Street. The food is genuine French, there is a nice atmosphere, and main dishes cost 40,000-140,000d. One of the newest places is **La Fourchette** (Tel: 231-101) at 9 Ngo Duc Ke Street. This small, friendly restaurant has already built a loyal following.

La Bibliotheque is a small restaurant in the library of a private home. The owner is Madame Dai, who was a lawyer and opposition senator before 1975. The restaurant, at 84 Nguyen Du near the cathedral, has no telephone and is difficult to find, but it is worth the effort. You need to make reservations for dinner, so you must go in person earlier in the day. Madame Dai prefers to speak in French, but at times there is lively English conversation. The ambiance is delightful.

There are several other European cuisines available in Saigon. **Le Chalet Suisse** (Tel: 293-856) is at 211A Dong Khai Street. It is a small place with a good menu and atmosphere above a delightful delicatessen. It opens for breakfast, lunch, and dinner. German and French food is available at **Gartenstadt** (Tel: 223-623) at 34 Dong Khoi Street. Downstairs is a traditional bar, and the dining room is upstairs. The very popular **Ciao Cafe** (Tel: 251-203) at 72 Nguyen Hue has Italian food, pizza, and sandwiches in a European atmosphere. Nearby, the **Napoli** (Tel: 225-616) at Number 75 offers Italian cuisine and pizza delivery. A further Italian option is **Capuccino Restaurant** (Tel: 291-051) at 9 Ho Huan Nghiep Street, while Tex-Mex food is available from the **Tex-Mex Restaurant** (Tel: 223-017) at 11 Hai Ba Street.

Maxim's (Tel: 296-676), at 15 Dong Khoi Street, has long been a favorite. Little has changed in the last twenty years, except the prices. The food is reasonable, the atmosphere is of the seventies, and there is live music and vocalists who try modern Vietnamese songs interspersed with old Western favorites. The service is good, and I have always found this to be a friendly place. There is an English menu. Prices are a bit high, but it is a good experience.

Liberty Restaurant (Tel: 299-820), at 80 Dong Khoi Street, is a more modern version of Maxim's. This airconditioned restaurant has a band

and some singers and an English menu. The atmosphere is pleasant and the place is often crowded. In my opinion, the food is nothing startling and neither is the service. Prices are on the high side—soup is around 15,000d here while it is 5,000d in many other places, and main courses are from 30,000 to 80,000d. A meal will cost around US$10 a head.

One place that I would like to recommend is **Seoul Restaurant** (Tel: 294-297) at 37 Ngo Duc Ke. I have been here several times and have always been the only Westerner in the place. That has been no problem because the pleasant waitresses speak English and explain the many food options. I recommend the Korean barbecue. The meal will cost around US$5.

Cafe Brodard (Tel: 225-837) is something else. It has been in existence for eighty years, and despite renovations it looks as if it came directly from the 1960s. The clientele is a mixture of foreign visitors, expatriate residents, trendy young groups, and families. There is a fairly basic menu, table staff who could have been there for most of the eighty-year history, sixties and seventies Western pop music, and food which is ordinary rather than exciting. Prices are reasonable. The coconut ice cream is a delight—order it and see for yourself. Cafe Brodard is at 131 Dong Khoi Street, on the corner of Nguyen Thiep Street. Around the corner is a patisserie with plenty of tempting offerings.

With a somewhat similar motif is **Givral Cafe**, which is at 169 Dong Khoi Street, overlooking Lam Son Square and the Opera House. At times, there are more foreigners than locals here—just like it was in the 1960s when this place was a great source of information and rumors for the foreign press corps of Saigon. The menu is not great, the food is a bit above average, and the decor is scruffy; but you haven't been to Saigon if you haven't eaten at this place. The patisserie next door has some great cakes and pastries.

Some other places worth trying are **Saigon Light** (Tel: 222-842), a nice pub-restaurant at 11 Mac Thi Buoi Street; **Chaplin** (Tel: 243-103) at 114 Ly Tu Trong Street for Vietnamese food, sandwiches, and spaghetti; **Jimmy's** (Tel: 223-661) at 57 Nguyen Du for a similar selection; and **Restaurant de Paris** (Tel: 298-956) at 7 Ton That Thiep Street, which has been operating since 1969 and offers a good selection of French and Chinese food.

There is a group of restaurants near the corner of Ham Nghi Boulevard and Nam Ky Khoi Nghia Street. Right on the corner is the large and impressive **Saigon Restaurant**, which has Japanese and Korean food and a good atmosphere. Next door is the **Yee Bo Chinese Restaurant and Nightclub**. Food here is excellent, but prices are high and an evening can cost more than you bargained for. Around the corner at 53 Nam Ky Khoi Nghla, you will find the **Thien Nam Restaurant** (Tel: 223-634), which was a favorite with U.S. troops during the early 1970s. It serves a famous sweet and sour sauce with almost anything you want, and the prices are very reasonable. Next door is the **Trong Dong Restaurant** (Tel: 292-600), which specializes in seafood. All of these restaurants are very popular, so to ensure a table you should arrive before 7 P.M.

There are several other restaurants that specialize in seafood. One of the best is the **Thanh The Restaurant** (Tel: 222-152) at 9 Nguyen Trung Truc Street. The chef here does a wonderful job with crab and fish, and the prices are most reasonable. **Sao Sang Seafood** (Tel: 223-354) is a large, well-patronized place with live seafood waiting to be cooked by Chinese and Vietnamese chefs. This place really jumps some evenings, so it can be hard to get a table. You find it at 100 Nguyen Du Street, near Unification Palace. You could also try the **Phuong Nam** (Tel: 294-045) at 1 Ton That Thiep. Prices are around 100,000 dong. The **Cha Ca Restaurant**, at 180 Nguyen Thi Minh Khai, cooks fish northern-style at your table like its Hanoi namesake. It is a worthwhile experience.

Along Le Duan Boulevard to the west, you will find the lovely **Angels Restaurant** (Tel: 231-340), which has excellent Chinese food in airconditioned surroundings. The decor is appealing, and I have found the staff to be particularly helpful and pleasant. Prices are not sky-high. For those lovers of Szechuan cuisine, the **Thien Phu Huong** (Tel: 241-248) at 55 Nguyen Hue, is the place to go. **Nang Dinh** (Tel: 299-137) at 2A Ton Duc Thang has Cantonese food with good food and super service. For those who must have Singapore food, the **Merlion** (Tel: 231-799) at 172 Pasteur Street may appeal. I had a bad experience here with overcharging, so I am wary.

Obviously, Vietnamese restaurants can be found throughout Saigon, but there are several worthy of note on Ngo Due Ke Street and Mac Thi Buoi Street—both of which are in the Me Linh Square area. Most have no names other than their street addresses. Several that I can recommend are: **15 Ngo Duc Ke**, **62 Mac Thi Buoi**, **5 Me Linh**, and **53 Nguyen Hue**. Additionally in central Saigon, it is worth trying **W Restaurant** on Nguyen Thi Minh Khai Street; the nearby **A-Phu Pancake House** at No. 99, where you eat Vietnamese rice flour pancakes wrapped around shrimp, pork, greens, and onion; and the **May Lan Nghe Si Restaurant** beside the Municipal Theater.

There are also several up-market Vietnamese restaurants worth checking out. The **Saigon Times Club** (Tel: 298-676) is at 37 Nam Ky Khoi Nghia. It is open for lunch and dinner, and you have a choice of airconditioned or open-air dining. **Lemon Grass** (Tel: 298-006) is at 63 Dong Khoi Street. Main courses run to US$3-6 and desserts US$1-2. Cocktails are US$2-4. Direct competition is provided by **Tan Nam** (Tel: 223-407) at 59 Dong Khoi Street. There are a few vegetarian dishes here for 20,000-40,000 dong. Similar prices apply at the large, smart **Vietnam House** (Tel: 291-623) at 93 Dong Khoi Street. Traditional music is played upstairs from 7:30-9:30 and a piano bar operates downstairs from 5 P.M.-10 P.M.

I shouldn't forget dining on the river. Apart from the restaurants in the Saigon Floating Hotel, there are several boats that operate short dinner cruises on the river. The **Saigon** and the **Ben Nghe** (Tel: 231-475) appear to be the most popular. Both depart each evening at 8 P.M. from berths opposite the Majestic Hotel. You need to arrive well before departure time to get one of the better tables near the bow. The scenery is good and the live band provides a nice atmosphere, but don't expect the food to be great. The cruise and meal will cost US$10-15.

This leaves a collection of places which are either memorable or horrible, depending on your taste. Lovers of Australian meat pies will head for **Shake's Pub** on Phan Van Dat Street, overlooking Me Linh Square. It also has some other Australian and Western food and a good atmosphere. The **City Bar and Cafe** on Dong Khoi Street is way up-market. It has good food and a sophisticated atmosphere with medium to high prices.

Although I have mentioned ice cream before, I must recommend that you visit a Saigon cafe or ice cream outlet. You will find it crowded with people, many of whom will want to talk with you. Take an hour or so and enjoy the experience. It will only cost a few thousand dong. There are two very popular places on each corner of the Le Loi Boulevard-Nguyen Thi Minh Khoi Street intersection and the **Saigon Connection Restaurant** (Tel: 242-176) at 114 bis Le Thanh Ton adds good cakes and coffee to an extensive ice cream selection.

For Karaoke fans, the large, airconditioned **Nhashang Damaght Restaurant**, at 138 Ham Nghi Boulevard, would be a delight. Finally, there is the **Pub International**, a strangely named place that has good French cuisine with a few Asian dishes thrown in. It is on Ngo Duo Ke Street, near Dong Khoi. Try the soufflé if you are desperate for a Western dessert.

6. Sightseeing

Central Saigon is a good place for walking. Many of the sightseeing attractions are within walking distance of the major hotels, the city is flat, and there is much of interest on the streets. Nguyen Hue Boulevard, Dong Khoi Street, and Le Loi Boulevard are attractions themselves, but there are a number of other specific attractions that should not be missed.

Unification Palace (also called Unification Hall) was known as Independence Hall or the Presidential Palace before 1975. This was the target of Viet Cong troops when they entered the city in April 1975. Many readers may remember the graphic television scenes of a North Vietnamese tank crashing through the gates of the palace and a soldier unfurling the Viet Cong flag from an upper balcony. The palace has been retained as it was in 1975, and it is now open to visitors each day for an entrance fee of 35,000d.

Unification Palace is interesting because of its size and modern architectural style, but it is its history that makes it fascinating. The first building on this site was a residence for the French governor general of Cochin China. It was started in 1868 and was called Norodem Palace. Many government services moved to Hanoi later that century; and for the next sixty years, it was only occupied intermittently. In 1954, the French authorities handed the building to the South Vietnamese authorities and it became known as Independence Hall. In February 1962, two South Vietnamese airforce jets bombed part of the building, so the whole structure was razed and the new Presidential Palace was built in its place. The architect was Ngo Viet Thu and the new building, which took four years to complete, was an excellent example of 1960s design.

The 20,000 square meters of usable floor area includes reception rooms, a cabinet meeting room, banquet room, conference hall, living and entertainment areas for the president and his family, and underground bunkers and command rooms. The guided tour, which is done in English, includes visits to all of these areas. You also have the option of viewing edited parts of a French documentary that briefly covers some of the history of southern Vietnam during the past one hundred years. Unfortunately, the print quality and English commentary are both extremely poor. The tour of the building will take around an hour, and you can wander the grounds later if you have the time. Currently the building is closed between 11 A.M. and 1 P.M. as well as when it is used for official receptions or meetings, which is fairly rare. Entrance to the grounds is through a gate on Nguyen Du Street, near the Nam Ky Khoi Nghia Street intersection.

When you leave the palace, head north along Nguyen Du Street. After two blocks, you will reach the **Notre Dame Cathedral**. This fine building was constructed by the French from 1877 through 1883; and for many years, it dominated Saigon's skyline. Even today, it is a good landmark as you walk the central city. The cathedral is built in a square that faces down Dong Khoi Street. Its neo-Romanesque, red brick facade is perhaps out of place in Asia; but in my mind, it looks fine because most of the surrounding area has a strong European architectural influence, and even the tree-lined streets and the square itself could be part of a provincial European city.

The two dominant features of the exterior are the European-style stained glass windows and the two square, forty-meter-high towers. The spires were added in 1900. The cathedral was consecrated in 1959. The interior is equally impressive, and it is worth the effort to locate a door that is open, so you can get in.

Just across the road from the cathedral is the **General Post Office**. This was built by the French a few years after the cathedral, and it is in a traditional European style that looks very much like a railway station. Postal services are available from early morning until 8 P.M., and telephone calls can be made until 10 P.M. There is an information desk where English is spoken, and several notices throughout the building are in English. It is not difficult to find the service you need. International services used to be exorbitantly priced, but some have been reduced recently as Vietnam tries to rejoin the world community. The following are late 1994 telephone charges in U.S. dollars for calls made from the post office:

Destination	First minute	Each subsequent minute
Laos/Cambodia	$3.10	$2.60
Thailand/Singapore	$3.10	$2.60
Australia/China	$3.80	$2.90
Japan/Canada/USA	$3.90	$3.00
Europe	$4.40	$3.40
NZ/Hawaii/Spain	$4.50	$3.70

You can purchase philatelic items, postcards, and envelopes; send telegrams and faxes; or use DHL Worldwide Express services at various counters within the building. Inquiries can be made by telephone at 296-555.

If you walk east down Dong Khoi Street, you reach the **Hotel de Ville** (City Hall) after two blocks. This building, which now houses the Ho Chi Minh City People's Committee, was built early in this century after years of controversy. It is not hard to see why there was disagreement about the architectural style. The white-on-yellow ornate facade would be controversial in Europe, and it is totally out of place in Asia, but I must admit that I love it. It has been called a folly, a disaster, and a joke; but it is probably the most distinctive building in Saigon. The authorities do not encourage entry to the building, but you can just walk in and wander around. The lovely crystal chandeliers are a reminder of another era.

Across from the Hotel de Ville, there is a nice park and a statue of Ho Chi Minh set in gardens. Walk through here to the intersection of Le Loi Boulevard and turn left. Immediately ahead of you is the **Municipal Theater**. This building was originally built as an opera house in the style of the Grand Palais in Paris. It was inaugurated in 1900, was damaged by bombing in 1944, and it became the seat of the National Assembly for the Republic of Vietnam in 1955. In recent years, it has reverted to being a theater.

Continue past the theater to Hai Ba Trung Street and turn right. It's a short distance from here to **Me Linh Square** with its statue of Tran Hung Dao. Anchored straight ahead is the Saigon Floating Hotel. A visit to a restaurant or bar takes you into another world. Just north of here on Ton

Duc Thang Street is the small **Ton Duc Thang Museum**, which is dedicated to the man who succeeded Ho Chi Minh as president of Vietnam. It opens every day except Monday, but is closed daily between 11 A.M. and 2 P.M. There are some interesting photographs and some other material, but the explanations are only in Vietnamese, so it has limited value to visitors.

If you are interested in **Ho Chi Minh**, you should visit the museum in the old customs house on Nguyen Tat Thanh Street which is given his name. The building is probably the best example of colonial architecture in Saigon. It was from here that Ho Chi Minh set sail for France in 1911 as a ship's cook using the name Van Ba. The explanations are only in Vietnamese, but you can follow the general picture from the photographs and exhibits. There is a copy of the Vietnamese Declaration of Independence used in 1945 and some early pictures of Saigon. The museum is closed on Mondays and Fridays and daily from 11:30 A.M. to 2 P.M.

There are several other museums to visit. The **Museum of the Revolution** (Tel: 299-741), at 27 Ly Tu Trong Street, is housed in what once was Gia Long Palace. This was the home of the French governor of Cochin China and the temporary home of President Diem while the new Presidential Palace was being built during the 1960s. The museum contains material from 1959 until the Communists occupied Saigon in 1975. There are many photographs, maps, and exhibits. You can see a model of the Cu Chi tunnels, look at a false bottomed rowboat used for smuggling arms, and see examples of Viet Cong and captured American equipment. In the garden behind the building, you can see a Soviet tank, an American helicopter, and an anti-aircraft gun. The museum is closed Mondays and daily between 11:30 A.M. and 2 P.M.

The **War Crimes Museum** was being heavily pushed a couple of years ago, but the Vietnamese government seems to be giving this less emphasis now. The museum is housed in the former U.S. Information Service building at 28 Vo Van Tan Street. The emphasis is on American atrocities committed during the late sixties and early seventies; but the Chinese invasion of a small area of northern Vietnam in 1979 also gets some coverage. Many of the photographs are from Western news services and most were well-publicized in the West, but having them concentrated in one place makes for very somber viewing. They certainly do not present humanity in a very good light. U.S. military equipment is displayed outside the building. The museum is closed on Mondays and daily from 11:30 A.M. until 2 P.M. Most of the displays are only labeled in Vietnamese.

The **Art Museum** (Tel: 297-059), at 97A Pho Duc Chinh Street, is much lighter. You can see a range of items from artifacts of early civilizations through to modern painting and sculpture. Most of the modern material has a political or social message, but some of it is quite interesting. The museum is closed on Mondays.

The **Museum of History**, formerly called the Asia Museum, is located just inside the gates of the **Zoo and Botanical Gardens** on Nguyen Biah Khiem Street. It was built in the 1920s in a neo-Vietnamese style by the Ecole Francaise d'Extreme Orient. There is an excellent collection displayed chronologically that covers the various cultures in Vietnam from the Bronze Age Dong Son civilization through the Chams, the Khmers, and the Vietnamese. Of particular note is the extensive pottery collection. There is an archaeological reference library with some material in English. The museum is closed Mondays and daily from 11:30 A.M. until 1:00 P.M. While here, you should walk around the zoo and the gardens. Giant trees thrive among the lakes and well-tended flower beds, while lawns provide an opportunity to relax, away from the bustle outside. There are some interesting and rare plant species, but they are hard to find these days. The gardens are 130 years old and were once the finest in Asia. Snacks and drinks are available at several places. The zoo has only a small collection of animals, but recent work has improved the enclosures and viewing facilities. The main gate is directly opposite Le Duan Boulevard.

While in this area, it is worth visiting the **Emperor of Jade Pagoda**, my favorite Chinese temple in the city. It is at 73 Mai Thi Luu Street, just north of Dien Bien Phu Street. The pagoda was built from public subscriptions early this century and is dedicated to a collection of Chinese and Vietnamese divinities in a mixture of Buddhism and Taoism. From the outside, the pagoda does not look particularly attractive; but once you are inside the building, you are surrounded by statues of all kinds, exquisite wood carvings, massive jars and artworks, and other treasures. This is very much a living temple. Joss stick aroma fills the air, locals come and go, paying homage to their own personal deities. Temple helpers are on hand to help the faithful.

The Taoist Emperor of Jade is the prime figure in the main sanctuary. He is flanked by his four guardians and surrounded by various other gods and their guardians. A doorway on the left leads you to another chamber that contains the Chief of Hell. To your left is the Hall of the Ten Hells, where carved wooden panels show the various torments awaiting in hell. At the far end of this chamber, there is a small room with ceramic figures of twelve women, each representing one year in the twelve-year Chinese calendar.

If you now return to the main chamber and pass right through it, you will find some stairs that take you to an upper level where there is another sanctuary and a balcony. One of the joys of this pagoda is the small nooks and crannies that allow you to escape from reality and perhaps have some time alone. I have been able to do this here without being disturbed by other tourists or local worshipers. It is a wonderful place.

Another pagoda worth visiting is the **Vinh Nghiem Pagoda** on Nam Ky Khoi Nghia Street, halfway to the airport. This is the largest pagoda in Saigon, and almost all of the buildings are modern. It was built with help from the Japan-Vietnam Friendship Association and was inaugurated in 1971. The eight-story tower with statues of the Buddha on each level is one of the most impressive in the whole country. Behind the sanctuary is another smaller tower containing funerary urns.

There are numerous other pagodas in the city, and all of them are interesting. Most visitors, however, will be content with visits to two or three, and my third choice would be the **Giac Lam Pagoda**. This is a long way from central Saigon, but it is worth the trip. To reach here, you need to go to Cholon, then take Le Dai Hanh Street in a westerly direction until you come to Lac Long Quan Street, where you turn right. The pagoda is about one hundred meters along here on your left. It is about eight kilometers from downtown.

This pagoda has been in existence for at least 250 years, and it is believed to be the oldest in the city. Outside the main building, there is a bodhi tree that was a gift from Sri Lanka, and a white statue of Quan The Am Bo Tat, the goddess of mercy. Inside, there are funeral tablets, portraits of deceased monks, countless gilded figures, various other religious items, and a large bell with lists of names attached. Prayer times (11 A.M. to noon and 4 P.M. to 5 P.M.) are particularly interesting because of the use of drums, bells, and gongs in the traditional ceremony.

While in Cholon, you may wish to visit **Cha Tam Church**, which is at the western end of Tran Hung Dao B Boulevard. It is an attractive white and yellow structure that was built about one hundred years ago, but gained notoriety in 1963 when President Ngo Dinh Diem and his brother took refuge here after fleeing the Presidential Palace during a coup. The brothers agreed to surrender, so the coup leaders sent an armored personnel carrier to pick them up; but before it arrived back in central Saigon, the soldiers had murdered the president and his brother. Masses in both Vietnamese and Chinese are held here every day.

Returning to central Saigon, you could visit the **Ben Thanh Market**, the city's largest. The range of goods for sale is quite amazing. Most Saigon people would have no need to visit any other place for their common needs. The market was built in 1914 by the French, and little has changed since. The main entrance, with its imposing gateway and clock tower, has become a well-known symbol of Saigon. Fruit, vegetables, meat, clothing, household items, hardware, and much more is available here. Food stalls can provide very inexpensive meals. Visitors should be aware, however, that the market and the surrounding streets are worked systematically by gangs of thieves and pickpockets. Foreign visitors are great targets for such people—I can personally verify that. A notebook and a few thousand dong were removed very professionally from a buttoned shirt pocket without me knowing until it was too late. Unfortunately, some of the detailed research for this book was lost in the process.

United States citizens and other visitors who remember the last days of the Vietnam War should visit the former **U.S. Embassy** on Le Duan Boulevard at Mac Dinh Chi Street. This building was finished in 1967 to replace the previous embassy, which had been destroyed by a huge car bomb. In January 1968, during the daring Tet offensive, a seventeen-man Communist commando unit dressed in South Vietnamese army uniforms managed to get inside the compound and cause some damage. The more long-term damage occurred as the incident was shown on American TV, devastating many American supporters of the war.

Also shown on the world's television screens were the emergency evacuation plans put into effect as South Vietnam's defenses crumbled in April 1975. Helicopters landed on the roof and the grounds of the chancery building as they ferried Americans and some Vietnamese to aircraft carriers waiting offshore. Many Vietnamese who had been promised evacuation were unable to leave because of the speed of the operation. The U.S. ambassador, Mr. Martin, boarded a helicopter in predawn darkness after most of Saigon had fallen into Viet Cong hands.

Today, parts of the embassy complex are used by the state oil company, but other parts remain empty because they can only be used with airconditioning. The public is not admitted, but even a look from the outside gives you a good idea why this was known as "the bunker."

OUTSIDE THE CITY

Apart from Dalat, which we cover in another chapter, the most interesting trips from Saigon are to the Cu Chi tunnels (northwest of the city) and to Vung Tau (southeast of the city).

The **Cu Chi tunnels** are spectacular for what they were, rather than what they are. What you see today is a sanitized, enlarged version of the real thing, but it still gives you some idea of what an amazing achievement this 250-kilometer network was.

The tunnels were built over a period of twenty-five years by the Viet Minh in their fight against the French. They were repaired and extended by the Viet Cong as they fought the South Vietnamese and American forces in the 1960s. The red earth of Cu Chi is ideal for tunnel construction, and the Viet Minh and Viet Cong took full advantage of this. All of the tunnels were dug by hand, and no timber or concrete was used to give them stability. Initially they were used as a means of communication between villages and as hiding places when the French army made sweeps through the area. Later they were used for mounting surprise attacks against the American and South Vietnamese troops, for infiltrating agents into Saigon and surrounding areas, and for controlling villages and "strategic hamlets" that were built and guarded by South Vietnamese forces.

The Americans realized that having a major Viet Cong presence so close to Saigon was a serious threat to the capital, so they constructed a major base in the Cu Chi area. Unknowingly, they built it over one of the existing tunnels, so with a little work, the Viet Cong had secret access to the base. It was not long before the Americans knew about the tunnels in the area, but they had great difficulty finding them. Wooden trap doors were camouflaged with earth, stumps, and tree branches. Some were in barns, others were under cooking pots.

Trained Alsatian dogs were used to smell out trap doors, air holes, and cooking exhaust vents, but the Viet Cong countered this by spreading peppers to confuse the dogs. They also used captured American clothing, American soap, American tobacco, and American shaving cream to throw the dogs off the scent. Even when the dogs did discover an entrance, they were often killed or maimed by booby traps. The Americans then began sending members of a chemical platoon into the tunnels. These slim-built, courageous volunteers became known as "tunnel rats." They suffered very high casualty rates.

The Viet Cong meanwhile were further developing the tunnels to include a network of command posts, living quarters, field hospitals, weapons factories, and training rooms. Tunnels were at several different levels and they crisscrossed and interconnected in a confusing and complex system that made it almost impossible for the Americans to navigate. Trap doors were installed to prevent tear gas, smoke, or water from moving from one section to another, and booby traps were deployed at regular intervals.

The U.S. Army eventually resorted to carpet-bombing the area with B-52 bombers, which destroyed many of the tunnels along with everything else. By this time, however, the tunnels had served their purpose, and the Viet Cong had won the hearts and minds of many of the local inhabitants. As the Americans withdrew, the Viet Cong took control of the whole area.

Today, there are two small sections of the tunnel system open to visitors. Both are about 1½ hours' drive from central Saigon. It makes little difference which one you visit. You buy a ticket that provides you with an English-speaking guide who takes you to a briefing room first. Here you see a large map that shows the extent of the tunnel system in the 1960s together with information on the locations of villages, South Vietnamese military posts, and the large American base. Another diagram shows the different levels of tunnels and associated works. You are then shown a short video that is high on propaganda, but also quite descriptive of the time and the living conditions of the inhabitants of the tunnels.

You are then invited to visit some of the underground chambers. Most have been enlarged so visitors can enter without too many problems, and some have even had their earth roofs removed and replaced with thatched versions that provide more light and space. Electricity is now supplied to most of them. Even the tunnels have been enlarged, so large-framed Westerners can move about. Despite this, many visitors balk at going down to the third level, and others avoid the thirty-meter crawl necessary to visit some of the rooms. Certainly anyone prone to claustrophobia should avoid trying it. Those that do the whole tour are rewarded with a great sense of satisfaction for themselves and a deep admiration for those who built, lived, and died in these extremely difficult conditions. There are facilities for buying cold drinks at the visitors' center, and you can also get a small selection of food. I became extremely ill about twelve hours after visiting here, so perhaps I should not be recommending the food to you.

There are guided day tours to the Cu Chi tunnels from Saigon, or you can rent a vehicle and driver to go there yourself. It is theoretically possible to get there by public bus, but the last five or so kilometers are a problem. You may be lucky to find a "Honda" to take you there, otherwise you can walk or hitchhike. It is best to round up a few other travelers and rent a vehicle from Saigon. The cost will be around US$35. Allow 1½ hours to get there, 1½ hours to look around, and 1½ hours to get back to Saigon.

If you leave Saigon early enough, you can extend your sightseeing by visiting the border crossing to Cambodia, or by going on to the town of **Tay Ninh**. This is about three hours from Saigon and is interesting mainly because it is home to an amazing "temple" of the Caodaism faith. This is something that you will not see anywhere else in the world. The building took twenty years to complete, and it is an extravaganza of sight that uses elements of East and West in a somewhat bizarre combination.

The religion of **Cao Dai** (high palace or God) is an attempt to create the ideal religion through an amalgamation of the best philosophies of East and West. There are bits of Buddhism, Confucianism, Taoism, Hinduism, Christianity, and Islam. Caodaism was founded by Ngo Minh Chieu, a civil servant. He became active in séances; and in the 1920s, he declared that he had been in contact with Cao Dai and had received a series of revelations which became a formal religion in 1926. Within a year, Caodaism had tens of thousands of supporters; and in 1927, a convert by the name of Le Van Trung seized the leadership, exiled Ngo Minh Chieu, and set about building the temple in the village of Long Hoa, some four kilometers from Tay Ninh. By the late 1930s, the sect had an estimated four million adherents and it virtually controlled its own independent territory.

The year 1955 saw a major confrontation between the South Vietnamese government and the Caodaist leaders. This led to the return of the Cao Dai territory to South Vietnamese control and the incorporation of the 25,000 Cao Dai army troops into the South Vietnamese forces. After 1975, the Cao Dai suffered persecution and lost all of their land and temples. However, most have now been returned to Cao Dai control. There are an estimated two million followers of Caodaism in Southern Vietnam today.

The temple that you can visit today is built on nine levels, representing the nine steps to heaven. The nave has columns decorated with dragons supporting a dome ceiling. Above the altar hangs a giant sphere containing the divine eye of Cao Dai with an eternal flame. There are statues and other colorful decorations throughout the building, giving it an atmosphere of high kitsch. Prayers are conducted each day at 6 A.M., noon, 6 P.M., and midnight. You are welcome to attend, and you can even photograph if you cause no disturbance.

About fifteen kilometers northeast of Tay Ninh, you can see **Nui Ba Den**, the mountain of the black lady. This is the highest point in Southern Vietnam, and there are several cave-temples on the mountain. Chua Linh Son Pagoda and Lang Chan Pagoda are places of pilgrimage, and you can avail yourself of the services of fortunetellers—some of whom speak English.

Vung Tau is 125 kilometers southeast of Saigon and is the closest beach resort to the city. The beaches are not great, but on weekends they can be crowded with people out for a bit of sun and surf. If you are going to central Vietnam, you could almost forget about Vung Tau; but if you are only spending time in Saigon, I recommend you take two days off and spend them in this resort.

The Vung Tau peninsula juts into the South China Sea. It is mainly flat and low-lying, but there are two small mountains immediately north and south of Vung Tau town. Vung Tau recently had a large number of Russians living here and working the oil rigs about fifty kilometers offshore. They lived in a compound separated from the rest of the population. Now many have gone home to be replaced by Australians, Japanese, and others who work for international companies who have recently won exploration permits. The compound no longer exists, but some of the better visitor accommodations are in this area.

Vung Tau has four beaches. **Back Beach** is the main bathing area and is by far the largest. It stretches for about eight kilometers, but the sand is only fair for much of its length and the water can be quite dirty at times. Sometimes there is a reasonable surf, but at other times it is completely calm. **Front Beach** is the area fronting Vung Tau town. It is rocky and fairly unattractive but the water is sometimes crowded with people. No one seems to swim, they just stand around in the water—often fully clothed. **Bai Dau Beach** is the

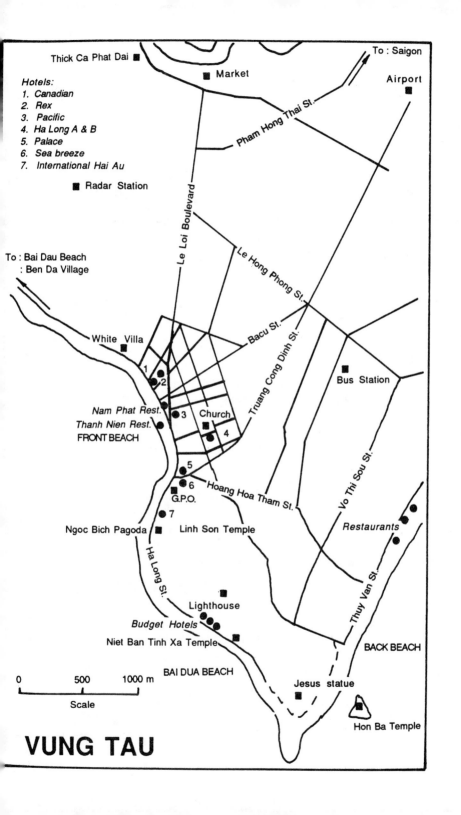

Thick Ca Phat Dai

Market

To : Saigon

Airport

Hotels:
1. Canadian
2. Rex
3. Pacific
4. Ha Long A & B
5. Palace
6. Sea breeze
7. International Hai Au

■ Radar Station

Pham Hong Thai St.

Le Loi Boulevard

Le Hong Phong St.

To : Bai Dau Beach
: Ben Da Village

White Villa

Bacu St.

Truang Cong Dinh St.

Bus Station

Nam Phat Rest.

Thanh Nien Rest.

Church

FRONT BEACH

Hoang Hoa Tham St.

G.P.O.

Ngoc Bich Pagoda

Linh Son Temple

Vo Thi Sou St.

Restaurants

Ha Long St.

Lighthouse

Thuy Van St.

Budget Hotels

Niet Ban Tinh Xa Temple

BACK BEACH

BAI DUA BEACH

Jesus statue

0   500   1000 m

Scale

Hon Ba Temple

VUNG TAU

prettiest and most relaxing of the beaches, and it has some coconut palms lining the shore. It is about three kilometers northwest of the city. **Bai Dua Beach** is a rocky cove with about two meters of sand, two kilometers south of the city.

Apart from the beaches, there are a few other places of mild interest. There is a great view from the lighthouse atop the Small Mountain (Nui Nho), however, for some obscure reason you are not allowed to photograph it. There is a narrow paved road to the lighthouse from the coastal road south of town. An enormous figure of Jesus, about thirty meters high, dominates the southern end of the Small Mountain. You can reach it by a footpath that heads up the hill from just south of Back Beach. Also in this area is the **Hon Ba Temple**, which is on a small island close to shore. You can walk across here at low tide.

Just north of Bai Dua, you can visit the large, modern **Niet Ban Tinh Xa Temple**. There is a huge reclining Buddha, a massive bell, and some other things of interest. At the other end of town, **Thick Ca Phat Dai** is a hillside park containing Buddhist statuary, a museum showing Con Son prison life under the French and South Vietnamese regimes, some restaurants, and a miscellaneous collection of other things that appeal to Vietnamese visitors.

Vung Tau has a large number of hotels and guest houses. There are two good modern hotels. The **Canadian Hotel** (Tel: 6-459-852), at 48 Quang Trung Street, overlooks the water and has good facilities. The hotel opened in 1991 and is well managed. There is a nice restaurant, a lobby bar, a disco, a business center, and a tennis court. The standard rooms are a good size with a balcony, and they come equipped with TV, telephone, refrigerator with mini bar, airconditioning, desk, and a small but clean bathroom. Bathrobes are provided for guests. Room rates start at US$40/50 single/double and rise to US$75/85 single/double. (Book by Fax: 846-459-851.) The alternative is the **Seabreeze Hotel** (Tel: 6-452-392), at 11 Nguyen Trai Street. This Australian-owned-and-managed property opened in 1992 and represents excellent value. Standard rooms are US$35 and come equipped with airconditioning, carpet, refrigerator, telephone, fans, TV with satellite programming, small but efficient bathrooms, and high-quality furnishings. There are nine super large rooms that rent for US$55 a night. They have the same amenities as the other rooms, but also have a three-piece lounge suite and table. There is a restaurant, a bar, and a nice swimming pool.

Down-market from here, there are numerous alternatives, but frankly I'm not very impressed by any of them. The **International Hotel Hai-Aur** (Tel: 6-452-178) opened in 1989 and looks as if it is thirty years old. It has the usual room facilities and two restaurants, a disco, massage, business center, and a swimming pool that was empty when I visited in the middle of summer. Room rates start at US$45. The **Palace Hotel** (Tel: 6-452-411) has 105 airconditioned rooms—all with telephone, TV, refrigerator, music desk, and table—but they are pretty unappealing. A few have no windows and are available for US$40, others go up to US$70. The hotel has two restaurants, a dancing hall, massage, a small shop, and a tennis court. It is about two hundred meters from the beach.

Budget accommodations are readily available in guest houses on most of the beaches and at a few hotels. The **Ha Long A Hotel** (Tel: 6-452-175), on Thong Nhat Street beside the church, has fan rooms from US$4 and airconditioned ones from US$7. There seems to be a number of women around this establishment, so there could be some short-time trade. The **Pacific Hotel** (Tel: 6-452-279), at 4 Le Loi Street, has airconditioned rooms with hot water and refrigerator for US$16 single and US$18 double. There are two restaurants, a massage, and a nightclub. The **Rang Dong** (Tel: 6-452-133) has 78 rooms from US$11 at 5 Duy Tan Street.

There are restaurants at all the beaches. At Front Beach, I had a good meal at the **Nam Phat Restaurant** on Quang Trung Street, near Le Loi Boulevard. The **Thanh Nien Restaurant**, which is actually on the seafront near here, has a lovely outdoor setting. At Bai Dua, there is a nice restaurant at **126 Ha Long Street** and a cafe with a nice view of the bay at **104 Ha Long Street**. On Back Beach, I had a reasonable, but overpriced meal at **Dai Duong 27 Restaurant**. I am told that the **Thang Muoi Restaurant** is good.

After dark, there is considerable action in Vung Tau. Most of the major hotels have dancing halls or discos. You will find that many locals stand outside the major hotels looking and waiting for something to happen. Some of these people speak English and will be glad to spend some nighttime hours with you. "Massage" parlors are flourishing in Vung Tau with the apparent support of the authorities. If all else fails, you can have a game of night tennis.

Buses for Vung Tau leave Saigon from the Mien Dong Bus Station or from the Van Thanh Bus Station (about US$0.60); but it may be better to take one of the "express" buses that leave from the foot of Nguyen Hue Boulevard or from outside the Saigon Hotel. These cost around US$5 for the round trip. A car from a tour agency will cost around US$50 for a day trip. A ferry service operates from central Saigon opposite the Majestic Hotel at 8 A.M daily. It returns from Vung Tau at 4 P.M. The round-trip fare is US$16 and the one-way journey takes 1 hour 20 minutes.

THE MEKONG DELTA

This is the richest agricultural region in Vietnam, and it is an essential region for the well-being of the whole country. Rice, sugar cane, fruit, and coconuts are the main crops. Some people rave on about how attractive the delta is; but frankly it is not one of my favorite areas. I acknowledge, however, that it is worth visiting if you are trying to get a good overview of the whole country.

The Mekong River is one of the great rivers of Asia. It has its source in the Tibetan plateau, and it flows through China, between Laos and Myanmar, through Laos, between Thailand and Laos, through Cambodia, and finally through Vietnam before discharging into the South China Sea. Through Vietnam, the Mekong has two major channels: the Mekong itself, which flows through Hang Ngu and Vinh Long, then splits into several branches to empty into the sea at five or six different points; and the Bassac River which flows through Phu Tan, Long Xuyen and Cantho. During September, the rivers are an awesome sight as they discharge the run-off from a huge area of southeast Asia. The silt that they carry continues to extend the shoreline of southern Vietnam by dozens of meters a year.

Highway 1 heads southeast from Saigon into the delta. The first major center you reach is **Mytho**, the capital of Tien Giang Province. There are day trips from Saigon to visit the town and surrounding area. Mytho was founded by Chinese refugees in the seventeenth century soon after the Nguyen Lords took control of the area from the Khmer. In the nineteenth century, it became an important center for French control of this region. In the twentieth century, it was an important American military base; and now it is a city of 100,000 people surrounded by rice fields and orchards. It is situated on the northernmost branch of the Mekong River.

The city is fairly ordinary, but the yellow Catholic church on the corner of Hung Vuong Boulevard and Nguyen Trai Street (Saigon Road) is worth seeing; and the central market along Trung Trac Street, near the Bao Dinh Channel on the eastern edge of town, is worth visiting. You can take a boat along the Mekong to visit Tan Long island, where you can see orchards, palm trees, and ship builders. **Vinh Trang Pagoda** is about two kilometers east of town. You approach it along an impressive tree-lined driveway and the ornate building itself is set on nice grounds.

There are several hotels in Mytho. Most are along Trung Trac Street. The **Song Tien Hotel** (Tel: 712-009), 36 rooms, is possibly the best in town. Room rates are US$15-20 for airconditioned rooms and from US$6 for fanned rooms. The highest-priced rooms have refrigerators. There are several restaurants along this stretch of road, and there are others in the market area. You can reach Mytho from Saigon by bus (about 1½ hours) or by passenger ferry (6 hours). A car ferry operates from Mytho to Ben Tre Province. This region managed to secure considerable independence under successive regimes since the eighteenth century, but was severely damaged during the 1960s and 1970s and the Vietnam War.

Although Saigon tour operators will not admit it, you can visit the major city of **Cantho** on a long day trip. This is probably the nicest city in the delta, and it is certainly the political, economic, and cultural center of the region. Cantho is on Highway 1 from Saigon and it is connected to most other major delta centers by road and water. There are two ferry crossings on the trip from Saigon—one at Vinh Long and one just outside Cantho. The trip can take three hours if you are lucky with the ferries, or up to 4½ hours if you are not.

In town, you can visit the university, which was founded in 1966. There is also an important rice research institute. The central market has taken over Hoi Ba Trung Street alongside the Cantho River, and it is quite fascinating to walk through here during a busy period. You will find that you become a center of interest as well. The **Munirangsyaram Pagoda**, on wide Hoa Binh Boulevard, is typical of the Khmer Buddhist pagodas you find in this region.

The highlight of a visit to Cantho is a boat ride on the one-and-a-half-kilometer-wide Bassac River. You take a boat from the Ninh Kieu Quay, near the market, and you can visit many rural areas of Hau Giang Province. It is also worth taking a boat to the floating market, where boats and junks are anchored side-by-side. There are boats piled high with shrimp and fish and others crammed with coconuts, watermelons, oranges, and durian.

The two best hotels in Cantho are probably the **Quoc Te Hotel** (Tel: 22-079) on Hai Ba Trung Street, and the **Hau Giang Hotel** (Tel: 21-851) on Nam Ky Khoi Nghia Street. Prices at each of these are around US$20-25 a room for airconditioned rooms and US$10-12 for fanned rooms. There are some good local restaurants which specialize in fish along the Cantho River waterfront.

If you have the opportunity to include it on your travel permit, I suggest a visit to Chau Phu on the Cambodian border and Rach Gia and Ha Tien on the Gulf of Thailand.

Chau Phu is a multicultural commercial center stretching along the right bank of the Bassac River. It has no memorable sights, but it is interesting for its remoteness and the Khmer influence that still exists there. In town, there are Buddhist temples, a Catholic church, and a temple for the worship of Thoai Ngoe Hau. Just across the river is a mosque for the Cham muslim population.

A special feature of Chau Phu and surrounding towns is the floating houses. Under each house, families keep fish in suspended nets, and they feed them scraps and other biological matter. The fish seem to thrive in the natural river habitat and are sold in the local market.

Twenty kilometers east of Chau Phu is the village of **Hoa Hao**. It was here that Huynh Phu So founded another influential indigenous religion that attempted to rid Buddhism of its pagodas and clergy. He banned alcohol,

230 MAVERICK GUIDE TO VIETNAM, LAOS, AND CAMBODIA

opium, and gambling; and he actively opposed injustice and poverty. After World War II, the Hoa Hao community created an anti-Marxist political party called Don Xa. As a result, Huyah Phu So was assassinated by the Viet Minh. When Ngo Dinh Diem came to power in 1954, the Hoa Hao opposed his regime—one faction even joined the National Liberation Front. After 1975, the Communists clamped down on the Hoa Hao, and the sect lost much of its influence.

Eighteen kilometers across the Bassac River, the **Tan Chau district** is famous for its traditional silk industry and luxury goods which are imported (smuggled) from Thailand via Cambodia. In the opposite direction, it is only about three kilometers to **Sam Mountain**. There are many pagodas and temples around the mountain. Several of these are worth visiting.

There are several hotels in Chau Phu, but none are great. The **Hang Chau Hotel** (Tel: 66-196) on the river near the Chau Giang Ferry terminal is probably the best. There are some reasonable restaurants on Chi Lang Street. Chau Doc is 120 kilometers from Cantho. The trip takes around 2 ½ hours.

Rach Gia is 115 kilometers west of Cantho via That Nat or Go Quao. This port city on the Gulf of Thailand is the capital of Kien Giang Province. The main part of town is on an island between two branches of the Cai Lan River. Here you find most of the hotels, restaurants, shopping areas, and markets. Here also is the century-old **Ong Bac De Pagoda**, built by the Chinese community, and the small **Rach Gia Museum**.

The two most interesting temples are north of town. **Phat Lon Pagoda** is off Quang Trung Street. This is a large Cambodian-style Buddhist pagoda which was founded about two hundred years ago. A block south of here, on Nguyen Cong Tru Street, the **Nguyen Trung Truc temple** is dedicated to the leader of the Vietnamese resistance campaign against the French in the 1860s. He was eventually executed in 1868. The temple has been rebuilt and enlarged over the years, and today it is quite impressive.

About twelve kilometers inland from Rach Gia is the site of Oc-Eo, a major trading city about 1,700 years ago. This was part of the Funan Empire, which covered most of southern Vietnam, southern Cambodia, and the Malay Peninsula. The archaeological excavations at Oc-Eo have proved particularly fruitful, and some artifacts can be seen in the History Museum in Saigon.

Reasonable rooms are available at the **To Chau Hotel** on Le Loi Street for around US$20 and the **Thang 5 Hotel** around the corner on Nguyen Hung Son Street. There are several good restaurants on the waterfront nearby. Phu Quoc island, near the Cambodian border, can be reached by boat from Rach Gia.

Ha Tien is on the Gulf of Thailand—almost on the Cambodian border. The main attraction for visitors is the white sand beaches that exist both east and west of the town. The best beaches close to town are at **Mui Nai**, four kilometers to the east. The most interesting is **Duong Beach**, which is noted for its white sand, clear water, and for the nearby **Chua Hang Grotto**.

Ha Tien was first settled by a Chinese escapee, Mac Cuu, who convinced the Cambodian king to make him governor of the Panthaimas District that centered on Ha Tien. Mac Cuu encouraged traders and settlers to come to the area, and prosperity followed almost immediately. Within a decade, it became a small thriving state. This brought attacks from the Siamese, which led Mac Cuu to seek help from the Vietnamese in Hue. For the next twenty-five years, he ruled as a prince under the protection of the Vietnamese. The last Mac ruler of this region was the seventh generation, Mac Tu Kham, who succumbed to the French in 1867.

7. Guided Tours

Saigon is the only city in Vietnam to have successfully developed a series of day tours that operate regularly. The initial planning and development was done by **Saigon Tourist** (Tel: 298-914), a government agency commissioned to run tours in southern Vietnam. Saigon Tourist has been hugely successful and is now a major player in the tourism stakes. I have found the staff to be pleasant and reasonably well informed, but the tours are highly priced and quite inflexible. Current prices per person for the four day trips operated by this organization are: city tour US$15, Cu Chi tunnels US$30, Mytho (delta) US$50, and Vung Tau US$60. Even if you are the only passenger, you still do the standard tour—whether you like it or not. Contact Saigon Tourist at 49 Le Thanh Ton Street, at the corner of Dong Khoi Street opposite the Hotel de Ville.

Several other operators have now gotten into the act. These include **Vietnam Tourism** in Ho Chi Minh City (Tel: 290-776). This organization specializes in tour packages for overseas tourists. It currently offers several 3-day/2-night packages in Ho Chi Minh City. A typical package includes "meet and greet" at Tan Son Nhut airport, transfer to the hotel, a city tour, a variety show at night, a day trip to Vung Tau or Mytho, and shopping and transfer to the airport. These tours cost US$230-400 depending on content and standard of accommodation.

Vietnam Tourism also has several 8-day/7-night packages from Ho Chi Minh City to Hanoi. Some use air travel, and one uses the train. The packages, which include accommodations, transportation, and meals, are amazingly expensive—about US$1,400 for one, US$950 each for two, and US$860 each for larger groups. An 8-day/7-night package from Ho Chi Minh City to Dalat, Nha Trang, and back to Ho Chi Minh City is a similar price. There are also fifteen- and twenty-one-day tours that include sightseeing in Ho Chi Minh City, Hanoi, and various points in between.

I have had limited contact with other operators, but **VYTA Tours** (Tel: 230-767) at 52 Hai Ba Trung Street appears to be a very active organization, and the equipment that I have seen is clean and modern. This company has budget day tours from Ho Chi Minh City at very attractive prices. Cu Chi is US$8, Mytho is US$9, Cu Chi and Tay Ninh US$13, and Vung Tau US$13. **Burotel Tourist** (Tel: 293-727) has package tours, but I have only used them for car rental services. The current rate is US$0.18 per kilometer for airconditioned car and driver. This is considerably cheaper than Vietnam Tourism, Saigon Tourist, and most of the hotels.

8. Culture

Saigon has several theaters where you can see various performances. Unfortunately, all performances are likely to be in Vietnamese, with not even a brief program note or announcement in English. Therefore, most have limited appeal to visitors. There are two theaters on Tran Hung Dao Boulevard and several in Cholon that fall into this category. The same can be said for the **Municipal Theater** (Tel: 291-249) on Dong Khoi Street and the huge **Hoa Binh Theater** complex (Tel: 655-199) on 3 Thang 2 Boulevard. Occasionally, however, these places have performances by international performers or companies. It is worth asking for information about what is playing when you arrive in Saigon.

The **Conservatory of Music** (Tel: 396-646) on Nguyen Du Street, near the Unification Palace, is the center for music teaching in Saigon. There are concerts here during certain times of the year from students, staff, and the occasional visiting teacher or performer.

A few restaurants and hotels have "cultural" performances on a semi-regular basis. If you have the opportunity to see one of these, I recommend that you do so. The culture is quite fascinating and it is interesting to see how different cultures have adopted different conventions for similar things. An example is the sixteen-string instrument that is akin to the Western zither. This has its bass strings toward the upper edge of the soundboard rather than the lower as we would expect.

The **Binh Quoi Village** (Tel: 991-833) has traditional music performances each Tuesday, Thursday, and Saturday from 5 P.M. to 8 P.M. The Classical Drama Group performs regularly at the **Long Phung Theater** (Tel: 297-674).

9. Sports

Golfers are catered for at the $30-million Song Be Golf Resort 20 kilometers north of Saigon. The 27-hole Vung Tau Entertainment Village course at seaside Vung Tau should open in 1995. A course is under construction in

Saigon's northeastern suburbs at Thu Duc. A golf driving range opened in late 1994 at this location (Tel: 960-756).

Most Vietnamese love exercise, and you can see this as thousands perform tai chi in the parks while thousands more can be seen jogging in the streets early in the morning. Badminton nets appear on sidewalks and soccer is played in the streets.

For a fee, swimmers can use the pools at the Saigon Floating Hotel, the Rex Hotel, and the Palace Hotel. The Floating Hotel pool is the best and the most expensive. There are also a few public pools scattered around the city that are in reasonable condition and appear to be well chlorinated. There are tennis courts for rent at the Saigon Floating Hotel and the Rex Hotel. The **Worker's Club** (Tel: 290-288), which occupies the site of the old Cerele Sportif on Nguyen Thi Minh Khai Street, has a swimming pool and several well-patronized tennis courts. Visitors are welcome to use the facilities for a price. There are also courts at 86 Le Thanh Ton Street (Tel: 292-186) and at 1107 Xo Viet Nghe Tinh Street, Binh Thanh (Tel: 991-517).

Bi Da is very popular throughout the city. This is a three-ball game played on a billiard table that has no pockets. The rules totally escape me, but I'm sure you could learn.

Horse racing is held most weekends at the **Phu Tho Racetrack** (Tel: 551-205) at 2 Le Dai Hanh Street, north of Cholon. The course is in fair condition, and betting is undertaken at a furious pace. For horse fans, it is an experience. Soccer and athletics are held at sports grounds near the airport, near the zoo, and just north of downtown Cholon.

10. Shopping   *Le Long Kieu - Antiques Street*

Saigon may be the best shopping center in Vietnam, but that doesn't mean that you will spend days roaming the shops and picking up bargains. Five years ago, it was difficult to buy anything in the city. Now there is a good range of basic necessities, but only a limited range of souvenirs and other things that you would want to take home.

Some of the hotels, such as the Saigon Floating Hotel and the Rex, have well-stocked shops, and they are a good place to start. Items in these shops have marked prices. Although they tend to be more expensive than some other places, you will know that you are not being charged an exorbitant price for an inferior product. In the markets and elsewhere, you can never be certain of this. Everywhere else, you run the risk of blatant overcharging, so know your prices before you venture out into the streets. It is a good idea to try bargaining everywhere. Even when prices are marked, you may get a ten-percent reduction. Elsewhere, foreigners can achieve a fifty-percent reduction and still end up paying twice what a local would.

There are souvenir shops scattered throughout the city, but as with many other items, they are particularly concentrated along Dong Khoi Street, between Le Loi Boulevard and Ton Duc Thang Street. **Lacquerware** is the most popular item and probably the best buy. Prices may initially seem high, but making the pieces is a complex and lengthy process. Even though wages are very low, weeks of work must be rewarded with a reasonable return. It can take up to eight weeks to make a medium-size piece.

You can visit a lacquer factory and buy pieces there; but in my experience, prices are no cheaper than they are in some of the retail outlets. It is interesting to see the manufacturing process, however. Cured wood is covered with cloth to prevent cracking, and a number of base coats of lacquer are applied. The artist then applies the design using paint, broken eggshells, or mother-of-pearl. This is followed by up to ten more coats of lacquer, with sanding between each coat. Finally, the item is polished by hand. If you are taking the item away from the tropics, it is very important to buy a piece that has had cloth applied to the wood. You can usually tell from a fine line that appears around the back edge of the piece.

Ceramics are also good, but you have the problem of transporting them. Dishes, bowls, and vases can be found in the markets, and they are inexpensive if you can get the local price. More unusual items, such as the imperial elephants, can cost around US$20-25 and can be bought in many shops in the Dong Khoi area. So-called antique ceramics are surprisingly expensive; and unless you know what you are doing, these should be avoided. I am told that many are fakes.

Paintings are numerous and reasonably priced. There are a number of galleries downtown containing oil paintings, watercolors, and paintings on silk in a variety of styles. One of the better places with a good selection is the **Art Arcade** on Dong Khoi Street, opposite the side of the Caravelle Hotel.

Excellent **leather goods** are available from many stores on Le Thanh Ton Street in the area surrounding the Norfolk Hotel. Handbags, wallets, briefcases, and overnight bags are all good buys. Most are genuine leather and would cost much more elsewhere. If you have small feet, you will find that there is a good range of leather shoes. The styles may not be the latest, but generally they are well made and serviceable. There is a small selection of leather clothes and hats. You can have shoes and even cowboy boots made to order, but this will take at least seven days and cost anything from US$20 to US$50.

There are **tailors** throughout the city—even some of the hotels have one on staff. While some offer a Hong Kong-style 24-hour suit-making service, others are more into quality and fit. I recommend that you allow at least three days for a suit or complicated woman's outfit, so there is the opportunity for

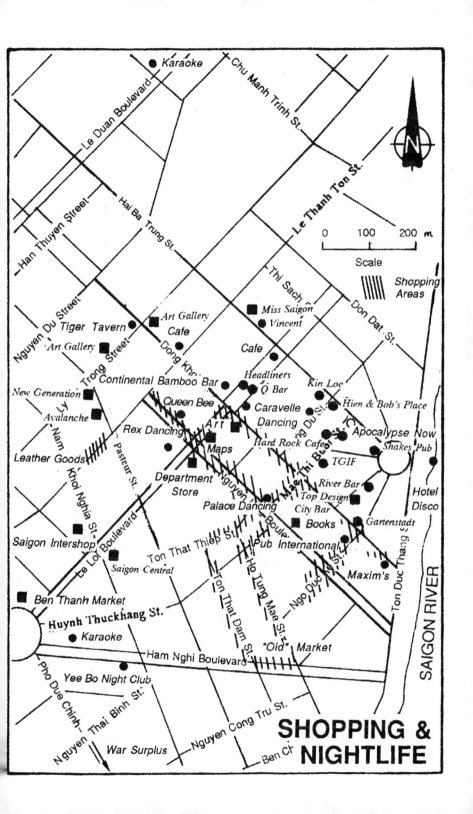

two fittings. Most tailors will attempt to follow a style from a book, but sometimes the results are less than satisfactory. Men's shirts cost around US$4-5; women's skirts are around US$8 plus material.

War surplus material is sold in the area near the Phung Son Tu Pagoda, on Nguyen Cong Tru Street and Ky Con Street. There are gas masks, parachutes, and flak jackets for those starting a private army, as well as the more useful canteens, mosquito nets, duffle bags, and boots. Many items are brand new and are the remains of items that "walked" from U.S. Army stores more than twenty years ago. Others are not. Back-alley manufacturers make a living by producing look-alike U.S. government-issue items. Gross overcharging of foreigners is common here, so you must bargain. If you can't get a fifty-percent reduction in price, forget about buying.

Books are popular in Saigon, so there are several bookshops worth visiting. There are learn-to-speak-English books by the ton, but you will also find a small selection of other material in English. The large bookshop at 40 Nguyen Hue Boulevard has a collection of used history books in English and some recently printed Vietnamese editions of old and new titles. The **Foreign Languages Bookshop**, at 185 Dong Khoi Street, has a fair selection of English material, including some real treasures hidden away in the back room. I haven't been there myself, but I am told that **Godfathers** down near Me Linh Circle has developed into the best bookshop in town.

The bookshops also have some **maps**, but I have found that the street stalls in Le Loi Boulevard, between Dong Khoi Street and Nguyen Hue Boulevard, have a better selection. You can buy a good Saigon map here, as well as Vietnam maps, Indochina maps, and maps of some of the other regions and cities in the country. This is by far the best selection available anywhere. If you need maps, buy them here, don't wait until later.

Film and film processing is readily available. There seem to be more processing stores in Saigon than in most cities of the world. Perhaps this is a reflection of the Vietnamese love for having their photographs taken. The equipment is modern, and the results for color prints are good. I don't recommend having slides developed in Vietnam. Take them to Thailand or back home with you. The x-ray machines at the airport are now said to be film-safe, but ask if you can hand carry undeveloped film, just in case.

It is well worthwhile to visit the **department store** on the corner of Le Loi Boulevard and Nguyen Hue Boulevard. A few years ago, this place was a dismal joke; but now it has been privatized and it is really buzzing. You can buy almost all necessities here as well as books, stationery, music and video tapes, and electrical goods.

For those who feel deprived without a supermarket, the good news is that Saigon, at last, has such a place. Head for the **Intershop** at the corner of Le Loi Boulevard and Nam Ky Khoi Nghia Street; and you will find imported canned goods, frozen foods, some local manufactured items, a whole range of household goods, jewelry, handicrafts, and so forth.

Don't forget the **Ben Thanh Market**. It has a wide variety of goods, but be warned about pickpockets. A similar comment can be made about the **Old Market** along Ton That Dam Street, Huynh Thuc Khang Street, and Ton That Thiep Street. This was the old black market, but now it is almost legal. You can find all sorts of electrical and electronic gear here at prices similar to those at home, but tapes and video cassettes are good buys, and there are some good food outlets appearing. The **Andong Market** in Cholon is worth a visit. The basement has many food stalls with low prices and above you will find almost everything imaginable including quite a range of imported goods.

There are a few up-market fashion outlets in town. These are aimed at the local "in-crowd," but could have some interest to visitors. **Miss Saigon** on Hai Ba Trung Street and **Avalanche** (Tel: 242-887) and the **New Generation** (Tel: 291-650) on Pasteur Street all have modern fashions and some interesting gear. **Top Design** (Tel: 290-711), at 13 Ho Huan Nghiep Street, is a modern hair and beauty salon with overseas styling.

11. Entertainment and Nightlife

Saigon is stirring. Although it is not back to its roaring sixties days, the city has at least thrown off some of the straightjacket restrictions that were imposed during the late seventies and eighties. Dancing is allowed. Cafeterias have sprung up. There are some discos. There are even a few straight bars.

Most visitors will explore their **hotels** first. Most will find that there is at least one Western-style bar, with or without music. Some of the best are the lobby bar at the Saigon Floating Hotel, the fifth-floor outdoor bar at the Rex Hotel, the lobby bar at the Mondial Hotel, the Club Bar at the Norfolk Hotel, and the Bamboo Bar at the Continental Hotel.

Also within the hotels, you can find **dancing halls**. These are places that have low lighting, a live band, and drinks at higher-than-normal prices. There are hostesses to dance with single men, and I am told that at least one place can provide the same service for single women. The Rex, the Palace, and the Caravelle all have well-known and popular rooms. The Majestic Hotel was not operating its dancing room when I was last in Saigon, but it should be by now. The music at these places is a mixture of Western and Vietnamese from the sixties and seventies, with lots of cha-chas, rumbas, and tangos thrown in. All have cover charges that are often waived for house guests.

The Saigon Floating Hotel has the best **disco** in town. It operates from around 9 P.M. to 2 A.M., and has a cover of US$5. Another place that is popular, and has just been renovated, is the third floor of the **Saigon Intershop** on Nam Ky Khoi Nghia Street. Also worth trying is **Queen Bee**, which is in the shopping center on Nguyen Hue Boulevard, opposite the Rex Hotel. This is a restaurant until 9:30 P.M., then a disco from 10 P.M.. A further possibility is the **Thai Son Disco Club** (Tel: 223-267) at 69 Dong Khoi Street. The cover charge rises as the end of the week approaches. Karaoke fans will like the **Saigon Karaoke Restaurant** (Tel: 298-474) at 55 Nam Ky Khoi Nghia Street.

Several restaurants have **floor shows** or at least a band and some singers. **Maxim's** on Dong Khoi Street is probably best. They also have dancing in an upstairs area. **Liberty**, a bit farther along this street, has singers in the restaurant and dancing upstairs. The **Yee Bo Night Club** on Ham Hghi Boulevard caters primarily to Chinese residents and visitors. The **Pub International** (Tel: 295-427) on Ngo Duc Ke is an option for those interested in meeting the locals. So too are a few old-style bars that have opened recently.

Hien & Bob's Place (Tel: 230-661) at 43 Hai Ba Trung is American-owned and serves cold Bud and ham and cheese sandwiches. Along the road a bit is the non-authentic **Hard Rock Cafe**, while two streets away you will find the **River Bar** (Tel: 293-734) with its snooker and food at 5 Ho Huan Nghiep. The most popular place in town at present is the up-market **Q-Bar** in the east side of the Opera House at 7 Cong Truong Lam Son. After 10 P.M. it really fills up with the Who's Who in the expatriate community. On the other side of the building is the **Saigon Headliners** (Tel: 225-014) with live music from 8 P.M. to midnight. It claims to be a jazz bar, but I think they are stretching the meaning of the word a bit. Two other places are **TGIF** (Tel: 243-977) at 23 Mac Thi Buoi Street and the **X.O. Pub** (Tel: 225-704) at 38 Hai Ba Trung Street. Both have meals. There is no "girlie bar" scene in Saigon, although ladies of the night will make themselves known to any single male who walks the streets after 9 P.M.

Saigon has a number of cafes. These are places for sipping an iced coffee during the daytime or a cold beer at night. Some have outdoor seating, where you can watch the world go by. Some of the most popular are at the corner of Le Thanh Ton Street and Dong Khoi Street, at the corner of Nguyen Thi Ming Khai Street and Nguyen Du Street, and on Nguyen Dinh Chieu Street and Le Quin Don Street. All of these are worth visiting. I would visit them in the order they are listed.

Two other places worth mentioning are **Tiger Tavern** (Tel: 222-738), at the corner of Dong Khoi Street and Ly Tu Trong Street, and **Apocalypse Now** at Mac Thi Buoi Street. Tiger Tavern has cold beer, a Western atmosphere, snack food, a good value set lunch and dinner, music late at night, and lots of trendy locals. Apocalypse Now has vintage music, a bulletin board, cold beer, a collection of odd-balls, and all the budget travelers in town. It is a good place to find out the latest travel information on the backpacker circuit.

12. The Saigon Address List

Airlines—Cathay Pacific, 49 Le Thanh Tong Street (Tel: 223-203); Vietnam Airlines, 116 Nguyen Hue Boulevard (Tel: 292-118).

Ambulance—(Tel: 296-485 or 15).

Banks—HCM City Bank for Trade and Commerce, 79 Ham Nghi (Tel: 290-494); Standard Chartered, 134 Dong Khoi (Tel: 298-335); Thai Military, 78 Nguyen Hue (Tel: 223-289).

Chamber of Commerce—171 Vo Thi Sau Street (Tel: 230-301).

Consulates—French, 27 Xo Viet Nghe Tinh (Tel: 297-231); Lao, 181 Hai Ba Trung (Tel: 299-262); Cambodian, 41 Phung Khac Hoan (Tel: 294-498).

Fire—(Tel: 18).

Foreign Investment Service Company—12 Nam Ky Khoi Nghia (Tel: 293-616).

Foreign Trade Development Center—92 Nguyen Hue (Tel: 222-982).

Hospital—Cho Ray—201B Nguyen Chi Thanh (Tel: 254-137).

International Freight—OHL—253 Hoang Van Thu (Tel: 444-268).

International Long Distance Call—(Tel: 13).

Office of Industry—101 Hai Ba Trung Street (Tel: 298-018).

People's Committee of HCM City—86 Le Thanh Ton (Tel: 291-054).

Police—(Tel: 13).

Post Office—125 Hai Ba Trung Street (Tel: 293-310).

Railway Station—1 Nguyen Thong (Tel: 443-952).

Saigon Tourist—49 Le Thanh Ton Street (Tel: 298-129).

Taxi—Vinataxi (Tel: 442-170).

Telephone Information—(Tel: 108).

Translation—Saigon Business Center—49 Dong Du Street (Tel: 298-777).

Vietnam Tourism—69 Nguyen Hue Blvd (Tel: 291-276).

Zoo—1 Le Duan (Tel: 298-146).

Laos

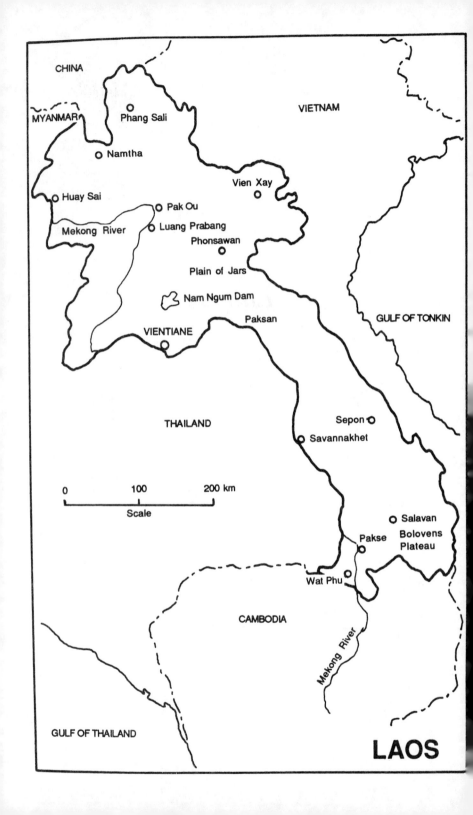

9

The Land, Life, and People of Laos

Neither nature nor history have been particularly kind to Laos. The landlocked country is mainly a place of crumpled mountains and narrow valleys that leave little space for good farming land.

With one notable exception, its history has been a battle to survive the power struggles of the masters of the region—the Khmers, the Siamese, the French, the Japanese, the Americans, the Vietnamese, and others. It is little wonder that this thinly populated Asian state, the size of the United Kingdom, has long been a remote backwater. That impression was reinforced when the Lao People's Revolutionary Party drew the bamboo curtain of communism around their borders in 1975, firmly shutting the doors to the West. Luckless Laos was in for another twelve years of pain.

Now things are different. Laos is still pathetically poor and underdeveloped, but no one is starving. A new optimism has emerged, and the country is opening itself to the world. Despite its past, the country still projects an inescapable charm. Visitors numbered a mere 185 in 1987; but since then the numbers have slowly grown. The country, which has been stuck in somewhat of a time warp, is about to blossom—if it can shake off its bureaucratic dust.

Geography

Laos stretches over one thousand kilometers from north to south, but is only about five hundred kilometers at its widest point. For much of its length, it is squeezed between the mountains on the east and the Mekong River on the west. It shares borders with Thailand, Vietnam, China, Myanmar (Burma), and Cambodia. It is entirely within the tropical zone of the northern hemisphere.

Seventy percent of Laos is mountain ranges, highlands, and plateaus. The Annamite Mountains, with an average height of around twelve hundred meters, separates Laos from Vietnam. All rivers to the west of this range drain into the Mekong River, which forms the border with Myanmar and a large part of the border with Thailand. These tributaries and the Mekong itself have been a dominant force in the existence of the Lao people for over a thousand years. The rivers have served as the country's lifeline, and the Mekong is still the major transportation link between the north and the south. The river is navigable year-round between Luang Prabang, Vientiane, and Savannakhet. The valley provides almost all of the country's wet rice lands and the largest population centers.

The country's highest mountain (about 2850 meters) is Phu Bia in Xieng Khwang Province. Close by is the Xieng Khwang Plateau, the best-known part of which is the Plain of Jars. This is about twelve hundred meters above sea level. In the south, the Bolevens (Bolovens) Plateau is an important agricultural area—particularly for tea, coffee, cardamom, and mountain rice.

Climate

The climate throughout Laos is monsoonal. In general, it is wet between May and October and dry between November and April. There are three distinct seasons with some variations between north and south.

The **cool dry season** occurs from November to January. In the Mekong Valley, temperatures can drop to around 15 degrees Celsius, and the mountain temperatures drop to zero degrees Celsius or lower at night. Humidity is low at this time of the year, and most visitors consider it the best time to travel to Laos.

The **hot dry season** follows through to May—although toward the end of this period there is high humidity and thunderstorms. Temperatures can reach 38 degrees Celsius in the Mekong Valley, which can be unpleasant for sightseeing or traveling. At this time, you will notice that the locals melt from the streets in the midday heat, and you should too.

The **wet season** generally lasts from June until October. It is typified by a consistent pattern of rain and low clouds, particularly through June, July, and August. The peaks of the Annamite Mountains can receive over three hundred centimeters of rain annually—most of which falls during this period. The far north, central, and southern provinces receive from 150 to

200 centimeters per year; while the central north, around Luang Prabang and the Plain of Jars, receives between 100 and 150 centimeters annually. Daytime temperatures at this time of year average around 28 degrees Celsius in the valley and 25 degrees in the mountains. Flooding occurs along the Mekong River and some of its tributaries.

History

There is little doubt that the Mekong River Valley was inhabited as far back as ten thousand years ago. Although evidence of their civilization and lifestyle is very limited, those people were probably related to the present inhabitants.

The present Thai and Lao people probably originated in southern China and started moving south in the eighth or ninth century. Under hereditary chieftains, they formed small communities throughout northern Thailand and Laos. Each group was based in part of a river valley, and some formed alliances for trade and protection. The early groups came under the control of the Mons or the Khmers, who had established earlier civilizations in the region. When the Mongols, under Kublai Khan, rose to power in China in the thirteenth century, there was a large southward exodus that contributed to the Thai rebellion against the Khmers. This resulted in the creation of the Sukhothai kingdom of northern Thailand.

Following an agreement between Sukhothai, Chiang Mai, and Phayao, a strong civilization called **Lanna** (million rice fields) was formed across north-central Thailand, and it included the region of Wieng Chan (Vientiane). This seriously eroded the Khmer empire's control over a vast region; so in the fourteenth century, Fa Ngum—with the support of the Khmers—conquered Wieng Chan, the northern region of Muang Sawa, and much of what is now northeast Thailand. He named these territories **Lan Xang** (million elephants) and established a capital at Muang Sawa, the present location of Luang Prabang.

Lan Xang is considered by many to be the first Lao nation, and it lasted for more than four hundred years. Fa Ngum made Buddhism the state religion, expanded the frontiers eastward to challenge the kingdom of Champa, and accepted the Pha Bang gold Buddha image from the Khmers. The Buddha was kept at Muang Sawa, which eventually led to the town changing its name to Luang Prabang (great Pha Bang).

Phaya Samsenthai had significant influence on Lan Xang. He reorganized the royal administration, built many temples and schools, and developed the economy such that Lan Xang became an important trading identity. The kingdom covered a large area, but was very much concentrated in Luang

Prabang with other areas under loose and indirect administration. When King Phothisarat moved the capital of Lan Xang to Wieng Chan in 1520, it forever changed the center of power in the region.

In 1545, Phothisarat overpowered what remained of Lanna and established his son Settathirath as ruler of that kingdom. Two years later, Settathirath inherited the kingdom of Lan Xang and moved back to Wieng Chan. He brought with him the Emerald Buddha (Pha Kaew) and built Wat Pha Kaew to house it. He also ordered the construction of That Luang, Vientiane's famous stupa. When King Settathirath disappeared in 1571, the kingdom rapidly declined, then disintegrated under the Burmese invasion of the late sixteenth century.

The kingdom was revived around 1637 when King Suligna Vongsa ascended the throne. He ruled for sixty years and reestablished Lan Xang as the most powerful kingdom in the region. These years were good for Lan Xang residents, and they are often regarded as the pinnacle of Lao achievement. When the king died without an heir, a succession dispute caused Lan Xang to collapse and become divided into three separate kingdoms. A nephew supported by Annam (northern Vietnam) took control of the area around Vientiane. The king's grandsons took control of the area around Luang Prabang, while a prince under Siamese influence established a southern kingdom at Champassak.

This separation lasted about eighty years, but gradually the Siamese expanded their influence over the Vientiane kingdom, and to a lesser degree over Luang Prabang. By the 1820s, this had become intolerable to Vientiane's Prince Anou, so he went to war with Siam. The result was devastating. Vientiane was almost razed, and many of its residents were forcibly taken to Siam. Some years later, Vientiane, Luang Prabang, and Champasak were all Siamese satellite states, and the Siamese also occupied the area now within Xieng Khwang and Hua Phan provinces in 1885.

This was the situation when the French entered the scene. They initially persuaded the king of Luang Prabang to accept French "protection" against the Siamese and the Chinese Ho Bandits. Then, with some blatant gunboat diplomacy, they forced the Siamese to cede all territories east of the Mekong River to France. The French then united all of the Lao principalities as one nation and called it Laos. However, their interest in the country was only marginal. In contrast to Vietnam and Cambodia, the French carried out little development in Laos. They built few roads, no railroads, and no universities; and they educated few local people. A Vietnamese-staffed French-style civil service was foisted on the country, effectively stifling indigenous efforts.

In 1941, the Japanese occupied the whole of French Indochina. The Lao offered little resistance to the Japanese, and they discovered that they had more local autonomy than they had under the French. Toward the end of the war, the Japanese convinced the king to declare independence; but this was seen as a farce by many. A nationalist movement called the Lao Issara was established under Prince Phethsarath to ensure that France did not regain control of the country.

France, however, had other ideas. French paratroopers landed in Vientiane and Luang Prabang in mid-1945 and declared Laos to be a French protectorate. Phethsarath and the Lao Issara countered by drawing up a new constitution and proclaiming Laos independent on October 12, 1945. The king refused to recognize the new document, so he was deposed by the National Assembly. However, in April 1946, he was reinstated. Two days later, the French invaded, smashing Lao Issara forces and forcing Phethsarath and many of the Lao Issara to flee to Thailand.

The French were not to stay long. In 1949, Laos was declared "an independent associate state of the French Union." This gave Laos the right to join the United Nations and be recognized as an independent nation, but this did not suit everyone. One major faction of the Lao Issara, led by Prince Souphanouvong, joined forces with the Vietnamese Viet Minh under Ho Chi Minh and established a resistance base in northeast Laos. They became known as the Pathet Lao. A government of resistance was formed in 1950 under Prince Souphanouvong. In 1953, France granted full sovereignty to Laos, but the Pathet Lao still saw the government as being Western-dominated and increased their liberation movement activities.

The U.S. government saw the Viet Minh Communists as a possible major influence on southeast Asia, so they began pouring money into Laos. This did not stop the Viet Minh and Pathet Lao forces, however, from effectively taking over the two northeastern provinces of Laos. After considerable maneuvering, a coalition government called the Government of National Union, was established under Prince Souvanna Phouma in 1957. It was probably doomed to failure from the start. In early 1959, a right-wing faction took over the government and arrested many Pathet Lao leaders and politicians. The Pathet Lao retreated to the countryside and instigated renewed guerrilla activity.

In 1960, a neutralist military faction leader and paratroop captain, Kong Le, led a coup d'etat in Vietiane and gave his support to the formation of a neutralist government headed by Souvanna Phouma. Four months later, the right-wing general, Phoumi Novasan, launched an attack on Vientiane and took control. Kong Le's troops and his government abandoned the capital and joined forces with the Pathet Lao in northern Laos.

A second attempt at a coalition government was made in 1962, but this was soon in disarray. In 1964, there were a series of coups that resulted in the Pathet Lao and some neutralists on one side and the other neutralists and the right-wingers on the other. This coincided with the commencement of U.S. bombing raids over Laos, as the direct participation of U.S. forces in South Vietnam increased. Before long, the Ho Chi Minh trail through eastern Laos and many targets in northeastern Laos were being attacked day and night. The country had become polarized and isolated. For the next eight years, there were effectively two governments—the Royal Lao government based in Vientiane and the Pathet Lao based in Sam Neva in the province of Hova Phan in the northeast.

In the late 1960s, northeastern and eastern Laos was almost bombed out of existence by saturation bombing. This caused depopulation over a wide area. The American CIA also carried out covert activities on the ground—including the training and arming of a special guerrilla force to fight the Pathet Lao. Many hired Thai soldiers also participated. Despite these efforts, the Pathet Lao—with considerable help from the Vietnamese, the Chinese, and the Russians—were able to expand their area of control until, by 1972, they controlled about seventy percent of the country.

With the U.S. wanting to pull out of Indochina, a political agreement and ceasefire was arranged for Laos in 1973; and the Provisory Government of National Unity, led by old faithful Souvanna Phouma, was organized in 1974. As with previous coalition governments, it almost immediately began to fall apart. The Pathet Lao were quick to take advantage of the situation, and they exerted considerable pressure on non-Pathet Lao ministers, army generals, and others. In May 1975, a number of ministers and generals resigned, and a mass exodus of certain groups began. Pathet Lao forces seized all major southern Lao towns and took Vientiane without resistance in August.

The Government of National Unity was dismantled, and the Lao People's Revolutionary Party held a Congress of People's Representatives in December, which accepted the abdication of the king and the proclamation of the Lao People's Democratic Republic. Kaysome Phomvihane was appointed prime minister. King Savangvathana was initially given a figurehead role by the new government, but in 1977 he and his family were banished to northern Laos and have not been heard from since.

The initial policies of the new government were harsh and unrealistic. Buddhism was curtailed, the private sector gave way to collectivization, and tens of thousands of people were either sent to re-education camps or imprisoned. By the end of the 1970s, at least ten percent of the country's population had fled to Thailand. The government realized that this situation could not continue, so they modified some policies to allow some free enterprise and more flexibility. By the mid-1980s, the exodus had stopped, and the Lao government has allowed many citizens to visit abroad since

1985. It has also launched a program to increase literacy and develop new political and administrative structures throughout the country. This has helped achieve a sense of national pride. The re-education camps, which held former royal army officers and royal government officials, were abolished in the late 1980s.

Important changes were introduced in 1987 when foreign capital was welcomed and many restrictions on private enterprise were lifted. The government has also come to an agreement with the Buddhist religion, and many of the severe restrictions have been lifted. The demise of European communism has caused many shock waves through Indochina, and Laos has not been immune. Government relations with Thailand and many Western countries are improving and further change is likely to occur in the near future.

The Government

The Lao People's Democratic Republic was formed in December of 1975. It has always been ruled by the Lao People's Revolutionary Party, who have a strong Marxist-Leninist political philosophy very similar to the Socialist Republic of Vietnam and the U.S.S.R. of the 1970s.

The party has a congress that meets every four or five years to elect party leaders and discuss policy; but the main seat of power is the Politburo, which makes all the major decisions. There is also the Central Committee and a permanent secretary. Many members of these bodies have been in power since 1975. The most influential was Kaysone Phomvihane, who held the posts of prime minister, secretary-general of the Politburo and Central Committee, and president of the Lao People's Revolutionary Party for seventeen years until his death in November of 1992. Kaysone had mixed Lao and Vietnamese parentage and was strongly influenced by the Vietnamese since the Viet Minh helped organize the Lao Issara resistance fifty years ago.

The Supreme People's Assembly (now the National Assembly) serves as the government's legislative body. It has between forty and forty-five members, two-thirds of which came from the Lao People's Revolutionary Party and the Lao Front for National Construction. The remaining third came from other bodies. The first national elections for the assembly were held in 1989, and a constitution was adopted in 1991. During the past five years, a series of laws have been issued, passed, and ratified covering common law, penal law, property law, labor law, foreign investment law, and so on.

Elections for district assemblies and provincial assemblies were held for the first time in 1988. Laos is divided into sixteen provinces and an independent prefecture for Vientiane. The present prime minister and chairman of the Lao People's Revolutionary Party is General Khamtay Siphandone, and the head of state is Nouhak Phoumsavan, who replaced Kaysone Phomvihane.

The Economy

Laos is classified as a least-developed country, and along with the rest of Indochina, it has one of the lowest per capita incomes in the world. About eighty percent of the Lao population is engaged in agriculture (mostly subsistence), fishing, and timber cutting. Much of the remaining workforce is employed by the army or the civil service.

The country has been dependent on foreign aid since the French left in the 1950s. In reality, the country is endowed with many natural resources—agriculture, timber, precious stones, minerals, and other things. Additionally, there is scope for hydroelectric power schemes, irrigation systems, and low-cost manufacturing. For various reasons, this potential has not been developed to date; but with the country opening up to more external forces, there is more hope now that development can occur.

The problems to date have been shortage of capital, shortage of skilled people, poorly developed transport and communications, poor educational and health resources, difficult terrain, small population, low population density, and restrictive government policies. While many of these remain, the government has made radical changes in monetary policy, commodity pricing, and its attitude toward private enterprise over the last few years. Foreign private investment is now welcomed, and joint enterprises with government agencies are encouraged.

The government has embarked on a program to transform some state organizations into semiprivate companies. The words "market economy" have suddenly become the catch cry, and dramatic change is occurring. The central government has also given the provinces freedom from most national budgetary controls, and it now requires them to raise most of their own revenues. The process has been painful, but it appears that the result will be a significant improvement.

As the policies have changed, Laos has managed to improve its image in the world, and this has encouraged the Asian Development Bank and several United Nations agencies to take an active interest in the country. Foreign aid from the West has increased recently and has helped offset the collapse of aid from the old Communist bloc.

Among the agriculture crops, **rice** is the most important. In the lowlands, rice is often grown under irrigation, making two and even three crops a year possible in some areas. In the highlands, dry rice is grown. In the late 1970s, a program of collectivization was instituted; but this was abandoned after most Lao peasants opposed the system. Now the rice crop is tended in much the same way as it is in Thailand—with private ownership and cooperative planting and harvesting. Other lowland crops are corn, cotton, fruit, and vegetables.

In the uplands, much of the agriculture still follows the slash-and-burn tradition, with some communities being somewhat nomadic. The government is trying to discourage this in order to protect forest resources and stop soil erosion, but it is only having partial success. One of the major traditional crops was opium, and the government permitted it to be legally cultivated and sold for some time because it was an important source of income for highland tribes in northern Laos. In the northwest of Laos, there was some refining of opium into heroin, which was then smuggled out through Thailand or elsewhere. Because of this, Laos has been known as part of the infamous "Golden Triangle." Today, Lao penal law forbids the production and trade of opium and other narcotics, and the government says that the opium refineries have been closed down and the operators brought before the courts.

Agriculture occupies only about three or four percent of the total land area, and it is estimated that only around ten percent of the country is suitable for this purpose. **Timber**, on the other hand, occurs over about two-thirds of the country, so forestry has become an important industry and a major exporter. Some logs are processed in Laos, but others are exported to Thailand and Vietnam. Teak is the most important timber and it commands good prices.

Fishing is undertaken by individuals, groups, and organizations. The rivers yield a steady supply of fish for local consumption, and fisheries within Nam Ngum lake are being developed for export purposes. **Minerals**, including coal, iron, copper, gold, oil, and zinc, have been discovered in commercial quantities; but exploitation of these resources is only just starting. Foreign countries have been invited in to assist with this development.

The Nam Ngum Dam, north of Vientiane, provides Laos with its largest foreign exchange revenue at present. **Electricity** produced at the dam is used in Vientiane and surrounding areas, but large quantities are exported to Thailand via power lines that cross the Mekong River and connect into the northeastern Thailand distribution grid. The Xeset hydroelectric power plant in the south of the country produces electricity for the southern provinces and for export to Thailand as well.

Manufacturing industry is being pushed in the Vientiane region. There are factories producing beer, cigarettes, soft drinks, cement, concrete cast components, and other goods. Several garment manufacturing plants have also been established, and these are providing valuable employment opportunities for a predominantly female workforce. A lack of trained personnel has been a major constraint in developing these industries, but the government is determined to make the country less reliant on imports—particularly from Thailand.

The People

The Lao people are primarily part of the Thai peoples who exist throughout southern China, southeast Asia, and parts of northeastern India. In general, they are a gentle, easy-going, slightly shy people with a positive outlook on life. The population of Laos is around four million people, and about half are classified as ethnic Lao. The remainder of the population is made up of the Lao Theung, who are semi-nomadic; the Lao Soung and the hill-tribes; other Asian groups (Chinese, Thais, Vietnamese, Indians, and some Cambodians), and a few Europeans.

The ethnic Lao are called **Lao Lum** or **Low Lao**. They traditionally reside in the Mekong River valley and along its tributaries, and they speak the Lao language. These are the people who moved from southern China about a thousand years ago and lived a subsistence lifestyle based on wet rice cultivation. Because they have lived in readily accessible areas and have been subject to various influences over the centuries, most of these people have given up their animist beliefs and are now mostly Buddhists.

Residing in some of the more remote river valleys are several tribal groups who are closely related to the Lao Lum. These people have not been completely absorbed into mainstream Lao culture, but they have similar roots. These people cultivate both wet and dry rice, and some still practice slash-and-burn cultivation in the remote areas. Collectively, these groups distinguish themselves from the Lao Lum by retaining strong tribal identity and mainly animist beliefs. The Black Thai (Thai Dam), who live in the upland valleys of northeastern Laos, are the most predominant tribe; but there are also groups known as White Thai, North Thai, Red Thai, and so on because of their clothing color or the area in which they live.

The **Lao Theung** are the second major group. These are mainly Mon-Khmer people who live on mid-altitude mountain slopes. In general, these people have a much lower standard of living than other Lao. The largest subgroups are the Khamu and the Lamet who reside in the north, but they also include some proto-Malays and others who live in the south.

The **Lao Sung** or **High Lao** are relatively recent immigrants from Tibet, southern China, and north Myanmar. They prefer to live at altitudes higher than one thousand meters above sea level, and they retain a strong tribal identity. The largest group are the Hmong (Meo), who raise cattle, pigs, and chickens, and grow dry rice, corn, and opium poppies. They have a sophisticated social structure, they are predominantly animist (although some are Christian or Buddhist), and they maintain tight tribal integrity. These are the people that were recruited by the CIA to oppose the Pathet Lao twenty years ago, and even now they provide some anti-government resistance at times.

The **Chinese** make up only a small percentage of the Lao population; and as in other southeast Asian countries, they are concentrated in the commercial area. Most restaurants, cinemas, hotels, and retail shops in Vientiane are owned by ethnic Chinese. There are also some Chinese in the southern towns along the Mekong, where they control much of the border trade. Some have lived here for centuries and have become integrated into the local scene.

Many **Thais** have come to Laos in recent years, but most have not settled. They engage in business and trade, but retain homes in Thailand. They are, however, providing valuable finance and business knowledge for future development of Laos. **Indians** and **Pakistanis** are not nearly as prominent as they are in Malaysia, for instance; but in Vientiane there is a visible number concentrated in the fabric and tailoring industries, at the markets, and in the business centers. The **Vietnamese** are not so obvious, but they are greater in number. Some came many years ago as French civil servants, but many arrived more recently. There are Vietnamese associated with the army, the government, and with trade to and from Laos. In the 1980s, some were associated with tailoring, repair workshops, restaurants, and boutiques.

During the 1980s, there were large numbers of workers from the Soviet Union and Eastern Europe, but most of these have now left. Some **Westerners** reside in Laos, but very few are permanent residents. Some work for the United Nations agencies, some are on bilateral aid programs, and others are employed by bodies such as the Red Cross or the Mekong Committee. In the last few years, there has been an increase in Western business people coming to Laos, some of whom have taken up temporary residence while business projects are under development. It is estimated, though, that there are less than five hundred expatriate Caucasians living in Laos, including embassy staff and all other categories.

Religion

More than five hundred years before the birth of Jesus Christ, an Indian prince attained Enlightenment and founded Buddhism. Over the next few centuries, the religion spread throughout Asia, molding attitudes, tempering morality, and coloring customs; but it was slow in reaching and spreading within Laos. Even today it has made few inroads to the Lao Sung or Lao Theung communities, but it is still by far the largest religion in the country and the only powerful religious force.

Buddhists believe that a person's life does not begin with birth and end with death, but it is a link in a chain of lives, each conditioned by acts committed in previous existences. The concept of earthly impermanence and the idea of uncertainty in an ever-changing existence have done much toward creating that relaxed, flexible, carefree mentality that is one of the most appealing characteristics of the Lao people.

Buddhism made its first significant impact in the late thirteenth century in the northern city of Luang Prabang. This was cemented when King Fa Ngum declared Buddhism to be the state religion when he accepted the Pha Bang Buddha image from the Khmers. Soon afterward, he built a temple to house this image and started the series of beautiful wats that can still be seen in Luang Prabang today.

In the sixteenth century, King Settathirath attempted to make Vientiane an important regional center of Buddhism, but this was never really successful. Even within Laos, it was another one hundred years before Buddhism began to be taught in the schools. The form of Buddhism practiced in Laos is the Theravada, or southern school, which is also found in Myanmar, Thailand, Cambodia, and southern Vietnam.

For the visitor, as for the Lao Buddhist, there are three obvious manifestations of Buddhism in all lowland towns and in some other areas. These are the Buddha in his sculptured form, which is found in temples, shops, and houses; the Dhamma, or teachings, that are chanted morning and evening in every wat; and the Sangha, or Buddhist brotherhood, which is represented by the orange-robed monks that you see in the streets and elsewhere.

Buddhist monks have always been accorded great respect for renouncing worldly pleasures and seriously undertaking study of the Buddha's teachings to attain "perfect manhood." In reality, a monk's life is not unduly severe, and daily contact with the general population is common. Except for the three months of the annual Rains Retreat, a monk is free to travel, and visitors will see many on the streets, in buses, in boats, and on aircraft.

It has long been a Lao custom for Buddhist males to be temporarily ordained as monks at some time during their lives. In practice, this often happens before the male starts a career or marries. Traditionally, the males spent three months in the wat, usually during the Rains Retreat, but today the period is often shortened—even down to two weeks. Merit is accrued by all who spend any time as monks. Women are welcome to reside in temples as lay nuns and engage in the same basic religious activities of meditation and Dharma study as the monks. You will sometimes see nuns with shaved heads wearing white robes on the street.

In the early days of the Lao People's Democratic Republic, Buddhist teaching was banned in schools, and people were discouraged from taking a monk's lifestyle or earning merit according to old Buddhist traditions.

Monks were forced to break their vows by raising animals and doing agricultural work. They were encouraged to participate in social development tasks, and many Buddhist schools were converted into training centers for this purpose. The government, however, had underestimated the feelings of the people for the sangha; and before long many of these restrictions were lifted. These days, the constitution of the country guarantees the liberty of confession and the right to believe in a religion.

Today, there is much greater religious freedom, and Buddhism is being taught and practiced by growing numbers of people. Many wats have been repaired, restored, and redecorated; and Buddhism is again playing an important role in the lives of many people. You again see the barefoot paddling of the monks as part of daily life.

Apart from Buddhism, animism is the only other important belief in the country. This form of spirit worship is practiced by many Lao Theung and Lao Sung groups. Even among the Lao Lun Buddhists, there are some who cling to animist beliefs as well. You see this at Wat Si Muang in Vientiane, where the prime temple image is not a Buddha figure, but a pillar in which the guardian spirit of the city is believed to reside. Similar non-Buddha images can be found in other temples.

Among the animists, there are priests who have been trained in dealing with spirits. You can see them at hill-tribe and other festivals. Each separate group has its own beliefs and traditions, and most restrict the spirit ceremonies to tribal believers, so little detail is known about some of these beliefs.

Christianity and Islam have some adherents in Laos, but neither is of great importance. There are Catholic and Protestant churches in Vientiane and some other centers.

Language

The official language of Laos is Lao, the language of Lao Loum that has developed and spawned a number of important literary works since the fifteenth century. There was an attempt to make the Vietiane dialect the official language, but this met a negative response from the population in other regions. The language is closely related to Thai, so native Lao and Thai speakers have no great difficulty understanding each other. Travelers in Thailand who spend time in the northeast of the country (Isan) will get a good introduction to Lao because there are more Lao speakers living in that area than there are in Laos.

In Vientiane, Luang Prabang, and some other areas, French is widely understood, and it remains the official second language of the country. In Vientiane, there are shop signs, restaurant menus, and some government notices in French. English is rapidly gaining popularity, however, particularly among the young people. Children will come up to you in the street and say a few words in English—especially when they realize that you are not Russian. Many Lao, however, will not be able to understand a question in English, so it is good to learn some basic Lao in order to at least try to communicate in the local language. This will earn you considerable respect.

Lao is a monosyllabic, tonal language that is fortunately is very flexible in everyday usage. You can begin speaking Lao without spending a lot of time learning all kinds of complicated grammar rules because, in everyday life, a sentence need not be a complete sentence. If the meaning is clear and understandable, no one cares or even notices that words have been left out.

The difficulty is that Lao has six tones that alter the meaning of a single syllable to produce six completely different words. The tones are mid, high, low, high falling, low falling, and rising. Most English speakers initially find it very difficult to distinguish or use the various tones, and it is almost impossible to successfully show the tones in written form. Nevertheless, it is still worthwhile to try to speak some Lao. Here is a selection of words and phrases that you will find useful in Laos.

Numbers

zero	—soon
one	—nung
two	—sorng
three	—sarm
four	—see
five	—ha
six	—hok
seven	—jet
eight	—paet
nine	—gow
ten	—sip
eleven	—sip-et
twelve	—sip-sorng
twenty	—sao
twenty-two	—sao-sorng
thirty	—sarm-sip
forty	—see-sip
one hundred	—nung roy
one hundred nine	—nung roy gow
two hundred	—sorng roy
one thousand	—nung pan
one million	—larn

Greetings

hello	—sa bi dee
how are you?	—sa bi dee baw
thank you	—kob chi
where are you going?	—pi si

Useful Words and Phrases

no—baw

Do you understand?—Kow ji baw

I do not understand—Baw kow ji

Where are you going?—Pi si

I want to go—oi yark pi

went—pi lao

I like—mark

I don't like—baw mark

How much?—thao di

Do you have . . .?—Me . . . baw

I need—Koi torng karn

buy—seu

expensive—paeng

small—noi

big—yi

shirt—sewa

trousers—sung

shoes—goueb

Lao skirt—sin

blouse—sewa kak

doctor—tarn more

headache—jep hwa

fever—ben ki

today—mu nee

now—do nee

much—li

good—de

bad—baw dee

Food

breakfast—kow sao

lunch—kow tang

dinner—kow leng

tea—narm sa

coffee—cafe

water—narm

orange juice—narm mark kiang

milk—nom

beer—bia

bread—kow chee

rice—kow

sticky rice—kow niaw

fried rice—kow patt

boiled egg—ki tom

fried egg—ki dao

pork—moo

beef—sin gwa

chicken—gai

fish—ba

shrimp—goong

spicy chicken salad—larp ki (gai)

orange—mark kiang

lemon—mark nao

banana—mark kooay

pineapple—mark nut

mango—mark mwang

papaya—mark hoong

sugar—harm tan

Traveling

tricycle—sarm lor	bed—diang
bicycle—lod teep	toilet—horng narm
taxi—lod taxi	bath/shower—arp narm
bus—lod mae	restaurant—harn aharn
plane—hua bin	market—talart
airport—dowen bin	post office—pi sa nee
hotel—hong haem	left—xi (si)
room—horng	right—kwa

Culture and Lifestyle

About eighty percent of Lao people live in rural areas, but the visitor is more likely to be associated with the twenty percent who are urban dwellers. In general, the urban people are more sophisticated, more likely to be able to understand some English or French, and more accustomed to seeing and dealing with foreigners. Unfortunately, most short-term visitors will have little opportunity to have in-depth relationships with any Lao people; but it will help you better understand the country and people if you know a little about the lifestyle and what influences the lifestyle of the lowland Lao.

Every family, both urban and rural, has within it a system of relationships and attitudes that governs personal contacts. It is repeated to some extent at all levels of society, which makes the Lao nation one large extended family. People learn a code of behavior in the house that they find perfectly viable when they go to school and later when they enter the workplace and deal with the government.

A typical Lao family will almost always extend beyond the nucleus of parents and their children to include grandparents, cousins, an uncle or aunt, or even the children of upcountry relatives, all living amicably together in the same house. This communal lifestyle, in which everyone lives together with little privacy, obviously requires tact, compromise, courtesy, and tolerance if social harmony is to be preserved. It has a major influence on people's attitudes.

Respect for elders is taught from a very early age and is universally accepted. This is formalized in language by using different words and titles for people older than oneself. The young Lao learns to defer to the superior age and position of the parents, the village leaders, and the workplace boss; and this attitude guarantees a strong degree of cultural conservatism. One of the primary responsibilities of the children is to take care of their parents in their old age. There is no feeling of being inconvenienced by caring for aged parents, and the parents' accumulated wisdom gives them an elevated place in the household.

The Lao are individualistic people, yet they believe that inner satisfaction is dependent upon an emotionally and physically stable environment. Social harmony is thus best preserved by avoiding any unnecessary friction in contact with others. This leads to an extreme reluctance to impose on anyone or disturb one's personal equilibrium by direct criticism, challenge, or confrontation. It can lead to frustration for visitors because when a problem arises, the Lao may have a natural tendency to go away, rather than face it and try to find a solution.

Outward expressions of anger are also discouraged. During normal social activities, strong public displays of dismay, despair, displeasure, disapproval, or enthusiasm are frowned upon. As a visitor, you will find that you usually make faster progress when you hold your temper and keep a smile on your face, than when you shout and cause a confrontation. When you shout and rage at a Lao, you lose his respect.

Life outside Vientiane revolves around the seasons. With rice being by far the most important of all crops, its seasons affect the entire community. Rice is the principal food for humans and animals throughout the country, and its importance can not be underestimated. Private ownership of rice land is now permitted in Laos, so the pattern of rice growing is little different from that in Thailand and northern Malaysia. The farmers' cooperatives that were established in the 1970s were abolished many years ago because of their low productivity and poor efficiency. In a widespread complex pattern of voluntary communal cooperation, farmers prepare their fields, repair bunds, plow, and transplant rice seedlings into each other's prepared fields. At this time, every active family member works in the field. If all goes according to plan, the monsoon rains arrive and the farmers can literally watch the rice grow.

When rice is ready for harvesting, cooperative work groups harvest each crop. Cut rice is spread in the field to dry, then it is taken to a compound where it is threshed. The harvest belongs to the farmer after he pays taxes of 80, 100, or 120 kilograms of rice per hectare, depending on the quality of the land. If the farmer wants to pay his taxes in cash, the amount is calculated according to the rice price at that time.

In the cities, the everyday lifestyle of people conforms to the universal urban pattern. Most people live in individual houses (although there are a few apartment blocks in Vientiane) or in shop houses, and they engage in some form of business or employment. Most businesses and government departments work 5½ or 6 days a week, and shops and markets are usually open seven days a week. Many people commute around the city on motorcycles.

However, even in the cities, the past is seldom far away. Lao music, dance, handicrafts, architecture, and sculpture have strong elements that go back centuries. Many of the customs and celebrations have roots reaching back over a thousand years. The **baci** is a typical example. Today it is a ceremony of prayers and good wishes, but it originated as a ceremony to honor and preserve the thirty-two guardian spirits that were thought to protect a body. It predates the arrival of Buddhism to Laos, but is still practiced today.

A number of people sit around the phakuan, an elaborate bouquet of flowers held by a cone of banana leaves and surrounded by rice wine, cakes, hard-boiled eggs, and rice. An elderly man with a white silk scarf will light the candles that have been placed among the flowers, then he addresses the gods in a fast, solemn monologue. The participants touch the rim of the phakuan, then have white strings tied around their wrists as more blessings and wishes are murmured. Jiggers of rice wine are passed around, then a meal is served. This is usually followed by a **lamvong**, the national dance, consisting of a slow revolving circle dance with expressive hand gestures.

Lao **folk dances** are another art form that has survived for many centuries. The numerous dances, most of which tell of the joys in life and work, are performed with the accompaniment of various musical instruments. The dances are quite different from those of Thailand, Cambodia, and Myanmar because the rhythm of Lao dance is very gentle. Some of the most popular dances are the Mahasay dance from central Laos; Yiam Viman, which is one of the oldest traditional dances; and Manola Bousayan, which was adopted from a fairy tale.

Lao **music**, as with Western music, has a classical and folk stream. Lao classical music was originally developed as court music, but it has been in decline for some time and is rarely heard at present. The music was played by an ensemble called the *sep nyai* that consisted of a set of tuned gongs, a xylophone-type instrument, a bamboo flute, and a double reed wind instrument similar to an oboe. Folk music instruments, on the other hand, are the khaen, a wind instrument having rows of reeds fitted into a sound box; and a bowed string instrument called a saw. Often there is also a vocalist. Most Lao pop music is based on vocal folk music.

The **maw lam** is a folk theater art consisting of witty, topical singing and talking covering a wide range of themes, but often alluding to sex. It can feature an ensemble of performers, a couple, or just one performer. You can see maw lam at temple fairs and other festive occasions, or hear it on Lao radio.

Lao **architecture** is concentrated on religious structures, and because of the country's history, only a few significant old structures remain. In my opinion, there are no significant modern architectural styles or achievements. The most unique structure in Laos is the That Luang in Vientiane. A *that* is a structure that commemorates the life of the Buddha. It is usually in the form of a tower. The That Luang shape has become the Lao standard, and many other stupas are modeled after it.

Temple architecture is the most obvious to the visitor, and the chapel, or *sim*, is the most prominent building. In Laos, there are two different styles—the Vientiane style and the Luang Prabang style. Neither is uniquely Lao. Most sim in Vientiane are large brick buildings covered with stucco, much like those in Thailand. The high peaked roofs contain several layers and are usually edged with a flame motif and have long, carved hooks at the corners. The front of the sim often features a large veranda made up of heavy columns, an ornamented roof, and a carved wooden frontispiece. These carvings are most impressive and represent one of the highlights of Lao art.

The Luang Prabang style is older and similar to some temples found in northern Thailand. Roofs are also layered; but they sweep down toward the ground, creating an unusually dramatic effect. The other significant feature is the complex carving or metalwork on doors and some outside walls. This is often overlaid with gold or gold leaf to produce a beautiful piece of art.

Within the temples, you will find many fine examples of Lao Buddha sculpture. The best of these come from the time of the Lao Xang kingdom (sixteenth-eighteenth centuries) and can be seen in Luang Prabang's National Museum and at Wat Visounnarat. In Vientiane, there are good examples at Wat Phra Keo and Wat Sisaket. There are two Buddha image styles that are distinctly Lao. One depicts the Buddha standing with his arms rigidly at his side and fingers pointing toward the ground. The other has his hands crossed in front of his body.

Weaving has long been a Lao tradition, and the art form remains viable today. You can see traditional wooden looms in lowland villages with women using both cotton and silk. Much of the weaving is done to make material for the phasin, a long wraparound skirt worn by almost all Lao women—even in the urban areas. Gold or silver thread is sometimes woven into the fabric to produce a material like the songket fabric from Malaysia. You can see and buy excellent weaving at Ban Phanom, a weaving village near Luang Prabang, or at the Lao Women's Textile Project in Vientiane.

Among the hill-tribe people, **silversmithing** is an important occupation. Many of the tribes have a tradition of wearing silver jewelry, ornaments, belts, and other pieces as a way of displaying wealth and preserving their inheritance for future generations. You can see good examples of this at Luang Prabang and other northern centers.

A visitor will find that once inside Laos, there are few difficulties in meeting local requirements or expectations. In fact, it is an easy country to become familiar with, and you will quickly feel comfortable. You must realize, however, that Lao culture is quite different from your own, and there are a few things that you should know to make life much easier for you. Everywhere in public, if in doubt as to what to do, look around you and do what the Lao do.

In a religious place, dress neatly and conservatively. Don't go shirtless, or in shorts, hotpants, or off-the-shoulder blouses. It is fine to wear shoes when walking around the compound of a Buddhist temple, but not inside the sim, where the principal Buddha image is kept. You should also remove your shoes when entering a Lao home.

Buddhist monks are forbidden to touch or to be touched by women or to accept anything from the hand of one. If a woman has to give anything to a monk or novice, she first hands it to a man who will present it, or she offers it on a tray or places it on a table or on the ground in front of him. Both men and women should kneel when putting money into the donations box in a wat.

It is considered rude to point your foot at a person, so try to avoid doing so when sitting opposite anyone. Take particular care when sitting with your legs crossed. If you are sitting on the floor in the company of a Lao, keep your feet tucked away. The foot is a low-class limb to most Lao, so don't point your foot to show anything to anyone—use your finger instead. Never put your foot on a table in the company of a Lao.

Lao people regard the head as the highest part of the body, both literally and figuratively. As a result, they don't approve of patting anyone there—even as a friendly gesture. Similarly, if you watch Lao people at a social gathering, you'll notice that young people go to considerable lengths to keep their heads lower than those of their elders to avoid giving the impression of "looking down" on them.

Public displays of affection between men and women are frowned upon. As a visitor, you should avoid this too. You will seldom see Lao couples holding hands, and you will never see anything more. It is quite common, however, for women to walk along a street holding hands, and you will sometimes see men doing the same. This denotes nothing more than friendship or shyness.

Always be circumspect when taking photographs. The government has a number of restrictions on the taking of photographs, and many of these are neither obvious nor make any sense to the visitor. Do not photograph official functions without permission, and if there is any doubt or if someone objects to your photographing anything, stop immediately. No photographs are allowed in the National Museum in Luang Prabang (a great pity because few people in the world know about this national treasure) or at the Nam Ngum Dam. You should always ask permission before photographing anyone within the temple grounds or before photographing inside a sim. In my experience, you will generally receive approval.

The local publication "Discover Laos" (Tel: 217-294) contains some useful information on customs and the culture.

Food and Drink

If you like Thai food, you will like Lao cuisine because there are many similarities. If you have spent time in northeastern Thailand, you will know what to expect. I think that the average visitor will be a little disappointed with Lao food, however, because it is difficult to get a good selection of true Lao dishes anywhere. At many restaurants, if you want Lao food, you must order ahead. At the restaurants that do have Lao food, the selection is often small, and the quality varies from poor to reasonable.

Traditional Lao food is simple and straightforward. Rice and vegetables plus perhaps some dried fish, soup, and a couple of sauces make an excellent meal for many households. Rice is the foundation of all Lao meals, and most Lao prefer the glutinous sticky rice to the ordinary white rice. Sticky rice is eaten with the hands by taking a small portion from the woven container in which it is served, then rolling it into a small ball and dipping it into the various dishes. It is an experience that you must try. In the restaurants in urban areas, foreigners are more likely to be served white rice because the Lao know that this is more familiar to Westerners. You eat white rice with a spoon.

Almost all Lao dishes are cooked with fresh ingredients whether they be vegetables, fish, chicken, duck, pork, or beef. Lime juice, lemongrass, and coriander leaf are added to give the food its characteristic taste, while tamarind juice, coconut milk, hot chilies, or various fermented fish sauces are used to create specific flavors.

One of the most common Lao dishes that is served fairly widely in restaurants is *larp*. There are several varieties, depending on what main ingredient is used. It is served cold and is usually accompanied by rice. Larp is made from minced meat, fish, or vegetables which are tossed with lime juice, garlic, powdered rice, onions, and chilies. It can be very hot, so be careful.

The Lao also eat a lot of what could be called Chinese food. This is available from Chinese restaurants or almost any restaurant, cafe, or food stall in the country. This food is generally less spicy and it can actually be quite bland at times. In Vientiane and some of the larger towns along the Mekong, French bread is a popular breakfast food. Sometimes it is eaten plain with coffee, sometimes with eggs, and sometimes with a Lao-style paté or pressed meat. Excellent croissants are available in Vientiane.

The Lao Brewery Company in Vientiane produces one draft and two bottled products. The draft beer is only available in Vientiane, where it is often served in two-liter plastic containers. It is inexpensive and popular with the

Lao and some foreigners. The cheapest bottled beer is Bia Lao, which comes in a bottle with a tiger's head on the label. It is readily available throughout Laos in small bottles (360 ml), or large bottles (700 ml). It has become the beer of choice for most people. Top of the range is 33 Export. This costs a little more (but is still inexpensive by Western standards) and may not be available outside the cities.

Imported beers are also available in Vientiane and some other places. The most common are Heineken and Tiger from Singapore, and Swan and Fosters from Australia. These imported beers often sell for less in Laos than they do in their countries of origin. It is rare to pay more than US$1.00 for a bottle or can.

Rice whisky, or *lao lao* is a popular local drink and is readily available by the bottle for around US$3.00. You can mix it with ice, soda, and lime or drink it with cola. In this form, it tastes somewhat similar to Thailand's famous "Mekong whiskey."

The Lao Soft Drink Company in Vientiane manufactures Pepsi Cola, Mirinda, and 7-Up under license, so these drinks are widely available at reasonable prices. Often they are the only thing available. Imported soft drinks in cans are appearing in the larger cities at prices somewhat higher than their Lao equivalents. Most locals buy iced drinks in plastic bags from young, streetwise vendors. You would be better off skipping the ice.

Chinese tea, instant coffee, Lao-produced tea, and Ovaltine are all readily available in the major centers. Milk, flavored milk, and yogurt are imported from Thailand and are available throughout the Mekong Valley. Be selective with ice in restaurants and food stalls. Some is made with boiled water, but much of it is not.

The most economical places to eat are the night markets. Food is inexpensive and generally quite good—although the choice may be limited. Noodle shops provide a good alternative and are often open all day. There are several in most towns. You will find a more varied selection of dishes at the Lao cafes and food shops. Many of these are owned and operated by Chinese, so amazingly these do not have any traditional Lao food. Sometimes they have a menu or blackboard on the wall, but usually it is only in the Lao language. You can often solve this problem by pointing to the food that you would like.

In Vientiane and the other larger centers, there are restaurants that are a step up from here. These will have a written menu (sometimes in English) and a good selection of food. The price may be more than double that of the market, but it is still inexpensive by most standards. Here is a short selection of dishes you may like to try while you are in Laos.

Spicy fish soup (tom yum par) is a favorite. It is usually served in a metal dish with coals to keep it hot. The Lao eat the meat, mushrooms, and other vegetables and often leave the liquid.

Omelette stuffed with vegetables and pork (ki yat si) is good when you want something less spicy and easy to eat.

Fried rice (cow padt) is a lunchtime favorite that is easy and inexpensive.

Chicken fried with chilies (gi padt mark pet) is obtainable almost everywhere. Sometimes the chicken has seen too many seasons.

Spicy minced beef (larp sin) is something you simply cannot miss if you go to any Lao restaurant. Often it is very good.

Papaya salad (tum mark hoong) is an ideal complement to larp. Green papaya is grated with tomato, carrot, lime rind, dried shrimp, garlic salt, and chili to make a most unusual dish.

Accommodations

The accommodation options in Laos are reasonably limited but are growing, particularly in the two-star and three-star category. There are few cheap guest houses of the style you find in Thailand. There are no student hostels or workers' dormitories available to visitors.

You will, however, find a reasonable selection of mid-range hotels and guest houses in Vientiane. In other parts of the country, there are usually some accommodations that will be adequate for a short stay. If you book a tour, you will sometimes be given a choice of "superior" or "standard" accommodations. Within these ranges, you will have no choice of hotels, and you will find that "standard" can be a government guest house without private facilities or hot water or a multi-story hotel with recently modernized facilities and good service.

In the next chapter, I have listed in some detail the accommodation options available in Vientiane, Luang Prabang, and some other centers. In these centers, you can obtain an airconditioned room with attached private bathroom facilities for US$20-$50. Outside these areas, you will usually have to settle for a non-airconditioned room, often without attached bathroom. The cost for this will vary from US$5 to US$20.

Most hotels in the major centers will have someone at reception who can speak English. You will be asked to register by filling in a card that has questions in English, which usually doubles as a police report as well. You will often need your passport at hotel check-in.

Health and Safety

In Vientiane, no abnormal health risks exist, but if you are planning extensive out-of-Vientiane travel, some precautions are necessary. These are more important than in other places because medical services in Laos are generally poor. If you become sick outside of Vientiane, you should immediately return to the capital. It may be necessary for you to be evacuated to Thailand if there is a significant problem. Medication required for personal use should always be brought with you because it probably will not be available in Laos.

Travel plays havoc with most people's systems, and minor diarrhea is common. This is partly induced by the tropical weather, the different water, and the hotter-than-normal food. You should bring tablets with you to combat this condition. The tropical sun can be a hazard to those unaware of its strength. Wear a hat and drink more liquids than you do normally. Bring sunscreen with you to apply to your skin when you are outdoors between 11 A.M. and 4 P.M.

Be aware that tropical temperatures and insanitation are a potentially dangerous combination. You should be conscious of the possibility of prickly heat, an itchy rash that often occurs on the buttocks; heat stroke, which is a serious condition caused when the body's heat-regulating mechanism breaks down; and fungal infections such as athlete's foot.

In hotels and restaurants, do not drink the tap water. Ask for water that has been boiled. Likewise with ice—ask if it has been made with boiled water. If you are not sure or cannot get an answer, don't use it. For the same reason, try to avoid all uncooked or unpeeled fruit and vegetables. Typhoid, cholera, and hepatitis may be uncommon, but they are extremely dangerous if not diagnosed and treated quickly.

Mosquito-borne diseases are common in Laos, so you should take precautions. Malaria is not a major problem in Vientiane, but it is prevalent elsewhere. There are no 100-percent reliable medical preventatives, but it is worth taking chloroquine tablets (for ordinary malaria) if you plan a long stay or will be spending time outside Vientiane. Your home physician will recommend other possible preventative treatments. Dengue fever is another possibility, as is the relatively rare encephalitis.

The use of insect repellent, mosquito sprays, electric mats, and mosquito coils all help. So too does wearing high-necked and long sleeved shirts and long trousers—particularly at dusk when mosquitoes seem to be most active. Always use mosquito nets if they are provided in hotels, and remember that dark clothing, perfume, and aftershave attract mosquitoes. A locally produced anti-mosquito soap appears to be successful.

Laos is a safe country for visitors, and theft is not a major problem. You should be aware, however, that what might be a few unimportant dollars to you may be a month's savings to a local. Don't put this temptation in front of hotel staff or others. Keep your hotel room locked when you are out and while you are sleeping at night.

I have never been concerned for my safety in Laos; and under normal circumstances, you will not either. The streets in Vientiane are much safer at night than many U.S. or European cities, and women can safely walk alone in most areas at any time of the day or night. Other centers are the same, although you will find that some areas are poorly lit and may therefore seem uninviting. Ask the hotel receptionist for advice.

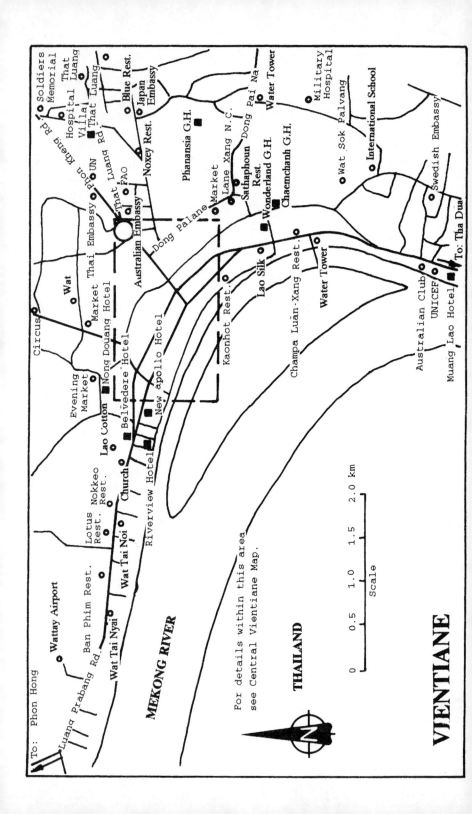

10

Vientiane and Other Places

1. The General Picture

Vientiane is the capital and largest city in Laos, but don't expect a modern, thriving metropolis. It is more like a large market town than a national capital. The city has a thousand years of history, but the total population is less than 200,000, so it is not difficult to find your way around once you understand a few facts.

Vientiane dominates central Laos, but it has less influence on some of the other regions of the country. Transportation and communications are still relatively poor in the provinces, so several regional centers are of significant local importance to their support areas. Notable among these are Luang Prabang in the north and Savannakhet and Pakse in the south. All of these cities are located on the east bank of the Mekong River.

At first glance, Vientiane is a city where little has changed in thirty years. There are some tree-lined boulevards and faded colonial buildings courtesy of the French and some older temples that appear to be timeless, but in reality, nothing is more than 180 years old. On closer examination though, it becomes obvious that many of the Vietnamese-Chinese shop houses and the nondescript Eastern bloc-style buildings are the result of more modern construction. Many, in fact, have been built since the open-door policy was launched by the government to encourage development about six years

269

ago. The city today is a hodgepodge of styles and influences. It is in a somewhat shabby condition, brightened here and there by something new or
an old building that is showing signs of love and care.

The city curves along the Mekong River in a northwest/southeast direction. The central area has a spine heading off in a northeast direction. As
the city grows, the areas between these development lines are gradually
being filled in, but the density of development is not high and the city
sprawls much more than most Asian counterparts.

Vientiane is not a city for action and excitement; it is rather a place to
savor at its own slow pace. Life for many here is as sluggish as the waters of
the Mekong passing by. Take the time to see and appreciate the various
influences that exist today, or have existed in the past—Lao, Thai, Chinese, French, Vietnamese, and Soviet—then talk to the local inhabitants
about their views on Laos, southeast Asia, and the world. You will find that
most people are proud to be Lao, yet are honest enough to realize that the
country must have more contact with the outside world if it is to grow and
prosper.

2. Getting There

Most visitors will arrive in Vientiane by **air**. At present, Bangkok is by far
the largest source of Laos-bound passengers, with both Thai Airways International and Lao Aviation offering several services a week. The flight takes
about one hour. It is an abrupt switch from booming high-rise Bangkok to
dreamy low-rise Vientiane.

Lao Aviation is actively looking at expanding its international routes; and
the current services to Hanoi, Bangkok, Chiang Mai, Saigon, and Phnom
Penh are likely to be joined by others in the future. Vietnam Airlines operates from Hanoi; Aeroflot flies from Moscow; and China Southern Airlines
operates from Guang Zhou and Kunming once a week.

Vientiane Airport (Wattay) is situated about five kilometers from the central city. It is a relatively small airport and facilities are meager. At present,
international flights are timed such that arrivals and departures do not coin-
cide, but the terminal still seems hard-pressed to handle the temporary rush
of one aircraft. Passengers are processed by two immigration officers and
several customs people. Fortunately, the procedures appear to be less strict
than in some socialist countries, so the process of deplaning, collecting baggage, and entering the country can be over in about thirty minutes.

The airport has a bank, a post office, and a restaurant; but it is not necessary to use any of these. Taxis are available to take you to the city for at about
4,000 kip, but they will usually accept Thai baht or U.S. dollars. A few taxis
with meters were introduced in late 1994 and are sometimes available at

the airport. You may be able to engage a tuk-tuk (three-wheel motorized taxi) to take you to town, but because they do not have an agreement with the airport authority, you will not find them lined up outside the terminal. If you do find one, the fare should only be around 1,200 kip. If saving money is your first priority, you can walk the five hundred meters to the main road and hail a samlor, pedicab, or perhaps even an infrequent bus. You must bargain with taxis, samlors, and pedicabs to establish a fare before you board.

Under some circumstances, it is possible for foreigners to arrive by **water**. This access to Vientiane and perhaps some other centers will probably become easier in the future. Each day, there are numerous ferries crossing the Mekong River from Nong Khai in Thailand to Tha Deua in Laos. These are used extensively by Lao and Thais; and if your visa permits you to enter Laos this way, there is no reason why you should not. The ferry fare is 30 baht, and you can quickly pass through immigration and customs in a small building at the top of the landing. There is an exchange booth, and transport to Vientiane is readily available. Your choices are bus (about 500 kip), tuk-tuk (about 3,000 kip), or taxi (as much as they can get).

It is theoretically possible to arrive in Vientiane by **road**. The Australian government built a road bridge from Nong Khai to Tha Na Leng (about twenty kilometers from Vientiane). This cost US$30 million and opened in early 1994, however, the Lao authorities are very reluctant to allow private vehicles to use it and bus connections have not developed as quickly as anticipated. This situation is likely to change.

3. Local Transportation

Although all Lao towns are small, there will be times when you will not wish to walk. In Vientiane, Luang Prabang, and Savannakhet, you have a choice of taxi, motorcycle taxi (tuk-tuk or samlor), or pedicab. **Taxis** tend to wait outside the main hotels, while **samlors** and **pedicabs** can be stopped anywhere on the street. Small cities and towns in other parts of the country generally do not have taxis, but they will have samlors and pedicabs.

In all cases, except the new metered taxis, you need to negotiate a fare. For a foreigner, the initial asking price will often be several times the amount that a local will pay, so take the time to find out what the correct value should be. In Vientiane, foreigners are often initially asked for 5,000 kip by taxis and 1,000 to 2,000 kip by samlors. After negotiation, the fares often come down to 2,000 kip and 500 kip respectively. Metered taxis in Vientiane operate with a 800 kip flagfall then 200 kip per kilometer.

Taxis and samlors can also be hired by the day. You may be able to get a taxi to run around town all day for less than 10,000 kip. I know of people

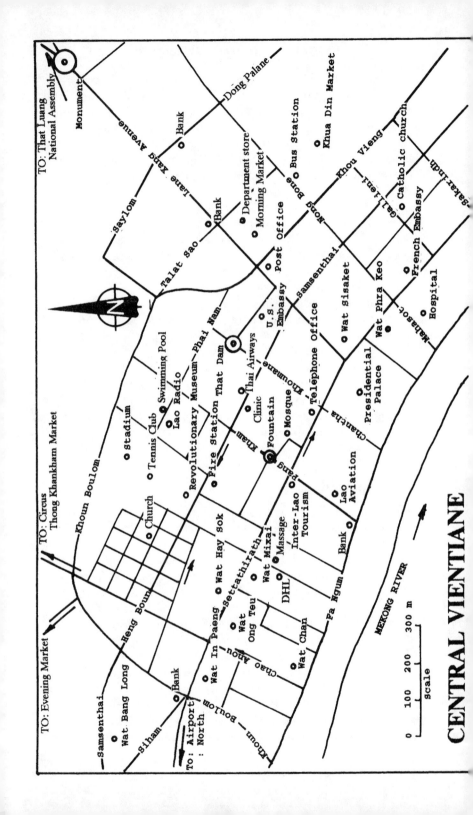

CENTRAL VIENTIANE

who have used a samlor for several hours of sightseeing and have been able to negotiate a rate of less than 4,000 kip.

If you crave to be independent, **rental bicycles** are available in Vientiane, Luang Prabang, Savannakhet, and possibly some other towns. In Vientiane, the asking price varies from 700 to 2,000 kip per day. There are several places along Samsenthai Road that have English signs advertising rentals. The motorcycle shop next to the Anou Hotel on Thanon Heng Boun sometimes has motorcycles for rent at US$10 per day.

Most major towns have a **bus** service that links outlying villages to the city. At times, these can be a fascinating and very cheap way to experience local color and atmosphere; but often they are old, crowded, and very uncomfortable. No city has a well-regulated commuter bus system.

Outside the cities, the most practical way to travel between provinces is by **air**. Lao Aviation has a reasonable service from Vientiane to most provincial capitals, and there are a few flights between some of the southern towns. Internal flights are handled by Chinese and French aircraft. There are no longer any scheduled helicopter services. French ATR42 aircraft were introduced in 1992 to replace the Russian Antonov 24s, and Chinese Y-7 and Y-12 aircraft were introduced in 1990 and 1991. There is a domestic departure tax of 300 kip.

Boats have traditionally been the best interprovince connections, and even today they serve an important purpose. The Mekong, the Nam Khan, the Nam Ou, and other rivers have regular river transportation on them. For long distances, diesel-driven ferries are used. Facilities are basic, but prices are cheap. Some ferries have food available on board, but many do not. Sleeping accommodations are often the timber deck.

Buses are extending their services as road improvements are carried out, but it will be many years before there are all-weather roads between Vientiane and most of the major provincial capitals. The exception is Luang Prabang where road construction may be completed in late 1995. In most of the country, road travel is a slow, uncomfortable experience because of the mountainous terrain and poor surface conditions. For part of the year, many roads are impassable. You should also remember that in rural Asia, buses are not just reserved for people. Pigs, chickens, ducks, bags of rice, and whatever else can be carried share the excursion. Most buses appear to have bulging sides from an excess of people, produce, and animals.

4. The Hotel Scene

Vientiane accommodations vary between basic and reasonable. There are no luxury hotels, no international chains, and no properties of outstanding value. Instead, you find a range of hotels and guest houses that crowd the mid-range category. By international standards, they are not expensive; but most only offer fair facilities and service.

As Laos tourism grows in the future, it is expected that several new hotels will open. In the last few years, development has been restricted to the upgrading of existing properties and the conversion of buildings to small guest house-style properties.

EXPENSIVE HOTELS

No hotels fit into this category at present.

MEDIUM-PRICE HOTELS

The **Belvedere Hotel** (Tel: 213570), 233 rooms, is the largest and most up-market hotel in the city. The rooms are large and well appointed, everything works, and there is 24-hour room service, a swimming pool, restaurant, tennis court, lounge, disco, Karaoke, gym, sauna, billiards, business center, reading room, and shop. The rooms have IDD telephone, mini-bar, and tea/coffee-making facilities. The hotel belongs to the Best Western network.

The location is not great but the facilities make up for this. The airport desk and pick-up service help too. Room rates are from US$90. (Book with the hotel at Samsenthai Road, Vientiane; Fax: 856-21-213572.)

The **Muang Lao Hotel** (Tel: 312380) is about three kilometers southeast of the central city, but it occupies a lovely position adjacent to the Mekong River. The hotel reopened in early 1992 after extensive renovations, and the new owners were determined to establish it as one of the best hotels in the city. Unfortunately, it has not made it.

There are four suites equipped with kitchenettes, which rent for US$40 a day, and twelve standard rooms from US$25. All rooms are airconditioned and have refrigerators, attached bathrooms with hot water, and a good standard of furnishings. There are two restaurants, conference facilities, and a nightclub.

The location is ideal if you have your own transportation or are involved with the Australian club, UNICEF, or the Soviet or Swedish embassies because these are all close by. It is less convenient if you are short on time or need to visit places in the central city on a regular basis. (Book with the hotel at Tha Deua Road, Vientiane, Lao P.D.R.; Fax: 856-21-212117)

The **Lane Xang Hotel** (Tel: 214102), 80 rooms, is on Fa Ngum Road in the center of the city. For many years, this was considered to be the best hotel in Vientiane, and I believe the management and staff became arrogant and unfriendly. Now there is more competition, and I'm not sure that this hotel is coping very well despite extensive renovations.

The public areas are large and quite attractive, but the rooms are nothing

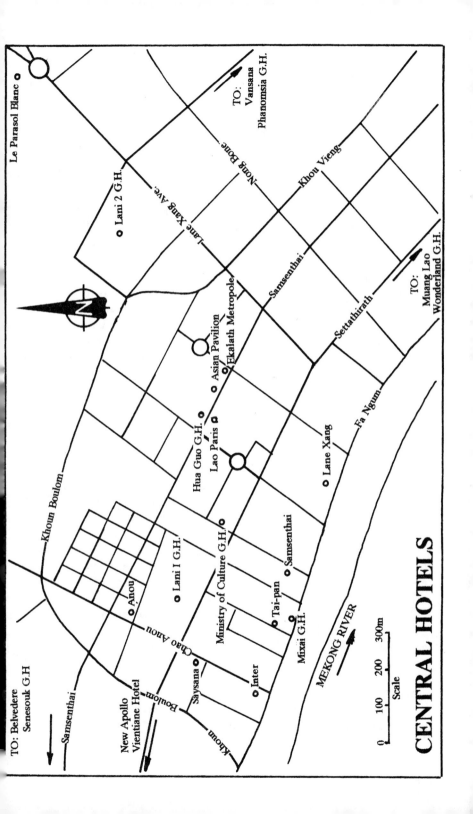

CENTRAL HOTELS

much. They are airconditioned and have their own attached bathrooms, but they are far from exciting or modern. The hotel has a swimming pool and some pitiful animals in metal cages in an area behind the parking lot. The four-story building has no elevator. (Book with the hotel at P.O. Box 280, Vientiane, Lao P.D.R.; Fax: 856-21-214108.) Prices are around US$60/70 single/double.

The **Tai-Pan Hotel** (Tel: 216907), 36 rooms, is a new, centrally situated hotel opened in 1994. The rooms are well equipped and well furnished. There are IDD telephones and satellite TV. The hotel has a good restaurant, a small lounge, and a business center. The staff is friendly. Room rates start at US$55. (Book with the hotel at 22/3 Francois Ngin Road, Ban Mixay, Vientiane, Lao P.D.R.; Fax: 856-21-216223.)

The **Asian Pavilion Hotel** (Tel: 213431), 50 rooms, is partly recycled and partly new, but you can hardly tell the difference. This was the site of the French-style Hotel Constellation, but nothing recognizable remains from those days. The hotel has reasonably sized rooms with nicely decorated attached bathrooms complete with toiletries. On the ground floor, there is a large lobby, a lounge area, a coffee shop, and a restaurant. All are bright, fresh, and attractive. The hotel is well located in the heart of the business area. Room rates vary from US$25 in the older building; to US$40 for standard rooms equipped with TV, airconditioning, telephone, and refrigerator; and US$60 for suites. (Book with the hotel at 379 Samsenthai Road, Vientiane, Lao P.D.R.; Fax: 856-21-213432.)

The **New Apollo Hotel** (Tel: 213343), 75 rooms, has emerged from the shell of the old Santhiphub Hotel but little remains of the original. The rooms are well presented and individually airconditioned. There are three restaurants and a nightclub. The staff is helpful and management efficient. Room rates start at US$69. (Book with the hotel at Sethathirath Road, Vientiane, Lao P.D.R.

The **Vansana Hotel** (Tel: 413171) is a modern facility at 9 Phonethan Road in suburban Vientiane. All 45 rooms are large, airconditioned, and have telephones, refrigerators, and satellite TV. All have a certain style that is missing from most other Lao hotels.

The low-rise building is situated on attractive grounds on Phonethan Road, about four kilometers from the central city. There is a small conference room and an attractive dining room. The gardens contain a swimming pool. At US$35, a twin room is a good value. The location is less than ideal if you do not have transportation, but I am told that it is not difficult to get a tuk-tuk during the day if you walk about three hundred meters to a nearby corner. For some, the garden, the peace and quiet, and the style outweigh any location difficulties. (Book with the hotel at P.O. Box 881 Vientiane, Lao P.D.R.; Fax: 856-21-413171.)

The **Ambassador Hotel** (Tel: 213003) is a strange place in the center of the city on Pang-Kham Road. The main building is colonial in style and is in reasonable condition, but adjoining buildings are in various stages of repair or rebuilding. The hotel is a joint enterprise of the Ministry of Foreign Affairs and a foreign company, but it appears to have run into severe financial problems.

The hotel has a large lobby with reception desk, lounge, TV, and bar which are all quite attractive. Some of the rooms are huge with ornate ceilings and concealed lighting. All are airconditioned and have attached bathrooms. The restaurant on the second level has little atmosphere, but the food is adequate. I found the staff to be helpful and friendly. Current prices are US$27.50 single, US$33 double, and US$40 for a suite. (Book with the hotel at Box 3188, Vientiane, Lao P.D.R.)

The **Saysana Hotel** (Tel: 213580), 36 rooms, has improved its facilities and service considerably in recent years, and it now represents a good value among the mid-range hotels. The central location is convenient to many restaurants and shops, and the hotel has friendly staff with some English abilities.

Rooms are reasonable. Most have telephone, airconditioning, and ceiling fan; and all have attached bathrooms with hot water, toilet, and shower. My room had no refrigerator, but I believe that some rooms do. Downstairs, there is a large restaurant that converts into a popular nightclub featuring a live band and various singers each evening. Current prices are around US$20/22 for single/double rooms and around US$33 for a junior suite. (Book with the hotel at Chao Anou Street, Vientiane, Lao P.D.R.; Fax: 856-21-213581.)

The **Anou Hotel** (Tel: 213631), 58 rooms, on Heng Boun Street is similar in standard to the Saysana Hotel and is only two blocks away. It shares a good central location with shops, restaurants, cinemas, and several Buddhist wats. The better rooms appear to be on the upper floor, so it can mean a climb up three flights of stairs.

The timber-floored corridors and rooms are well kept and clean. All rooms are airconditioned and have a ceiling fan. Attached bathrooms have hot and cold water, but like most bathrooms in Laos, everything gets wet (including the toilet paper) when you try to take a shower. Downstairs, the lobby is fairly small, but there is a large restaurant that has a band at night and Asian and European food from 7 A.M. to 11:30 P.M. Room costs are from US$15 to US$30 single/double. (Book with the hotel at P.O. Box 3655, Vientiane, Lao P.D.R.)

The **Ekalath Metropole Hotel** (Tel: 213421), 32 rooms, is at the corner of Samsenthai Road and Chantha Khoumane Road. The pluses for the hotel are its location, the very friendly owners, and the helpful staff. The minuses are room doors that are difficult to open, electrical wiring that is borderline dangerous, and many staff that do not speak English.

Most rooms have airconditioning, ceiling fans, and refrigerators. There is a restaurant, bar, and TV in the lobby. Room rates are around US$22/29 for single/double, including breakfast. (Book with the hotel at P.O. Box 3179, Vientiane, Lao P.D.R.)

The **Lao Paris Hotel** (Tel: 216382), 21 rooms, is a good proposition at present. The newly opened property has large, clean rooms with all the usual facilities. There is a Lao-Thai restaurant on the first level. Room rates are US$25-35. (Book with the hotel at 100 Samsenthai Road, Vientiane, Lao P.D.R.)

Lani Guest House (Tel: 215839), off Settathirath Road in central Vientiane, is one of those delightful discoveries you occasionally make. The guest house is situated within a nice building on a lane next to Wat Haisok. The eight rooms have been tastefully decorated and the owners/managers are a delightful, friendly couple who aim to please. The guest house advertises itself as "your home in Vientiane," and this is the atmosphere that prevails. Although the guest house only opened in 1990, it is no surprise that there are many repeat guests, including U.N. and diplomatic staff.

All rooms have airconditioning and attached bathrooms and are nicely furnished. There is a nice large lounge area adjacent to the reception desk and a delightful terrace where breakfast and drinks are served. Other meals are available by order. For short-term visitors, the location is excellent because shops, restaurants, offices, and other places of interest are within easy walking distance. Room rates are around US$25 a night. (Book with the guest house by writing to P.O. Box 58, Vientiane, Lao P.D.R.; Fax: 856-21-216103.)

Lani Two Guest House (Tel: 213022), at 268 Saylom Road, is operated by the same management and is, in many ways, a copy of the successful Lani Guest House. It opened in 1991 and is already very popular. The location is close to the morning market development, and only a short tuk-tuk ride from the shopping and office area. (Book through the same address as Lani Guest House.)

Villa That Luang (Tel: 413370) is on That Luang Road, out toward Pha That Luang (the Great Sacred Stupa). This is about two kilometers from central Vientiane. The friendly owner speaks good English and is helpful and enterprising. The facilities and service are both good.

All rooms are airconditioned and have refrigerators and attached bathrooms. Current room rates are from US$14-30, which includes laundry service. There is a nice restaurant for all meals, a lounge with TV, and a popular bar. In my mind, the older building has more atmosphere, but that is very much a personal choice. (Book with the villa at Thanon That Luang, Vientiane, Lao P.D.R.)

Le Parasol Blanc (Tel: 216091) was originally known as a delightful piano bar and restaurant (in fact it is one of my favorites in Vientiane), but has now developed into one of the most popular hotels in the city. It has progressively expanded from four rooms to 55 rooms in a period of five years. The rooms are nothing very special, but they are a good size and are clean. Many have outdoor areas for walking or talking. The staff is friendly. There is a swimming pool, nice gardens, and the delightful bar and restaurant, of course.

Le Parasol Blanc is tucked away on Sibounhevang Road behind the former National Assembly building and in front of the Ministry of Commerce and Tourism, near the Pratuxai Monument (Anousavali). There is no transportation to the front door; but if you walk three hundred meters, you are on Lane Xang Avenue and only a few minutes from the Morning Market. The hotel is owned by the diverse Vico Group of Companies headed by entrepreneur Vinay Inthavong, one of Vientiane's high-profile operators. You will often see him in the restaurant with friends and associates. (Book with the hotel at P.O. Box 815, Vientiane, Lao P.D.R.; Fax: 856-21-215628.)

The **Vientiane Hotel** (Tel: 212926), 15 rooms, is on Thanon Luang Prabang, about one kilometer west of the central city. There is a restaurant on the ground floor and the hotel reception is on the second floor. Fan-cooled rooms are available for US$20, while basic airconditioned rooms with telephone, refrigerator, and a very small bathroom are US$25-30. The hotel does not appeal to me, but it appeared to have a number of guests on the last occasion I visited. (Book with the hotel at Luang Prabang Road, Vientiane, Lao P.D.R.)

The **Samsenthai Hotel** (Tel: 216287), 20 rooms, is a bit run-down, but the rooms are well-equipped with airconditioning, TV, telephone, and hot and cold water in the bathroom. Prices are US$15 and US$20. (Book with the hotel at 15 Manthathurath Street; Fax: 856-21-212116.)

The **Riverview Hotel** (Tel: 216244), 32 rooms, is next to the Mekong River, about 1½ kilometers west of the central city. The hotel sees its location as an attraction to guests and charges heavily for rooms with river views. All rooms are airconditioned and have telephones and attached bathrooms; but US$40 for a normal double, US$50 for a river view room, and US$80 for a special river view room seem overpriced for what you get. There is a ground-floor restaurant that overlooks the river. It can be an attractive place for lunch. (Book with the hotel at Luang Prabang Road, Vientiane, Lao P.D.R.; Fax: 856-21-216232.)

The **Inter Hotel** (Tel: 213582) is also overlooking the river, but is close to the central city. All rooms are airconditioned, some have river views, and the hotel has a popular restaurant and bar. The hotel has resisted steep price increases, so the rooms are a good value at US$12-20, including Continental breakfast. Don't expect great facilities or service at this price; but on my last inspection, the hotel was clean and I was told that it is often full. (Book with the hotel at Chao Anou Road, Vientiane, Lao P.D.R.)

The **Nong Douang Hotel** (Tel: 21-6768) is on Nong Douang Street, opposite Nong Douang Market. The building is a two-level villa with a spacious front court holding an attractive garden restaurant. The hotel has one suite for US$20 a day and nine double rooms with attached bathrooms for US$15 a day. Only three of these have hot water. All rooms are airconditioned and are equipped with ceiling fans. There is a restaurant on the second level. (Book with the hotel at Nong Douang Street, Vientiane, Lao P.D.R.)

The **Chaemchanh Guest House**, 9 rooms, is a popular place. Some way out of town at 78 Kuvieng Road. All rooms are airconditioned and have hot water. Prices are US$20.

BUDGET ACCOMMODATIONS

Vientiane has no tradition of budget guest house accommodations, youth hostels, or workers dormitories that are available to foreigners, so the choice of really inexpensive accommodations is very limited.

The best you can hope for is inexpensive guest house accommodations or very poor standard basic hotel rooms. I strongly recommend the guest houses.

The **Santisouk Guest House** (Tel: 215303), 9 rooms, is above the restaurant of the same name on Nokeo Kouman Street near the Revolutionary Museum. Rooms with outside bathrooms are US$10 and with a bathroom US$12. The location is good.

The **Mixay Guest House** (Tel: 216213), 6 rooms, is also well located at Fa Ngum Street by the river. The rooms are fairly basic, but the US$10 price tag is reasonable.

The **Hua Guo Guest House** (Tel: 216612), 12 rooms, has clean rooms from US$8. Add a bathroom with cold water and it's US$10. With hot water it becomes US$12. You find it at 359 Samsenthai Road in the center of the city.

The **Dok Champa Guest House** (Tel: 314412), 15 rooms, is out on the Thadeva Road about three kilometers from town. There is a nice restaurant here, and the rooms are all airconditioned and have telephone and hot water. Price start at around US$12.

The alternative is the **Manthaturath Road Guest House** (Tel: 21-2362), which is run by the Ministry of Culture in the central city. All rooms have attached bathrooms with cold water. Fan-cooled rooms are US$7 and airconditioned rooms are US$10. The guest house has a coffee shop for meals and drinks, and there is a small handicraft shop. (Book through P.O. Box 2911, Vientiane, Lao P.D.R.)

5. Dining and Restaurants

Although Vientiane is a small city, there are numerous dining opportunities that cover a wide range of cuisines, prices, and standards. In the last few years, a number of privately owned mid-market restaurants have joined the hotels and basic Lao-Chinese eateries in the city; and the variety continues to grow.

Some visitors will be reluctant to leave the familiar surroundings of the hotel at night to search out a restaurant in streets that often lack adequate lighting and are in poor repair. While I understand this feeling, I urge you to resist this temptation. There are several restaurants, bars, and entertainment places that offer good food and a unique look into another side of Lao life that you don't see if you only eat with other visitors.

HOTEL RESTAURANTS

Most hotels in Vientiane have at least one restaurant; and although I have not eaten at all of them, I have found the ones that I have tried to be acceptable and, in some cases, quite excellent. I have yet to find anyone who has said, "Don't eat at such-and-such hotel restaurant because it is terrible." That is probably comforting to those who are somewhat wary of Asian cuisine, health standards, and possible aftereffects.

My favorite Vientiane restaurant is actually a hotel restaurant, and I do not say that about any other city in the world. **Le Parasol Blanc** (Tel: 216091) is delightful. The restaurant is in a lovely old mansion set in landscaped gardens. You can start or finish the evening in the downstairs bar and lounge, listening to the music as you sip your favorite cocktail, beer, or soft drink. The whole atmosphere is subdued, quite sophisticated, and totally relaxing. You will find that guests are a mixture of visitors, local Lao business or government people, and embassy or United Nations expatriate workers.

Food orders can be placed while you are listening to the music, and the waiter will tell you when your table is ready. The restaurant is situated in a large downstairs area, in an outdoor terrace, and upstairs in two beautifully furnished rooms, each containing four or five tables and some outstanding plants and flower arrangements. You can chose between Asian and European dishes, and requests such as "half a serving of this and half a serving of that" are handled without difficulty. A meal for two can cost as little as US$10.

The restaurant is open for lunch and dinner and is located on Sibounhevang Road, behind the old National Assembly building, adjacent to the

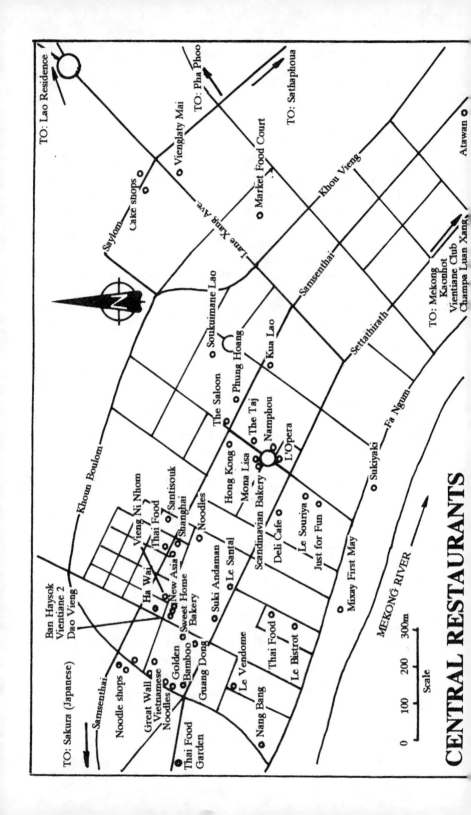

CENTRAL RESTAURANTS

Pratuxai monument. It can be difficult to find at night, but it's worth making the effort. Most taxi and tuk-tuk drivers know where it is.

The renovated **Muang Lao Hotel** (Tel: 312380) has a nice restaurant on the second floor that is open for lunch and dinner. It serves a selection of Asian and European dishes.

The restaurant at the **Vansana Hotel** (Tel: 413171) is probably a place most visitors will not visit unless they are staying in the hotel; but this is another small, attractive restaurant with nice, personal service and good food. If you are staying at this hotel, do not leave without at least one meal in the restaurant. You will not be disappointed.

The **Asian Pavillion Hotel** (Tel: 213431) has an attractive restaurant as well as a more casual coffee shop. Both are acceptable for lunch or dinner; and because this hotel is in the center of the city, it attracts some visitors who are not actually staying in the hotel. The same can be said for the **Lane Xang Hotel** (Tel: 214102). Its large dining room is a meeting place for many. At night, **Sukiyaki Restaurant**, which is operated by the hotel, but is across the road on the riverbank, specializes in "steamboat" and has Lao music by a local group.

The **Belvedere Hotel** (Tel: 213570) has a popular restaurant and also has regular barbecues in an attractive outdoor setting. The Apollo Restaurant at the **New Apollo Hotel** (Tel: 213343) is large and contemporary, while the restaurant at the **Tai-pan Hotel** is smart and informal.

Among the other hotel restaurants, the **Riverview Hotel** (Tel: 216244) has a restaurant overlooking the river which is attractive, particularly at lunchtime. The **Snake Bar and Restaurant** (Tel: 413370) at Villa That Luang is a nice, quiet hideaway for lunch or dinner, with a choice of Lao, Thai, and Western cuisine. The **Inter Hotel** (Tel: 213582) has an attractively furnished restaurant with excellent sizzling steaks at good prices. The **Ambassador Hotel** (Tel: 213003) has an upstairs dining room with reasonable food, but absolutely no atmosphere. The **Metropole** (Tel: 213421), the **Anou** (Tel: 213631), and the **Saysana** (Tel: 213580) are all acceptable, but are not worth going out of your way to find.

LAO AND LAO/CHINESE/THAI FOOD

My introduction to dining in Vientiane was in a ramshackle timber building with open sides on the banks of the Mekong River. The **Ban Mixay First May Cooperative Restaurant** (Tel: 216312) was doing a roaring trade in draft beer in large plastic jugs. There were rough timber tables and chairs, goats wandered around the no-man's-land between the river and the restaurant, and Western country music was being played on a ghetto-blaster. It was a very strange scene. After spending two hours there, sampling the *laap* (a mixture of ground meat, lime juice, garlic, green onions, and chilies) and the local 33 export beer and watching the sun set and Thailand light up across the river; I decided that this was a great place. I have since revisited many times. Very little seems to change. The crowds come and go, the beer sometimes runs out, the rubbish on the riverbank increases, but the attraction remains. The menu is not extensive and the food is probably overpriced for what you get, but I recommend that you visit just before sunset and enjoy the next few hours in a uniquely Lao way. You find it about five hundred meters west of the Lane Xang Hotel, almost opposite the Mixai Guest House.

Lao food can also be enjoyed in other surroundings. At the **Dong Palane Market**, about one kilometer southeast of the city center, you can sit at an open-air stall and enjoy the food the locals eat. At times it is dusty, other times it is wet. Sometimes there are mosquitoes and other times there are flies; but the food is always cheap and, in my experience, quite good. This is probably not the best place for your initial introduction to Asian dishes, but after you have a feel for Vientiane, this will have considerable appeal. This is a good place to try the local roast chicken, fried rice, stir-fried vegetables, or spicy green papaya salad.

The road between the central city and the airport has several restaurants of note. As you travel out, you pass the **Nokkeo Restaurant** (Tel: 214252) on your right. This green building decorated with colored lights, comes into its own after dark. The food is a combination of Lao and Thai and is quite tasty. The restaurant has a live band playing nightly, so if music does not appeal to you, go early. Next is the **Lotus Restaurant** (Tel: 414741), which is also on the right. I have never been here, so I have nothing to report. The last place of interest is **Ban Phim Restaurant** (Tel: 214700), about 2½ kilometers from the central city. This is a little off the road to the right and is quite attractive. The decor is Lao-style, as is much of the cuisine. Western food is also available. The large bar can provide you with your favorite drink, and the evening can be relaxed and pleasant.

Back in town, there is quite a selection. The **Nang Bang Restaurant** (Tel: 217198) is on Thanon Khoun Boulom, near where it joins Thanon Fa Ngum. This small, local restaurant hardly rates for looks, but the food is rather good. Some locals claim that it is the best Lao food in Vientiane. The **Golden Bamboo Restaurant** (Tel: 414174) is a little more upscale. This is on Thanon Settathirath, just around the corner from Khoun Boulom. I have a soft spot for this place because they have a poster of my hometown hanging on the wall. I asked how they got it, and I was told that they bought it in the market because they liked the picture. They had never heard of the place featured on the poster.

Several new up-scale Lao restaurants have opened in the central area. The **Ban Haysok Restaurant** at 34 Heng Boun Street (opposite the Anou Hotel) is operated by the owner of the Lani Guest House. It serves high-quality Lao and Southern Chinese food in a nice setting. **Soukuimane Lao Food** is less impressive, but the food is genuine Lao and is excellent. If possible, go with a Lao speaker to get the most from the evening. The restaurant is tucked away in a small street immediately west of That Dam (behind the Metropole Hotel).The **Kualao Restaurant** (Tel: 215777) is close by in Samsenthai Road. This place opened in late 1994 in a restored French-style mansion. The setting and food are both impressive.

Just north of here along Thanon Heng Boun and Thanon Chao Anou, there are numerous restaurants and **noodle shops**. This is the unofficial Chinatown, and eating becomes a very serious business. There are many Chinese-style open-fronted, concrete-floored, bare-walled eateries here that sell noodle soup, fried noodles, or fried rice. Most will also serve a plate of rice with chicken, pork, or duck on top to anyone eating alone. You should just wander along and choose a place that appeals to you. The food in any of them will be good. If you find a place where no one speaks English, just wander over to the cooking area and point to what you want. That is perfectly acceptable.

In this area, there are a few more conventional restaurants, where the eating area is separated from the street by a wall or window. There is a small unnamed restaurant next to the Vientiane Colorlab on Thanon Heng Boun that you could try. It serves Lao and Chinese dishes. So too do the **Restaurant Vientiane 2** and the **Restaurant Dao Vieng** (Tel: 213945), which are almost side-by-side on Heng Boun, opposite the Hotel Anou. The Dao Vieng is extremely popular at lunchtime. At night, meals are served upstairs in a large, open room, where there is a Chinese singer and a live band. The best food here is Chinese cuisine. The menu is in French and Lao. The **New Asia Chinese Restaurant** (Tel: 312575) is a new place at 278 Samsenthai Road, and is rapidly developing a good reputation. In the same block you will find the **Shanghai Restaurant**, and two blocks east there is the excellent and very popular **Hong Kong Restaurant** (Tel: 213241). Across the road and one block farther east, the **Phung Hoang Restaurant** (Tel: 216474) has Vietnamese and Chinese food.

Two other places worthy of mention are on Tha Deua Road, south of the city. The first is the **Champa Luan Xang Restaurant**, which is built adjacent to a recreation lake near the water tower, about two kilometers from the city. There are covered tables and chairs set in an attractive area around the lake's edge—ideal for a quiet drink or light snack. There is a large, air-conditioned room where Lao, Thai, and some Western food is served before and during a heavy music session from 9 P.M. until midnight. The second place is the **Mekong Restaurant** (Tel: 312480), which is about four kilometers from the city. This is the largest restaurant in Vientiane, and it serves

Lao, Chinese, Vietnamese, and French food. The restaurant is airconditioned and is adjacent to the Mekong River. It is very popular with mid-
dle-class Lao people and also with the expatriate community. Taxis and
tuk-tuks are readily available for transport back to your hotel.

The **Lao Residence Restaurant** is an attractive up-market place on That
Luang Road not far from the Monument. Lunch time is particularly popular because of the good value lunch specials on offer. Cuisine and service
are of high quality. The **Pha Phoo Restaurant** at the Bank Tennis Club serves
Lao food in reasonable surroundings although the price always surprises
me.

THAI FOOD

Laos has close links with Thailand, so it is no surprise to find several Thai
restaurants and much Thai food in Vientiane. Many of the restaurants mentioned in the previous section serve some Thai dishes, but the following specialize in Thai cuisine.

My favorite Thai restaurant is **Vanh Mixai** (Tel: 3090) on Francois Ngin
Street. The owner is a friendly Thai lady, who will chat to you in English and
suggest a menu that might appeal. The atmosphere is that of a suburban
street with friendly neighbors. The menu is not brilliant, but it is quite adequate with all the Thai standards. The dishes that I sampled were excellent. Service and prices are both good.

Also worth checking out is the **Thai Restaurant** at the Lao Paris Hotel
(sometimes called the Pimmasane Guest House) at 100 Samsenthai Road.
The food is good, the service a bit slow, and the prices about average.

The **Thai Food Restaurant** (Tel: 214283) on Samsenthai Road, one block
west of the Revolutionary Museum, is another popular spot. There is an
open-fronted Chinese-style eating area and an airconditioned room. Much
of the food is precooked and available as take-out meals.

Another is the **Thai Food Garden** on Luang Prabang Road to the west
of Khoun Boulom. This place has a good reputation among the expatriate
community for its Thai seafood dishes.

The **Sathaphoun Restaurant** on Dong Pai Na Road not far from the Lan-
Xang Nightclub serves reasonable food in an attractive outdoor setting.
Prices and service are acceptable.

WESTERN FOOD

Laos was occupied by the French for more than half a century, and one
reminder can still be seen today. French breadsticks are widely available in
the mornings; croissants are popular for breakfast; as are baguettes filled
with a type of pressed meat or paté.

Western (American) breakfasts are also popular at the hotels and some other places. The **Sweet Home Bakery**, at 109 Thanon Chao Anou, has a wall menu that includes a choice of either egg, ham, and sausage; egg, ham, and bacon; or omelette and ham—all served with toast, butter, jam, and coffee for about US$1.50. There is also the alternative of muesli, fruit, and fiber; natural muesli; or apple muesli—all served with fruit, yogurt, and coffee for the same price. Sweet Home, and the adjacent **Vinh Loi Bakery** at 111 Thanon Chau Anou, both have good selections of small cakes, sandwich loaves, ice creams, sundaes, and large decorated cakes. If someone is having a celebration, this is the place to head.

There are several restaurants that specialize in Western food, and some of these are excellent. Certainly most of them have more atmosphere than the Lao/Chinese/Thai establishments. The **Namphou Restaurant** (Tel: 216248) is at 20 Place Namphou (Fountain), just off Settathirath. It is a popular bar and restaurant among expatriates staying in Vientiane because of the food, the service, and the ambience. The cuisine has French influence, but you can also get some good Lao dishes if you order ahead. Just opposite is the **L'Opera Restaurant** (Tel: 215099), which serves Italian food. This has become a serious rival to the Namphou. Currently it is open from 11:30 A.M. to 2 P.M. for lunch and from 6 to 11 P.M. for dinner. Not far away, the **Le Souriya** (Tel: 215887), at 3½ Thanon Pang Kham, is another place with good food and service and attractive decor. **Le Vendome** on Soi Inpeng around the corner from the Saysana Hotel is probably my favorite. The atmosphere is that of a provincial French restaurant, and the food matches perfectly. The salad bar is a big hit. So too are the pizzas. These four restaurants are the closest you will get in Laos to an intimate Western eatery. The standards in each are high; and for Laos, the prices are high too, but they will not break the bank of most visitors. Main dishes cost US$4-8, and cocktails and imported beer are around US$2. Local beer is about US$1.50.

The **Santisouk Restaurant** (Tel: 215303) on Thanon Nokeo Khoumane, near the Revolutionary Museum, is unfortunately only a shadow of the famous Cafe La Pagode that it once was. There is some atmosphere, but the room is rather plain and I was not excited by the service. The restaurant has European, Thai, and Lao cuisine; but most dishes are served in a Western manner on individual plates. The menu is in French and Lao. Main courses range in price from around US$2.50 to US$3.50.

Le Santal is another French restaurant that has a big following. The food is well priced and the pizzas are particularly popular. It is situated at 101 Settathirat Road. A newly opened place called the **Mona Lisa Restaurant** (Tel: 217251) is at 73/2 Pang Kham Street at the fountain. The cuisine here is French. Almost next door is the **Scandinavian Bakery** (Tel: 215199) where donuts, cakes, coffee, and snacks are the rage. Around the corner, the **Deli Cafe** (Tel: 215651) has just what you would expect — pate, meats, breads, coffee, and so forth. **The Saloon** (Tel: 212990) at 78 Pang Kham Road has snacks, videos, and some Western grills in a casual atmosphere.

The **Arawan Restaurant** (Tel: 3977) at 474 Thanon Samsenthai is an agreeable alternative. This bar and restaurant has French cuisine and a range of other Western dishes. Main courses include filet mignon, pork chops, and fried chicken served with French fries and are priced around US$4. Ice cream is around US$1.50 and fruit is similar in price. There are also some special dishes, such as deer (US$8), New Zealand T-bone steak (US$12), sauerkraut (US$5), and duck in green pepper sauce (US$5).

The Blues Restaurant is a small Russian casino eatery on Dong Si Sung Wun Road opposite the Japanese embassy.

OTHER CHOICES

The Taj (Tel: 212890) at 75/4 Pang Kham Road is a stylish Indian restaurant serving tandoori, curries, and vegetarian dishes with considerable flair. **The Sakura** (Tel: 212274) is a Japanese restaurant on a small soi off Luang Prabang Road near the Belvedere Hotel. An unfortunate incident with the bill has put me off this place.

Kaonhot (Tel: 214592) on Thanon Sakarindh is also known as the Snooker Club because of its billiard room. This bar, restaurant, and discotheque seems to come and go in popularity, so ask someone when you get to Vientiane. The restaurant specializes in grills at reasonable prices. **Vienglaty Mai** (Tel: 215321) on Lane Xang Avenue is primarily a nightclub. It opens from 8:30 P.M. to midnight each day and offers food while you listen to the band or dance the night away. The **Golden Fish Food Garden** is one of a number of small seafood places on Road 13 north of the city (actually it is on the road to the south). This is possibly the best of them and is about 12 kilometers from downtown. The **Win-West Pub and Restaurant** (Tel: 217275) is a delightfully decorated place with a Filipino singer and Western and Asian food. This is probably the best "pub" in the city. It is on Luang Prabang Road opposite the New Apollo Hotel. **Just For Fun** on Pang Kham Road has vegetarian and variable quality Thai food in a nice homey atmosphere.

6. Sightseeing

The sightseeing attractions of Vientiane can be classified as monuments, thats and wats, and lifestyle activities such as markets. The first two categories can all be seen in one day, whereas the lifestyle attractions will take as long as your interest holds. It is impossible to overemphasize the influence that Buddhism has had on the Lao lifestyle, and the best way to appreciate it now is to visit several *thats* (stupas) and *wats* (temples).

A good place to start is at **Pha That Luang**, probably the most important monument in Laos. That Luang is about three kilometers northeast of central Vientiane. You reach it by traveling along Lane Xang Avenue past the Pratuxai Monument, then out Thanon That Luang. The present construction was started in 1566, but it is thought that it was built over a much older structure. One theory is that an original stupa was built in 307 B.C. by Phraya Chanthabury Pasithisak, the founder of Vientiane, to house a holy relic of Lord Buddha. That structure is said to have been nine meters high and made of stones. It is possible that the Khmers later built a monastery on this site.

When King Settathirath, ruler of Chiang Mai and Luang Prabang, decided to move his capital to Vientiane, he embarked on a plan to build a great stupa. When it was completed, it was a magnificent structure with a top covered in gold leaf. Unfortunately, That Luang has been attacked, ransacked, abandoned, restored, and damaged on many occasions over the years by Burmese invaders, the Siamese, Ho pirates from southern China, and even by lightning strikes. A cloister with small openings and a strong gate was built in the early nineteenth century by King Anouvong as a defense measure, and a major controversial repair was carried out by the French in 1900. In the 1930s much of the building was demolished and rebuilt.

The stupa has three levels that the public can visit. The lowest is a base measuring 69 by 68 meters that has 323 ordination stones (simas), four prayer pavilions with staircases leading to them, and a special pavilion on the eastern side that houses a small decorated stupa said to be one of 8,400 stupas originally built by King Ashoka in 220 B.C. The second level is forty-eight meters square and is surrounded by 120 lotus petals. There are 288 simas and thirty small stupas on this level as well as additional praying places. The third level is thirty meters square and supports the four-sided, elongated lotus-bud-shaped spire that emerges from a bowl-shaped base. That Luang is forty-five meters high and can be seen from many areas around the capital.

The stupa is nominally open from 8 to 11:30 A.M. and 2 to 4:30 P.M. daily, except Mondays. Foreign visitors pay an entrance fee of US$0.30. You can buy a small booklet called *The Short History of Phra That Luang* in Lao and English for about US$0.25 at the entrance gate. The That Luang festival is held each November and is a major celebration within the city.

As you head back toward central Vientiane, you will pass by the **Pratuxai Monument** (often called Anousavari). This imposing structure is rather reminiscent of the Arc de Triomphe in Paris. It was built in 1969 to commemorate those Lao who died in wars over the centuries. There is a small restaurant within the structure, and there is a staircase that takes you to the top for a good view over the surrounding city.

Continue southwest along Lane Xang Avenue, and the **Morning Market** is on your left. This has been extensively redeveloped in recent years and now consists of three major buildings containing the Vientiane Department Store and a wide range of small stall holders that sell household goods, jewelry, fabrics, electrical goods, clothes, and so forth. This has become the major shopping area of Vientiane and is frequented by locals, expatriates, and visitors who are in-the-know. The market operates all day until around 4:30 P.M. It is a great place to browse—even if you are not buying. The department store has a fair range of imported items (mainly from Thailand, China, and Vietnam) at reasonable prices, and there is a supermarket and a small snack bar. The small stalls in the other two buildings compete among themselves, so prices are good. No matter what you are looking for, you will have a choice of up to twenty different outlets for your purchase. At all of them you need to bargain. In the first one or two, try to establish what the lowest price is likely to be, then move to another one and enter into serious bargaining.

At the back and side of the Morning Market, there are many small restaurants that open early in the morning and many mobile stalls offering snacks, drinks, flowers, vegetables, fruit, and other items. Inside the department store there is a cheap, airconditioned food hall that is very popular at lunch time. This whole area needs several hours of your time to explore and enjoy.

At the end of Lane Xang Avenue, you will find the **Presidential Palace**. This has recently been repainted, and visitors are now allowed to photograph the building. The Presidential Palace is occasionally used for receptions and entertaining official visitors to Laos.

When you reach the Presidential Palace, turn left on Thanon Settathirath. There are two interesting temples here that together form the **Museum of Hokprakow.** This opens from 8 to 11:30 A.M. and from 2 to 4:30 P.M. daily except Mondays. Foreign visitors are required to pay a US$0.30 entry fee. **Wat Sisaket** is the first part that you come to. This temple was constructed in nineteenth-century Thai style in 1818 by King Anouvong. When the Siamese almost destroyed Vientiane in 1828, this building was saved, so it is the oldest wat building in Vientiane today. The main building in the compound (sim), which contains the important Buddha image, is surrounded by an extensive cloister. This cloister contains over two thousand silver and ceramic Buddha images and three hundred larger wood, terra-cotta, stone, or bronze images in different forms. Most of the images are between one hundred and three hundred years old, but a few have survived from the fifteenth century. There is also a Khmer-style Buddha of unknown age.

The sim itself is quite lovely. The interior walls have hundreds of Buddha niches in them, as well as murals depicting the Buddha's life story. The decorated ceiling is said to be copied from Siamese temples in the old capital of Ayuthaya. The sim contains several large Buddha images as well, bringing the total number of images at this temple to over six thousand. The sim is surrounded by a colonnaded terrace, and the whole structure is topped by a five-tiered roof. As you wander around the grounds, you will notice a five-meter-long carved wooden trough that is used once a year for the ritual cleansing of the Buddha images. You will also see a raised library building in the compound that once contained some important scripture documents. This whole compound is extremely interesting and great to photograph, and I urge you to visit—even if your time in Vientiane is short.

The second part of the museum is nearby **Wat Phra Keo**, which was originally the royal temple of the Lao monarchy. It is said to have originated in 1565, when it was built to house the so-called Emerald Buddha, which is now in Bangkok. The Emerald Buddha was once in Chiang Rai, then in Chiang Mai, Thailand; and it is supposed to have been brought to Vientiane by King Settathirath. It is believed that the Siamese seized it back in 1779, then destroyed Wat Phra Keo when they invaded Vientiane in 1828.

The present temple was built about fifty years ago in a style that was popular about 150 years ago. The building is interesting without being outstanding, but the interior, which now houses some of the best museum pieces, is a "must see." There are Buddha images from various periods, a range of wooden carvings, palm-leaf manuscripts, Khmer inscriptions, a gilded throne, and other antiques. Unfortunately, there are no English explanations for any of the exhibits. The surrounding terrace also contains some treasures, including a thirteen-hundred-year-old stone Buddha, several bronze Buddhas, and some inscribed tablets. The garden contains a large stone jar from the Plain of Jars in northern Laos and some other objects. It is well worth exploring every corner.

While you are in this part of the city, go about three blocks southeast to **Wat Simuang**. This temple contains the city's foundation pillar—said to have been erected in 1563 by King Settathirath. Tradition says that a volunteer was needed as a sacrifice to the spirits before the huge stone pillar could be firmly put in place. The sim was erected over the foundation pillar. The original sim was destroyed by the Siamese in 1828, and the present building was not constructed until 1915. Today, the stone pillar is wrapped in sacred cloth, and it forms the center of the altar. It is surrounded by several Buddha images, including one which is supposed to have the power to grant wishes. Those who believe their request has been granted later return with an offering of bananas and coconuts.

If you now take Thanon Sansenthai back toward the central city, you will pass close to the **Catholic church** on Gallieni Street. There is a multilingual service (including English) each Sunday at 8:30 A.M. If you turn right at Lane Xang Avenue and continue for one block, you will see the **General Post Office** on your right. Business hours are 8 A.M. to 5 P.M. Monday through Saturday, and 8 A.M. to noon on Sunday. The outbound mail service seems fairly reliable, and friends may like to receive Lao stamps. Before you reach the post office, a small street named Bartolini leads off to the left. This passes the **United States Embassy** and leads to **That Dam**, the Black Stupa. The exact age of this is unknown, but it is believed to have been built about six hundred years ago. As such, it is by far the oldest structure in Vientiane. Unfortunately, That Dam is not well cared for, but it is still an impressive structure. Some Lao will tell you about the legend of a seven-headed dragon that lives in That Dam and came to life to help protect the city against the Siamese in 1828.

Turn left and return to Thanon Samsenthai. You are now at the start of what could be called the central business district of Vientiane. It consists of one block on Samsenthai and a short length of Thanon Pang Kham toward the fountain. This area contains many jewelers, tailors, and souvenir shops. There are also some food outlets, clothing shops, and tourist traps. The **fountain** is an attractive centerpoint for this area. A small **mosque** is situated down a lane to the east of the fountain. Friday prayers are at 1 P.M.

Back on Samsenthai, the **Lao Revolutionary Museum** is on the right, two blocks ahead. This is of interest to history or political science students, but will not thrill most visitors. While it is theoretically open to the public each day, in practice it appears to open only on special occasions. Continue straight ahead, and you enter the unofficial **Chinatown** of Vientiane. Along Thanon Samsenthai, Heng Boun, and Chao Anou, there are several cinemas, many Chinese restaurants, minimarts, bakeries, hardware shops, and so forth.

When you reach the corner of Thanon Chao Anou and Thanon Settathirath, you are surrounded by temples. How many you wish to visit will depend on the time you have available and your interest in architecture, religious art, Buddhism, and present-day lifestyles. From the outside, **Wat In Paeng**, to the right, is one of the most impressive. The grounds are well kept and the entrance from Settathirath leads directly to a highly decorated temple with a very impressive veranda facade. The sun shining on the ornate decorations and the tropical vegetation closing in on the building present great photographic opportunities.

Ahead and to your left is **Wat Ong Teu**. The present buildings have all been constructed in the past 150 years, but the temple was originally founded in the early sixteenth century. The wat contains an important Buddhist training school for monks, and you will see many students as you walk through the grounds. The temple itself contains a large and impressive sixteenth-century bronze Buddha. Other points of interest are the beautiful temple doors and the carved wooden facade to the veranda. These are well worth seeing.

Wat Mixai is next to Wat Ong Teu. The main building is attractive with verandas on all sides, and the guardian giants at the gates can hardly be missed. The compound has an elementary school. Across the road is **Wat Hay Sok**. The temple has been beautifully restored; and the narrow, soaring, five-tiered roof is probably the most impressive in Vientiane. The last temple in this area is **Wat Chan**. This is behind Wat Ong Teu, overlooking the river. The sim is quite recent, but it has been well constructed in a typical modern Lao style. Housed inside is an impressive, large, and beautiful Buddha that was once in a previous building that is now long gone. There is also the remains of an ancient stupa that was once guarded by Buddha images.

Now that you are down by the river, it is worthwhile to just find a quiet spot to sit, rest, and watch life around you. This is Vientiane as it has been for many years—quiet, slow, attractive, and dependent on the river. This part of town is also the center for tour and travel information and bookings. **Lao Aviation** has its head office on Thanon Pang Kham, at the side of the Lane Xang Hotel. This is where you reconfirm onward flights and make internal air bookings. **Thai Airways International** has moved from this area to an office next to the Asian Pavilion Hotel. The Lao National Tourism office, which has had its name changed to **Inter-Lao Tourism**, is on the corner of Pang Kham and Settathirath, facing Nam Phou Square. This organization is primarily set up to run guided tours, but you can get some verbal information (but unfortunately no printed matter) in English.

There are a few other places to see within the city. If you head north along Thanon Chao Anou, it leads to Thanon Thong Khoun Khan Kham. About 750 meters along here, you come to the **Thong Khan Kham Market** on the corner of Thanon Dong Miang. This is the largest produce market in town. There is meat, fish, vegetables, fruit, rice, groceries, and some cooked food. The market is still not properly developed, so it can be muddy after rain. A little farther out, you will find the **Vientiane Circus** building. The building was a Soviet aid project, and was built from a Soviet design that is clearly unsuitable for Vientiane's hot humid weather. The other problem is that Vientiane is hardly large enough to regularly support such a facility, so performances are restricted to about one a month. If you hear of one while you are in Vientiane, it would be fun to go—if the weather is good.

If you go west instead of north, you will find yourself on Luang Prabang Road. You pass the **Three-headed Elephant** on the right (at the intersection of Samsenthai) and a succession of wats on the left. The **Textile Center** is on a lane to the right, opposite Wat Oup Moung. There is a workshop and shop where you can see handwoven cotton fabrics being made, and buy the articles produced. It is open Monday through Saturday from 8 A.M. to noon and 2 to 4 P.M. Back on Luang Prabang Road, the **Evangelical church** has services every second Sunday at 9:30 A.M. Services are in Lao, but there is an English order of service. Farther out, there is a **Bahai Center** behind Wat Tai Noi. Another 1.5 kilometers brings you to the **airport**.

The **Revolution Monument** (sometimes called Unknown Soldiers Memorial) is on Thanon Phon Kheng, which leads to Route 13 to the south. This white edifice was built to commemorate those who died in the War of Resistance in the 1960s and 1970s. Close by is the new National Assembly building facing That Luang Square; and on the opposite side of Thanon Phon Kheng are the **Army Museum** and the **Ministry of Defense**. About a kilometer southeast is the **That Luang Market**, which is known to locals as a good place to buy exotic food and animals. Another market worth visiting is **Dong Palane Market**, which is located on Thanon Dong Palane, not far from Wat Dong Palane. This is best at night when there are many stalls selling precooked foods.

Southeast of the city, there are two wats that are noteworthy—partly because they have facilities for saunas. **Wat Sok Paluang** is about three kilometers from the central city. The sauna is located in the nuns' quarters, which is to the left of the main temple. You take the path that leads between the stupas, to the left of the large, white entrance gate. The sauna takes some time to prepare, so it is best to make prior arrangements. You need a towel and an hour or more of time. The sauna is prepared with herbs and is quite relaxing. The room is large enough for several people, so it's best to go with friends. You go in and out of the room for as long as you like. While cooling off afterwards, the nuns provide tea, and there is the option of a massage. There are no private changing rooms or showers. The nuns make no fixed charge for a sauna, but it is customary to leave about US$3.

Wat Sri Amphorn (Tel: 312531) also provides saunas, but has better facilities, although it appears to be less well known. You can telephone ahead to make your arrangements. There are restrooms, an exercise room, and a shower. Herbal tea is served to you after you finish the sauna. Both of these wats are relatively close to the Swedish Guest House.

AROUND VIENTIANE

There are several points of interest along Route 2 to the south of Vientiane. At kilometer six, you come to the Chinamino roundabout. Stay to the left on Route 2, and you pass a number of factories that may represent the future for Laos. At kilometer fourteen, there is a park (with a small entry fee). If you follow the road to the end, you will find a lake with Chinese temples, a refreshment area, and to the left a small **zoo**. There is another small entry fee for the zoo, where you can see elephants, deer, and a few other animals.

A few kilometers farther along the main road, you come to the new Laos-Thailand bridge. The bridge was funded by the Australian government, and it opened in 1994. It is a few kilometers to **Tha Deua**, which is the arrival and departure point for ferries across the river from Nong Khai, Thailand. There is really very little here except a customs and immigration office, a collection of open-sided restaurants along the riverbank, and a rabble of taxis, tuk-tuks, buses, and motorcycles dropping off and picking up people who cross the river in small motorized boats sporting Thai or Lao flags.

Three kilometers south of the town is a fascinating attraction called **Wat Xieng Khwan**, or **Buddha Park**. Here, on the riverbank, you will find an amazing collection of concrete statues of Buddhist and Hindu figures strangely mixed with mythology. The whole thing is bizarre, yet as an attraction for visitors, it is fascinating. Photographers will go wild. At one end, there is a ten-meter globe that you can enter to experience a stylized version of Hell, earth, and Heaven. If you think the construction looks somewhat suspect, you may be assured (or concerned) to know that it is over thirty years old. The last stairway to the top is not for the elderly, but the view from the top of the globe is outstanding. Climb it if you can.

The "priest" who organized the construction left Laos in about 1975, and he has since established a somewhat similar park outside Nong Khai in Thailand. This park is kept in much better condition than the Lao one and is worth visiting if you plan to spend some time in Thailand.

The other main attractions around Vientiane are to the north or northeast. Your ultimate destination is **Nam Ngum Dam** and lake, which can be reached by bus from Vientiane. Ask at the bus terminal behind the Morning Market. If you have your own transportation (taxi or motorcycle), you can visit several other places of interest as well. I suggest you make a round trip by going out Route 10 and returning by Route 13. The whole trip is on sealed roads, and it is around ninety kilometers each way.

You leave Vientiane along Thanon Phon Kheng, past the Revolution Monument and along Route 13 (south). Twelve kilometers from Vientiane, the road forks with Route 13 going to the right and Route 10 almost straight ahead. Take Route 13 (south) for four kilometers, then take the road on the right to a lake and picnic area. It is sometimes known as **Paddleboat Island**. You can walk across a suspension bridge to the island, where you will find a restaurant that will sell you drinks and basic food. You now need to go back to the Route 10 intersection and follow this road north.

Route 10 crosses the Nam Ngum River by a new bridge, then passes through some interesting country as it winds toward Ban Keun. About four kilometers before Ban Keun, a sealed road leads off to the right to a deer park on the left. Back on Route 10, you pass through Ban Keun, beside the

Nam Ngum River, then it is a relatively short distance to the dam wall and the hydroelectric plant. For some obscure reason, photography is banned in this area and frankly there is little to see. It is best to follow a road off to the right that takes you to a point on the lake where there are restaurants, fresh fish for sale, and boats that will take you around some of the hundreds of islands in the lake. I am told that on Peace Island there are some accommodations for those who would like to get away from it all. Some of the boat owners can arrange basic accommodations at some of the villages around the lake as well. There is also a restaurant and lodging on one of the large boats that cruise the lake. This is also available for seminars and conferences.

The best accommodations in the area are probably the airconditioned rooms available from the Electric Company at a site about four kilometers from the dam, near the village of **Thalat**. This village has a market that is fascinating because of the many animals for sale. This is also the location of the popular **Thai Longngouam Restaurant**, which is crowded on Sundays, but less rushed during the week. The way back to Vientiane is via Route 13, which is fourteen kilometers from Thalat, at the town of **Phon Hong**. Route 13 to the right would ultimately take you to Luang Prabang in northern Laos, but at present it is not recommended for conventional vehicles.

In Phon Hong, turn left and head south. You can get back to Vientiane in about 1½ hours, but it is worthwhile to do some sightseeing on the way. The first stop should be at the 62 kilometer mark, in the village of **Phone Ngeun**. Turn off the road to the left and drive a few hundred meters past some well-maintained houses. You leave the vehicle at the end of the track and walk for about two kilometers through the countryside. I found it fascinating. There is jungle, rocky hill slopes, cultivated areas and more. As you walk along the track, you will meet children, women collecting food, and water buffalo going about their normal daily routine. This is Laos as it really is. After about forty-five minutes, you reach a lovely Khmer Buddhist shrine nestled at the foot of a rock wall. It is known as **Vang Xang** and was built in the eleventh century. Few foreigners have been here and most Lao have never heard of it. This really is a special spot. Don't miss it.

Back on Route 13, there are several small waterfalls off in the hills on the right. You reach **Nam Suong Rapids and Waterfall** by taking a gravel road at around the 40 kilometer mark. There is a sign indicating that the road leads to the Lao-Australian Livestock Project Center. After three kilometers, you reach the river. There is a pleasant picnic spot with sheltered tables and a small kiosk about half a kilometer to the right, near the rapids. The waterfall is about half a kilometer to the left.

Tat Son Waterfall is reached by turning off Route 13 at approximately the 22 kilometer mark and following a dirt road for about fifteen kilometers to a picnic area on the river. **Khu Kana Waterfall** is ten kilometers off Route 13. You turn onto a gravel road at Ban Nasai Tong, about sixteen kilometers from Vientiane.

LUANG PRABANG

Without any doubt, this is my favorite city in Laos. It is a sleepy town of about 25,000 inhabitants serving a province of about 300,000. The attraction is its location, at the junction of two rivers hidden among the folds of jungle-covered mountains, and its long and fascinating history. Luang Prabang can be reached from Vientiane by truck or bus for much of the year, but the two-hundred-kilometer drive (each way) is not recommended at the moment due to poor road conditions and occasional rebel attacks. It is possible to take a river ferry, but the three-day trip is not very comfortable, so most foreigners prefer to fly. Lao Aviation has two daily services at 9 A.M. and midday, which are sometimes supplemented with other flights. Flying time is about thirty-five minutes, and you experience a sense of journeying into a long-lost world as you look down on the rugged, empty country. The view along the way is quite spectacular, particularly as the aircraft approaches Luang Prabang. Try to get a window seat on the left side of the aircraft.

Luang Prabang is the oldest city in Laos. Sixty-three kings, from Khoun Lo to Sisavang Vathana, ruled over Luang Prabang for twelve hundred years. Its great power really began when the first Lao kingdom, Lan Xang, was established here by Fa Ngum. When the king accepted a gilded bronze statue from the Khmer monarchy, the city acquired its present name, which means "royal capital of the golden Buddha (holy image)." The city became an independent kingdom when Lan Xang broke up at the end of the seventeenth century, and it remained more or less in this state until the French made Laos a protectorate in the early twentieth century. The monarchy remained until 1975.

The choice of accommodations in Luang Prabang is quite clear. The **Phouvao Hotel** (Tel: 7233), 55 rooms, is considered to be the best hotel in town. It has a nice entrance lobby and restaurant, and the rooms are reasonable—except for the airconditioners, which make it sound as if you are sleeping in the cargo compartment of a 747 jet. The hotel has a swimming pool, but the water was too dirty for swimming on my last visit. It is now under new management, and I understand things have improved. The location is pretty (on a hill at the edge of town), but it is too far to walk to the center of town in the heat of the day. Room prices are around US$55-80 a night. The **Phousi Hotel** (Tel: 7024) is right in the center of town. Airconditioned rooms cost around US$20. The hotel is much older than the Phouvao, but it is kept in good condition. The dining room is adequate, and the outdoor bar can be very attractive when the weather is right.

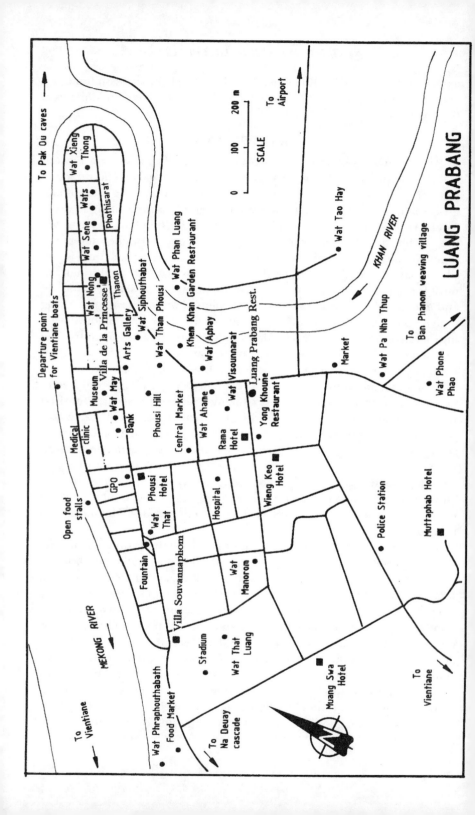

The **Villa de la Princesse** (Tel: 7041) on Sackaline Road has 11 comfortable airconditioned rooms with private baths. The building is French-Lao colonial style and was once the residence of Crown Princess Khampha. This is my favorite place to stay. There is also a good dining room with regional cuisine. A viable alternative is the **Villa Souvannaphom** (Tel: 7224) in Phothisarat Road. Recent renovations have improved this place considerably and this is reflected in the price of US$55-80 for a room. Princesse rooms are US$40.

The **Muang Swa Hotel** (Tel: 7056), a privately owned facility on Phouvao Road, has seventeen airconditioned rooms, each with marble floors, minibar, telephone, TV, and fan. The very small bathrooms have no hot water at present. There is an elaborate restaurant, bar, and nightly entertainment. Everything is neat and clean, and the management is friendly. Rooms cost US$20 a night. The **Rama Hotel** (Tel: 7105) is a noticeable step down from here, although its position is better. There are fifty-two fan-cooled rooms without airconditioning. Rooms are reasonably clean and are self-contained. There is a nice second-floor breakfast terrace, and a ground-floor restaurant with nightly entertainment. Twin rooms are priced at US$10 a night, and singles US$8. The **Wieng Keo Hotel** (Tel: 7048) has eight rooms with twin beds. Each has a shower, but no toilet or airconditioning. Rooms cost US$5 a night. The **No. 4 Guest House** (Tel: 7264) is on No. 13 Road. There are 10 rooms with fans that rent for US$10 a night.

Luang Prabang has three attractions for me. The first is its general ambience, then there are the wats and the national museum, and finally there is the river and the chance to see the Buddha caves. I could quite easily go back to Luang Prabang and do no sightseeing for the first day. I would walk the streets watching the bicycles, pedestrians, chickens, and buffalo jostle the few cars on the dusty roads; sit in an open-fronted restaurant watching the children wander through the temple grounds; and soak up the old-world atmosphere that has disappeared from most places in the world. This is something best left to the individual, but you would find me near the main market early morning, late morning at the Khem Khan Garden Restaurant overlooking the Khan River, early afternoon along the banks of the Mekong, late afternoon along Thanon Phothisarat, and early evening outside the Pousi Hotel. Sometime during the day, I would probably rent a bicycle from the Rama Hotel to go a little farther afield.

When it comes to sightseeing, the museum and the wats are head and shoulders over everything else. Do not miss the **museum**. This was the royal palace from 1904 until 1975, and it is beautiful. Unfortunately, although the museum is supposed to stay open until late afternoon, in practice it often closes early, so go in the morning if possible. You enter the museum grounds from Thanon Phothisarat, and the museum is straight ahead.

Before you enter the main building, you can gaze through bars at the museum's most valuable pieces, including a replica of the Pha Bang, an eighty-centimeter-tall gold Buddha presented by the Khmers. There are several other Buddhas, elephant tusks carved with Buddhas, some beautiful embroidered silkscreens, a carved frieze, and other objects. While these items are no doubt very valuable, the visitor loses much by not being able to see them in better surroundings.

Inside the museum, it is a different story. You can walk through the formal quarters of the Lao monarchy, then visit their private quarters, which have been preserved much as they were left in 1975. The formal quarters are magnificent. You can visit the king's reception room, the queen's reception room, the throne room, and a room filled with gifts from nations around the world. There are paintings, some huge murals by French artist Alix de Fautereau, replicas of sculpture from India's National Museum, gold, silver, and crystal Buddhas, the king's elephant chair, and much more. Many of the items are treasures in their own right; together they make a fascinating display.

You can visit the royal bedrooms, the dining room, and the king's study. There is a room containing old musical instruments, dance masks, and other personal objects. The museum guides have reasonable knowledge of what you see, but are reluctant to discuss the royal family, previous royal residences, or where the last king and queen may be today. These questions, of course, are just what many visitors will want to ask. As you leave, you will be asked to add your name to the visitors' book. There is a small admission fee.

After visiting the museum, you can easily spend the rest of the day visiting some or all of the thirty or so temples that exist within the city. Most visitors will want to be selective with these, so here are my recommendations. **Wat Xieng Thong** is not to be missed. It is located near where the Mekong and Khan rivers join, and it is the city's most beautiful temple. It was built in 1560 in what is now known as classic Luang Prabang style, with roofs that sweep low and wide. Richly decorated timber columns support an ornamental ceiling. Wood carvings and bronze relief work occur on each end of the main chapel. Within the large grounds, you will find several other buildings. One of these is the royal funeral chapel, which houses the royal urns and a seven-headed serpent carriage made by the famous Lao sculptor Thid Tun. In the Red Chapel, you will find a bronze reclining Buddha that was displayed earlier this century at the Colonial Exposition in Paris.

Wat May, on Thanon Phothisarat between the museum and the Phousi Hotel, is one of the most beautiful and interesting wats in Luang Prabang. It was built in the eighteenth century and its construction took seventy years, so it is a "new" temple. At one time, it was the residence of the head of Lao Buddhism, and it was the home of the Pha Bang from the late nineteenth to the mid-twentieth century. This statue is returned here for public display during the Lao New Year celebrations. The style of the sim is fairly typical of Luang Prabang temples with its five-tiered roof, but the front veranda is outstanding for its highly decorated columns and gold-relief panels depicting the legend of Phravet, one of the last reincarnations of Buddha. **Wat Sene**, which is halfway between these two temples, is outstanding because of its gilded facade and octagonal columns.

Wat Visounnarat (also known as Wat Wisun) was built in the early sixteenth century and was home to the Pha Bang from 1513 to 1894. The present sim was rebuilt in 1898 following a fire, but this is the oldest operating temple in Luang Prabang. Today, the temple is outstanding because it contains the largest Buddha in the city as well as a unique collection of other Buddha statues and ancient ordination stones. The grounds contain several items of interest, including the gigantic That Mak Mo (watermelon stupa), which was built in 1504.

Nearby is **Wat Ahame**, which was once the residence of the head of Lao Buddhism. From here, it is a short distance, but a hard walk, to the temples that adorn Phousi Hill. The main entrance to the hill is from Thanon Phothisarat past Wat Pahouak, but if you are approaching from the south, there are stairs leading to **Wat Tham Phousi** and a rough path to the top of the hill. From here, there is an excellent view of the town and surrounding countryside. You look down on curving temple roofs and a huddle of simple houses peeking out from behind a curtain of tropical greenery. The old antiaircraft gun, which still exists here, was strategically placed. On the north side, **Wat Siphouthabat** has nice grounds and a Buddha footprint shrine. There is another Buddha footprint at the modern **Wat Phraphouthabath** on the riverbank, behind the food market. This is supported by the Sino-Vietnamese community of the city.

Without commenting on each and every one, let it suffice to say that all the thirty or so operating temples have their individual appeal. After seeing my recommendations, you may want to make your own discoveries. However, there are a few other places around town that you should see. The **central market** on the corner opposite the hospital is a good place to browse and do some people watching. It is quite common to see hill-tribe people in traditional dress buying and selling items to stall holders. There is a good range of cloth, jewelry, household goods, and clothes. The main fresh **food market** is on Thanon Phothisarat at the western end of town, near Wat Phraphouthabath. It opens early in the morning and is best visited before 9 A.M. There is another small market with open-air food stalls behind the post office on the riverbank.

Luang Prabang is not particularly well endowed with conventional restaurants, but here are three recommendations. An old favorite, the

Yong Khoune Restaurant, is still opposite the Rama Hotel and is good for lunch. It has a Lao and English menu with fried noodles, fried rice, and salad for 500 kip; fried egg with meat for 1,000 kip, and roasted duck and fried chicken for 1,200 kip. The **Maly restaurant** is on the edge of town on Phouvao Road. This serves Lao food, and the choice is fairly limited but the taste and price are both good. The **Khem Khan Garden Restaurant** (Tel: 7168), on the bank of the Nam Khan River, has a lovely atmosphere at night, when the colored lights reflect on the water and the locals arrive to drink some beer under a starry sky. Tom yum, pork, and chicken dishes are all around 2,000 kip, but they are large enough that two dishes are enough for three people. The menu is in Lao and English.

Probably the best food in town is available at the dining room in the **Villa de la Princesse**. The cuisine is Lao and Lao-French and there is a selection of wines and liqueurs. The **Luang Prabang Cafe**, along from the Yong Khoune Restaurant, has sandwiches, hamburgers, and so forth.

Outside the city, there are various points of interest, but getting to some of them is difficult. **Luang Prabang Tourism** may provide some of the answers. It operates several organized tours ranging from 2 days/1 night through to 6 days/5 nights. This organization is also prepared to offer special sightseeing tours to small groups (of two or more); and if you have little time and some money, this may be a good way to quickly see as much as possible. The office is presently in a building near Villa Souvannaphom on Thanon Phothisarat (Tel: 7224).

Luang Prabang Tourism offers a trip to **Ban Phanom weaving village**, or you can take a public bus from town. The village is about four or five kilometers on a poor road from town. Most of the inhabitants are Lu people from southern China, and they are well known for their cotton and silk handweaving. You can wander around the village and see hand looms being operated under houses, then visit a large display area where up to fifty women sit around offering material for sale. Initially, it is a daunting task to decide what you want and where in the room you will buy, but after making the rounds two or three times, you will sort out your needs and the prices. Expect to be able to bargain for a reduction of about twenty-five percent. Prices here are excellent. They are probably twenty-five percent lower than at the Luang Prabang market, and up to fifty percent lower than what you pay in Vientiane. Most people come away with several pieces of cloth.

Four kilometers to the west of Luang Prabang, you will find the **Na Deuay Cascade**. This is a nice picnic spot on a hot day, but is hardly in the spectacular category. **Tatse Waterfall** is fifteen kilometers southeast of town, but is only worth visiting during the wet season. Unfortunately, this is also when local roads are in their worst condition, so there are times when this is not reachable. I have been told about the **Kuangsy Waterfall** and water-driven rice mill, thirty kilometers southeast of Luang Pradang, but I have never visited myself. Some locals rave about this location, so ask around to see if there is a trip or local transport that you can take. Another point of interest is **Long Laih**, a Hmong village forty-one kilometers along a poor road east of town. This is no tourist trap—it is a working village set in dramatic countryside. It provides a good glimpse into a lifestyle that is totally foreign to most of us.

The major attraction outside Luang Prabang is the **Pak Ou Caves** and the associated trip on the Mekong River. The caves are about thirty kilometers upstream of town and are famous for the number of Buddha images that are packed inside. The lower cave, called Tham Thing, is little more than a large gash in the cliff face not far above river level. It is easily seen without artificial light. A path leads around the cliff, then up to Tham Phum, the upper cave which is much deeper and requires light to be explored. Fortunately, Luang Prabang Tourism has a caretaker here, and he will light a series of candles to let you see the hidden secrets. The effect is very beautiful, with hundreds of dancing lights piercing the natural blackness.

Going to and from the caves, you will see the importance of the river to this region. Many villages have no road connections, so life is centered around the water. You will see families washing, children swimming, boat builders working, and many other activities on the riverbank or in the water. It is a good idea to get the boatman to stop at one or more of the villages, so you can see local life close at hand. One village close to the caves manufactures Lao rice whiskey. You can see families tending the stills that are built close to the riverbank. The liquor is stored in earthenware jars and sold to traders who ply the river. Much of it ends up in Luang Prabang. As you walk around the villages, you will see the fish traps, the coconuts, and the rice baskets that are so much a part of daily life.

Getting to the caves involves either taking a tour with Luang Prabang Tourism or renting your own boat. The tourism company has a nice covered boat that is operated by two or three boatmen, but the US$55 cost for the rental is quite exorbitant. You may be able to rent a smaller long-tail boat from a private operator at a quarter of the price. The trip will take about 1½ hours upstream and less coming back.

Back in Luang Prabang, you may wish to sample the nightlife before you leave. The choice is small. There are one or two cinemas, but these will have no appeal to most people. The Muang Swa Hotel and the Rama Hotel both have bands and singers, and these can be good places to spend an hour or so.

Luang Prabang endures as an outpost of old Asia. Here you can appreciate what much of the region was like before someone invented the package tour. Luang Prabang moves softly. Go there, but please do not disturb the tranquility.

THE PLAIN OF JARS

This mysterious area is in Xieng Khuang Province, east of Luang Prabang. You reach it by a 45-minute Lao Aviation flight from Vientiane or by a long, torturous road journey that cannot be recommended at present. The province has a population of around 130,000, and the capital is the town of **Phonsawan**. The countryside consists of green mountains, lush valleys, and a rolling plateau. There is little of great interest, except for the intriguing stone jars that dot the countryside.

It is the mystery surrounding them, as much as the jars themselves, that is the attraction. At present, there are about three hundred jars scattered over a twenty-five-kilometer square area. Many are grouped on the slopes and on top of two small hills. The jars range in height from about one meter to 2.5 meters, and their diameters range from 0.6 meters to 2.6 meters. They weigh up to six tons. Just who built them, how they were built, and what they were used for remains a mystery to this day. French archaeologists came to the conclusion that the jars were burial urns, where ashes were stored more than two thousand years ago. Local legend says that the jars were built for the fermentation of rice wine. Another theory is that they were used for rice storage.

Whatever their purpose, their construction is a mystery. The jars appear to be made from solid stone; and if so, it was obviously an awesome task to manufacture them. One story is that the jars were made from a strange concrete using animal skin, sand, water, sugar cane, and a secret ingredient that was then heat treated at a nearby cave kiln. It seems more likely, though, that the cave was used to make pottery products. Some of these have been found near the stone jars.

For those wanting to stay in the area, the **Mittaphab Hotel**, 15 rooms, or the **Muong Phuoan Hotel**, 8 rooms, in Phonsawan are probably the best choices. The Mittaphab is near the governor's offices but is some distance from the commercial center. The Muong Phuoan is near the airport and several shops and restaurants. Prices start at K3,000 at the Muong Phuoan, and there are no rooms with bathroom facilities. Rooms at the Mittaphab are from K7,500. Other options are the **Hotel No. 5**, 21 rooms, and the **Haghin Hotel**, 14 rooms.

The town is not big on restaurants, but the food at the Sornwaney Restaurant, the Buarsenwan Restaurant, and the Phonsavan Restaurant, all in the main street, is acceptable but not outstanding. There are several noodle shops if all else fails.

The market is worth a visit but closes by 6 P.M. The town has electricity

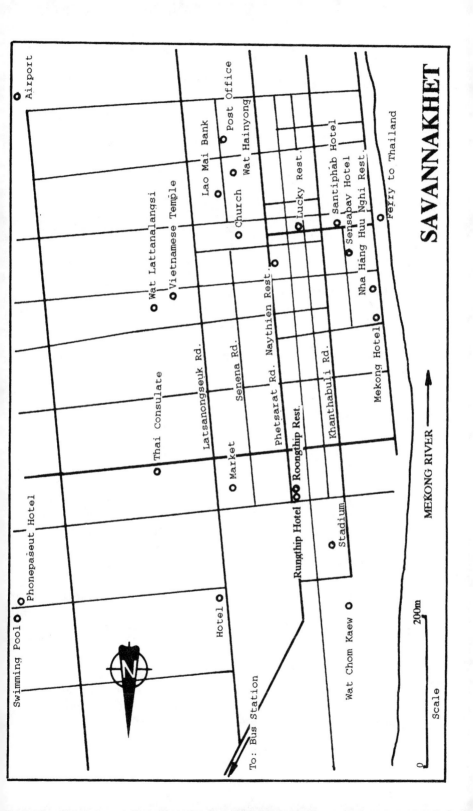

until 9:30 P.M. but no street lights so it is very quiet after dark. There are no bars or night life.

If you have the time and can find a rental vehicle, it is worthwhile traveling to **Muang Kham** then on to **Baw Yai** mineral springs. There are bungalows and bathing facilities here which are not particularly great, but the trip along the Vietnamese-built road is through interesting country and you will see several Hmong villages.

SAVANNAKHET

This is the most populous province and one of the most important trade centers in Laos. The provincial capital is on the Mekong River across from Mukdahan, Thailand. There is a growing trade across the river, and much of this product continues on to Vietnam via Road 9. Trade goods may enter Laos at this point, but foreigners (except Thai tourists) are not permitted to do so at present. These restrictions are likely to be removed shortly.

Lao Aviation has daily services to Savannakhet, which take about one hour; but during the wet season these often have to return to Vientiane without landing. Road access is possible most of the time, but is not recommended in a conventional vehicle. Government and privately owned long-distance buses operate during the dry season. The fare is inexpensive, but the comfort level is poor. There is a river ferry and some other boats operating between Vientiane and Savannakhet. The ferry takes two days downstream and about three days upstream.

Accommodations in Savannakhet are available at the **Phonepaseuth Hotel** (Tel: 7620), 31 rooms, on Santisouk Road in the north-east part of town. The rooms are built around a courtyard and are clean and airconditioned and equipped with refrigerator, TV, and hot showers. There is a reasonable restaurant and across the road is a nice 25-meter swimming pool. For those wanting to be in a central location, the **Rungthip Hotel** (Tel: 7744), 25 rooms, on Phethsarat Road is best. Rooms are well fitted out, and there is a restaurant and very popular nightclub. Rooms at both hotels are around US$25 a night.

There are three choices in Senena Road. The old **Savanbanehova Hotel** (Tel: 7661), 25 rooms, has a wide choice of fanned or airconditioned rooms from around US$12. The **Nanehat Hotel** (Tel: 7522), 39 rooms, is more up-market with airconditioned rooms at US$25, while the small **Mekong Guest House** (Tel: 7731) has seven rooms from US$7.

The best value budget rooms are at the friendly **Sensabay Hotel** on Radsavong Road. They cost US$5 but are not great. The nearby **Santiphab Hotel** (Tel: 7639), 23 rooms, is similar but costs US$6. An alternative is the old **Mekong Hotel** which is potentially attractive on the river. Rooms cost around US$10.

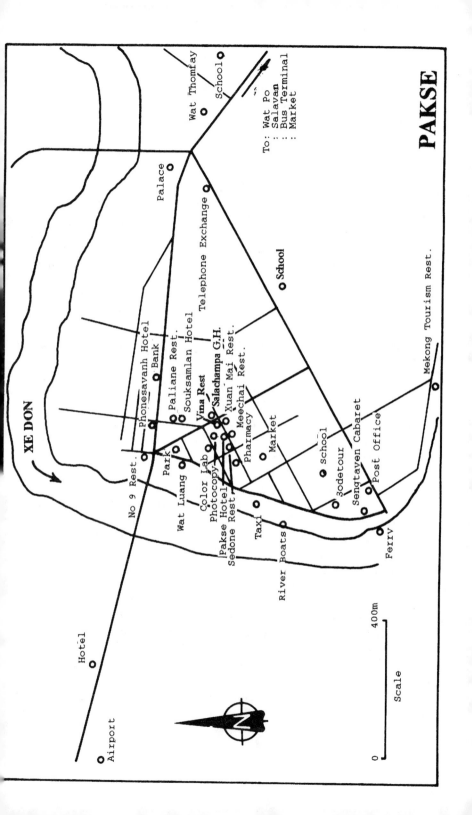

The choice of restaurants has improved in recent years, but is still not large. Most of the bigger hotels have restaurants but none are outstanding. As alternatives you could try the **Lucky Restaurant** in Phethsarat Road or the **Naythien Restaurant** on the road between the church and the river. Both have good Lao/Thai food. The **Nha Hang Huu Nghi Restaurant** on the waterfront is also OK. The **Rungthip Nightclub**, next to the hotel on Phethsarat Road, is the top night spot in town.

Savannakhet is not big on sightseeing attractions, but a pleasant day can be spent wandering around town and taking in the sights. **Wat Xainyamungkhun** by the river is the old French-style part of town. **Wat Chom Kaew** behind the stadium, **Wat Lettanalangsi** and the nearby **Chua Bao Quang** Vietnamese temple, and the large market on Latsanongseuk Road are worthy of a visit. You could also visit **That Inghung**, a famous stupa from the eighth century. It is situated on Road 9, between Savannakhet and Seno.

Elsewhere in the province, there are some interesting Khmer ruins at **Ban Hwan Hin** (stone house) in the Dong Hayn district; and some of the villages close to town are among the most beautiful in the country. **Kaeng Kok** is particularly noteworthy.

PAKSE AND WAT PHU

Pakse is the capital of Champassak Province in the south of Laos. This area has had strong links with Cambodia over the centuries, particularly during the Khmer period; but the town itself has existed for less than one hundred years. The town is situated at the confluence of the Mekong and Se Don rivers. The most practical way to reach Pakse is by air. Lao Aviation has a daily service from Vientiane, which sometimes travels via Savannakhet.

In spite of its reputation as the metropolis of southern Laos, Pakse has little of interest to visitors. It is, however, a gateway to the former royal city of Champassak, the eleventh-century Khmer ruins of Wat Phu, the lovely Bolovens Plateau, and the spectacular Khone Waterfall. While in town, it is worthwhile making a visit to the active market. You will probably end up staying at least one night in Pakse. The **Souksamlan Hotel** (Tel: 8002) has reasonable accommodations for US$16-18. This is operated by **Lan Xang Tours**, which is an excellent contact for anyone wanting advice on this region. There is an office in Vientiane (Tel: 212469). Another prominent operator is SODETOUR, Société de Développement du Tourisme (Tel: 8056 or 8054). This organization has a representative office at 114 Fa Ngum Road in Vientiane (Tel: 219023).

Other accommodation options are the attractive **Salachampa Guest House** (Tel: 8254), 14 rooms, on No. 14 Road in an old French villa, the noisy and ordinary **Hotel Pakse** (Tel: 8065), 24 rooms, and the down-market **Phonesavanh Hotel**, 18 rooms. The Salachampa has an attractive terrace for breakfast and room rates from US$20. The Pakse has rooms from US$8, while the Phonesavanh has some from US$5. Top accommodation in 1995 will be at the **Champasack Palace**, a hotel emerging from the unfinished Bounome Palace, the former residence of a local prince who fled Laos in 1974.

Eating options are not great. The food at the Salachampa is quite good and the Souksamlan Hotel has a reasonable restaurant. You could also try the **Paliane Restaurant** next to the Souksamlan, **Restaurant No. 9** near the river bridge, and the **Xuan Mai Restaurant, Meechai Restaurant, Vina Restaurant**, and **Sedone Restaurant**, all in the street beside the Pakse Hotel. There are two nightclubs in town. The **Mekong Tourism Restaurant and Nightclub** and the **Sengtavan Cabaret**, both have Lao food, live music, dancing, and dancing partners.

The **Bolovens Plateau** is on the border between Champassak and the provinces of Salavan and Se Kong. The plateau stretches over the area of Paksong, Lau Ngam, and Thataeng districts and is home to many of the highland tribes of southern Laos. The area has a lovely climate, fine scenery, and has developed quite a reputation as a spot for rest and recreation. The area produces high quality arabica coffee, tea, and cardamom. On the Se Set River, there are several waterfalls—one of which supports a forty-five-megawatt power plant.

Se Set Waterfall has become one of the most visited sites in southern Laos. The location is spectacular but unfortunately water only flows during the wet season. A few kilometers downstream, the Tat Lo has water all year, and this is a good spot for swimming. The adjacent **TadLo Resort** has some accommodation for top government people but there is also some public accommodation in bungalows and simple rooms, and there's a nice restaurant. The resort offers elephant rides, and you can walk through the jungle. Room rents are from US$8 to US$30. Some prehistoric sites have been discovered in the region. You are welcome to visit the highland tribe villages of the Laven, Laveh, and Nhahoen people.

Champassak is about thirty kilometers south of Pakse. You can reach it by road or by river. The town contains some gracious old French-style homes and memories of a long-forgotten time. The kingdom of Champassak was established here under Siamese influence, and there were three kings in the 1713-1811 period; but eventually the Siamese destroyed much of the city and forced many of the residents to resettle in Siam (now Thailand).

It is only about ten kilometers from here to **Wat Phu**, an Angkor-period Khmer temple. You approach from Ban Nongsa, past canals and a large reservoir with a terrace of carved stones. Here there is a more recent pavilion, which served as shelter for the king and other dignitaries at official ceremonies or when watching games in the pool. There is a 280-meter-long avenue from here to the monument. Ancient buildings, now in ruins, line this avenue and adjacent open spaces.

To the north and south, two palaces were erected; and behind each was a courtyard surrounded by a gallery. The style is similar to those you see at Angkor Wat. From the open space, a long avenue and stairway lead to the upper temple. This upper section is the main sanctuary, where you see much evidence of the original Hindu sculpture even though it was converted into a Buddhist temple a few centuries after it was constructed.

Unfortunately, Wat Phu is in urgent need of restoration. Some work has been carried out, but it needs an international effort to save this masterpiece from further destruction. Despite its condition, it is well worth visiting now. You can rent a vehicle in Pakse to reach Wat Phu. If you happen to be in the area during the full moon in February, you can visit for the Bun Wat Phu festival. Pilgrims come from southern Laos and Cambodia for this three-day event. Another festival in June involves the ritual sacrifice of a water buffalo. It is not for the squeamish.

While in the Champassak region, you should not miss the **Four Thousand Islands** and the associated waterfalls. This spectacular feature is on the Mekong River just north of the Laos-Cambodia border, about 120 kilometers from Pakse. You can reach it by bus, except during the height of the wet season. The falls, which are really rapids, are quite extensive; and the size of the river will surprise you. Most visitors make a stop at **Khong Island**, where there are some basic accommodations and good fish restaurants at Muang Khong, a short ferry ride from Hat Xai Khun. About 50,000 people live on this island. You can also visit some other smaller islands of the Siphandone archipelago (Four Thousand Islands). The insular villages and their inhabitants seem to be left back in time. The biggest kettledrum ever found in the world was discovered here. It is more than three thousand years old.

The two most interesting islands are Don Det and Don Khon, south of Khong Island. One hundred years ago, the French built a narrow-gauge railway across the islands to avoid the Mekong River rapids. You can still see the remnants today, together with several old French-style villas in the main villages. At the western end of Don Khon, you can visit the spectacular Li Phi Falls.

The other main point of interest is the **Khon Phapheng Falls** near the village of Thakho. There is a pavilion where you can buy food and drinks while you watch the spectacular water movement, There are passenger trucks to this area from Pakse, but you will need to change several times.

7. Guided Tours

There are several organizations in Laos that offer guided tours of the country, but I could not find one that had any literature in English. **Diethelm Travel** (Tel: 215920), which has an office at the fountain in Vientiane, was happy to talk to me about two- and three-day trips to Luang Prabang, Champassak, and other places, but they referred me to their Bangkok office for literature. This is hardly satisfactory for the average visitor in Laos who is wanting to do a tour. It appears that guided tours are available for one or more people, so obviously local expectations on tourist numbers are not high. A 2-day/1-night trip to Luang Prabang was being offered for US$221 for one passenger, US$174 each for two passengers, and US$159 for four passengers. The same trip to Champassak was US$533, US$397, and US$338 respectively. The **Lao Air Booking Co. Ltd.** (Tel: 216761), at 38 Thanon Settathirath Road, can also help with plane tickets and general travel services.

The only organization that I have had direct experience with is **Inter-Lao Tourism** (originally called Lao National Tourism). This company is associated with the Ministry of Commerce and Tourism, and I have found it to be excellent. The company office is on the corner of Thanon Settathirath and Pang Kham, facing Nam Phou Square (Tel: 214832). There are weekly tours to Luang Prabang, the Plain of Jars, Pakse, the Bolovens Plateau, and Savannakhet. The company also operates a day trip to Nam Ngum Lake and half-day excursions around Vientiane. I strongly recommend all visitors to consider one or more of these tours—particularly if their time is limited. Guides can speak excellent English and are well informed, and the vehicles are satisfactory. I believe that these tours are a reasonable value and are generally well organized. **Lan Xang Tours** (Tel: 212469) is a good outfit if you plan to visit the south of the country.

The **Lao Travel Service** (Tel: 216603) on Lane Xang Avenue, **That Luang Tour** (Tel: 215803) on Khemkhong Road, and **Vienchampa Tour** (Tel: 314412) on Thadeva Road are three other recommended operators. As noted earlier, **Sodetour** (Tel: 219023) has extensive connections in the region around Pakse, but it also operates elsewhere.

8. Culture

The major cultural elements in Vientiane consist of the museums, memorials, and wats that were covered in the sightseeing section. The other significant activities are the festivals, parades, and holidays that occur throughout the year. The traditional Lao calendar is based on both solar and lunar phases, and it commences 638 years before the Christian calendar that we know in the West. Festivals (buns) are usually based on either historical Buddhist holidays or agricultural seasons. Their celebration dates vary each year because of the phases of the moon. The first month of the Lao year is actually December, but the celebrations are traditionally held in April, the fifth month.

The first celebration in the Western year is **Vietnamese Tet and Chinese New Year**. This is in late January or early February; and in Vientiane, it is celebrated with visits to Vietnamese and Chinese temples, fireworks, and parties. Many businesses close for several days.

Pi Mai (Lao New Year) is celebrated in mid-April. This is a major festival, and there are three public holidays to allow everyone to join in. Prior to the festival, houses and rooms are repainted and decorated, young girls are chosen as "Miss New Year," and many Lao send cards to their friends. On the first and second day of the celebrations, crowds gather in the temples with candles, flowers, perfume, and water. The monks and people wash Buddha images as they pray for good "merit." They then wish for happiness and wealth throughout the new year. A procession is held in Vientiane and many of the other main towns, then everyone takes to the streets to dowse friends and strangers with water to help wash away all the bad things of the last year. This is a time to wear casual, quick-drying clothes because you are bound to get wet. The third day is the start of the new year, and many women rise early to give some food to the monks. Many people organize the *aci*, give parties, and visit friends.

International Labor Day (May 1) is celebrated in Vientaine and a few other centers with a parade. This is a national holiday.

Visakha Buja falls on the fifteenth day of the sixth lunar month (usually in May). It is an important Buddhist day, and activities are centered around the wats. At night, there are beautiful candlelight processions. The **Rocket Festival** (Bun Bang Fai) is now held around the same time. It lasts for two days, with the first day consisting of crowds bringing rockets and offerings to the temple then sports, dancing, and drinking at night. On the second day the rockets are first paraded through the towns, then launched from a nearby field later in the day. The one that soars the highest and goes the farthest brings a prize and honor to its creator. The rocket firing is designed to remind the heavens that rain is needed for the rice fields.

Khao Phansa is at full moon in July and is the beginning of Buddhist Lent, or the three-month "rains retreat," during which Buddhist monks fast during the day and remain in a single monastery. It is also the traditional time for men to temporarily enter the monkhood to gain knowledge and merit for their future lives.

Awk Phansa celebrates the end of the rains retreat. There is often a Kathin ceremony in which the monks receive offerings of new clothes and other useful items from the people. Monks are now free to leave the monasteries to travel until the next year. **Bun Swang Hwa** (Boat Races Festival) and **Bun Lai Hwa Fai** (Decorated Illuminated Floating Raft Festival) are among the important festivals organized both before and after the Awk Phansa day. On the evening of Awk Phansa, the full moon of October, there are candlelight processions in the wats. The huge boat-shaped candlestick (Hwa Fai Khok) is then illuminated in the wat's courtyard. Also illuminated are the windowsills and veranda ledges of all pagodas, houses, and public buildings in town. It is a very special sight.

In Vientiane, there is a great atmosphere. After the wat ceremonies, participants head for the Mekong River and Fa Ngum Road. North of the Mahosot Hospital, it is very crowded. Most people bring small decorated rafts to set afloat on the river. Each is illuminated with candles. Usually a large raft has been prepared and anchored near the Lane Xang Hotel; and at the height of the activity, this raft is illuminated and set afloat. The following day is the time for the boat races. Each has a crew of fifty or more. Women participate in the morning and men in the afternoon. There is a large riverbank fair, which stretches north from the Lane Xang Hotel. Similar celebrations are held in Luang Prabang, Savannakhet, and some other riverside towns.

The **That Luang Festival** is held at the full moon in November. The festival lasts for three days, with hundreds of monks assembling for religious ceremonies. On the third day, large crowds gather at Pha That Luang in the morning for prayers and alms giving. In the evening, there is a magnificent candlelight procession around the that, and small rockets made by the monks are discharged into the sky. A week-long carnival takes place at the same time as the festival. There are many stalls and music and entertainment late into the night.

Lao National Day is December 2. This is a public holiday throughout Laos. In Vientiane, it is traditionally celebrated at That Luang Square with a military parade followed by a dance parade from the Fine Art School. Bands play and flowers are presented to government leaders, then groups of workers and others march through the square in a big parade.

9. Sports

Sporting facilities for short-term visitors are very limited, and the general condition of these facilities combined with the hot weather mean that few visitors will want anything other than a swimming pool.

Few hotels in Vientiane currently have **swimming pools**—the Lane Xang Hotel, the Belvedere, the Vansana Hotel, and the Le Parasol Blanc are the only exceptions that I can think of. If you are not a guest at these establishments, you will generally not be welcome to use their pools. There is a public pool in what was once the French Dongpassac Bar at Wattaynoi on Luang Prabang Road, out toward the airport in the northern part of town. In the southern suburbs, the Sokpaluang pool (Tel: 2361) is, by no surprise, on Sokpaluang Road. There is another one near the National TV and radio offices in the center of town. Hours are usually from 10 A.M. to 5 P.M. The nicest pool in town is the one at the Australian Embassy Recreation Club, but this is only open to members. The club has a facility for short-term membership (not more than three months); and if your stay in Vientiane extends into weeks, it could be advantageous to join. You fill in a membership application; and when accepted, you pay a US$10 joining fee and US$20 a month. In my experience, the management is helpful toward short-term members.

There are some **tennis** facilities in town. The Australian Embassy and the U.S. Embassy residence have courts, and arrangements can be made to use them at off-peak times. The Vientiane Tennis Club, which is near the center of town, behind the Revolutionary Museum, has several well-used courts and coaches available if you want instruction. This is mainly a members club, but foreign visitors can often make arrangements to play. Both the Banque tennis court, off Nong Bone Road, and the Luk Saam court on Thanon Thadeva, about 2½ kilometers from town, have private coaching facilities and offer access for foreign visitors. Ball boys and girls are available at most courts for a rate of around US$0.30 per child per hour.

Vientiane has a fledgling **golf course**, which currently operates nine holes. There is a small clubhouse and barbecue facilities, so the whole affair is very relaxed. To find the course, go south on Route 13, about two kilometers past the Revolution Monument, then turn right. At the first fork, keep left and keep right at the second. You can follow the signs from there. A Japanese-controlled, up-market course is planned near Thadeva.

Hash House Harriers has a weekly run open to everyone. There is a different venue each week, and it is advertized on the notice board at the Australian Embassy Recreation Club. Participants pay US$3 for the run, beer, soft drinks, and light meal. Monday at 5:15 P.M. is the assembly time.

Squash is available to members at the Australian Club, and the court is also used for other activities. **Yoga** is held there every Thursday between 2:30 and 4 P.M., and **aerobic exercises** are held every Tuesday and Thursday at 5:30 P.M.

Saunas are available at Wat Sok Paluang and Wat Sri Amphorn, which also has an exercise room; and there are also saunas at several of the hotels and at several health centers such as the **Eden Club** next to Wat Phia near the Mekong River. A **bridge** group meets every Monday at 2 P.M. at the

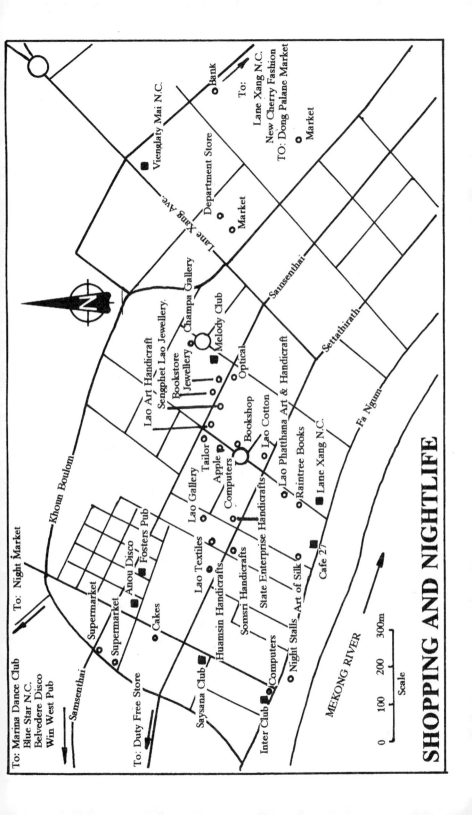

SHOPPING AND NIGHTLIFE

316 MAVERICK GUIDE TO VIETNAM, LAOS, AND CAMBODIA

Australian Club, and duplicate bridge is played every Tuesday at 7:30 P.M. at the Swedish Guest House. There is a gymnasium next to the Lam-Xang Nightclub on Dong Palane Road.

10. Shopping

Laos offers some interesting shopping opportunities—primarily in hand-made items produced within the country. My recommendations are jewelry (but only buy inexpensive items unless you know the business), hill-tribe crafts, handwoven fabrics, wood carvings, and antiques.

In Vientiane, there are three shopping options. Each is small, so serious shoppers will visit each area. The new **Morning Market** on Lane Xang Avenue provides the largest concentration of shops and stalls selling hardware, ready-made apparel, materials, shoes, silver and gold, and general handicrafts. It is a place that visitors cannot ignore, even though it can be hot, crowded, and frustrating. There are three major buildings, which are connected along the back. All have two levels, except the central one, so it is quite a complex. The central building contains a supermarket, a few fast-food outlets, and department store-style counters for electrical, kitchen, and sporting goods as well as local and imported items that appeal to better off Lao people, foreign workers, and visitors.

The rest of the complex is a collection of shops and stalls, and the competition should be good for prices. In this area, you have to bargain. Be satisfied if you get ten to fifteen percent off the price, even though you will not know what the locals would pay. I asked a friend to check the price of a small silver bracelet. At the market, it was US$3; in a jewelry shop in central Vientiane, it was US$4; and in Bangkok, it was US$6.50. I suspect that in the United States, Canada, or Australia, it could easily be US$12. Of course, at this price, you can hardly guarantee the quality, but you are not risking a fortune and it is fun to make a purchase where the locals shop.

The second area is along **Thanon Samsenthai** and **Thanon Pang Kham**. This is a long-established retail area that partially serves as the town center. There are several hotels in this immediate area, so many visitors find this to be the most convenient place to shop. On these two streets, you will find dressmakers and tailors, jewelry shops, food outlets, leather goods, weaving and handicraft outlets, and antique shops. You can browse without being pressured to buy, and there are never the crowds that you sometimes get in the market. Some people will prefer to buy here, even though the price may be higher.

If your time is short, you may like to follow my suggestions; but otherwise the area is small enough to make your own choices. I believe these shops are satisfactory. For dressmaking or tailoring, try **Adam Tailleur** at 8 Thanon Pang Kham for men and boys, **Queen's Beauty Tailors** (Tel: 214191) at Number 21, **Nora** at 364 Thanon Samsenthai, or **R.V. Chuong** at 395 Thanon Samsenthai for Thai silk jackets and suits. For jewelry, **Bari and Sons** (Tel: 212680), **Handmaker Jewelry**, and **Lao Jewelry** (Tel: 215383) are all on Samsenthai Road, and they all manufacture on the premises. **Bari and Sons** also deals in precious stones.

Teng Liang Ki, at 51 Thanon Pang Kham, makes shoes and handbags and will repair all leatherwork. **Bob's Dry Cleaning** operates a dry cleaning and laundry service at 267 Samsenthai. The friendly people at the **Phimphone Minimart**, at 94/6 Thanon Sansenthai, sell ice cream, cheese, milk, chocolate, canned goods, wines, spirits, soft drinks, cigarettes, and much more.

When it comes to weaving, handicrafts, and antiques, there is a big selection. **Kanchana** (Tel: 213467), on Quartier That Dam, opposite the Ekalath Metropole Hotel, has a good selection of upscale silk and cotton fabrics, silver, wood carvings, and gifts. By Vientiane standards, quality and price are high. **Lao Phattana Art** (Tel: 212363) at 29/3 Thanon Pang Kham, offers similar goods. **Nang Xuan Antique Shop** (Tel: 213341), at 385 Samsenthai, has Asian antiques from throughout Indochina.

Nguyen Ti Setto, at 350 Samsenthai, has Lao and Vietnamese jewelry, handicrafts, and gifts. **Lao Cotton**, at Nam Phu Square on Thanon Settathirath, has a wide range of handwoven all-cotton fabrics, linen, and ready-made items. This is a very successful Lao Women's Union/UNDP project, and the items are of outstanding quality. The **Gold Color Lab**, at 386 Samsenthai, is open seven days a week for rapid film processing, films, batteries, and so forth.

The third area is **Thanon Chao Anou** and **Heng Boun**. This is unofficially known as Chinatown, and it is an excellent eating area. It is worth mentioning that **Sweet Home Bakery**, at 109 Thanon Chao Anou, has an excellent range of croissants, cakes, breads, ice cream, and some grocery items. Right next door, the **Vinh Loi Bakery** has a similar range, but adds fishing tackle to the list. The **Foodland Minimarket**, at No. 117, offers cheese, milk, fish, meat, chicken, canned goods, Japanese food, and ice cream. To complete the food picture, there are two modern supermarkets on Khoun Boulom between Samsenthai Road and Heng Boun.

Chansons Lao, at 7-9 Thanon Heng Boun, sells Lao music on tapes. The **Sourinhong Inthavong Sports Store**, at 117 Chao Anou, has the best range of sporting goods in town. Try **New Photo Express** on Khoun Boulom for quick developing of film. It is open six days a week.

There are a few other places that are worth seeking out. The **Arawan**

Charcuterie, next to the Arawan Restaurant at 472 Thanon Samsenthai, is probably the best place in town to buy smoked meats, paté, sausages, pickles, and other delicatessen items. **Jeanine's Coiffeur Pour Dames**, at 14 Thanon Settathirath, does shampoo, cutting, styling, tinting, facials, and manicures. It is open Monday through Saturday at 8 A.M.

Lao Textiles (Tel: 21213) at 84 Nokeo Khoumane Street sells high-priced antique and contemporary textiles collected or designed by American Carol Cassidy. The **Art of Silk** (Tel: 214302) on Manthaturath Road opposite the Samsenthai Hotel is a non-profit organization for the preservation and promotion of Lao textile. There is a small textile museum and some interesting items for sale. **Lao Vilai Fashion** (Tel: 216716) at 107 Samsenthai Road specializes in contemporary Lao women's clothing. **New Cherry Fashion** out on Dong Palane Road is somewhat similar.

Artisanat and Handicrafts on Luang Prabang Road has a kiln and shop creating beige, brown, or blue ceramics. **Somsri Handicrafts** (Tel: 216236), at 18 Thanon Settathirath, has a good selection of wall hangings, Lao dolls, bags and purses, and antiques.

Raintree Books on Pang Kham Street has a range of English books and magazines including some regional newspapers.

11. Entertainment and Nightlife

Vientiane is a small city with no recent tradition of nightlife, but the government is lifting many of the harsh controls on lifestyle, and there is an emerging night scene. Much of it is centered on the hotels and restaurants in town, and it includes dancing to live bands or to music at discos. There is no obvious raunchy Bangkok-style nightlife—remember that Vientiane is an early-to-bed city. After midnight, not a person, chicken, or even a dog stirs on most blocks throughout the city.

The **Lane Xang Hotel** has a band and singers in its snack bar each night. It has an entrance on Thanon Pang Kham, next to Lao Aviation. The **Melody Club** at the Metropole Hotel is popular from around 9:30 P.M. The **Inter Club** on the river at the Inter Hotel has a solid following. The Anou Hotel sports the **Anou Cabaret**, where there is food, live music every evening, and a unique ambiance that occasionally attracts some eccentrics. It can be fun. The **Saysana Hotel** also has a nightly cabaret. On my last visit, this was very popular; but you must recognize that these outlets are aimed at the locals more than visitors, so much of the music, language, and atmosphere is Lao. The **Belvedere Hotel** has a popular disco, while the **New Apollo Hotel** has a live band and singers in its renovated room, and the **Muang-Lao Hotel** has its lovely room swinging some nights.

Apart from the hotels, there are a few other nightspots. One of the most prominent is **Vienglaty Mai Nightclub** (Tel: 215321) on Lane Xang Avenue, just north of the Morning Market. It has meals and a live band every night from 8:30 until midnight. Beer sells for US$2 a bottle, and Pepsi-Cola for US$1.50. This is probably the most "sophisticated" nightspot in town. The **Dao Vieng** (Tel: 213945), at 40 Thanon Heng Boun, has a band, Chinese or Lao singers, and dancing every night. This is popular with visiting Thai business people, but the very large room is often short on customers during the week. The **Champa Luan-Xang Restaurant and Nightclub** by the lake on Tha Deua Road, two kilometers from town, has food, drinks, and a band every night from nine until midnight. The crowd here tends to be older, and there will be a few "expats" among the customers.

Other places you could consider are **Nokkeo Latrymai**, on Luang Prabang Road toward the airport. You won't miss this green building with colored lights. There is a live band every night and meals are available, but you are welcome just to stop in for a drink. On this same road you will find the new **Marina Night Club** (Tel: 616978) which opens from 8:30-11:30 P.M. for dancing action. Back toward town, the **Bluestar Night Club** (Tel: 213287) is similar. In the opposite direction from town, the **Lane Xang Nightclub** on Thanon Dong Palane, a little south of Wat Dong Palane, is very popular some nights. The **Kaonhot Disco** is at the Snooker Club on Thanon Sakarindh. The best nights are Saturday and Sunday.

The **Piano Bar** at Le Parasol Blanc has a lovely atmosphere and some fine keyboard playing. The **Sukiyaki Restaurant** has traditional Lao music played by a local group.

For a quiet place to drink, the **Namphu Garden** around the fountain can be delightful on a still evening. A small bar on the riverbank at the end of Quai Si Thane is popular with expatriates. It's sometimes called the French bar. **Foster's Modern House** on Touran Street just off Sansenthai has a late night following for its cold beer and good music.

There are three local **cinemas** in Vientiane. These show Thai, Chinese, and Indian movies. Soviet movies were once shown regularly, but are much less common now. The admission cost is around US$0.20, but the facilities and print quality are likely to be poor. There are no facilities for English translation or subtitles. If you need a shot of American culture, the **American Embassy Movie Theater**, on Thanon Bartolini, screens movies every Wednesday evening. Admission cost is around US$2.00; and beer, soft drinks, and popcorn are available. **Le Club France Movie Theater**, on Thanon Settathirath, screens movies or videos every night of the week: Monday, Wednesday, Friday at 6:15 P.M.; Tuesday, Thursday, Sunday at 8 P.M.; and Saturday at 5 P.M.

12. The Vientiene Address List

Airport—Flight information (Tel: 212066).

Banks—Banque Pour le Commerce, Thanon Pang Kham (Tel: 213201); Joint Development Bank, 31 Lane Xang Ave (Tel: 213530).

Car Rentals—Burapha Consultants, 14 Thanon Fa Ngum (Tel: 216600); Vico Trading, Thanon Phon Kheng (Tel: 214810).

Club—Australian Embassy Recreation Club, Thanon Tha Deua (Tel: 314921).

Church—Anglican English, ARDA English School (near Santisouk Restaurant) (Tel: 217162).

Dentist—Dr. Sisario, 165 Thanon Settathirath (Tel: 214991).

Embassies—Australian, Thanon Phonxai No. 1 (Tel: 413601); French, Thanon Settathirath (Tel: 215258); German, 26 Sokphaluang (Tel: 312111); Japanese, Thanon Dong Si Sung Vong (Tel: 414400); Swedish, Thanon Sok Pa Luang (Tel: 315018); Thai, Thanon Phon Kheng (Tel: 214582); U.S., Thanon Bartolini (Tel: 212580).

Fire Station—Thanon Samsenthai (Tel: 212708).

General Post Office—Lane Xang Avenue (Tel: 215403).

Health Clinics—Australian Embassy Clinic, Thanon Phonxai No. 1 (Tel: 413603); Swedish Clinic, Thanon Phonxai No. 1 (Tel: 315015); International Clinic, Mahosot Hospital (Tel: 214022).

Lao Language Instruction—Australian English Language Center, That Luang Road (Tel: 414873).

Medical—Dr. Khanh Soulinthong (Tel: 216770).

Ministry of Foreign Affairs—Thanon That Luang.

Police—Emergency (Tel: 190).

Taxi—Metered Cars (Tel: 213918).

Telephone Office—Thanon Settathirath (Tel: 16).

Tourism—Inter-Lao Tourism, Thanon Settathirath/Pang Kham (Tel: 214232).

Translation—Vientiane International Consultants, 234 Thanon Samsenthai (Tel: 214182).

Transportation—DHL Worldwide Express, Thanon Nokeo Khoumane (Tel: 212050); Lao Aviation, 2 Thanon Pang Kham (Tel: 212149).

Cambodia

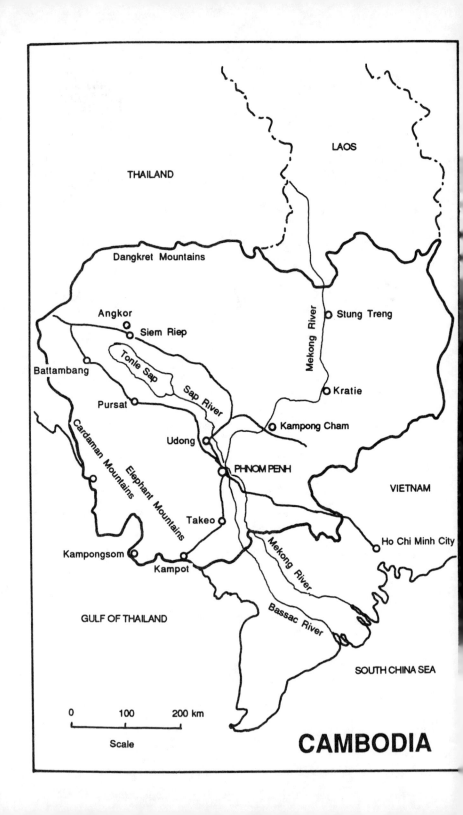

11

The Land, Life, and People of Cambodia

Cambodia is probably better known around the world than most small nations of six million people. The reason is the succession of wars, genocide, and tragedy that have plagued this nation for the past fifty years. Most people have lost sight of the fact that today's Cambodia is what remains of the mighty Khmer Empire that ruled much of central southeast Asia for five centuries.

A visitor today sees a nation in the midst of rapid change. Although the civil war continues in various forms, communism has died; Sihanouk has returned; the United Nations has a huge presence; and the capital at Phnom Penh is in the middle of an unprecedented boom.

The people in Phnom Penh are responding to the changes with enthusiasm. Those caught up in the rural fighting, however, are in a much less happy position—many are homeless and destitute. This contrast seems to symbolize Cambodia today.

Geography

Cambodia is surrounded by Thailand, Laos, Vietnam, and the Gulf of Thailand. It is a country that is roughly half the size of Vietnam, extending about 580 kilometers in an east-west direction and 450 kilometers in a north-south direction. Much of the land border regions are mountainous,

323

and there is even a mountain range toward the southwest, between the central region and the Gulf of Thailand.

The central region of the country is a vast alluvial plain that is dominated by the Mekong River, the Sap River, and Tonle Sap (the Great Lake). The Mekong River, which has already passed through or by Tibet, China, Myanmar, Laos, and Thailand, flows south through eastern Cambodia before reaching Phnom Penh. Here it splits into two streams—the Mekong and the Bassac—that flow through southern Vietnam to the South China Sea. The Sap River joins the Mekong at Phnom Penh. For part of the year, it discharges water from Tonle Sap; but when the Mekong is flooding, it reverses its flow and starts filling the lake again. This has a major effect on the Mekong's flow all year, reducing it during the peak time and topping it up when flows are low. During this period, the size of Tonle Sap doubles then halves, and the depth changes from two meters to ten meters and back again.

It is in the central region that most people live and most development has occurred over the years. Much of the area has been cleared and used as rice fields or for other agricultural pursuits. The mountainous areas, in contrast, remain heavily timbered.

Climate

The weather pattern is similar to that of Bangkok and northern Thailand. The cool season runs from around November to February, with maximum temperatures in the mid twenties (Celsius). This is followed by a short hot season in March, April, and early May during which maximum temperatures rise to 35 degrees Celsius. From mid-May to October, the southwestern monsoons bring high humidity and heavy rains that result in about eighty percent of the yearly rainfall.

Rainfall varies considerably between different areas. The wettest areas are the seaward slopes of the mountains that front the Gulf of Thailand. This is the area that also receives a battering from strong winds sweeping across the gulf.

History

The earliest confirmable history of this area dates to the first through sixth centuries, when much of Cambodia was part of the Kingdom of Funan, which ruled the southern part of Indochina. This kingdom had trading relations with both India and China, and it adopted large slices of Indian culture that later shaped the direction of future Khmer states. Both Hinduism and Mahayana Buddhism found homes in Funanese society.

Funan came to a rapid end when the Kambujas people, who lived in what is now northeast Thailand, southern Laos, and northern Cambodia, broke away and established their own state, Chinla. It was not long before Chinla absorbed Funan; but one hundred years later, Chinla itself divided into north and south. It appears that the north was fairly stable for the next one hundred years, but the south was in a constant state of conflict and was invaded and occupied by the Javanese empire at one point.

The height of Khmer development started around 800 A.D., when Jayavarman II arrived from Java. It is believed he was distantly related to earlier Chinla dynasties. Jayavarman II reigned from 802 to 850 A.D., and he soon controlled an area nearly as large as present-day Cambodia. The king established a new state religion with himself as a god-king. He installed himself in the Tonle Sap lake region and built several capitals. The last of these was at Rolvuos, thirteen kilometers east of the present town of Siem Reap.

Jayavarman II was succeeded by Jayavarman III, who built the earliest large, permanent temples to be constructed by the Khmers. This was the beginning of Khmer classical art. The next king, Indravarman I, constructed a vast irrigation system in the Tonle Sap region, which allowed the Khmer to develop and maintain a highly centralized state. Indravarman I's successor moved the capital a few kilometers to the northwest, to what we know as Angkor.

During the next century, the Khmer empire went through a dramatic expansion until, by the middle of the tenth century, the Khmers dominated a vast area of what is now Cambodia, Thailand, Laos, and Vietnam. The empire expanded until it encountered territory controlled by other major kingdoms—the Burmese, the Chams, and the Vietnamese.

For the next two centuries, the Khmers fought with their three neighbors. Often they won, but in 1177 they suffered a major defeat when the Chams captured and sacked Angkor, leaving the Khmer empire in ruins. During this period, there was also a change in religious focus from the Hindu cult of the god Shiva to that of Vishnu, and then to a form of Mahayana Buddhism.

The Cham invasion was overcome by Jayavarman VII, who ruled from 1181 to 1201. He expelled the Chams, then began a huge building program centered on his new capital, the massive city of Angkor Thom. His most important work was the huge Buddhist temple called the Bayon. Angkor Thom was a magnificent and thriving metropolis, and the huge system of reservoirs and canals that surrounded the capital allowed for intense cultivation and high yields in the densely populated nearby countryside.

This huge building program took its toll on the kingdom, however, and after the death of Jayavarman VII, the decline of Angkor began. At first, it was gradual—progress and change continued in some areas. The Khmer state abandoned its love for Hinduism and embraced Hinayana Buddhism instead. The use of Sanskrit was discontinued, and Pali became the sacred language. At the same time, the Siamese made repeated incursions into Khmer territory, slowly weakening the resolve and the defenses of the Khmers. In 1431, the Siamese launched a major attack and succeeded in capturing Angkor. The Khmer court dramatically abandoned the city, moving their capital eastward to a site near Phnom Penh.

The next 150 years represented a period of almost continuous warfare with the Siamese and confusing dynastic battles at home. The Khmers gradually recaptured some of their lost territory, but the Siamese delivered a crushing blow when they captured the Khmer capital in 1594. The Khmers never recovered. Despite their victory, the Siamese had no desire to take over the Khmer kingdom, so they allowed the Khmer king, Satha, to remain. To bolster his position, the king asked for help from the Spanish who had taken over the Philippines. The Spanish responded by sending an army expedition to Cambodia in 1596. When they arrived, they discovered that Satha had been deposed, so they attacked and ransacked the Chinese quarter of Phnom Penh, attacked the palace, killed the new king, installed one of Satha's sons on the throne, and set up a garrison in the city so they could control the region.

It was not long before resentment surfaced against the power wielded by the Spanish forces; and in 1599 there was an uprising that massacred the entire contingent. The Spanish government failed to act in retaliation, so shortly thereafter the Siamese were instrumental in installing Satha's brother to the throne.

For the next 250 years, Cambodia was ruled by a succession of weak kings who depended on the support of Thailand or Vietnam for survival. This support was supplied at a price—the Vietnamese occupied the eastern section of Cambodia that is now part of southern Vietnam, and the Thais dominated the western provinces of the country. The Thais also exercised increasing control over the Khmer royal family, which culminated in one king being crowned in Bangkok before being taken to Cambodia by the Thai army.

Asian control over Cambodia effectively ceased in 1863 when French gunboats arrived to intimidate King Norodom into signing a treaty of protectorate over the country. The French were initially more interested in Vietnam than they were in Cambodia, so little changed. However, in 1884, King Norodom was forced to sign a treaty giving the French almost total control. This sparked a two-year rebellion, which only ended when the king and the French agreed to return to the pre-treaty arrangement.

Despite the agreement, the French gradually took over the day-to-day administration of the country; but at the same time, they deliberately enhanced the symbolic status of the monarchy in order to stifle any opposition to their rule. It was surprisingly effective. King Norodom was succeeded by several other kings until 1941, when the French governor general of Japanese-occupied Indochina placed eighteen-year-old Prince Sihanouk on the throne. In 1946, the French retained de facto control of Cambodia, but declared the country an "autonomous state within the French Union."

This proved to be an unsatisfactory arrangement, and in January 1953, King Sihanouk dissolved the parliament, declared martial law, and embarked on a campaign for independence. He was spectacularly successful, and independence was proclaimed on November 9, 1953. In March 1955, Sihanouk abdicated in order to pursue a career as a politician. He established the Peoples Socialist Community Party and won every seat at the September elections. He then served as prime minister until 1960, when he became chief-of-state.

Sihanouk initially declared Cambodia neutral in international affairs, but he broke diplomatic relations with the U.S. in 1965 and embraced North Vietnam, China, and by default the Viet Cong. Shortly afterwards, he agreed to allow the North Vietnamese army and the Viet Cong to use Cambodian territory in their battle against South Vietnam. This eventually led the United States to begin a bombing offensive on large parts of eastern Cambodia.

It was not smooth sailing for Sihanouk. The population was becoming fed up with the corruption that had become endemic in government. The army put pressure on him to take action against powerful left-wing elements that were emerging, and other sections of society were dissatisfied with the lack of political dissent that was allowed in the country. In March 1970, while Sihanouk was on a trip to France, General Lon Nol deposed him as chief-of-state. Immediately, violence broke out against ethnic Vietnamese, who were seen as North Vietnamese supporters, and many of them left the country. A month later, U.S. and South Vietnamese forces invaded eastern Cambodia in an attempt to eliminate the North Vietnamese troops who had taken up residence there while they attacked South Vietnam.

Sihanouk went to China and set up a government-in-exile, which supported the Cambodian revolutionary movement known as the Khmer Rouge. For the next five years, savage fighting erupted throughout Cambodia. The U.S. government gave support to the Lon Nol regime, while the Chinese supported the Khmer Rouge. Slowly, the Khmer Rouge gained the upper hand as they undermined all attempts by the government to win the trust of the people. The government helped the process by failing to control the greed and corruption of many of its leaders.

The world hardly noticed as several hundred thousand people died in the savage fighting, and hundreds of thousands more were made refugees in Phnom Penh. One by one, the provincial capitals fell to the rebels; and on April 17, 1975, the Phnom Penh government collapsed and the Khmer Rouge took over the country. Pol Pot became the country's ruler and policy maker. What followed was one of the most appalling episodes in the world's history.

Within two weeks of coming to power, the Khmer Rouge evacuated the entire population of Phnom Penh and the provincial capitals to the countryside. Here they were placed into work teams under teenage Khmer Rouge cadres; and they were made to do manual work for up to fifteen hours a day. The aim was to achieve a radical transformation of Cambodian society into a Maoist, peasant-dominated collective that would have little contact with the outside world. To help achieve this end, all air flights were halted, borders were closed, money was abolished, the central bank was blown up, religion was banned, and postal services were discontinued. The date was proclaimed year zero.

Hundreds of thousands of people died of malnourishment, disease, and inhumane treatment in the camps. Almost as many were tortured to death or executed in a campaign to rid the country of its intellectual elite. The "elite" included anyone with a tertiary education, anyone who wore spectacles, anyone who could speak a foreign language, and anyone who looked as if they had soft hands. Within four years, more than one million people—more than fifteen percent of the country's population—were killed.

Although the Khmer Rouge were ardent Communists, they had little time for the Vietnamese Communists across the border. Pol Pot ordered a series of raids on Vietnamese border provinces that left hundreds of Vietnamese civilians dead. Within Cambodia (renamed Kampuchea), the Khmer Rouge rounded up the remnants of the Vietnamese population, accused them of being spies, and systematically killed them. On December 25, 1978, Vietnam reached the end of its patience with the Pol Pot regime and launched a full-scale invasion of Cambodia. Two weeks later, the Vietnamese seized Phnom Penh, and the Khmer Rouge fled westward toward Thailand.

The Vietnamese installed a new government led by two former Khmer Rouge officers, Hun Sen and Heng Samrin. Their first main problem was a widespread famine that swept the country in 1979. Hundreds of thousands of Cambodians fled to Thailand while a massive international relief effort sponsored by the United Nations was put into place.

Sihanouk, who had returned to Cambodia as chief-of-state for a brief period in 1975 when the Khmer Rouge came to power, was flown to China when the Vietnamese invaded. With China actively opposed to Vietnamese influence in Cambodia, Sihanouk was forced to head a military and political front opposed to the Phnom Penh government. This consisted of the

Cambodian National Front for an Independent, Neutral, Peaceful, and Cooperative Cambodia (FUNCINPEC), the Khmer People's National Liberation Front (a non-Communist group formed by former prime minister Son Sann), and the Party of Democratic Kampuchea (the Khmer Rouge). The various members of this loose alliance were slowly forced from Cambodia into camps established across the border in Thailand by the estimated 170,000 Vietnamese troops in the country in the 1980s.

From 1985 until 1990, the factions engaged in guerilla warfare aimed at harassing the Phnom Penh government forces and demoralizing them—just as the Khmer Rouge had done fifteen years earlier. In these activities, they were supported by money and arms from China, the United States, Thailand, Malaysia, and Singapore. The immediate result was the killing of thousands of defenseless Cambodian civilians. Due to economic problems and the need to reduce its international isolation, Vietnam announced in 1990 that it had withdrawn all its troops from Cambodia. Although this claim was doubted in some quarters, it was the signal for the Khmer Rouge to launch a series of offensives within Cambodia aimed at recapturing territory from the Phnom Penh government. In 1992, despite all the efforts by the world community, this was continuing.

A major diplomatic success occurred in September 1990, when a plan proposed by the U.N. Security Council was accepted by the Phnom Penh government and the three factions of the resistance coalition. This established the Supreme National Council, comprised of six individuals selected by the government and six selected by the opposition under the chairmanship of Sihanouk. The plan was finally put into place in late 1991, when Prince Sihanouk returned to Phnom Penh.

United Nations peacekeepers and election experts arrived in Cambodia in 1992 and elections were held in mid 1993. Prince Sihanouk became the official head of state when a new constitution was promulgated in September 1993 and the monarchy re-established. His official title is His Majesty Preah Bat Samdech Preah Norodom Sihanouk Varman, King of Cambodia.

The Government

The elections of 1993 produced a new government to replace the previous Vietnamese-based regime. The result was an uneasy coalition of former enemies and the amazing situation of joint prime ministers. First prime minister is H.R.H. Samdech Krom Preah Norodom Ranariddh and second prime minister is Samdech Hun Sen, the former premier. The Khymer Rouge currently play no part in the government and, in fact, they have recommended a guerrilla war against the government. Political instability was heightened following an abortive coup in July 1994. The situation is further complicated by the poor health of King Sihanouk who moved to a Beijing hospital in mid-1994.

In his youth, King Sihanouk ruled Cambodia as his personal fiefdom with the support of the French. Later, he abdicated in favor of his father, so he could form his own political party. Sihanouk was prime minister until the death of his father in 1960. He then became chief of state. In 1970, he was deposed, so he took up residence in China. In 1975, he was briefly head of a Khmer Rouge state. Now he is back once more as Cambodian head of state.

The Economy

The devastating Khmer Rouge years, which were followed by thirteen years of international isolation, have left Cambodia struggling to regain the levels of development that existed in the 1960s. Most of the educated population was killed by the Pol Pot regime, and years of war have devastated the male working-age population. Today sixty-four percent of the adult population is female, ill health is rife, food production is barely adequate, and infrastructure is still severely damaged.

Before 1975, Cambodia's economy was based on rice, rubber, and fish. Since then, however, international politics and civil war have severely reduced rural production, and food had to be imported from Vietnam and the Soviet Union during the 1980s. Before Pol Pot, about eighty percent of farmers owned the land they farmed. Most lots were small, but they produced enough to sustain a family. All private ownership was abolished in 1975, so huge disruption has occurred throughout the country. In the late 1980s, when social dogma was discarded in favor of free-market principles, private ownership was again allowed; but the civil war has discouraged settlers moving into many areas.

Other economic activities almost ceased during the seventies, but recently there has been a surge in private enterprise and small business. Shops are opening again in Phnom Penh and elsewhere, and importers are operating with the support of the government to offer some consumer goods, motor vehicles, and so forth from the West. It is estimated that approximately seventy percent of the economy is now in private hands, and the percentage is still rising. Foreign investment laws have been promulgated to encourage overseas investment, and Asia-Pacific countries are expanding their contracts with Cambodia.

In mid-1992, the United Nations Secretary-General Boutros Boutros-Ghali launched an appeal for US$595 million to restore basic services and infrastructure in Cambodia. Although this aid is essential, Cambodia needs an upgraded administration and more trained people if the aid is to be absorbed effectively. The United Nations is trying to earmark assistance for the public sector, but it faces opposition from the Khmer Rouge, who see this sort of aid as directly benefiting the Phnom Penh government, which is its chief adversary.

Another huge challenge to the economy is the reintegration of up to 700,000 people into the urban and rural areas of the country. The resettlement program, which began in mid-1992, is an integral part of the peace agreement and involves more than 360,000 refugees from Thailand as well as more than 180,000 displaced people within Cambodia and 200,000 soldiers, who are to be disarmed and demobilized by the United Nations.

The original U.N. plan was for resettlement of refugees on small farm lots, which would sustain a family through farming; but there were several problems with this. Theoretically, there is much land available for farming, but much of it has been mined by the government or the rebels. In addition, most of the Thai refugees have had little or no experience in farming for many years, and in the camps they have been accustomed to regular food supplies, safe water, and health facilities. In rural Cambodia, none of these conditions exist.

The United Nations' presence in Cambodia has already had an effect on the economy. Prices in Phnom Penh are skyrocketing. Everyone wants to work for the United Nations and the foreign agencies because the rate of pay is far higher than local companies or the government are able to pay. Hotel rates are rapidly rising, office accommodations are at a premium, and many ordinary Cambodians are already suffering. There are already great gaps between the rich and the poor, and these are rapidly growing. Imported cars and beggars are both strong growth areas in Phnom Penh.

The United Nations planned to hold elections in May 1993. The new government is likely to need substantial aid for several years to handle the country's many socio-economic problems. Cambodia, however, will have to compete against many other countries for a piece of the limited financial pie. Achieving continuing financial commitment will not be easy.

The People

Cambodia is one of the most homogenous countries in southeast Asia. More than ninety percent of the people are ethnic Khmers; and the ethnic Chinese, ethnic Vietnamese, and Chams are the only other significant races. The country's population is estimated to be around seven million, which equates an average population density of less than forty people per square kilometer—a very low figure by Asian standards.

The Khmers have inhabited Cambodia for at least the last two thousand years. Over the years, they have mixed with other groups such as the Javanese, the Thais, and more recently the Vietnamese and Chinese. Their culture and religion were strongly influenced by Indian values, and many of these influences can still be seen today. The Khmers live side by side with the Chinese, the Vietnamese, and the Chams, but there are undercurrents of antagonism among the races. The Chinese and Vietnamese are disliked because of their aggression, and the Khmers refer to them as "barbarians." The Chams are looked down on for their poverty and religion.

The Chinese city dwellers suffered very severely under the Pol Pot regime, and many have chosen to leave Cambodia over the last fifteen years. The Vietnamese suffered right through the 1970s under both the Lon Nol government and the Khmer Rouge; but after 1979, thousands of Vietnamese poured into the country to claim farmland and become fishermen in the Tonle Sap. When the Vietnamese troops left Cambodia in 1990, many of these Vietnamese went with them.

Cambodia also has some minority hill-tribe people who live in the country's mountainous regions. They include groups such as the Pear, the Brao, the Saoch, and the Kuy; and they have been mistreated for centuries by the Khmers, who refer to them as "savages." It is believed that these people now number around 60,000.

Religion

Buddhism is the dominant religion in Cambodia. It was the state religion for about a thousand years until 1975, then it was reintroduced as the state religion in the late 1980s.

During various periods, Buddhism has exercised enormous control and influence over Cambodian life. Between 1975 and 1979, the Khmer Rouge attempted to eliminate the religion entirely by killing the vast majority of monks and destroying or damaging almost all of the country's three thousand wats. Now religious activity is tolerated, but the government still imposes many restrictions on the monks and the religion.

Hinduism flourished for many centuries, and the worship of Shiva and Vishmu was prominent in the Angkor and later-Angkor periods. Today Hinduism plays little part in religious activities.

There are some Muslims in Cambodia. The majority of these are descendants of Chams who migrated from central Vietnam. The Khmer Rouge also attempted to eliminate the Muslim religion, and the Cham community suffered great losses during that time. In 1975, there were around 110 mosques in Cambodia; but by 1990, there were less than twenty.

Christianity is not significant in Cambodia despite many years of French influence.

Language

The Khmer language is quite different from Thai, Lao, or Vietnamese and is difficult and confusing to learn. Unless you are planning a long stay or frequent trips to Cambodia, it is unlikely that you will want or need to learn any Khmer. Cambodians realize that their language is unique, and they have little expectation of foreigners to use it. There are thirty-three consonants and many vowels in the language. The pronunciation of a vowel depends on what consonant precedes it. Consonants written at the end of words are barely pronounced.

English has become the second language of choice for Cambodians, and thousands of students crowd the private language schools in Phnom Penh. French is still used as a second language in government, and some restaurant menus are in French. Some people, who were trained in Cuba, speak Spanish, and others trained in East Germany can speak German. A few people speak Vietnamese and Thai.

Here are a few basic words that you may like to use.

yes (by men)—bat	meat—saach
yes (by women)—jas	fish—trei no te
please—suom	chicken—maan
thank you—ar kun	noodles—mee
excuse me—suom tous	eggs—poung sat
doctor—krou peit	

Culture and Lifestyle

Cambodia's cultural achievements undoubtedly peaked during the Angkorian era (ninth to fourteenth centuries). From then until the French protectorate period (starting about 1865), the culture went into decline, and little emphasis was placed on keeping the artistic traditions alive. When the French arrived, there was some encouragement given to reviving these traditions; and by the 1930s, there was a growing artistic and cultural community. This struggled during the forties, fifties, and sixties; and was almost totally destroyed when Pol Pot came to power. The Khmer Rouge set about destroying all the old cultural values—including many of the best and most valuable pieces in museums and wats. They also killed as many "culturally-inclined" Cambodians as they could. Since the mid-1980s, there has been a revival in interest in Khmer culture, but lack of funds has severely restricted what can be done.

The government has recently re-established a national **classical dance** troupe, which gives performances for visiting dignitaries and delegations. Unfortunately, at present it does not give public performances. The troupe performs works adapted from dances performed at Angkor a thousand years ago. Many are based on stories and legends taken from Hindu epics. There are many similarities to Thai classical dance.

Khmer **architecture** is exemplified by the wonderful structures of Angkor Thom and the temple of Angkor Wat. Since that period, little of particular merit has been built. The Royal Palace and the National Museum in Phnom Penh are modern buildings of some merit.

There are a number of **lifestyle** considerations that you should remember while in Cambodia. The first is that the country has been through twenty years of incredible trauma that must have affected everyone. It has affected different people in different ways—some have turned to religion; some have become detached. Some have been hardened by the process; some don't want to talk about the experience. You must make allowances for this in your contact with people. Despite this, you will find that most Cambodians will give you a great welcome to their country and will go out of their way to help if you ask for it.

Cambodians traditionally have greeted each other by pressing their hands together in front of their bodies and bowing. Today this practice has been partially replaced by the Western practice of shaking hands when men meet each other. Foreigners are excused if they offer to shake hands with Cambodians of both sexes.

Modesty is considered important in Cambodia, as it is in Thailand. The women are much more modest in their dress than the Vietnamese. At home, both men and women wear sarongs, but on the streets most men wear Western clothes. During the day, some women wear colorful variegated silk shirts called *hols*, but many others can be seen in T-shirts and long skirts. Topless or nude bathing is unacceptable—even for foreigners. Please remember to act and dress with respect when visiting wats or other religious sites. This includes many of the temples at Angkor.

Health and Safety

Cambodia has one of the poorest health records in the world. Life expectancy has fallen in the last twenty years and is now below forty for both men and women. As a visitor, you should be aware that there are significant dangers to your health—particularly if you require treatment for an accident or sickness.

Almost all of Cambodia's doctors were killed by the Khmer Rouge, so there is a chronic shortage of trained medical help, especially in the rural areas. In addition, Cambodia's hospitals have either been destroyed by the civil war or suffer from a chronic shortage of almost everything. Most hospitals stock virtually no pharmaceuticals, so you will have to buy your own medications if you go to the hospital and need anything. Many of these have been stolen from aid agencies or imported illegally from Thailand. Some will have passed their expiration date. Others will be nothing more than a mixture of sugar, flour, and coloring.

Fortunately, I have had no direct experience with Cambodia's hospitals; but I am told by aid workers and others that injections are routinely carried out using unsterilized equipment, most IV solutions are not sterile, and anaesthesia is often not handled properly. The word is that you should avoid treatment in Cambodia, unless it is a life-threatening situation. Evacuation to Thailand is strongly recommended.

Until the civil war ends, travel in many areas is risky. There are still many illiterate, nervous, and heavily armed teenagers in the armies of the various factions; and until they are disarmed, your life may depend on their good judgement. No one in Phnom Penh really knows the true situation in the provinces, and rumors spread like wildfire. The deployment of U.N. troops may be helping the situation, but already some have been injured by gunfire and others have encountered undetonated mines. In mid-1992, there were still several areas of the countryside where I would not go, even if a travel permit had been made available.

As with Vietnam and eastern Laos, you should never touch any rockets, bombs, artillery shells, mines, and so forth that you come across. In Vietnam and Laos, these are likely to be twenty years old; but in Cambodia, they may have been put there only last night. The Khmer Rouge and the government were still laying new minefields in mid-1992, so you are at risk. Never walk away from well-worn paths under any circumstances—even in the Angkor area—and avoid walking through jungle areas—even on paths. There are many better and more healthy places in the world to bushwalk and see rainforest. If you need further incentive to follow this rule, just look around at the large number of limbless people all over Cambodia.

The number of HIV-positive cases diagnosed in recent times has climbed rapidly, and the authorities are now taking the situation seriously.

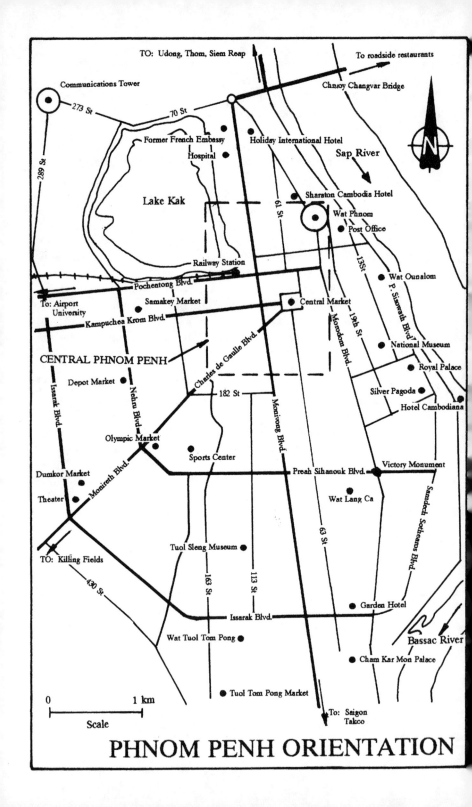

PHNOM PENH ORIENTATION

12

Phnom Penh and Other Places

1. The General Picture

Phnom Penh is the capital and only major city in Cambodia. The city came into prominence in the mid-fifteenth century and reached its peak in the time of the French. Since then, it has had a dramatic and amazing history, due to the Indochina War of the early 1970s, the Khmer Rouge regime of the late 1970s, the nationwide civil war of the 1980s, and now the U.N. peace-keeping efforts in the 1990s.

The dramatic population changes that have occurred in the city are evidence of this. In the 1960s, the population was around half a million people. By 1975, it had swelled to over two million. From 1976 to 1979, it was almost zero. Now it is back to approaching one million.

Unfortunately, what was once considered to be the most beautiful of the French-built cities in Asia is now just a shadow of its former beauty. Twenty years of strife have devastated vast areas and robbed the country of much of its appeal. What has returned in the last few years, however, is the vitality and enthusiasm that disappeared during those decades of violence, political chaos, and dilapidation.

The city is built adjacent to the Mekong River, although you don't actually see the river from the city itself. The water you do see is the Sap River, which is a Mekong tributary, and the Bassac River, which is a Mekong branch that forms part of the delta. The city stretches about seven kilometers in a north-south direction and about five kilometers in an east-west direction. The inner sections have a high population density, but some of the outer areas consist primarily of single-level dwellings on individual blocks. Newly named Monivong Boulevard is the major north-south arterial, and Pochentong Boulevard is the primary east-west arterial. Issarak Boulevard and Preah Sihanouk Boulevard connect these two arterials by forming roughly parallel semicircles.

2. Getting There

At present, most visitors arrive in Phnom Penh by **air** . The number of airlines serving Phnom Penh is rapidly growing. In late 1992, the major ones were Bangkok Airways, Thai Airways International, and others from Bangkok; Vietnam Airlines from Ho Chi Minh City; Lao Aviation from Laos; Silk Air and others from Singapore; Malaysia Airlines from Kuala Lumpur; Dragonair from Hong Kong; and Aeroflot and Air France from Europe. Cambodia International Airlines operates to several Asian capitals including Bangkok and Singapore.

Phnom Penh Airport (Pochentong International Airport) has recently been expanded, and the international terminal is quite acceptable. The arrival procedure is complicated, however, by some passengers having to fill in arrival and customs forms and obtain visas upon arrival at the airport. Unless you are met by a tourguide at the entrance to the arrivals hall, it can all be very confusing—particularly for travelers who have little knowledge of Khmer or English. The correct procedure is to fill in two copies of the arrival form and two copies of the customs form, then go to the visa issuing counter to have the prearranged visa issued to you. You can then pass through immigration, collect your baggage, and go to customs. It appears that most tourists do not have their bags inspected on arrival, but returning residents are often treated differently.

There are facilities for changing money at the airport, and you will need some U.S. dollars or Thai baht to pay for transportation to the city. There is a limousine service to the city for US$10 or you can negotiate with a private vehicle for around US$5. If you have reservations at the Hotel Cambodiana, the hotel bus will pick you up. If all else fails, you can walk the 150 meters to Highway 3 and get some form of public transport into town. The Cambodians (Khmers) like visitors, so you will receive help if you stand somewhere looking helpless.

The procedure on departure has become less complicated, and you should be able to arrive one hour before your flight and have no problems. The departure terminal is smart and clean with good English signs. Departure tax is US$8. The airport has a duty-free shop (with identical prices to Bangkok), a drink and snack food outlet, and television entertainment.

You can also get to Phnom Penh by **car** or **bus** from Ho Chi Minh City, provided your paperwork is in order. This includes ensuring that your Vietnam visa stipulates that Moc Bai is your exit point, and you have been able to arrange a Cambodian visa in Ho Chi Minh City or elsewhere that allows a land entry. At the time of this writing, it was still difficult to do this (but not impossible).

3. Local Transportation

Cyclos (samlors) are a cheap and effective way of getting around inner Phnom Penh and most other urban areas. You can hail them on the street, or you can find them clustered outside hotels, markets, and other places where people gather. In Phnom Penh, some drivers will be able to speak a little English or French; but you can still have difficulty communicating your desired destination. Most drivers appear to have no knowledge of maps, so even pointing to the destination doesn't necessarily help. The only certain way is to get your hotel receptionist to write the destination in Khmer, so you can give it to the driver. Cyclo travel is very cheap if you are adept at bargaining; but most visitors are not, so expect to pay US$1 for a short trip in town and US$2 for anything longer.

Phnom Penh has some **buses** and converted trucks serving the suburbs, but few visitors will be attracted by the service. Buses depart from terminals near the Central Market and the O Russei Market; but generally they are dirty and unreliable, and it is difficult to determine where each vehicle is heading. If the destination is unimportant, hop aboard, give the driver US$1, and he will probably let you travel all day.

Central Phnom Penh is safe for **walking**, and it can be very interesting to do this—except during the summer when it is just too hot. You can travel a little farther afield by **bicycle**. These can be bought for around US$25 and can be a good investment if you are staying in the city for longer than a few days. I have not been able to find a reliable rental shop in Phnom Penh, but you could inquire at your hotel to see if one of the staff would like to rent his bicycle to you for a few hours.

Travel around Cambodia is still quite restricted to foreigners, but hopefully this will open up in the near future if the political and civil war situation is kept under control. You need a travel permit to leave the city; and these are issued by the Ministry of the Interior, which is located on Tou Samouth Boulevard, out toward the Monivong Bridge. At present, you will

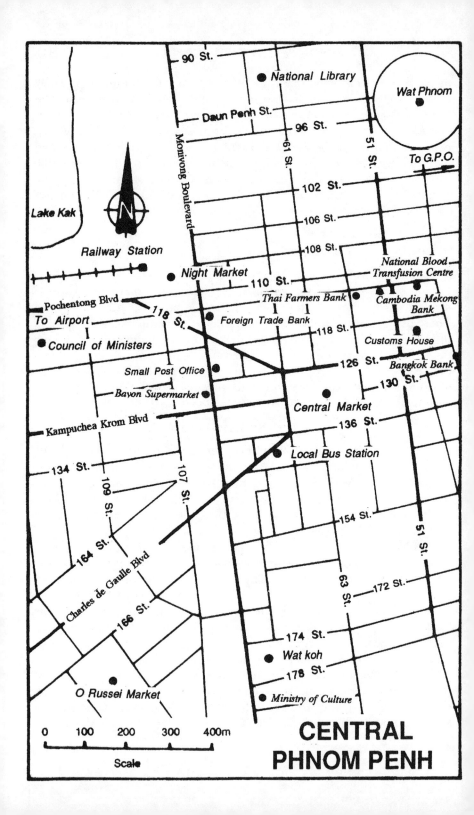

CENTRAL
PHNOM PENH

not be given a permit to travel by bus, except to Ho Chi Minh City, or by train. You may get a permit for car travel to some nearby locations—particularly if you indicate you plan to rent one of the ministry's vehicles.

Air travel to Siem Reap (also spelled Siem Riep) is no problem, and you may get permission to fly to Stung Treng if you have a plausible reason. The situation is changing rapidly, however, so make inquiries as soon as you reach Cambodia to learn the current situation. **Boats** have always been an important method of transportation in Cambodia on the 1,500 kilometers of waterway. Of most interest are the half-day excursions from Phnom Penh and the trip to Siem Reap.

4. The Hotel Scene

Phnom Penh is currently enjoying a hotel boom as commercial life recovers after three decades of chronic problems. Tourism is also showing healthy growth, so at times Phnom Penh hotels put out their "no vacancy" signs. The Hotel Cambodiana (a Sofitel hotel) and the Novotel Hotel, currently under development, are the first international chain hotels in the country; but there is little doubt that others will follow. The city can now offer a reasonable choice in price, location, and facilities. Here is a selection of properties that I have experienced or inspected.

EXPENSIVE HOTELS

The **Sofitel Cambodiana Hotel** (Tel: 26392), 320 rooms, is a well-run property built on the bank of the Sap River, about 1½ kilometers from downtown. You could believe that you were in a better Bangkok or Singapore hotel, but all the staff are clearly Khmer. The rooms are a good size and have all the necessary facilities—airconditioning, telephone, refrigerator with minibar, television, and clean attached bathrooms.

The hotel has two bars, each with live music in the evening; the Mekong Restaurant featuring Cambodian and international food; the Royal Pavillion, which specializes in Chinese food; a business center with fax, telex, and typing facilities; a large outdoor swimming pool; and a tennis court. It is all that you would expect from a four-star international hotel. Room prices are from US$175, with suites starting at US$240. (Book with the hotel direct at 313 Sisowath Quay, Phnom Penh; Fax: 855-23-26290; in U.S. and Canada Tel: 800-221-4542.)

The **Allson Star Hotel** (Tel: 62-008), 67 rooms, is a nice property in the heart of downtown. The rooms are well equipped, the lobby is peaceful, and there is a business center, a restaurant, and a bar. The level of service is high. Room rates start at US$90. (Book with the hotel at Monivong Boulevard at 128 St., Phnom Penh; Fax: 855-23-62018.)

The **Cambodiana Inn** (Tel: 26771), 25 rooms, is situated next to the Sofitel Cambodiana Hotel and has the same address. It has a series of bungalows built in nice grounds. All rooms are airconditioned and nicely furnished. Room prices are around US$100.

The **Ambassador Hotel** (Tel: 26029) is on the corner of Pochentong Boulevard and Boulevard Issarak, on the way to the airport. The hotel opened in 1992 but has struggled to establish itself. Room rates are US$150, US$120, and US$110.

The **Royal Phnom Penh Hotel** (Tel: 60026), 40 rooms, is a deluxe property with plans to develop to 362 rooms. Rooms are modern and comfortable, the Rose Garden Lounge is a good place to unwind, and there is the Bassae Restaurant and Night Club. The hotel is several kilometers from downtown so it can feel somewhat isolated. Room rates are US$150. (Book with the hotel at Samdech Sothearos Boulevard, Phnom Penh; Fax: 855-23-60036.)

MEDIUM-PRICE HOTELS

Phnom Penh has a good choice of hotels in this category, and the number is growing. It is very difficult to rate the hotels in any order of priority because of the spate of renovations and improvements to various properties that is currently occurring. Because of this, I have decided to group hotels by location, rather than strictly by price or facilities. The first group of hotels is those in the central city.

The **Pailin Hotel** (Tel: 22475), 81 rooms, would be my choice at the moment. The hotel has been extensively renovated in recent years. This has included a new reception area, two new elevators, new hot water heaters in the rooms, and general care and attention. It is still not great, but it will be adequate for most people looking for a mid-market hotel. Its location on Monivong Boulevard at the intersection with Boulevard Charles de Gaulle places it right in the center of the action. Many of the rooms are very large, and all are airconditioned and have a telephone, refrigerator, and minibar. The attached bathrooms are not great, but they are quite large and clean. There are no shower curtains. The hotel's Hong Kong restaurant is one of the most popular in the city.

I have a soft spot for the Pailin because I have found its staff to be very helpful and friendly, and it seems to lack the "rip-off" mentality which has developed in some areas of tourism in Cambodia. A good example is the minibar prices. The Pailin probably has some of the lowest prices in the world—beer at eighty cents a can, soft drinks at sixty cents a can, and drinking water at thirty cents a bottle. That is less than you pay on the streets. Room prices are climbing rapidly, but are still reasonable. A small single is US$50, large double US$80. (Book with the hotel at 211 Monivong Boulevard, Phnom Penh; Fax: 855-23-26376.)

Going south, the **Hotel Neak Poan** (Tel: 22485), 24 rooms, is the next place you reach. This relatively new hotel has fair rooms and good facilities for US$20. There is a large restaurant, which is often packed in the evening, and a first-floor disco that is heavily promoted and operates from 7 to 11 P.M. nightly. The staff that I met were all helpful. (Book with the hotel at 331 Monivong Boulevard, Phnom Penh; Fax: 855-23-26543.)

Across the street and just a little south, you will find the **Mittapheap Hotel** (Tel: 23464), 40 rooms. Rooms have both fans and airconditioners and are of acceptable standard. Prices are US$20 for a double. All rooms have a refrigerator and television. The hotel has a nice, reasonably priced restaurant. (Book at 262 Monivong Boulevard, Phnom Penh.)

The **Orchidee Hotel** (Tel: 22659), 40 rooms, is actually around the corner on 174 Street, but it still has a Monivong Boulevard address. This place appeals to me because it is quieter than the hotels on the main boulevard and it appears to have a nice "feel" about it. All rooms are airconditioned and have telephones, refrigerators, and televisions with video movies. The bathrooms have hot water. (Book with the hotel at 262 Monivong Boulevard, Phnom Penh; Fax: 855-23-26576.) Room rates are US$25, US$30, and US$35.

The **Hong Kong Hotel** (Tel: 27108), 37 rooms, is a new place a little farther south. Rooms are OK, and there is a reasonable restaurant. Room prices start at US$20. (Book at 419 Monivong Boulevard, Phnom Penh; Fax: 855-23-27094.)

There are just as many possibilities going north from the Pailin. Immediately north is the new **Paradise Hotel** (Tel: 22951), 100 rooms, and a very nice ground-floor restaurant. Room prices are US$25-40, an excellent value. (Book at 209 Monivong Boulevard, Phnom Penh; Fax: 855-23-27280.)

Across the road is the attractive **Diamond Hotel** (Tel: 27825), 86 rooms. This has all required room facilities, a restaurant, and good service. Room prices are from US$70. (Book at 172 Monivong Boulevard, Phnom Penh; Fax: 855-23-26635.)

Next is the renovated **Asie Hotel** (Tel: 27826), 120 rooms. This incorporates the old Santepheap Hotel. Rooms are airconditioned and have TV and refrigerator. Rooms without windows start at US$25. With a window it is US$35. The ground-floor Miramar Restaurant is popular. (Book at 136 Street/Monivong Boulevard; Phnom Penh; Fax: 855-23-26334.) Almost next door is the **Singapore Hotel** (Tel: 25552), 25 rooms. This is a newly opened no-frills hotel, but the rooms have airconditioning, TV, telephone, refrigerator, and hot and cold water. Room prices start at US$20. (Book by Fax: 855-23-26570.)

The **Sukhalay Hotel** (Tel: 22403), 85 rooms, has been on the scene for a long time. The old hotel used to reduce room prices as you climbed the seven-floor building, but now with a new elevator and some refurbishing, the prices rise as you go higher. Rooms are nothing wonderful, but the staff is friendly and there is quite a reasonable restaurant on the ground floor. External rooms are priced at US$25-34, while internal ones are US$21-30. There is an annex mentioned in the budget section. (Book with the hotel at 132 Monivong Boulevard, Phnom Penh; Fax: 855-23-26140.)

The **Monorom Hotel** (Tel: 24799), 68 rooms, has also been around for some time. This hotel is operated by Phnom Penh Tourism and is one of the best-known hotels in the city. Recent renovations have improved its image. All rooms have attached bathrooms, airconditioning, and refrigerators. The higher-priced rooms have televisions with video movies. There is a ground-floor bar and restaurant, which is a popular place with guests and locals, and a nice sixth-floor restaurant, which opens from 5 A.M. to 8 P.M. for Asian and Western food, then operates later as a discotheque. (Book with the hotel at 89 Monivong Boulevard, Phnom Penh; Fax: 855-23-26149.)

The **Dusit Hotel** (Tel: 22188), 50 rooms, also known as the Mekong Hotel, is diagonally opposite the Monorom. This has been renovated in the last year or so and is now quite acceptable. All rooms are airconditioned and have refrigerators, TV with satellite programs, and telephones. Doubles are priced from US$20. (Book with the hotel at 118 Monivong Boulevard, Phnom Penh; Fax: 855-23-27209.)

There are three other central city hotels in this category. The **Hotel London** (Tel: 25778), 12 rooms, is on Charles de Gaulle Boulevard near Monivong Boulevard. Rooms have airconditioning and refrigerator and cost from US$15. (Book by Fax: 855-23-27778.) **La Paillote Hotel** (Tel: 22151), 20 rooms, is on 130 Street opposite the main market. The reception is upstairs above the large, popular ground-floor restaurant. Rooms have airconditioning, TV, video movies, refrigerator, and hot water. Prices start at US$20. (Book by Fax: 855-23-26513.) Best of all is the **Hawaii Hotel** (Tel: 26652), 68 rooms. The rooms are attractive and well appointed, and the restaurant has good Thai, Chinese, and Western cuisine. Room rates start at US$35. (Book at 18, 130 Street, Phnom Penh; Fax: 855-23-26652.)

There are some good hotels in other parts of the city as well. They may not be so convenient for those who like to wander the shops, but they all offer something—they may be quieter, more spacious, or more personal.

The **Hotel Le Royal** (Tel: 23051), 82 rooms, remains an old favorite even though it is a bit run-down. It is rumored that the Raffles group from Singapore will restore it to its former glory soon. The hotel is set on nice grounds, and the location is convenient to many of the attractions of the city. Some of the rooms are very large, and all have attached bathrooms. My room (second class) was airconditioned and had a refrigerator and minibar. The bathroom had a full-size bath. There is a swimming pool out back, and a bar and restaurant. The hotel has a discotheque that operates every night. Room prices start at US$26, and bungalows are available for US$50. (Book with the hotel at 1 Daun Penh Street, Phnom Penh.)

Farther north from here the **Holiday Hotel** (Tel: 27402), 41 rooms, has some of the better modern rooms in the city. The location, however, is not convenient without access to a vehicle. There is a 24-hour room service and the attractive Palm's Cafe, and there is a business center and upcoming swimming pool. Room rates start at US$70. (Book at 84 Street, Phnom Penh; Fax: 855-23-27401.)

The **White Rose Hotel** (Tel: 23421), 15 rooms, would be another good choice, although its location three kilometers south of the central city is not particularly convenient. Rooms here are very nice. They are all airconditioned and have refrigerators, but no telephones. The attached bathrooms have hot water and are neat and clean. The hotel has a lovely outdoor restaurant, which is attractive during the cooler time of the year. There is also a large airconditioned restaurant, which is popular in the evenings. (Book with the hotel at Issarak Boulevard, Khand Chamcarmon, Phnom Penh.)

Nearby, at 160 Issarak Boulevard, is the **Punleu Pich Hotel**, 24 rooms. This new hotel has airconditioned rooms with refrigerators, but there is no restaurant at the hotel or close by, so that is somewhat of a problem. Room rates are US$30.

There are several other mid-range hotels in this area south of the city. The **Sydney International Hotel** (Tel: 27907), 40 rooms, is a reasonable property with nice rooms and a restaurant. Room rates start at US$30. (Book at 360 Street, Phnom Penh; Fax: 855-23-27907.) The **Phnom Penh Garden Hotel** (Tel: 27264), 22 rooms, is a newly renovated property in a quiet area. Rooms are very well appointed with airconditioning, satellite TV, in-house movies, IDD telephone, refrigerator with minibar, carpet, and hot and cold water. There is a restaurant, private Karaoke rooms, 24-hour room service, and a swimming pool. Rooms start at US$30. (Book at 66, 57 Street, Phnom Penh; Fax: 855-23-27345.) Then there's the **Green Hotel** (Tel: 26055), 30 rooms, at 145 Norodom Boulevard. Rooms with breakfast start at US$25. (Book by Fax: 855-23-27359.) The **Gold Hotel** (Tel: 27558), 33 rooms, is not far from here. Rooms are OK and are available from US$20. There is a restaurant. (Book at 10, 280 Street, Phnom Penh; Fax: 855-23-27558.)

The **Renakse Hotel** (Tel: 22457), 23 rooms, is another French-style hotel built on nice grounds. It is near the river, opposite the Silver Pagoda. To be really attractive, the hotel needs to spend quite a bit more money, but the present 1950s ambiance will appeal to some people. All rooms are airconditioned, some are quite large, and all have attached bathrooms. Rooms have refrigerators and hot and cold water, but no telephones. There is a nice lounge area, and the restaurant is adequate. Room rates are US$30-35. (Book with the hotel at Samdech Sothearos Boulevard, Khand Don Penh, Phnom Penh; Fax: 855-23-26036.)

There are several properties to the west of downtown. The **Juliana Hotel** (Tel: 66070), 51 rooms, is a comfortable low-rise development with nice rooms, friendly service, a restaurant, lounge, business center, conference room with fitness center with sauna and massage. Room rates are around US$100 with a discount usually available. (Book at 152 Road, Sangkat Veal Weng, Phnom Penh; Fax: 855-23-66072.) **Le President Hotel** (Tel: 27055), 123 rooms, is a modern property a little farther out. I have never stayed here, but the hotel seems to operate efficiently. Rooms are fine, and the restaurant/bar/nightclub facilities are good. It is a bit far to walk to the downtown area. Room prices start at around US$60. (Book at 682 Kampuchea Krom Boulevard, Phnom Penh; Fax: 855-23-27460.) The **China Nanjing Hotel** (Tel: 27101), 65 rooms, opened in late 1994 so there has been little time to assess its performance. Facilities are reasonable. Room prices start at US$30. (Book at 219 Kampuchea Krom Boulevard, Phnom Penh; Fax: 855-23-66269.)

BUDGET ACCOMMODATIONS

True budget accommodations of the hostel or backpacker-style are just emerging in Phnom Penh. There are two central guest houses offering low-cost dorm beds and small private rooms. The **King Bar** in 130 Street has dorm beds from US$2 and rooms with bed, table, chair, and fan from US$3. There is a restaurant on the ground floor with English movies on video. The **Lotus Guest House** is around the corner on 53 Street. This has dorm beds from US$3 and rooms from US$4. Both fan and airconditioned rooms are available. There are laundry and ironing facilities, a reading room, an Indian restaurant, and an ice cream parlor.

There are also several hotels offering rooms in the US$10-15 range. Two of these are downtown. The **Pacific Hotel** (Tel: 26926), 16 rooms, is on Monivong Boulevard almost across from the Pailin Hotel. The night club is the big thing here, but if you want a room in this atmosphere they are available from US$10. The **Hotel Ripole** (Tel: 22713), 26 rooms, is more of a hotel. Rooms are airconditioned and have TV, refrigerator, telephone, and bathtub with hot water. Rates are US$15. (Book at 118 and 126 Street, Phnom Penh; Fax: 855-23-27192.)

Farther out along Monivong Boulevard, the **Tai Seng Hotel** (Tel: 27220), 53 rooms, has reasonable accommodation from US$10. (Book at 56 Monivong Boulevard; Fax: 855-23-27551.) West of downtown on Monireth Boulevard, the **Sangker Hotel** (Tel: 26663) 29 rooms, at Number 5, and the **Borei Thmei Hotel** (Tel: 25229), 47 rooms, at Number 13, both have reasonable airconditioned rooms for US$15.

An emerging area for this type of accommodation is the area adjacent to the Monivong-Preah Sihanouk intersection. The **Fortune Hotel** (Tel: 27393) at No. 2, 67 Street has rooms from US$10. All are airconditioned and some have refrigerators. There's a restaurant, sauna, and massage. The **Tokyo Hotel** (Tel: 62079), 30 rooms at No. 15, 278 Street, and the adjacent **South East Asia Hotel** (Tel: 62446) at No. 157, 63 Street, both have airconditioned rooms with TV for US$15. The **Hotel Yang Chou** (Tel: 27423), 19 rooms, is similar at No. 27, 252 Street. This place also has a large Thai-style massage facility at US$5 per hour.

5. Dining and Restaurants

Dining opportunities in Phnom Penh are growing rapidly. You can get an acceptable meal at many of the hotel restaurants; you can buy local food from the markets or the food stalls that set up at various places in the evening; or you can visit a regular restaurant and have a choice of Khmer, Chinese, Thai, or Western food. Despite years of trouble and strife, the Cambodian natural love for food, which was cultivated over a long period by the French, has refused to die. Now that there are more opportunities for locals to enjoy themselves, they are doing so with gusto. You will quickly notice that the tables in most bars and restaurants are piled high with mostly unopened beer cans. Status demands that you appear able to finance the consumption of an ocean of beer, even if half the cans remain intact at the end of the evening.

HOTEL RESTAURANTS

I don't particularly recommend that you seek out hotel restaurants other than the one in the hotel at which you are staying; but there are some that are worth trying if you are in the area. At haute top of the list would be the **Mekong Restaurant** and the **Royal Pavillion** at the Hotel Cambodiana. The Royal Pavillion's Chinese cuisine is probably the best. At times it is very popular, so reservations are suggested (Tel: 26288).

The **Hong Kong Restaurant** (Tel: 25485) at the Pailin Hotel has good food, reasonable prices, and plenty of customers. The **Hollywood Cafe** at the Allson Star Hotel has a fresh, bright atmosphere. The upstairs restaurant at the **Monorom Hotel** is adequate for both food and atmosphere.

One of my favorites is the ground-floor restaurant at the **Paradise Hotel** (Tel: 22951) It is bustling with life at lunch time and in the evening as business people, families, and singles meet over a meal. I have never eaten at **Le Cyrene Restaurant** at the Hotel Le Royal, but I have been told that it

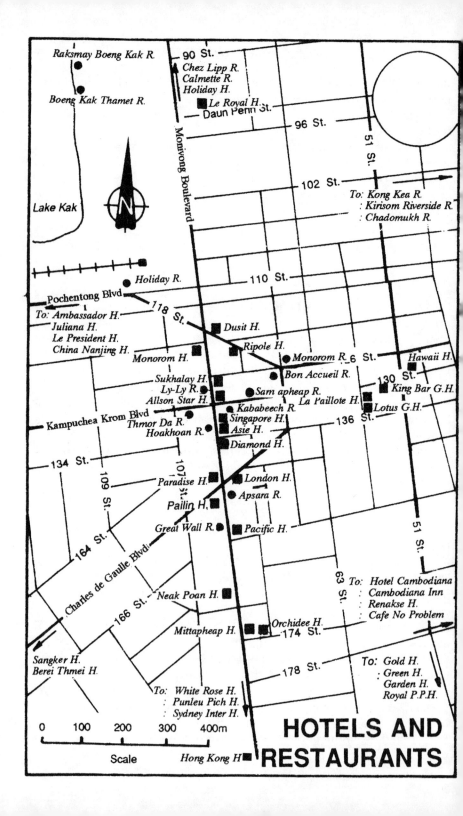

HOTELS AND
RESTAURANTS

has good French food and other dishes. The **Hawaii Hotel** restaurant has good Thai, Chinese, and Western food.

RIVERSIDE/LAKESIDE RESTAURANTS

One of my favorite things to do in Phnom Penh is to eat by or on the water. The city has a good choice of places to try. At Boeng Kak, the large shallow lake north of the city center, I like the **Raksmay Boeng Kak Restaurant** (Tel: 23850). There is an extensive menu covering Cambodian, Chinese, and some seafood and Western cuisines. The atmosphere is nice because you actually dine out over the water; and the food is good without being too expensive. A reasonable meal for two people will cost around US$10. The nearby **Boeng Kak Thamet Restaurant** is noisier and has a discotheque at night.

There are also restaurants on the Sap River. In my experience, the **Kong Kea** (Tel: 22651) is the best. This is close to the destroyed Chruoy Changvar Bridge. It has dancing and a band at night and is a very lively place. I find the inside to be too noisy, but outside on the deck watching the river drift by is quite delightful. The food is reasonable and prices are not high. Fish is one of the most popular dishes. Male diners without female partners are likely to be approached at their tables by Cambodian or Vietnamese "dancing girls." Most of the girls will not speak English, but they will be hoping to dance with you and go home afterwards for a fee. A simple "no" solves that problem.

Two other restaurants south from here are the **Kirisom Riverside Restaurant** and the **Chadomukh Floating Restaurant**.

OTHER RESTAURANTS

Excellent French food is available at **Cafe No Problem** (Tel: 127250), and the upstairs **La Mousson Restaurant** at Number 55, 178 Street opposite the National Museum. There is a real Parisian atmosphere at this place, which is established in an old French mansion enhanced by attractive lighting. Prices are heading upward, but they are still a fraction of what you would pay in France (or New York, for that matter). Special lunch and dinner options are from US$6, and it's all imported meat.

The **Apsara Restaurant** (Tel: 22860), at 208 Monivong Boulevard, is a very popular place for lunch. The menu is in English and French, and there is a choice of Cambodian or Western food. The menu has no prices on it, so you would be wise to ask the price before you order; but in my experience, prices are reasonable.

Deja Vu (Tel: 27654), at No. 22, 240 Street, is a very attractive place. It has fine European food served within an interesting building surrounded by a nice garden. It opens from 11:30 A.M. until midnight and has main meals for

US$3-5 and desserts at around US$2.50, I like it. Guests are welcome at the **Foreign Correspondents Club** (Tel: 27757) at 363 Sisowath Quay where there is a bar, restaurant, and pool table. In the same general area, the **Ban Thai Restaurant** (Thai and Khmer food) on 306 Street has lunch specials from US$2.50.

The **Chez Lipp Restaurant** at 40 Monivong Boulevard, near the corner of 84 Street, is a relaxing place with good food and a nice personality. This is a good place for dinner when the temperature is not too high. The open-sided restaurant with its tropical roof looks out over a nice garden. **Restaurant Calmette** is just a little farther north on the opposite side of the road. It is similar in style.

Back near the railway station on Pochentong Boulevard you will find the **Holiday Restaurant and Disco** (Tel: 25516). This place comes to life after dark; but the food is good enough reason for going here—even if you don't want the entertainment.

In the center of the city, there are all sorts of restaurants. The **Ly-Ly Restaurant** is a typical Chinese-style eatery at 117 Monivong Boulevard. All the popular dishes are available at US$1 or $2. The **Hoa Khoan Restaurant** (Tel: 25537) in the next block at Number 165 is very much the same. Both offer good value. The **Restaurant Monorom** (Tel: 24162), on the corner of 126 Street and 118 Street, has a similar selection. Unfortunately, nobody seems to speak English, so what you get is somewhat of a gamble. **Restaurant Bon Accueil** is diagonally across the street, facing the market. Locals sit out on the footpath, watching the passing scene, but I am not impressed by this place because it always looks dirty. **Uncle Sam's Family Restaurant** (Tel: 26038) with its fried chicken specials is actually within the central market complex. This is a good place to have an imported Tiger or Anchor beer while you soak up some of the local color and atmosphere. The **Great Wall Restaurant** at 229 Monivong Boulevard has a Chinese buffet meal each evening.

In this area, there is a collection of restaurants along Kampuchea Krom Boulevard. Two of the best are **Restaurant Samapheap** at No. 39, where Cambodian dishes cost US$1-2 and there are always crowds of people, and the **Thmor Da Restaurant** at No. 90, where you can get ice cream, hamburgers, sandwiches, and Cambodian food in a large, clean room. Others that you could try are **Leem Tear Hae Restaurant** at No. 8, which has Cambodian and Chinese food; and **Cafe Champa**, No. 46, and **Cafe Khanara**, No. 50, which have TV sets and crowds of square-eyed people who probably hardly notice the food.

Close to the Monivong-Preah Sihanouk intersection there are many options. For French food, try **Le Cordon Bleu Restaurant** on Sihanouk Boulevard opposite Lucky Market. There is a set lunch for US$5 and set dinner menus at US$8 and US$15. Close by, the **Royal Kitchen** (Tel: 018-810607) at Number 130 has excellent Thai food and steam boat. At Number 55, **California's Restaurant** (Tel: 25645) has a selection of Western food. The **King of Kings Restaurant** (Tel: 62407) on the corner of 63 Street has a range of French and Chinese food at reasonable prices. Further down-market, the **Restaurant Makara** appeals to the locals and the backpacker market. Finally, you could try the **Long Beach Restaurant** (Tel: 018-810223) at 477 Monivong Boulevard. The restaurant is upstairs past a waterfall and has an English menu. Good steaks range from US$7-9.

MARKETS AND FOOD STALLS

There are ten major markets in Phnom Penh, and each has food stalls where you can buy very cheap local food. Visitors always wonder about the cleanliness of these places; and frankly in Cambodia, I'm not too sure. If you have been touring Asia for some time and eating from the street markets without ill effects, you may like to take the risk here. If on the other hand, you have come straight from home and want to make the most of every minute of a tight schedule, gambling with the market food just doesn't make sense. I have eaten at the **central market** (on the western side), at the **Orasey Market**, and at the **Toul Tom Pong Market** on 163 Street without ill effects; but this is no guarantee that you can too. I recommend that you be careful.

You will be much better off sampling the food at the restaurants that set up at night around the city. In my opinion, the best of these are on the riverbank, just north of the Royal Palace. The location is appealing as well.

6. Sightseeing

Phnom Penh has several good sightseeing attractions; but for many people, the fact of just being there will be a huge attraction in itself. These days, it is rare for travelers to be able to visit a place that most people know about, but few have visited. Phnom Penh is one of these places, so being there is exciting. When you discover that it is interesting, safe, and fascinating to explore on foot, that's all a bonus.

The **Royal Palace** is once again occupied, so it is no longer open to the public. I turned up one day with an official from the General Direction of Tourism, the government tourism agency, but no amount of talking would convince the guards to allow me to go through the gates for about ten meters to photograph the main palace building. The buildings have been recently refurbished, and what you can see is very attractive. The Chan Chaya Pavillion, which forms the main palace entrance, can be photographed anytime. Early morning gives the best results.

The main building within the palace is the Throne Hall. This was built in 1919 to replace a large wooden building built fifty years earlier. The hall, which is topped with an Angkor-style tower, was used for coronations and ceremonies involving foreign diplomats. Since the palace has been reoccupied by King Sihanouk, many of the former functions of the palace buildings have been restored.

The **Silver Pagoda** compound is something not to be missed, but you need special authorization from the Ministry of Information and Culture. This department has offices at 398 Monivong Boulevard, on the corner of 180 Street. Once you have your permission paper, you must present it to the guards at the entrance to a laneway between the Royal Palace and the pagoda. This gate is supposed to be open from 7 to 11 A.M. and 2 to 5 P.M. You can pay US$2 for permission to photograph within the grounds, but not within the main building.

The Silver Pagoda gets its name from the five thousand or so silver tiles that cover the floor. To many Cambodians, it is known as Wat Preah Keo. The original building was constructed in 1892 and was said to be inspired by Bangkok's Wat Phra Keo at the Grand Palace. The present building dates to 1962.

An English-speaking guide will take you around the pagoda compound and show you the colossal mural painted on the compound wall that depicts the epic of "Ramayana." You can also see several royal stupas, an equestrian statue of King Norodom, a forested artificial hill once used by the Royal family for relaxation, and a bell tower.

However, it is the Pagoda itself that is the highlight. Although more than fifty percent of the contents were destroyed by Pol Pot's forces, what remains today is quite breathtaking. There are gold, silver, bronze, crystal, and marble Buddhas; various items showing the grandeur of Khmer civilization; and gifts from foreign heads of state and governments. It is unfortunate that there are no English descriptions on the objects, but even without them you can wander around and just take in the beauty of everything. It is priceless.

The **National Museum** collection is housed within a fine Cambodian-style building, which was opened in 1920. The site is just north of the Royal Palace on 13 Street. It opens every day except Sunday from 8 to 11 A.M. and from 2 to 5 P.M. Entry for foreigners is US$2, and you will have an English-speaking guide to take you around. Photography within the building is prohibited.

Much of the museum collection was stolen or destroyed by Pol Pot's forces, but a sufficient amount has been saved to show the magnificence of Khmer art and craftsmanship. The earliest pieces come from the fifth and sixth centuries, and include a stone musical instrument, a bronze drum, and some sandstone lintels. Some of the highlights for me were the huge wooden statues, the eighteenth-century king's houseboat, the old weaving equipment, some of the beautiful ceramics, and the royal carrying chairs. It is fascinating to see the change in carving techniques over the centuries and how some periods showed extreme attention to detail, with muscles and bone structure on the statues and carvings, while other periods had humans and other objects in stylized forms.

Unfortunately, the museum building is in a fairly bad state of repair. Birds and bats fly around some of the galleries, and the noise of bats can be heard in the ceiling. The smell of bat guano is never far away. Despite these negatives, this is a place that you must see.

Wat Phnom is the ancient heart of the city. The buildings are on and around a twenty-seven-meter-high hill, which has a grand naga-balustraded staircase on the eastern (river) side. It is said that the first pagoda on this site was built in the fourteenth century. Nothing remains of that now, and the sanctuary that you see today actually was built in 1926. There is a large stupa that is said to contain the ashes of King Ponhea Yat, who reigned in the early fifteenth century, and several other shrines, stupas, and other structures. The whole area is attractive because of the extensive landscape that has developed over the years. You will often see monkeys in the trees, and there may be elephants in attendance on weekends.

Wat Ounalom is interesting to visit and photograph, but it is sad to hear of the enormous destruction brought about by Pol Pot. This is the headquarters of Cambodian Buddhism, and the complex was founded in 1443. It once held the extensive library of the Buddhist Institute, but this was completely destroyed in 1975. So too were many of the valuable Buddha images, while other objects were thrown into the river. A statue of Huot Tat, the fourth Patriarch of Cambodian Buddhism, suffered this fate; but it was retrieved after 1979 and is back in the main building. Huot Tat himself was murdered by the Pol Pot regime when he was eighty-four years of age. Fortunately, Wat Ounalom is recovering. Some of the buildings have been restored and are very attractive, and the number of monks in residence is again growing. You find it on Preah Sisowath Boulevard at the corner of 154 Street.

The **Independence Monument** (or Victory Monument), at the intersection of Preah Sihanouk Boulevard and Norodom Boulevard, is a major landmark for the southern part of the city. The structure was built in 1958 and shows considerable French influence in its design. Adjacent **Wat Lang Ka** was almost completely destroyed by Pol Pot's regime, but much restoration work has taken place and the compound is certainly worth visiting.

The **Tuol Sleng Museum** (Tel: 24569) carries a warning from me. I have visited many places in my travels throughout the world, but few have been as depressing or moving as my visit to this museum of crime. In 1975, the school that houses the museum was taken over by Pol Pot's forces and converted into a security prison called S-21. Here, more than 20,000 people were imprisoned and systematically tortured in the most barbaric ways imaginable. Most were then taken to an extermination camp at Choeng Ek, just outside Phnom Penh. Each prisoner was photographed before or after torture. Among them were several foreigners from the United States, Australia, and France.

The only "crime" committed by most of these victims was being educated. Many were teachers, engineers, and doctors. Others were friends of educated people or workers in the previous government's public service. Most had nothing to "confess," so the torture had no political or military purpose. The inhumanity displayed by the torturers is chilling. You can feel it today, nearly twenty years after this insanity ended.

The museum may be too graphic for some visitors. You are shown the rooms where fourteen prisoners were tortured and killed, just twenty minutes before liberating troops captured the prison. The shackles, the pitiful furniture, and the blood are all still there. The graves are nearby in the schoolyard. You then visit the classrooms, which were converted into holding cells for hundreds of prisoners at a time. They were not fit for pigs. At the height of the madness, a hundred victims a day were being tortured and killed. The museum has room after room with walls covered with photographs of the men, women, and children who were "processed" through here. Finally you are shown a bizarre map of Cambodia made from the skulls of some of the victims. There was no way I could photograph such a thing.

The museum is on 113 Street, near 350 Street. It opens daily from 7 to 11:30 A.M. and from 2 to 5:30 P.M. Go, but be aware that you will come away with a different outlook on life and humanity.

The **Central Market** is an amazing art deco building. Its central domed hall has four wings, which are filled with shops selling all sorts of items—from jewelry to designer jeans. Outside the main building, there are stalls offering different goods or food. The best time to visit is early to mid-morning, before it gets too hot. In the afternoon, it can become stifling.

Few people think of Cambodia without thoughts of the fall of Phnom Penh in 1975 and the aftermath as told in the movie *The Killing Fields*. You can visit many of the sites that were portrayed in the film, but remember that the film was made in Thailand, not Cambodia. The former **United States Embassy**, at the corner of Issarak Boulevard and Norodom Boulevard, is now a government office. On April 12, 1975, U.S. Marines evacuated 275 people by helicopter to ships in the Gulf of Thailand. One of the last to leave was U.S. ambassador John Gunther Dean. Many Cambodians seeking escape from a crippled country were left behind. The **Chruoy Changvar Bridge** across the River Sap is near where the *New York Times'* correspondent Sidney Schanberg and his companions were captured by the Khmer Rouge and threatened with execution on the day the Khmer Rouge took over the city. The former **French Embassy**, on Monivong Boulevard north of 80 Street, is where eight hundred foreigners and six hundred Cambodians took refuge later that same day. Two days later, the Khmer Rouge ordered all Cambodians, except for women married to foreigners, to leave the embassy. Most Cambodians were taken away and killed. The foreigners were later transported by truck out of the country.

AROUND PHNOM PENH

There are several points of interest between Phnom Penh and the old capital of Udong. Route 5 goes north from Monivong Boulevard. A few kilometers from the city, you pass **Nur ul-Ihsan Mosque**, which was founded early in the nineteenth century. The original minaret was destroyed by Pol Pot's forces and the building was used as a pig sty, but the mosque is again being used for worship today. Just a short distance north is the new **An-Nur an Naim Mosque**, which replaced a lovely structure that was completely destroyed by Pol Pot.

Thirty-two kilometers north of Phnom Penh, there is a major ferry crossing to the right, where Highway 6 and Highway 7 cross the Sap River. The Prek Kdam Ferry can be a major cause of delay for vehicles heading for north and northeastern Cambodia, so there are numerous food stalls here to help pass the time.

To reach **Udong**, you continue north on Route 5 for a few kilometers. Udong served as the capital of Cambodia on several occasions during the seventeenth, eighteenth, and nineteenth centuries. Unfortunately, many of the best ancient remains were blown up during the 1970s. These include the wonderful Vihear Preah Ath Roes, other temples, numerous Buddha statues, the Ta San Mosque, and untold stupas. Some restoration work has started on part of the site, but it will be impossible to re-create a fraction of the former grandeur. Close by is a building showing murals of Khmer Rouge atrocities and a memorial containing some bones taken from the over one hundred mass graves containing Pol Pot's victims. You can reach Udong by bus from Phnom Penh, but foreigners are discouraged from doing that at present.

Route 1 leaves Phnom Penh via the Monivong Bridge over the Bassac River in the south of the city. About twelve kilometers from the bridge, a road leaves Route 1 and goes to **Koki Beach** on the Mekong River. On Sundays, this is a hive of activity as Phnom Penh residents come to picnic, swim,

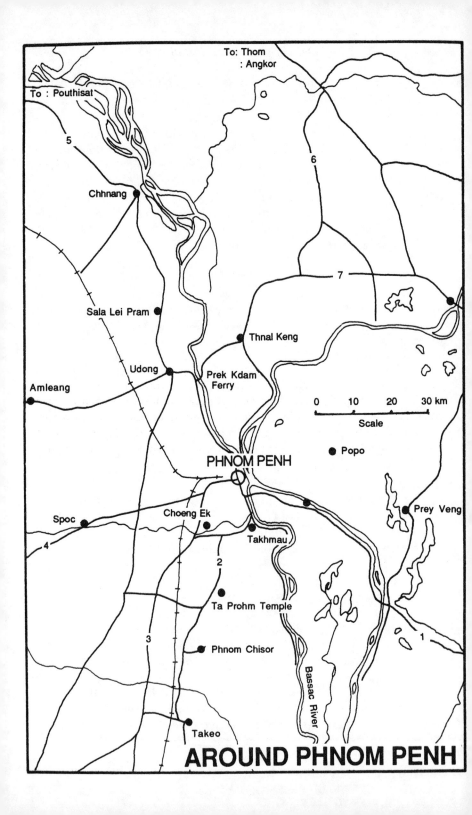

AROUND PHNOM PENH

and sleep. Most visitors like to rent an area of thatch-covered bamboo pier. Here they lounge around, talk, and nap. All sorts of food are available.

If you take Monireth Boulevard out of the city, you will be heading for the **Killing Fields of Choeng Ek**. This is where most of the tortured prisoners from security prison S-21 were taken to be executed. One hundred and twenty-nine communal graves have been located on this site. Some bodies have been exhumed, while other graves remain untouched. Over eight thousand skulls have been assembled in the memorial stupa that has been built on this site. It is estimated that this is where about 20,000 people were killed. Most were beaten to death. The site is about fifteen kilometers from central Phnom Penh.

There are several ancient temples south of Phnom Penh that can be visited in a day. You reach them by taking Route 2, an extension of Norodom Boulevard, south of the turnoff to Monivong Bridge. The first area is about thirty-five kilometers from the city, and the highlight is the temple of **Ta Prohm**. This laterite structure was built in the twelfth century on the site of an earlier sixth-century shrine. The temple was damaged by the Khmer Rouge, and many of the statues and carvings were destroyed; but there is still enough left to make this an interesting and valuable site. Nearby there is a small structure called **Yeay Peau Temple** and the modern **Wat Tonle Bati**. On weekends, these sites are very popular. So too is the nearby river promenade, where you can buy food, laze around, or have a swim on Sundays. There is a two-kilometer-long road from Route 2 to the temples.

The second area of interest is **Phnom Chisor**, about fifty-five kilometers from Phnom Penh. Here a laterite and brick temple complex from the eleventh century stands on a hilltop about five kilometers from Route 2. The temples were built by Khmer Brahmins, but today there are Buddha statues within the sanctuary and a modern Buddhist temple nearby. On the plain below Phnom Chisor, there are two other Khmer temples and the remains of a sacred pond. You see that these form a straight line when viewed from the top of the central shrine, and they were once connected by a stone walkway.

ANGKOR

The famous temples of Angkor are one of the wonders of the ancient world, and they represent one of mankind's most significant architectural achievements. What you see today are the remains of a succession of cities built over nearly five centuries by the kings of the mighty Khmer empire. At its height, the kingdom ruled an area covered today by modern Cambodia, southern Laos, southern Vietnam, and much of Thailand. It is probable that its then capital, Angkor Thom, had a population of a million people. That is more than any European city of the period.

The Khmer kings built several cities on the northern shore of the great lake in the area of Siem Reap, starting in about the ninth century. The successive cities were built around natural or artificial hills, which were identified with Mount Meru, home of the gods in Hindu cosmology. Temples such as Bakong, Bakheng, Phimeanakas, Baphuon, and Bayon are examples of this. The Khmers also built a huge system of reservoirs and channels that allowed intensive cultivation of areas around the cities, ensuring a readily available food supply.

Although there is still some debate over what exactly happened, it is now believed that the Khmer empire gradually declined in the thirteenth century, and the Siamese armies from the west eventually captured Angkor. Certainly the Khmer court abandoned the city in a hurry, moving eastward to a site near Phnom Penh. Angkor was then lost to the world for centuries.

References to a lost city overgrown by jungle were made by European missionaries in the sixteenth and seventeenth centuries; but it was not until 1860, when the French naturalist Henri Mouhot visited the site and told the world about his find, that the "lost city of Angkor" became the center of both popular and scientific interest. Early in this century, archaeologists from the Ecole Francaise d'Extreme Orient began the task of painstakingly reclaiming the ruins from the jungle. They labored there for nearly sixty years, until their efforts were overcome by the civil war.

For the past twenty years, the Angkor region has been the scene of heavy fighting between government and rebel forces. The nearest modern town, Siem Reap, has suffered considerable damage—as have the temples themselves—and the area has been littered with mine fields. Despite these problems, there was great world desire to open this region to tourism; and the process has started. The success and rate of progress will depend on the political and military situation; but if peace can be restored, tourism is sure to boom.

At present, the only way for visitors to reach Angkor is by air from Phnom Penh or by boat during the wet season. There are several daily flights to Angkor in the morning and return flights to Phnom Penh in the afternoon. The number of aircraft used is governed by the number of visitors wishing to travel. Additionally, there are several hotels in Siem Reap available for visitors who wish to stay overnight, so there is now the chance to really spend a decent amount of time at the ruins. All visits to Siem Reap and Angkor are controlled by Angkor Tourism, so you need to be on some sort of package tour. I understand that all visitors are charged US$100 by Angkor Tourism for transportation from the airport to the ruins and back, for the provision of a guide, and for lunch at one of the hotels. The airfare is extra. This is an outlandish price, but there is currently no alternative.

The day trip from Phnom Penh only allows you five hours in Angkor, and

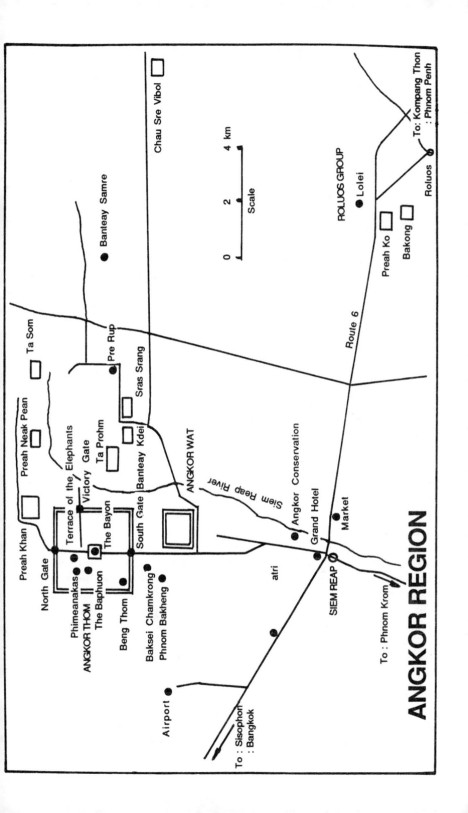

ANGKOR REGION

more than one hour of this is taken up by lunch. Nevertheless, you still see enough to agree that Somerset Maugham was correct when he wrote, "I have never seen anything in the world more beautiful than the temples of Angkor."

The two most magnificent temples at Angkor are the **Bayon**, which faces east and is best visited and photographed in the morning, and **Angkor Wat**, which faces west and is best seen in the late afternoon. You can see them both on the day trip, but unfortunately not at their best times. The Bayon is within the fortified city of Angkor Thom, while Angkor Wat is outside the city, a few kilometers away.

Angkor Thom is a walled city about ten square kilometers (four square miles) in size, which was built in its present form during the late twelfth century. The city was built on the site of previous towns, and incorporates some of those earlier structures into its framework. It was enclosed by a wall approximately twelve kilometers long and eight meters high, which was encircled by a one-hundred-meter-wide moat. The city had five monumental gates and numerous giant statues.

The city was built by King Jayavarman VII, who came to power just after the Cham civilization of central Vietnam had overrun and destroyed much of the old capital. The Chams were subsequently defeated, and the king went on a building spree to reestablish Khmer glory. With Angkor Thom, he was brilliantly successful.

The Bayon is the most outstanding feature of Angkor Thom. The temple is built in the exact center of the city and was connected to four city gates by roads which were used by people and elephants. The temple, with its fifty towers and more than 170 enigmatic giant faces, was a masterpiece that was slightly spoiled by the addition of a third level at some later time, when the original building—which was dedicated to the worship of Shiva—was converted to a Buddhist temple. Later, some of the Buddhist elements were removed when Hinduism again became popular.

Today, as you approach the complex, it seems to be a once imposing structure in a very poor state of repair; but as you gaze at it further, you realize that this impression is partly given by the sheer complexity of the building. Certainly there is much damage inside from time and man, but the restoration work that has been done intermittently over the past twenty years has been quite successful, and you can now walk around inside the complex without difficulty.

Visitors will find the faces and the amazing bas-reliefs to be the principal attractions of the Bayon. You can climb to the third level and come face to face with some of the faces. They are fascinating. If you have a fifty-riel note in your pocket, you can identify the sketch on the note with one of the faces. The expressions on the stone faces are all different, and they seem to change with the light. It used to be possible to visit here at night to see the temple in the moonlight. That must have been spectacular. If you have the chance to do this, grab it with both hands.

The Bayon bas-reliefs stretch for twelve hundred meters and incorporate over eleven thousand figures. The time spent creating this masterpiece is difficult to imagine. The reliefs show both Hindu and Buddhist influence, but most show scenes of everyday life in the twelfth-century kingdom. You see meals being prepared, women selling fish in the market, people picking lice from their hair, cock fights in progress, and several other occurrences that are as common in modern Cambodia as they were eight hundred years ago. Violent scenes of battle, victory, and defeat are shown. The Cham army is shown advancing; battle scenes show a Cham victory and the wounded Khmer king being helped from his elephant. Later you see the Cham army being defeated and expelled from Khmer territory. Some of the sections remain unfinished.

There are numerous other structures in Angkor Thom, but most are in fairly poor condition. Hopefully some further restoration work will be possible if permanent peace returns to the area. If you have the time, you should visit the **Baphuon**, which was the center of a town in existence before Angkor Thom. The central structure is over forty meters high and was once described as the "copper tower"—presumably because of its color. Some reconstruction work was carried out in the 1960s, but it has never been completed. Next to this is the so-called **Terrace of the Elephants**, which was used as a viewing platform for the king during public ceremonies or games. Here you will see the famous frieze of the elephant parade. The terrace forms part of the surroundings of the **Royal Enclosure**, which has now been overtaken by the jungle. At one time, there were numerous buildings in this area, but even the most impressive Phimeanakas, or celestial palace, is now very dilapidated.

Just outside of Angkor Thom at the south gate, you will see **Baksei Chamkrong**, one of the few brick structures in the Angkor area. It was built in the early tenth century, 250 years before Angkor Wat. At one time, it was covered in mortar. Although it is only a few hundred meters from the road, guides currently warn visitors against visiting this site—presumably because of the possibility of undiscovered mines or explosives in the area.

Angkor Wat is a spectacular monument in anyone's language. It covers an area about 1.5 by 1.3 kilometers and is one of the largest temple complexes in the world. The temple was built in the first half of the twelfth century to honor Vishnu, then to serve as the funerary temple for King Suryavargman II. By the fifteenth century, the wat had become a Buddhist religious center. Today, there are still monks within the Angkor Wat grounds; and over the years, they have protected the monument and stopped the encroaching vegetation.

Angkor Wat is the only temple at Angkor that faces westward. You cross the 190-meter-wide moat on a laterite causeway to the main entrance, West Portico. This 220-meter-long, richly decorated structure contains a 3.3-meter-high statue of Vishnu, which was carved from a single sandstone block. To the left and right, you see other statues, carvings, and friezes. Ahead is the 475-meter-long stone paved avenue that leads to the main temple. From this point, the main temple appears to have three towers; but in reality there are five. You need to leave the avenue and walk to the side of the compound before you see this.

The central structure of Angkor Wat is a three-level building. Each level has interlinked galleries and open space. The corners of the second and third levels have towers with lotus buds carved into them. In the center of the complex, a huge tower that soars thirty meters above the third level ties all the other work together into a majestic whole. At one time, this held a gold statue of Vishnu.

The other major feature of Angkor Wat is the 800-meter-long bas-reliefs that encircle the lower gallery of the temple. The figures tell stories about the king and depict scenes from Hindu classics such as the "Ramayana." The most famous of the bas-relief scenes at Angkor Wat is the "Churning of the Ocean of Milk," which depicts devils and gods churning up the ocean by rotating an immense serpent, so they can extract the elixir of immortality. Various Hindu deities are seen watching or participating in the event. Another panel known as the "Days of Judgement" shows the rewards of heaven and the punishments of hell. Those who proceed to heaven are shown in beautiful mansions, leading lives of peace, while those condemned to hell suffer horrible tortures.

Angkor Wat represents the pinnacle of Khmer architecture in many ways. While it is immense, it is well proportioned, brilliant in its detail, and thoroughly marvelous to explore at your leisure. If you are staying at Siem Reap, you could easily spend a whole day here. The temple is currently under restoration, and most of it is being cleaned. I am not sure that I like the result. To me it is too clean and too sterile; but I guess if we want to keep it for future generations, we have to put up with this from time to time.

Angkor Wat is about six kilometers from the Grand Hotel in Siem Reap. It is too far to walk, but you can rent bicycles, which are a great form of transport around the area, from the hotel for US$2 an hour. Do, however, stick to well-worn tracks when you are riding around. Between the hotel and the temple, you will see a large theater which was started in 1967, but has never been finished. There is also a high school that was destroyed by the war, and a small new sports stadium that is a hopeful indication that general building or rebuilding may commence in this area soon.

Other sites can be visited, but none are nearly as spectacular as those already described. For a different feel about Angkor, you should visit **Ta Prohm**. This was built as a Buddhist temple during the twelfth century, and it has deliberately been left just as it looked when the first French explorers saw it in 1860. You can imagine that you are an explorer as you walk the narrow and sometimes overgrown paths into and around the complex. The massive carved-stone building blocks have been strewn in all directions by current and long-gone trees. Great trees tower overhead, blocking the sun and encouraging the lichens and mosses to carpet the bulging walls and sagging floors. Here and there, bas-reliefs can be seen among the tree roots and creepers that now engulf everything. It is a place crowded with mystery. Nearby, you can visit **Banteay Kdei**, a massive temple surrounded by four walls. The inside of the central tower was never finished, but the four outer entrances have some nice decorations.

The **Roluos Group** is about thirteen kilometers east of Siem Reap along Route 6. These are among the earliest large temples built by the Khmers. They date from the late ninth century. The **Bakong Temple** is the most impressive, but much of it has crumbled away. You can still see the five-tier central sandstone pyramid, eight brick and sandstone towers, and the remains of other buildings. The complex is surrounded by three walls and a moat. **Preah Ko** was erected at about the same time. Here, six brick towers are aligned in two rows. Similar towers can be seen at **Lolei**, which is about two kilometers away.

Accommodation choice is improving in Siem Reap. The **Grand Hotel** (Tel: 15-911292) and the **Villa Apsara** (Fax: 855-15-911291) are both controlled by Angkor Tourism and have rates of US$25/32 and US$32/40 respectively for single and double rooms. Meals are available at the Grand Hotel for US$3 for breakfast and US$6 for lunch or dinner. The **Banteay Srei Hotel** (Tel: 15-913839), 53 rooms, is controlled by Bopha Angkor Tourism and has good rooms at similar rates. The **Hotel de la Paix** (Tel: 15-912322), 40 rooms, in Sivutha Street, and the **Ta Prom Hotel** (Tel: 15-911783), 58 rooms, are another two alternatives. More accommodations will be needed as the tourist numbers increase. This will happen as soon as the world sees that Cambodia has its civil war under control. Already there are moves to open the Thai border, so visitors can travel to Angkor by bus or car. This is still premature for political and military reasons, as well as the dilapidated state of most roads in the region. Change will come, however, and it may be very rapid, so ask in Phnom Penh for the latest information.

7. Guided Tours

At the present time, most visitors to Cambodia come on package tours. These are outlandishly expensive, but they effectively eliminate the problem of visas, travel permits, and transport arrangements. There are a wide variety of programs available in Bangkok, Singapore, Hong Kong, and other cities to visit Cambodia or Cambodia in conjunction with Vietnam and sometimes Laos. Generally, these are full-scale programs providing airport transfers, all meals, sightseeing, accommodations, and the services of an English-speaking guide. They can be bought separately from the airfare, so it is possible to buy a short program and have some extra time on your own after the package finishes.

Within Cambodia, there are several organizations that operate one-day or extended tours of the country. Most of these organizations welcome you to join one of their programs—even one specifically geared to a Thailand or Hong Kong market. Be aware that Cambodian tour prices are high due to the low number of tourists currently visiting the area. If you can round up half a dozen people yourself, the price comes way down. A one-day Phnom Penh sightseeing tour will cost you US$80. If you want to go out into the countryside (to Ta Prohm for example), a day tour will cost US$100. The one-day Angkor trip, including round-trip airfare from Phnom Penh, is around US$250.

Tours are operated under the control of the **Ministry of Tourism** with offices on Monivong Boulevard at 232 Street (Tel: 26107; Fax: 855-23-26364). My experience with this organization has been good. The staff whom I have met are courteous and helpful. **Phnom Penh Tourism** is the agency of Phnom Penh municipality. Until 1990, it had a monopoly on tourism and sold high-priced three-day tours through Saigon Tourist in Ho Chi Minh City. Now that there is competition, it has become more cooperative. The main office is at 313 Sisowath Quay (Tel: 24059; Fax: 855-23-26043).

There are also private tour operators. I have only had experience with one of these—**Aroon Tours Company, Ltd.** at 99 130 Street (Tel: 26303; Fax: 855-23-26300); and I have no complaints about the professionalism and service. Other operators that have significant operations are **Bopha Angkor Tourism** (Tel: 27933; Fax: 855-23-27406) at 797 Monivong Boulevard, who specialize in Angkor visits; **Diethelm Travel** (Tel: 26648; Fax: 855-23-26676), the big Thai-Indochina tour company at 8 Samdech Sothearos Boulevard; **Hanuman Tourism** (Tel: 26194; Fax: 855-23-26194) at No. 188, 13 Street near the National Museum; and the **Tourism Group** (Tel: 25535; Fax: 855-23-27809) at 246F Monivong Boulevard.

8. Culture

Cambodian culture looks longingly back to the Angkor period for inspiration and tradition. In some ways, since the fall of Angkor in the fifteenth century, the cultural and artistic traditions of the Khmer people have slowly lapsed due to civil war, political instability, and foreign influences. Since the arrival of the French in the mid-nineteenth century, there has been more interest in and appreciation for Cambodian culture; but there has been a conservatism that has led to few major developments in art, music, architecture, or handicrafts.

Recently, there has been another major discouraging influence on interest in art and culture. During the disastrous Pol Pot years, anyone who wore glasses, spoke a foreign language, had any artistic talent, or looked as if he might have an interest in history, past cultures, or artistic development was designated a threat to the state; and most people in these categories were killed. It is estimated that up to ninety percent of all classical dancers in the country were killed, as were sculptors, painters, architects, historians, and others. In effect, the country's efforts in developing these talents really only commenced again in 1979, and they have been slowed by a lack of people.

At the moment, there is nowhere in Phnom Penh to see any regular cultural performances. A national classical dance troupe has been formed, but they only perform for visiting delegations. The Soviet-funded circus building is unfinished and unfit for performances. The National Theater appears to be rarely used. Modern Cambodian culture in the form of Western pop music bands can be seen in a number of restaurants and discos around town.

With life returning to some sense of normality for some of the country's population, there is a growing interest in traditional holidays and festivals. Additionally, there are several politically inspired celebrations that are supported by the government. The following are the major events during the year.

National Day is celebrated on January 7. This commemorates the Vietnamese overthrow of Pol Pot in 1979. It is likely to have less significance in the future.

Tet, the Vietnamese and Chinese New Year, is celebrated by these sections of the population, but not generally by the Khmer people. Tet falls in late January or early February, depending on the lunar calendar.

Cambodian-Vietnamese Friendship is celebrated on February 18, during anniversary reminders of a treaty signed in 1979.

The **Cambodian New Year** is a three-day celebration held in mid-April. This is the major festival of the year for the Khmer people.

Visakha Buja occurs in late April or early May and is a celebration of the birth and enlightenment of the Buddha.

International Workers' Day is celebrated on May 1.

Genocide Day is May 9. Memorial events are held to mark the atrocities of the Khmer Rouge regime.

The **Royal Ploughing** ceremony is held in late May.

The **Spirits Commemoration Day** is held in early October.

The **King's Birthday** is celebrated on 30 October and 1 November.

Independence Day is on November 9.

The **Water Festival** (or Festival of the Reversing Current) is celebrated in late October or early November. It traditionally corresponds to when the Sap River changes its direction of flow and begins to drain the Tonle Sap Lake back into the Mekong River. Longboat races are held in Phnom Penh at this time.

9. Sports

There are almost no opportunities for sports other than swimming and tennis in present-day Cambodia. Several Phnom Penh hotels have **pools**, and there are some **beaches** on the Mekong River and elsewhere used by people who want to lie in the water. The **Hotel Cambodiana** has a tennis court, a jogging track, and a health center. Tennis facilities are also available at the **Cafe No Problem**, opposite the National Museum. This also has billiard tables. The **National Sports Center**, at the corner of Boulevard Sivutha and Boulevard Pokambor, has facilities for athletics, swimming, boxing, volleyball, and other sports. There are no golf courses, squash courts, or deep-sea fishing available in Cambodia at present.

10. Shopping

I find shopping in Phnom Penh to be rather disappointing, but others have told me of great bargains that are available. Antiques, silver items, and jewelry are supposed to be the things to buy. There are many places in central Phnom Penh where you can buy these items. A cluster of them is on the road fronting the western side of the Central Market. You could also try **Khemara Souvenirs** at 139 Monivong Boulevard; **Souvenir Khmer Rarchana Cachnay** at 101 Monivong Boulevard; or **Khmer Rachakna Souvenirs** at 97, 126 Street, opposite the northern side of the Central Market. If you are a serious shopper, I recommend you visit **Kheng Song Souvenirs** at 99 Monivong Boulevard. The owner speaks good English and is very obliging. He has silver, gold, antiques, precious stones, and some nice pottery.

In other areas, you could try **Green House II** on Sihanouk Boulevard, east of the Independence Monument for imported fashions and accessories and local cards and gifts. There is also a florist and newsstand. Close by is **La Boutique** at Number 36. **Tan Sotho Fine Antiques** (Tel: 26194) is at No. 188, 13 Street. The **New Art Gallery** (Tel: 15-911360) at No. 20, 9 Street has original art by local artists. The **English Bookstore** (Tel: 62291) at No. 213, 51 Street has a good range of magazines and books.

There are many tailoring shops in Phnom Penh, but the styles look very dated. Some of the more progressive seem to be **Mondial Tailleur** at 197 Monivong Boulevard and **Nobel Tailleur** at No. 169. There are a few shops with ready-made clothes. Try **Phnom Penh Clothing Shop** at 153 Monivong Boulevard or the **House of High Style** at No. 263. The **Paris Perfumerie** at 81, 126 Street has a range of perfumes of unknown origin at good prices.

Film processing is available at **Diamond Film and Processing** at 209 Monivong Boulevard; **City Color Photo** (Tel: 23137) at No. 123, and **Photo Selpak** at 56 Kampuchea Krom Boulevard. There are many pharmacies, but the stocks are very limited. **Pharmacy Chok Chey**, at 41 Kampuchea Krom Boulevard; **Pharmacy Santepheap** (Tel: 22413), on 118 Street opposite the Dusit Hotel; **Asie Pharmacy**, at 177 Monivong Boulevard; and **Pharmacy Monorom**, at 103 Monivong Boulevard, are some of the better ones. Hair-dressing is available at **Prom Bayon Hairdressing**, at 189 Monivong Boulevard, **Kampuchea Hairdressing** at No. 227; and the **Phnom Penh Beauty Parlor** (Tel: 24830), at No. 245. A more up-market alternative is **Madame Beauty House** (Tel: 23116) at No. 73, 115 Street just off Preah Sihanouk Boulevard.

There are several minimarts where you can buy Western goods. The **Bayon Market** (Tel: 29962) at 133 Monivong Boulevard is particularly convenient. **Lucky Market** at 160 Sihanouk Boulevard serves a similar purpose. **Le Shop** (Tel: 26644) at No. 129, 118 Street, and **Suntan Foodmarket** (Tel: 018-810223) at 477 Monivong Boulevard are two alternatives.

The markets are worth a visit, but you need to bear in mind that items are not necessarily what they appear to be. The **Tuol Tom Pong Market** in the south part of town is considered to be the best place to look for antiques, old coins, and general souvenirs. The old market on 13th and 15th streets has some jewelry for sale, as does the huge **Central Market** building.

Duty-free goods are available at **Bayon Duty Free** (Tel: 27756) at No. 34, 214 Street or at **TAT Duty Free** (Tel: 26412) at Pochentong Airport.

11. Entertainment and Nightlife

The Cambodian government has been rather schizophrenic about night-time activities for quite a long time. Until 1989, a curfew operated in Phnom Penh. When that was lifted, discos and other nightspots started up immediately; but the government cracked down again a few months later, and most closed up. Since then, there has been a gradual easing of restrictions, although there is still a close watch kept on this activity.

Hotel lounges of the Western-style with music, drink service, and nice relaxing atmosphere are few and far between in Phnom Penh; but as more larger hotels develop, these will come. At present, the only two that I know of are the Cyclo Bar and the Lobby Bar at the Hotel Cambodiana. Both have live music commencing late in the afternoon, and both are well patronized by hotel guests and a growing number of well-heeled locals. The Crystal Night Club at the Ambassador Hotel is popular late at night.

Hotel "discos" have also appeared. This is a complete misnomer because most do not have a D.J. or recorded music. Instead, live bands play a selection of Cambodian and Western music while people gyrate on a small dance floor. These places come in and out of fashion very quickly, but you could try those at the Hotel Le Royal, on the sixth floor of the Monorom Hotel, and at the Hotel Neak Poan. All operate nightly.

There are several nightclubs in the city and a growing number of Karaoke outlets. The nightclubs tend to be glamorous and expensive. The most popular at present is **B Boss** (Tel: 27079) at 254 Monivong Boulevard where Filipino bands provide the beat. The **Pacific Nite Club** (Tel: 18-810289) is at 234 Monivong Boulevard, and the **Pacific International Nightclub** is on Kampuchea Krom Boulevard near the Central Market. The **Martini Pub Disco** at 402 Issarak Boulevard is down-market from here.

Discos exist outside the hotels and are very popular with the locals. Some—such as Kong Kea Floating Restaurant and the Boeng Kak Thamet on the shore of Boeng Kak Lake—are used by visitors and expatriates. There are many more—such as the Chbouk Kak Restaurant and Disco on Issarak Boulevard and the Holiday Restaurant and Disco on Pochentong Boulevard—where you could easily be the only foreigner in the place. As far as I am aware, all of these places are considered safe by most people.

Bars and bar girls are not found much in the central city, but their numbers are growing since the crackdown on the Tuol Kork red light area. There are also some Thai-style massage parlors. The **Rain and Fire** pub at 42, 178 Street has billiards, darts, Karaoke, a cozy atmosphere, and Filipino hospitality.

Theater, cultural events, and so forth are non-existent at present.

12. The Phnom Penh Address List

Airlines—Kampuchea Airlines, 152 Norodom Boulevard (Tel: 18-810274); Bangkok Airlines, No. 61, 214 Street (Tel: 26707); Cambodia International Airlines, No. 19, 106 Street (Tel: 26248); Dragonair (Tel: 27652); Lao Aviation, 58 Sihanouk Boulevard (Tel: 26563); Malaysia Airlines, 207 Monivong Boulevard (Tel: 26688); Silk Air, Pailin Hotel, Monivong Boulevard (Tel: 22236); Thai International, No. 19, 106 Street (Tel: 22335); Vietnam Airlines, 527 Monivong Boulevard (Tel: 27426).

Bank—Foreign Trade, corner Monivong Boulevard and Soeung Ngoe Ming (Tel: 24863); Standard Chartered, 95a Sihanouk Boulevard (Tel: 26685).

Church—Nazarene, 217 Street; Church of Christ our Peace (English 8 A.M.), No. 21, 294 Street.

Hospital—Calmette, Monivong Boulevard (24-hour emergency) (Tel: 23173).

Medical—Access Medical, No. 203, 63 Street (Tel: 15-912100).

Ministries—Foreign Affairs, Sisowath Quay (Tel: 24441); Information & Culture, Monivong Blvd. (Tel: 24769).

Museums—Crime, 103 Street at 350 Street; National, 178 Street at 19 Street.

Overseas Courier—DHL, No. 17, 90 Street (Tel: 18-810838); TNT, 38 Kampuchea Krom Boulevard (Tel: 26694).

Phnom Penh University—Pochentong Boulevard.

Post Office—GPO, 13 Street at 102 Street (Tel: 24511).

Railway Station—Monivong Boulevard (Tel: 23115).

Telecommunications—Telstra Australia, 58 Norodom Boulevard (Tel: 26022).

Index

Huong Pagoda (Perfume Pagoda), 120; Festival, 130-31

Imperial City (Hue), 146, 147
Independence Hall. *See* Unification Palace
Independence Monument. *See* Victory Monument
Indira Gandhi Park (Hanoi), 111
Indochina War, 337
Indravarman I, 325
Industry, 70-71
Infrastructure, 71
Inter-Lao Tourism, 293, 311
Investment, 71
Islam, 53, 255, 332

Japan, 80-81
Japanese Covered Bridge (Hoi An), 176
Jayavarman II, 325
Jayavarman III, 325-26
Jayavarman VII, 327-28

Kaeng Kok, 308
Kampuchean Airlines, 21, 23
Kaysone Phomvihane, 249
Keo Pagoda, 125
Khai Dinh, tomb of, 151-53
Khammuan Plateau, 15
Khamtay Siphandone, 250
Khanh Hoa Tourism, 188
Khenark, 313
Khe Sanh, the town, 155; Combat Base, 155
Khmer People's National Liberation Front, 329
Khmer Rouge, 327-29, 330, 337
Khmers (in Vietnam), 50-51, 75; (in Laos), 243; (in Cambodia), 323-26, 331-32
Khong Island, 310
Khon Phapheng Falls, 310
Kim Lien, 157

Kim Lien Bus Station (Hanoi), 91, 116
Kip, 30
KLM, 21
Koki Beach, 355-57
Kong Le, 247
Kratie, 26
Krong Laa, 184
Khu Kana Waterfall, 297
Kuangsy Waterfall, 303
Kublai Khan, 245

Lake of Sighs, 187
Lake Tay (Hanoi), 97
Lake Xuan Huong (Dalat), 168, 173, 185
Lambrettas, 165
Lam Dong Province Tourism, 165, 188
Lam Son Square (Saigon), 213
Lam Son Uprising, 75-76
Lam Ty Ni Pagoda, 187
Lamvong, 260
Lang Co, 158; Railway Station, 158
Lang Son, 128
Lanna, 245
Lan Xang, 245-46, 297
Lan Xang Tours, 308, 311
Lao Air Booking Co. Ltd., 311
Lao Aviation, 21, 23, 270, 273, 293, 297, 304, 306, 308, 338
Lao Bao, 26, 155
Lao Cai, 128
Lao Issara, 247
Lao Lum (Low Lao), 252
Lao People's Revolutionary Party, 243, 248
Lao Revolutionary Museum (Vientiane), 286, 287, 292
Laos, 243-320; architecture, 260-61; culture, 258-63; economy, 250-52; holidays and festivals, 27, 311-13; food, 263-65; government, 249-50; history, 245-49; language, 255-58; population, 252-53; religion, 253-55
Lao Sung (High Lao), 252
Lao Theung, 252

Please tell us about your trip to Vietnam,
Laos, and Cambodia.

(This page can be folded to make an envelope.)

Place your check or money order
inside this envelope. Please do not send
cash through the mail.

CUT OFF

CUT OFF

FOLD

RE: 3rd edition, Vietnam

Place
first-class
postage
here

THE MAVERICK GUIDES
Pelican Publishing Company
1101 Monroe Street
P.O. Box 3110
Gretna, Louisiana 70054